Layla Zami
Contemporary PerforMemory

Editorial

The series is edited by Gabriele Brandstetter and Gabriele Klein.

Layla Zami (Dr. phil., Dipl.-Pol.) is Visiting Assistant Professor at Pratt Institute in Brooklyn, NY, where she teaches in the fields of humanities, performance studies, and art history. She also works as Interdisciplinary Artist-in-Residence (music, spoken words, physical theater) with Oxana Chi Dance & Art, and is Co-Curator of Dance at the International Human Rights Art Festival. Zami obtained a PhD from the Center for Trandisciplinary Gender Studies at Humboldt-University in Berlin, where she was awarded a Teaching Quality Prize for her seminar *Performing Memory*. She received an ELES/BMBF Doctoral Fellowship, graduated from Sciences Po Paris, and was a Visiting Research Scholar at Columbia University. Zami is also the co-director of *Memory2Go*, a documentary film produced alongside this book. www.laylazami.net

Layla Zami

Contemporary PerforMemory

Dancing through Spacetime, Historical Trauma,
and Diaspora in the 21st Century

[transcript]

To Oxana Chi, whose dancing grace set this book in motion.

This book was published with the support of:
Stiftung Zeitlehren, Publication Fund
Humboldt University of Berlin, Faculty of Humanities, Cultural and Social Sciences
Pratt Institute, History of Art & Design Department

=== STIFTING ===
ZEITLEHREN   **Pratt**HA&D
HISTORY OF ART AND DESIGN

HUMBOLDT-UNIVERSITÄT ZU BERLIN

This book resulted from research supported by a Doctoral Fellowship from:
Ernst Ludwig Ehrlich Studienwerk / German Federal Ministry of Education and Research
(ELES/BMBF, Jüdische Begabtenförderung - eine Geschichte mit Zukunft)

ELES Ernst Ludwig Ehrlich
Studienwerk

This book project is accompanied by a documentary film project called *Memory2Go*.
For audiovisual impressions and updates, see: laylazami.net/film

Bibliographic information published by the Deutsche Nationalbibliothek
The Deutsche Nationalbibliothek lists this publication in the Deutsche Nationalbibliografie; detailed bibliographic data are available in the Internet at http://dnb.d-nb.de

Cover concept: Kordula Röckenhaus, Bielefeld
Cover illustration: Front: Oxana Chi in *Through Gardens (Durch Gärten)*, Berlin, 2008. Photo by Annette Hauschild, courtesy of Oxana Chi. Back: Layla Zami in *Through Gardens*, Dresden, 2014. Photo by Sebastian Loeder, courtesy of the artist.
Cover Design: Doro Tops, Berlin
Copy-editing: Fatin Abbas, PhD
Proofread: Dr. Layla Zami

Print-ISBN 978-3-8376-5525-4
PDF-ISBN 978-3-8394-5525-8
https://doi.org/10.14361/9783839455258

Contents

PREFACE... 7

TUNING IN: OF STORY-HUNTERS AND DANCING LIONS 11
Inspiring, or Whom to Acknowledge... 11
Imagining, or What an Academic and Artist Aims to Find Out about Dance and Memory......16
Innovating, or Which Contributions I Wish to Make to Existing Scholarship 30
Investigating, or Why Epistemology and Methodology Come into Play..................... 35
Inventing, or Whence the Outline Comes From.. 49

1   MEMORY DANCESCAPES 53
Archiving a Repertoire of PerforMemory 56
    Dancing counterhegemonic choreobiographies...................................... 60
        THROUGH GARDENS – OXANA CHI.. 60
        THEY CALL YOU VENUS – CHANTAL LOÏAL 64
    Dancing after the ancestors: family, trauma and movement 68
        ALL ABOUT NOTHING – ZUFIT SIMON 69
        DIGITAL MIDDLE PASSAGE – ANDRÉ M. ZACHERY............................... 71
    Dancing without borders: geopolitical and physical islands 74
        IMPRESSIONS BY WAN-CHAO CHANG 75
        CHOC(S) BY CHRISTIANE EMMANUEL 77
        PAROLE, PAROLE, PAROLE BY FARAH SALEH.................................. 80
Memory as a Site of Movement 84
    Performing memory in the age of Postmemory 84
        Imagining perforMemory.. 84
        Moving center stage 88
    Embodying history, HERstory, theirstories... 90
        Defining choreography... 91
        Between telling history and performing memory............................... 92
        Emotions in motion 94
    Memory2go.. 96
        Escaping and shaping memory.. 96
        From the choreography of power to the power to choreograph 98

2   DIASPORIC MOVES 101

Moving Through Diaspora 106

    Inhabiting diaspora 106

    Jewish/Black/Feminist diasporas 114

The Stage as a Diasporic Space 125

    Diasporic space is the place 126

    Finding a home space in the dance place? 132

3   DANCING THE PAST IN THE PRESENT TENSE 143

The Timescapes of PerforMemory 145

    Stretching time: bending hegemonic timelines 146

    The quantic dance of memory: moving through and beyond past,

    present and future 165

The Moves of PerforMemory: Shaping the Dancescapes 175

    Turning 177

    Jumping 183

    Crossing 188

4   DANCE DIALOGUES: IN CONVERSATION WITH... 195

OXANA CHI 202

CHRISTIANE EMMANUEL 215

CHANTAL LOÏAL 223

FARAH SALEH 231

ZUFIT SIMON 239

WAN-CHAO CHANG 245

ANDRÉ M. ZACHERY 255

TU(R)NING OUT: TRANSFORMING THE BODY INTO A SPACETIME OF RESIST(D)ANCE 265

Bibliography 273

PREFACE
THE WORDS OF A DANCER, SEEDED IN TIME

[She] liked to look
at the drops of water
in her garden.
She often stopped
to notice how the
light shone through
their delicate shapes [and]
she loved to draw forms
in the [earth] with her bare feet.
Andrea d'Aquino[1]

Time, much time, went by.
I saw how time disappeared.
How hours, minutes, seconds, spun away.

I witnessed how Dr. Layla Zami and I, wrapped in metal,
flew through the clouds,
immersing into one time zone to emerge in another time zone,

       to land,

       to step out,

       to linger,

       to step back in,

       to fly further.

---

1   Andrea D'Aquino, *A Life Made by Hand: The Story of Ruth Asawa*, Hudson: Princeton Architectural Press, 2019.

Berlin – San Diego,
San Diego – New York,
New York – Fort-de-France,
Fort-de-France – Paris,
Paris – Taipei,
Taipei – New York,
New York – Vienna,
Vienna – Berlin.

Time, as it seems to me today, just flew by.
Time – in days...weeks...years – pulse.

I experienced all this precious and inspiring time,
I lived through it along with Layla.

This time, filled with experiences, impressions, theater visits, performances, workshops, farewells, hourlong lingering in bookshops, libraries, universities and online platforms, by the ocean and in coffeeshops, this time stretched itself out, at various paces, on the blank pages that became this book.

Step by step, letter by letter, syllable by syllable, words, which the author elicited from the heads, bodies, and passionate hearts of seven artists...

...accompanied by and paired with Dr. Zami's insightful and sensitive thoughts, and her deep interest in precisely this art of dance, which the choreographers create. To a dance-interested audience-readership thirsty for knowledge, she hands in her words in a crystal glass that opens, clears, and enlightens minds, filled with ice-cold pomegranate juice that expands horizons.

I experienced, saw, spoke and listened, when the author visited and interviewed us artists in theaters, dance studios, cafés, and apartments. I witnessed how the scholar stood herself on stage as a Resident Artist with my company Oxana Chi & Ensemble Xinren (also known as Oxana Chi Dance & Art), moving, performing movement, music, and words in my dance productions, to dive deeper and deeper in the expressive medium called dance art.

I was shocked, as days turned into nights, the nights almost disappeared, were abolished. Time seemed to be stretched out to the splits, as Dr. Layla Zami sat at her laptop, with pearls of sweat on her forehead, to transform all the voices of the dance-makers in the digital realm.

The words, movements, dances, ideas, musics, (hi)stories, and moods of all the involved moving bodies are archived in this book. Enriched by Dr. Zami's research and additional expert voices from the fields of dance, dance and performance studies, gender studies, history, memory studies, physics, ecology, and general knowledge, health and healing wisdom, it all becomes readable, hearable, and perceptible. What a knowledge-building art work!

Politicized dance art, research, and creative writing nourish this book with the spirit of our times, and bring together in the dance roundelay a rich, beautiful and atrocious past, a turbulent now, and the hope of a friendly and inclusive future for all dance lovers.

Warmly,
Oxana Chi
Brooklyn, June 27th, 2020

TUNING IN
OF STORY-HUNTERS AND DANCING LIONS

ich sehe dich im garten stehend
träumend, dich bewegend

(i see you, in the garden standing,
dreaming, you are moving)

May Ayim, Afrekete[1]

Inspiring, or Whom to Acknowledge

I developed a deep interest in the conscious linking of dance and diaspora, storytelling and struggles, bodies and battles, performance and politics, movements and memories, after being introduced to Oxana Chi's work in 2009 and working with her on stage since 2012. Like the figure dancing in the garden in the above quoted poem, it was the sight of Oxana Chi dancing her solo *Through Gardens (Durch Gärten)*, that led me to follow this research path. My first encounter with the piece, in which Chi tells the powerful and tragic story of the Jewish-Chinese-Russian-Latvian dancer Tatjana Barbakoff (1899 Liepaja - 1944 Auschwitz), took place on October 7th, 2009, at the Werkstatt der Kulturen Theater in Berlin, Germany. I was mesmerized by the impressive quality of the solo dance, by the astounding interplay between sounds and live-music, by the astute and emotional storytelling, by the alternating energies of tenderness and struggle embedded in Chi's moves.[2]

Through Gardens originally awakened me to the tremendous power of dance art to perform memory. It also piqued my interest in the role of performance in preserving and re-creating memories of the past grounded in the present, and in imagining a future when and where persecution, discrimination, oppression and genocide are no longer imaginable. The experiences of the piece are the roots that nurtured my concept of *perforMemory*. However, at this time, I was far from

---

1   Ayim, *Blues in Schwarz-Weiss*, 40 [My translation].
2   See Zami, "Tanzkunst als lebendige Erinnerung."

knowing that I would collaborate with Oxana Chi. I was even further away from imagining that I would conduct academic research and publish my first monograph on the relations between dance and memory.

My deepest gratitude for this project therefore goes to Oxana Chi, whom I am blessed to call my life and work partner. I feel grateful for the path that we have walked together from Berlin to New York over Surakarta and Istanbul, and for the worlds we have encountered on the way. I also want to express deep gratitude to the six other dancers-choreographers whose bodily work forms the core of my research: Zufit Simon, Chantal Loïal, Farah Saleh, André M. Zachery, Wan-Chao Chang, and Christiane Emmanuel.

My heartfelt thanks go to all of you for carving precious time within your busy schedules, expressing enthusiasm and trust, sharing fascinating conversations and performances. Like a performance, this work required patience and perseverance to be materialized, and I thank you for understanding it. I admire your moving efforts to fill the stage and our hearts with beauty and complexity. Your inexhaustible discipline and creativity are the fuel that powers my research.

Oxana Chi's creative spirit has shaped Berlin's and more recently Brooklyn's artistic landscapes in many ways. She is a trendsetting and internationally ac-claimed dancer-choreographer, artistic director, filmmaker, author, and curator. Between 2010 and 2014, I had the pleasure to participate in her film project about her dance *Through Gardens*. The production took place in Indonesia, Germany, and France, and resulted in the feature-length documentary-fiction film *Dancing Through Gardens (Durch Gärten Tanzen)*. During that time, I also published my first essays and journalistic articles about dance in English, French, and German.[3]

In 2011, within the context of the exhibition *Tanzende Erinnerungen (Dancing Memories)* curated by Oxana Chi at the Galerie Gondwana, we commissioned the placement of a "Stolperstein" stone for Tatjana Barbakoff in the center of Berlin. Stolperstein literally means "a stone to stumble upon." The stones are a commem-orative project by the artist and activist Gunter Demnig, who places them on side-walks all over Germany to render visible the names of people who were deported during the Nazi rule.[4] The increasing presence of the stones throughout the coun-try marks public space with a material, daily, individualized memory-reminder. While the stones are usually placed in front of the building where people had lived, we asked Demnig to place the Barbakoff stone in front of the Renaissance Theater where Barbakoff performed, thus shifting the focus from her place of residence to

---

3   Zami, "Rendre sur scène son corps à Sawtche." and Zami, "Mit Oxana Chi Durch Gärten."
4   The artist started the project in 1996 in Berlin-Kreuzberg, defying the lack of municipal au-thorization. The city legalized the stones later, and by now Demnig has placed 50,000 stones all over Europe. Some cities such as Munich continue to forbid the stones, which continue to be placed individually by hand by the artist-artisan, funded by private individual and insti-tutional donors. http://www.stolpersteine.eu/en/

her place of work, in order to signify her major role in the cultural history of the city. The memory stones, like the *performemory* I sketch in this study, generate a dynamic remembering, situated in the present and negotiated by the movement of individual bodies within collective spaces.

In 2012, Oxana Chi invited me to work with her in the development of her production *I Step On Air*, commissioned by Dr. Natasha Kelly, who taught the May-Ayim-seminar at Humboldt-University at that time. With the choreographer's mentorship, I created and performed music, physical theater, and poetry in dialogue with the dance. This was my first experience as an Interdisciplinary Artist-in-Residence with Oxana Chi & Ensemble Xinren, also known as Oxana Chi Dance & Art. I have been touring universities, theaters, festivals and conferences with the company ever since, gaining invaluable artistic experiences that inspired and shaped my academic reflection on dance-making.

I Step On Air commemorates and celebrates the legacy of May Ayim, a Ghanaian-German author, activist, scholar and teacher, whom Chi likes to call the "Afro-German Audre Lorde," knowing that Ayim was indeed a close friend of Lorde. Ayim's words (cited at the beginning of this introduction) connect dream and motion in a fashion that resonates with Oxana Chi's commemoration-celebration of dancer Tatjana Barbakoff in *Through Gardens*. Ayim's dreamlike imagery echoes Barbakoff's account of "dreaming herself into" the Chinese silk clothes of her mother as a child, an experience which she subsequently defined as her first attempts to make dance.[5] As you will see, the layers of diaspora's costumes carry patterns that resurface throughout this book.

Tatjana Barbakoff was a successful expressionist dancer-choreographer who inspired many artists in the 1920s/30s Europe, yet is often unacknowledged in what pretends to be "the" Western dance historical canon. The experience of *Through Gardens*, as well as the kitchen table conversations and office desk discussions with its choreographer, made me realize the importance of writing about and documenting how cultural memory and historical trauma are performed on stage. I deem it important to specifically address the issue of (in)visibility of certain artists in an academic context because universities devote material resources such as funding, time, and curricula to historiographical and epistemological matters.

In 2013, I became a doctoral candidate at Humboldt-University in Berlin, where I conducted research within the Cultural Studies department, and later within the Center for Transdisciplinary Gender Studies. I wish to thank my doctoral advisors at Humboldt-University, starting with Professor Claudia Bruns, Chair of the Institute for Cultural Studies, for showing interest in the initial iteration of the project.

---

5   Straus-Ernst, "Bei Tatjana Barbakoff"; Printed in Chi, *Tanzende Erinnerungen*, 2011, 15–17. Originally printed in Goebbels, *Tatjana Barbakoff: eine vergessene Tänzerin in Bildern und Dokumentation*.

My thanks also go to the bold scholar Dr. Lann Hornscheidt, formerly Professor for Gender Studies and Language Analysis at Humboldt-University, and currently founding director of the publishing house w_orten & meer. I appreciate the empowering support I received from you, our deep conversations on the topic of voices, privileges, visibility, and the encouragement to expand the definition and goals of what is known as "Gender Studies."

From 2013 onwards, I had the great pleasure and privilege to be a Doctoral Fellow in the Jewish Talents Program "Jüdische Begabtenförderung" administered by the Ernst-Ludwig-Ehrlich-Studienwerk (ELES Scholarship Fund) and funded by the Federal Ministry of Education and Research, known as BMBF in Germany. A special acknowledgement goes to my program advisors at ELES, PD Dr. Eva Lezzi and Dr. Dmitrij Belkin for their constant availability. ELES, along with Humboldt-University's KSBF Women's Fund, also funded some of my international research stays and presentation travels.

In the summer of 2013, I accompanied Oxana Chi on a networking trip to New York City, and took a deep dive into open-air and air-conditioned spheres of dance and research. I attended dance classes at the CUMBE Center for African and Diaspora Dance, where I met the wonderful founding director of Evidence, Ronald K. Brown. I want to acknowledge the generosity of Ronald Brown, and company member Annique Roberts, for precious interviews that informed the orientation of my research. At the top of the Brooklyn Library building, I found the monograph *Urban Bush Women – Twenty Years of African American Dance Theater, Community Engagement, and Working It Out*[6] written by Professor Nadine George-Graves.

I am grateful that Professor George-Graves, former President of the Congress for Research on Dance, and currently Chair of the Dance Department at Ohio State University, accompanied part of this journey as a doctoral advisor. Thank you for inviting me to be a Visiting Research Scholar at the Department of Theatre and Dance at the University of California San Diego in 2015, and for inciting me to find what became the book structure as early as possible. I appreciated our intellectual exchanges on the short islands of time whose diasporic shores we lingered on. At UCSD, I also thank Marybeth Ward for keeping it sunny on the administrative side of the street.

As a Visiting Research Scholar at Columbia University in New York in 2015/2016, I had the pleasure to meet and exchange with Professor Tina Campt during her time at the head of the Barnard Center for Research on Women (BCRW). I was a Visiting Scholar in the Institute for Research on Women, Gender and Sexuality (IRWGS), led by Professor Marianne Hirsch, who became my doctoral advisor. I am grateful to Marianne Hirsch for her trust, curiosity and availability, and for the gift of her presence at my dissertation viva in Berlin in May 2017. The defense

---

6   George-Graves, *Urban Bush Women.*

was also attended by committee members Dean Professor Ulrike Vedder, PD. Dr. Bettina Bock von Wülfingen, Professor Susanne Gehrmann, Dr. Pepetual Mforbe Chiangong, and my students Marie Springborn and Jan Dammel. I thank them for their presence, as well as my special guests Dr. Ika Hügel-Marschall and Dr. Dagmar Schulz, who were close friends of Audre Lorde during her Berlin years.

Several enthusiastic experts assisted me on my writing journey. I warmly thank my editor Dr. Fatin Abbas, a creative writer and Harvard alumna, for her precious edits and her careful attention to detail. In Berlin, Dr. Jacob K. Langford (artist and lecturer at Humboldt-University) gave wonderful feedback on the first chapter, and Professor Michelle M. Wright (Northwestern University) shared helpful thoughts during a graduate workshop. Professor Jill Strauss (City University of New York, Department of Theatre and Communication), dance expert Judy Pritchett (Frankie Manning Foundation, Board), Aradhana Hinds (New School, Doctoral Candidate), and Kerry Downey (RISD faculty member, interdisciplinary artist and former MoMA educator) took up the torch in New York, gifting me with many helpful edits and suggestions. For assistance with interview transcription and translation, I thank dancers-writers Jaya Chakravarti (Berlin) and Nubian Néné (New York, Glasses & Laces). Warm thanks also go to my friend and comrade AnouchK Ibacka-Valiente (community organizer, activist, and spiritual leader) for always having more than two ears to listen and more than one word of encouragement to express.

In 2016, it was a pleasurable challenge to develop and teach my first graduate seminar at Humboldt-University, entitled "Performing Memory," which was selected for the Education Quality Program (Berliner Qualitätsoffensive für die Lehre), and led me to obtain the First Prize in the Faculty Teaching Award (Fakultätspreis für gute Lehre) from the Faculty of Humanities and Social Sciences.

For financial support that contributed to making this publication possible, I thank the German Foundation Stiftung Zeitlehren; the Faculty of Humanities and Social Sciences (KSBF) at Humboldt-University; and the History of Art and Design Department at Pratt Institute. At Pratt, I also benefited from Mellon Research Funds awarded through the Department of Humanities and Media Studies. At these institutions, my special acknowledgements go to Dr. Agnes Hartmann, Professor Arlene Keizer, Professor John Decker, Jill Song, Professor Jennifer Miller, Professor Heather Lewis, and Mirland Terlonge.

It is a wonderful opportunity to publish my first monograph in the influential Critical Dance Studies series. At transcript publishing house, I thank Jenso Scheer, Johanna Tönsing, and the series editors Professor Gabriele Klein and Professor Gabriele Brandstetter for receiving my book project with openness and enthusiasm. I also thank my project manager Dr. Mirjam Galley for her availability and clear communication, and the marketing team for their efforts. For the beautiful cover design, my thanks go to the talented Doro Tops and to Kordula Röckenhaus.

Warm thanks also go to my colleague and friend Professor Jens R. Giersdorf (Marymount Manhattan College) for believing in this book.

None of this would have been possible without the love of my parents Dr. Ketty Smith and Alex Zuckerman. I also wish to acknowledge my grandmother Germaine, who made space for my steaming laptop in her Caribbean diaspora dining room; and my grandmother Friedel, a Folkwang alumna, whose dance career was brutally disrupted in Germany in 1933. To all my ancestors and all the deities and spiritual beings twirling around this and other universes, I send endless gratefulness for helping me to overcome, circumvent, and jump over structural barriers of racism, antisemitism, genderism, classism, homophobia, and transphobia. Thank you for always carrying me into the crea(c)tive flow.

Imagining, or What an Academic and Artist Aims to Find Out about Dance and Memory

The connection between traumatic cultural memory and corporeality has come to the fore in recent years, especially with the vanishing of the last generation of Holocaust survivors, and the digitalization of oral history – slave narratives, for instance. The role of performing bodies within collective and individual cultures of remembrance, however, has been contested. Memory scholarship has foregrounded the role of visual and literary arts in representing, reclaiming and recasting history.[7] Feminism and performance scholars have argued that the body functions as an archive.[8] Some scholars of African-American studies have situated Black[9] bodies as receptors and generators of culture, and highlighted how dancers perform and negotiate the intersections of race and gender on stage.[10] Yet to date, little research has thoroughly examined the function of dance as an epistemological practice of

---

7   See Bruns, Dardan, and Dietrich, Anette, *Welchen der Steine du hebst*; Hirsch, *The Generation of Postmemory*; Kelly, *Afrokultur*; Mandel, *Against the Unspeakable*; Landsberg, *Prosthetic Memory*; Rothberg, *Multidirectional Memory*; Tillet, *Sites of Slavery*.

8   See Anzaldúa, *Borderlands*; Cvetkovich, *An Archive of Feelings*; Lepecki, *Exhausting Dance*; Taylor, *The Archive and The Repertoire*; Wehren, *Körper als Archiv in Bewegung*; Zenenga, "Power and the Body."

9   I use the word "Black" to refer to people of the African diaspora. I choose to capitalize the word "Black" to acknowledge the fact that Black is a proper name on par with Jewish, Latinx, or Irish. On this controversial question, see for instance Lori L. Tharps, "The Case for Black With a Capital B"; Kapitan, "Ask a Radical Copyeditor: Black with a Capital 'B.'"

10   See for example Dixon Gottschild, *The Black Dancing Body*; George-Graves, *Urban Bush Women*; Johnson and Rivera-Servera, *Blacktino Queer Performance*; Kusser, *Körper in Schieflage: Tanzen Im Strudel Des Black Atlantic Um 1900*; DeFrantz, *Dancing Revelations: Alvin Ailey's Embodiment of African American Culture*; DeFrantz and Tara A. Willis, "Black Moves: New Research in Black Dance Studies."

cultural memory in relation to historical trauma. Pursuing this research path represents a vital step in opening up new viewpoints on memory, and gaining new insights into the value and function of the body within the humanities.

From writing history to dancing memory

How can dancers embody the afterlives of traumatic pasts, in ways that render the sensation of the present meaningful, and the imagination of the future possible? This overarching question is the canvas on which I examine moving bodies as nodal points between cultural, performance and gender studies. My aim is to analyze how dance performances and cultural memory intersect in the 21st century. I am interested in finding out how selected works handle and generate knowledge about historical trauma in relation to current sociopolitical contexts. My research explores how movement and, more specifically, contemporary dance productions, may inform and transform access to traumatic pasts, current power relations and perceptions of (post)human futures at a personal and a societal level. Contending that corporeality is a site and a source of power, I ask what happens when bodies propel the past into the present, metaphorically and materially. By challenging the presumed ephemerality of dance,[11] I contend that it can be read as a dynamic epistemology that mobilizes memory, in a way that has a long-lasting impact on the production and transmission of memory. Eventually, this book argues that dance as an epistemological medium functions as a fundamental tool for processing historical trauma in relation to current sociopolitical relations.

I hope to contribute to knowledge production located at the crossroads of gender studies, cultural memory studies, postcolonial studies, performance studies, and critical dance studies. Working towards the recognition of dance as a vital field for academia, I argue that it should be acknowledged as knowledge, thus rejoining dancer-scholar Ananya Chatterjea, who makes the case for:

> [...] situating dance and choreographic work in the larger frame of cultural production as a potent source of information, analysis, and critique, linked intimately to the processes of sociocultural and political change.[12]

Here Chatterjea suggests that dance can, or even should be a matter of academic inquiry, and that interpreting dance works can lead to sociopolitical transformation. In Germany, scholars such as Gabriele Klein and Gabriele Brandstetter have sharpened the reflection on the epistemological role of dance, and contributed to

---

11   See for instance the performance-as-disappearance paradigm of Peggy Phelan in *Unmarked: The Politics of Performance*; and Schneider, *Performing Remains*, for arguments against the ephemerality of performance.

12   Chatterjea, *Butting Out*, 30.

"the ongoing process of de- and re-thinking questions of dance and theory."[13] Their much appreciated *TanzSkripte* and *Critical Dance Studies* series, in which this book appears, is part of this effort. Klein even argues that

> [...] the customary separation of dance from other areas of society, but above all the demarcations within the dance field itself – for example between dance as art, dance studies and dance education – are irrelevant.[14]

If we finally achieve a much needed increase in dance and performance studies departments at German universities (starting with Humboldt-University, where my research stood out through its focus on dance), what does this statement imply? We could re-envision these dance "demarcations," and strive for increasingly inter- and transdisciplinary networks that are conceived so as to promote a constant flow of knowledge between research, practice, and education. With my project, publication and film production, I undertake a small, yet hopefully significant step in this direction.

Years before I started reading any dance theory, it is live dance itself that sharpened my awareness of its crucial sociopolitical role, as mentioned in the preceding section in reference to the milestone encounter with *Through Gardens*. Its choreographer Oxana Chi, the first artist interviewed for this book, suggested that her dance-making overlaps with a process of memory-making. The (hi)storytelling dance maker emphasizes the intent to use dance as a medium to counter hegemonic storytelling and, the will to use her body as a counterweight to mainstream historical narratives:

> [My work on] Tatjana Barbakoff led me to increasingly question: Who writes or is allowed to write history in Germany, in Europe, in the world? It then became clear to me how important it is, for contemporary artists like myself, to write history ourselves. And if I do not have the means to write a book, then I shall step on stage, and dance it out, this history. I must create alternatives to all this mainstream that actually, very intentionally, narrates a single story, which is, for my taste, extremely truncated.
>
> ([Meine Arbeit zu] Tatjana Barbakoff hat mich mehr und mehr dazu gebracht, zu hinterfragen: Wer eigentlich in Deutschland, wer eigentlich in Europa, wer eigentlich in der Welt Geschichte schreibt, oder schreiben darf. Dann wurde mir klar, dass es ganz wichtig ist, für zeitgenössische Künstler_innen wie mich, Geschichte selbst zu schreiben. Und wenn ich nicht die Mittel habe, ein Buch zu

---

13   Brandstetter and Klein, *Dance [and] Theory*, 13. This anthology offers important insights derived from contributions presented at the international congress on *Dance [and] Theory* held at the Uferstudios in Berlin in April 2011. See also Klein and Noeth, *Emerging Bodies: The Performance of Worldmaking in Dance and Choreography*.

14   Klein, "Dancing Politics: Worldmaking in Dance and Choreography," 26.

schreiben, dann muss ich mich auf die Bühne stellen und muss sie dort vertanzen, die Geschichte. Ich muss Alternativen schaffen, zu diesem ganzen Mainstream, der im Prinzip ganz ganz berechnend eine einzige Geschichte schreibt, die für mein Geschmack, sehr sehr beschränkt ist.[15])

Chi emphasizes her will to use her own body as a tool to challenge and displace hegemonic narratives. This does not mean that she rejects the practice of writing. Her own reflections on her work appear in self-published publications as well as in academic anthologies such as *Sisters and Souls*.[16] What I read in the quotation however is the will to explore dance art as a corporeal alternative to conventional instruments of historiography.

Dance indeed enables the expression of stories, characters and imaginations that are otherwise marginalized, invisibilized, or erased in Western narratives of the past, as we will see in this book. Focusing on the role of social categories in the production of historical narratives from a transnational feminist Afro-diasporic perspective, Samantha Pinto asks,

> How do race, gender, and diaspora interact with the concept of 'history', both as it is constructed as a Western narrative of dominance and in counternarratives of resistance?[17]

This book offers some responses through the lens of dance. I contend that because the categories of race and gender are constructed as bodily markers, the analysis of bodily engagements with history provides necessary tools to answer Pinto's question. I examine how selected choreographic works negotiate hegemonic conventions and definitions of memory, and how they contribute to reflecting upon concepts of diaspora, time, space, body and self. Dance does not only signify and represent meaning, it also enacts power dynamics on multiple levels, as pointed out by Susan Foster:

> [...] as a *cultural practice* that cultivates disciplined and creative bodies, as a *representational practice* that explores rigorously strategies for developing bodily signification, as a *cultural endeavor* through which cultural change is both registered and accomplished [...].[18]

To analyze dance, one must therefore take into consideration the interplay of its cultural, representational, and interventional dimensions. Because my book focuses on artists who work outside of mainstream structures of cultural production, I found it particularly relevant to look at how they negotiate the stage as a

---

15   Chi, Interview.
16   Chi, "Von Hier Nach Dort - I Step On Air."
17   Pinto, *Difficult Diasporas*, 78.
18   Foster, *Corporealities: Dancing Knowledge, Culture and Power*, xii. [My emphasis]

strategic site for bodies to not only represent (themselves or others), but also to intervene by reclaiming visibility and agency. The performances discussed here have not only remained relevant to our society, they actually offer significant embodied contributions to worldwide debates on bodily movements, distance and proximity, survival, and how to navigate space and time individually and institutionally, topics that now appear more urgent than ever.

Seven dancers, seven dances

In the precious hours that I spent counterbalancing the academic activities of sitting/reading/writing, I encountered the eight limbs of yoga, a fundament on which a yogi is meant to build their home. My research material rests on seven limbs. (Seven is a great yogic number too, think of the seven chakras!). The book discusses seven works by seven dancer-choreographers who are currently active in the dance scene: Oxana Chi, Zufit Simon, Christiane Emmanuel, Chantal Loïal, Farah Saleh, Wan-Chao Chang, and André M. Zachery. Commonalities include the fact that all of them are able-bodied cis-gender identifying artists (six women and one man).

Based in Germany, Taïwan, Martinique, Palestine, France and the USA, their choreography sometimes relates to their genealogies located in Afro-descendent (Afro-European, African-American, and Caribbean), Jewish European, Palestinian and Chinese diasporas. I regroup these artists who vary greatly in terms of style, location, race, age, and education under a broadly defined "diasporic dance" umbrella. Just as a dancer's pieces of work form a repertoire, this research is my own repertoire of perforMemory.

My study focuses on concert dance productions, meaning works that have been choreographed, rehearsed, and performed by professional artists on a stage for an audience, often in a conventional theatrical setting. Consequently, my research scope does not encompass social dance, such as club dancing, or street dance.[19] While most pieces discussed belong to the realm of concert dance, Farah Saleh's *Parole, Parole, Parole* is an interactive lecture-performance with and about dance.

For the sake of clarity, capacity, intensity, and sanity, the written analysis focuses on one piece per dancer-choreographer. The book spotlights one solo dance per artist, meaning that the choreographer interprets her/his/their own work on stage, without other dancers involved (the only other performers occasionally being musicians). Here, again, the dance solo *Through Gardens* inspired me to concentrate on single, individual corporealities dancing onstage, performing movements they

---

19   For research on social dance I recommend: Ramón H. Rivera-Servera, *Performing Queer Latinidad*; Bragin, "Shot and Captured: Turf Dance, YAK Films, Nad the Oakland, California, R.I.P. Project."; Cyrille, "Musique, Danse et Résistance En Guadeloupe et En Martinique."

created for their own bodies. I was also incited to choose this lens of analysis because I found that most of the academic readings dealt with group choreographies and/or collective dances.[20] This does not mean that solo dance is the exclusive or preferred mode of expression for all the dance-makers discussed. In fact, most of these artists are prolific group choreographers, for instance Chantal Loïal as the Founder-Director of Difé Kako and André Zachery with his Renegade Performance Group (RPG). Focusing on dancer-choreographers – rather than dancers or choreographers – also offered an additional insight into the power of agency I was interested in exploring in relation to perforMemory.

Since the artists perform their own choreography, it was particularly interesting to conduct interviews and listen to their perspectives. In this context, I opened the conversation to other works, including some of their group choreographies. You will find these riveting discussions in the last chapter entitled Dance Dialogues. These interview transcripts, rather than being a mere appendix, constitute a book within the book, allowing the reader to zoom out and to discern a broader picture of each choreographer's repertoire and artistic intents. Here you will read about other creations dealing with historical trauma from a diasporic perspective, for instance Oxana Chi's *Neferet iti* and *I Step On Air*; Wan-Chao Chang's *Keep Her Safe, Please!*; André Zachery's *The Inscription Project* and *Dapline!* (with Renegade Performance Group); Farah Saleh's *Ordinary Madness* (with Sarreyet Ramallah); and Chantal Loïal's *Noirs de Boue et d'Obus* (with Difé Kako). The film *Memory2Go*, which shall complement this book, also includes excerpts and discussions of several works by the artists, thus giving simultaneously a broader and a more precise impression of their performances of memory.

The decision to write only about works I appreciate and admire is a natural pendant to the methodology described later. It echoes the approach of performance scholars such as Jill Dolan, who writes about "works that inspired [her] emotionally, intellectually, and politically."[21] Moreover, the selection of the performances comes from a conscious will to acknowledge the works of artists whose active and important presence onstage has received less exposure in academia.

However, this claim too must be relativized, as some of the seven artists discussed here are becoming increasingly present in academic settings. *Through Gardens* has been included in the curriculum of Humboldt-University's Gender Studies department since 2016, and is now discussed in several academic publications.

---

20   For an interesting discussion of race and gender in solo theater pieces, and a dynamic collection of academic essays, artists interviews, and performance scripts, see the anthology: Johnson and Rivera-Servera, *Solo/Black/Woman*. See also Gabriele Klein, (co-editor of this *Critical Dance Studies* series), *Pina Bausch's Dance Theater* for a discussion of the lesser investigated solo dances in Pina Bausch's repertoire.

21   Dolan, *Utopia in Performance*, 33.

Since 2013, Oxana Chi's performances have increasingly been featured at universities, and she performed at prestigious universities including New York University's Jack Crystal Theater, Humboldt-University, Goldsmiths University (London), Bielefeld University, Yeditepe University (Istanbul), Tampere University (Finland), among others. In 2016, Farah Saleh was a choreographer in residence at Brown University and a Visiting Scholar at the Pembroke Center. André M. Zachery recently published an article reflecting upon his *Afrofuturism Series* in the Yale Drama journal.[22] He was a 2017-2018 Guest Professor at Virginia Commonwealth University (VCU).

In the desire to explore contemporaneity, this study highlights concert dance productions from the 21st century. All pieces discussed are original creations, and premiered between August 2008 and November 2015 in Germany, the USA, France, Martinique and Taiwan. Although I formally began doctoral research in 2013, I relate to live experiences of the works between 2009 and 2016. I conducted interviews between 2013 and 2016 in Berlin, Paris, Vienna, New York City, Fort-de-France (Martinique), and Taipei. Since then, the artists and their creations have not only remained relevant, they offer increasingly urgent responses to current issues of representation, corporeality, migration, and movement at individual and societal scales.

I limit the scope to recent works because my intent is to engage with dance productions which are currently part of the cultural landscape. Although or because contemporary choreographic inquiries of the past are often re-enactments of past works or events, I chose to highlight a less explored field, namely original creations that engage with the past. This also works towards bridging the gap between cultural productions and their inscription into academic knowledge production, and generating knowledge in synchronicity with its societal surroundings. The following chart is meant to offer a clear and concise overview of the seven performances at stake here.

---

22   Zachery, "Futurity and the Containment of Blackness in Twenty-First-Century Performance."

Overview of the main dance productions discussed in this book

Perfor-mance	Artist	Synopsis	Premiere
Through Gardens (Durch Gärten)	**Oxana Chi**	A tribute celebrating and commemorating the successes and struggles of dancer and muse Tatjana Barbakoff in 1920s/30s Europe.	September **2008** House of Democracy and Human Rights, Berlin, **Germany**
Choc(s) (Shock(s))	**Christiane Emmanuel**	An assessment of body memory at the confluence of political, economic, physical and spiritual shocks on a global and local scale.	November **2010** Aimé Césaire Theater, Fort-de-France, **Martinique**
On t'appelle Vénus (They Call You Venus)	**Chantal Loïal**	The story of Sawtche, aka Sarah Baartman, her experience as "Black Venus," and a return to her Khoi San roots.	January **2011** Aimé Césaire Theater, Fort-de-France, **Martinique**
Impressions	**Wan-Chao Chang**	A corporeal retrospective on Chang's inner and outer journeys in search of artistic and cultural identity.	September **2012** Taipei Fringe Festival, **Taiwan**
Parole, Parole, Parole	**Farah Saleh**	The (im-)possibility of a Gaza/Ramallah love story within political-physical barriers.	April **2013** Ramallah Contemporary Dance Festival, **Palestine**
all about nothing (un-emotional Series)	**Zufit Simon**	A body collage on trauma and emotions, inviting the audience to activate their own memories	June **2014** Schwere Reiter, Munich, **Germany**
Digital Middle Passage (Afrofuturism Series)	**André M. Zachery**	An exploration of the movements of African-American diasporic identity between past, present and future.	November **2015** Irondale Center, New York, **USA**

By no means do I attempt to give an evenly balanced discussion of each piece, as it would contradict my epistemological and methodological framework, described in the next section. Firstly, the pieces vary greatly in terms of duration, for instance a full hour for *Through Gardens*, 27 minutes for *Digital Middle Passage*, or 15 minutes for *Parole, Parole, Parole*. Moreover, my knowledge of the pieces and my proximity to the artists also vary greatly. While I have followed the works of Oxana Chi, André Zachery, and Chantal Loïal closely over several years, I encountered other choreographers more recently. Sometimes, I had the chance to witness a choreographer's process within her own dance studio, as is the case with Christiane Emmanuel in Martinique, other times I used the internet technology to find out about new artists, for instance with Farah Saleh. After having reached out to her per email, I travelled to the Tanzquartier Vienna to attend her performance about work created in Palestine. The research phases and interviews I conducted in Taiwan and Martinique (still a French colony) were opportunities to research outside the West. This disparity of perception infers a diverse engagement with the works. I found that all choreographers have a different understanding of (cultural) memory, and do not necessarily refer to their work as works of memory in the performance descriptions or public statements. It is rather through my interpretation that they come to co-exist as diverse voices in the conceptual body of perforMemory.

Jumping between the gaps of hegemonic narratives

The dance performances engage with various historical traumata, such as the European Holocaust, the Transatlantic Slave Trade, the Maafa,[23] the Nakba,[24] and other forms of colonial-racist violence. The dances explore tropes of displacement, migration, oppression, empowerment and resistance from the micro-level of the individual body cells to the meta-level of society networks. All the dancers-choreographers situate their dance practice in the now, meaning that their interest in knowing the past goes hand-in-hand with the desire to shape the present.

Through a reflection upon these pieces, my book examines how dance art intervenes in memory discourses and practices. My main research goal is to discover how dance can accomplish what bell hooks calls "a politicization of memory [...], remembering that serves to illuminate and transform the present."[25] In my view,

---

23   The term Maafa means "catastrophe" in Ki-Swahili. It was introduced by Marimba Ani to name the physical, economic, and psychological violence perpetrated against Afro-descendant bodies in the Transatlantic Slave Trade and other forms of imperial domination, past and present. See Ballé Moudoumbou, "Erste Annäherung zu Maafa."

24   The word Nakba means "Catastrophe" in Arabic, and is used to refer to the forced displacement of approximately 750,000 Palestinians that began with Israel's establishment, and that continues to this day. Originally the term was used to call 1920 the "Nakba year", in reference to the colonial partition of the Ottoman Empire, which led to uprising in Palestine, Syria and Irak. See Jewish Voice for Peace. "Facing the Nakba."

25   hooks, "Choosing the Margin as a Space of Radical Openness," 155.

these seven pieces share the capacity to *politicize memory* on stage, by embodying biographies, themes, and perspectives usually marginalized in dominant narratives of history. Thus, my research is also about political matters: the interaction between the power of performance and the performance of power.[26]

Institutional memory, as it is transmitted via official textbooks, media, and monuments, often does not adequately represent and address the perspectives of people of color[27] and/or marginalized groups. In the German context, Kien Nghi Ha calls "Ent_innerung"[28] (dis_remembering) the active process of writing minoritarian perspectives out of institutional memories of national-socialism and colonialism. Ha's scholarship demonstrates how the failure to acknowledge the colonial-racist past pervades contemporary memory discourses and practices.[29] Using the example of the medial representation of the 1992 Rostock-Lichtenhagen pogrom directed against Vietnamese migrants, he further unveils dis_remembering as a root of racism in the present. On June 21st 2012, Ha released an anthology on Asian-German diasporic presences.[30] As part of the book release event, organized jointly with the Federal Agency for Civic Education, he curated Oxana Chi's *Through Gardens*. After the performance, Ha expressed a strong emotional reaction to the piece. He joined the performer on stage to express openly how the dance form set into motion, in the theater, and in his body, an unusually visceral engagement with topics of diaspora, identity, discrimination, and memory. Indeed, Chi is able to fill the gaps of dis_remembering with her movements, creating space for the complexity of Tatjana Barbakoff's Asian-European-Russian cultural heritage and for the possibility of a narrative in which success and persecution co-exist. The performance reminded the audience of the role of the body in defying the epidemic disease of Ent_innerung or dis_remembering.

In the context of the Americas, there is an equivalent for dis_remembering in the scholarship of Diana Taylor. She cites the word "dememorazido"[31] used by the Peruvian performance group Yuyachkani, which leads her to speak of "percepticide."[32] The term is a powerful wording suggesting that epistemic violence, and the

---

26   Zenenga, "Power and the Body."
27   I understand "people of color," following Kien-Nghi Ha, as a generic, political term referring to racialized humans who possess either or many of these genealogical origins: African, Asian, South American, Arabic, Kurdish, Jewish, Indigenous, Pacific. Ha traces the origins of the words to a 1966 Black Panther manifesto. Without masking differences, the appellation aims to foster solidarity among people experiencing racialized discrimination. See Ha, "People of Colour."
28   Ha, "Macht (T)raum(a) Berlin," 105.
29   Ha, "Die Fragile Erinnerung Des Entinnerten"; Ha, "Rostock-Lichtenhagen: Die Rückkehr Des Verdrängten."
30   Ha, *Asiatische Deutsche*.
31   Taylor, *The Archive and The Repertoire*, 209.
32   Taylor, 28.

erasure of certain perceptions in memory transmission is part of and/or is itself genocidal violence.

Michel Rolph-Trouillot also argues that "any historical narrative is a particular bundle of silence."[33] In *Silencing the Past*, he reflects on historiographical omissions and erasure with case studies touching upon such diverse themes as the Haitian Revolution, the Holocaust, and Disney's plans for an amusement park themed around slavery in Virginia. What Rolph-Trouillot shares with Chi, Ha, and Taylor as cited earlier, is an attention to the relations between present power structures and historical narratives. All of them show how omissions are not haphazard occurrences, but rather fundamental rules of the storytelling game. While Ha and Taylor use nouns to name silencing practices, Rolph-Trouillot emphasizes the verb form:

> By silence, I mean an active and transitive process: one "silences" a fact or an individual as a silencer silences a gun. One engages in the practice of silencing.[34]

What this uncanny imagery suggests is the intricacy of material and historiographic power: hegemonic violence operates not only through physical weaponry but also through epistemic practices of erasure. Moreover, like a silencer aimed at rendering the shot inaudible, historical silencing is a practice that renders certain events, biographies and perspectives invisible. In our film *Dancing Through Gardens*, Oxana Chi reflects on the connection between physical, linguistic, and epistemic erasure. On her way to her daily rehearsal, she crosses the former border between East and West Berlin, speaking into the camera "Der Fluss hat nicht nur ihre Körper fortgespült, sondern auch Ihre Namen," which can be translated as "The river has not only flushed their bodies away, but also their names."[35] This is especially true of those actresses of history, who happen to be women, and more so women of color. My book aims to foreground dance as a practice of re-membering that has the power to counteract hegemonic practices of historical erasure.

When dancers embody history on stage, they can bring the past into motion, and emotion, and bring life to what at times become numb words or numbers. As a practice, dance often works through the expression of emotion, for instance in the German expressionist dance form of Ausdruckstanz, and in the Indian emphasis on *rasa*. In the academic world, Sara Ahmed makes the relation between emotion, bodies and time particularly clear:

> Emotions tell us a lot about time; emotions are the very 'flesh' of time. They show us the time it takes to move, or to move on, is a time that exceeds the time of an individual life. Through emotions, the past persists on the surface of bodies.

---

33   Trouillot, *Silencing The Past: Power and the Production of History.*, 26–27.
34   Trouillot, 48.
35   Chi and Zami (dir.) *Dancing Through Gardens (Durch Gärten Tanzen)*.

Emotions show us how histories stay alive, even when they are not consciously remembered; how histories of colonialism, slavery, and violence shape lives and worlds in the present. The time of emotion is not always about the past, and how it sticks. Emotions also open up futures, in the ways they involve different orientations to others.[36]

Although she does not refers to dance, Ahmed hints at possibilities for using emotions and body memory to transcend spatiotemporal boundaries. While all art forms can express emotional states, dancers channel emotions through their own bodies moving through space and time, or spacetime. If emotions tell history, then a body-in-motion-through-emotion is a strong vector of history. Dancers activate their bodies – and thus their emotional surfaces – in the present, and also use them to represent the possibility of transformation in the future. Bodies in movement can thus become, and be read as the location of re-emerging pasts, but also as living nodes channeling a past, present, and future connection.

Ahmed's take on emotions echoes the definition of diaspora offered by Anita Gonzalez and Thomas DeFrantz's in their introduction to *Black Performance Theory*:

Like skin, [diaspora] is porous and permeable, flexible and self-repairing, finely spun and fragile. And like skin on a body, diaspora palpably protects us. We wrap ourselves in its possibilities, and they remind us of impossible connectivities. In this reminding—this bringing into consciousness of the intangible experience of a mythic past—we wear memory on our bodies; we see each other in skins that go together or sometimes belong apart.[37]

Here again, bodily surfaces are understood as the embodiment of past trauma and present connections. The duality of fragility and protection, past and present seems to be an attribute of emotions as well as of diaspora, both of which are metaphorically conceived here as skins. If diaspora is like a skin on the body, what happens when diaspora dances on and with the body? I would like to suggest that the body is the meeting point between overlapping conceptualizations and realizations of memory, diaspora, spacetime, and movement. These four elements become the signposts for the chapters you will encounter as you travel further along the book.

Thinking of spacetime, let's pause a moment on temporality. Porousness, permeability and flexibility are also attributes of time. Temporality sustains both memory and dance, and is therefore at the core of this book, with a thorough discussion in chapter three. I ask how the dancers negotiate emotional, temporal and spatial perimeters not only to represent, but also to enact, through their own flesh, alternative realities. By looking at the temporality of historical narratives

---

36   Ahmed, *The Cultural Politics of Emotion*, 202.
37   DeFrantz and Gonzalez, *Black Performance Theory*, 11.

and dancing narratives, I argue that dance can offer a compelling alternative to chronological approaches to the past. For instance, I discuss André M. Zachery's *Digital Middle Passage* as an example of other conceptions and realizations of time and identity-formation. I show how Zachery's work bears affinities with Michelle M. Wright's critique of the "Middle Passage Epistemology,"[38] in which she assesses Western conceptions of linear time as they affect the production of historical and contemporary definitions of blackness.

Because the temporality of performance is the present spacetime, the art of dance is an appropriate medium to address the continuity between historical trauma and contemporary sociopolitical conflicts, between a "haunting past" and an "ongoing violence."[39] In a kindred spirit with Nicola Lauré al-Samarai's interest for Black German visual artists' productions as the possibility to "provide their own plot"[40] to historical narratives, I am interested in how minoritized performing artists officiate the stage, re-write the storyline of historical matter from a diasporic perspective, and intervene directly into present power relations. Presence, which may be physical, political, historical, and charismatic, becomes a main protagonist in my research. At the intersection of memory, self, and agency, I strive to map into words the trajectories of moving bodies within their self-traced dancescapes. Wandering, I wonder how selected dance solos *contemporize* the past and how they stand in the present in the hope of a future. Roaming, I follow the dancers as they move within and beyond current coordinates of race and gender, and explore how they manifest the relation between embodying the past and enacting change in the present.

PerforMemory as a compass

In order to navigate these moving territories, I came to conceptualize *perforMemory* in order to better describe, understand and investigate the innovative ways in which the performances produce memory. Orientating the present research as it navigates through dance, memory, trauma and diaspora, perforMemory can serve as "a compass that traces historical linkages that were never supposed to be visible."[41] The very selection of the performances draws such unexpected lineages. PerforMemory conceptually unfolds throughout the book, and is meant to be expanded conceptually and materially beyond this book. It is a form of expression and an intervention. It is both a performative process and a result. It is a shape-shifting force in collective and individual landscapes of cultural memory. The idea of perforMemory shifts

---

38   Wright, *Physics of Blackness*.
39   Schwab, *Haunting Legacies*, 2.
40   "die Möglichkeit schaffen, ihre Geschichten und Gegenwarten mit einem eigenständigen Plot zu versehen" Lauré al-Samarai, "Inspirited Topography," 118.
41   Omise'eke, "Black Atlantic, Queer Atlantic," 208.

the focus to understanding memory as a site of movement: moving back and forth, and blurring the borders between past, present and future, between countering absence and performing presence, between understanding and imagining, between emotions and reflections, between science and fiction, between transformation and liberation, between knowledge and truth. PerforMemory foregrounds corporeality as a mode of production and transmission of cultural memory. Through my analysis of selected dances, I argue that perforMemory is a remedy to the epidemic silencing that erodes the memorialization of political trauma.

My research is situated chronologically and thematically after the "performative turn in memory studies,"[42] which foregrounds agency and embodiment. The concept of perforMemory shares with Toni Morrison's "rememory" the capacity to be both a noun and a verb. In the novel *Beloved*, first published in 1987, Toni Morrison uses the word "rememory"[43] to describe how the trauma of slavery re-emerges in the lives and bodies of African-Americans in the 20th century. Analyzing *Beloved* alongside Jewish, Kurdish and Palestinian post-traumatic art, Marianne Hirsch theorized the paradigm of "postmemory,"[44] in which memorial identifications also happen across boundaries of race, gender, family and generation. Hirsch works from a refreshing feminist perspective, applying her concept to literature and visual art works that deal with historical trauma. While she asks why visual media has come to occupy the primary place in the field of memory studies,[45] I pose the corollary question: why is dance marginalized on the academic memory stage? Furthermore, Hirsch identifies a challenge for postmemorial artists: to create work that reinvents the past from an affiliative, but not appropriative perspective, and to engage with historical trauma without inducing re-traumatization.[46] The dances of perforMemory presented here take on this challenge successfully, and negotiate traumatic memory in an empowering and healing way.

I believe my concept of perforMemory to be relevant to artists and works beyond this book. Here I think for instance of Julian Carter's discussion of the piece *Lou* (2009), choreographed by Sean Dorsey in memory of the transgender activist Lou Sullivan, and interpreted by four dancers. Carter contends that Dorsey's work "stages the tension between the material reality of historical loss – the past as dead and gone – and the equally material reality of physical rememory - the past as embodied in the living present."[47] The dynamic "tension" between loss and recovery, between countering absence and performing presence, is also relevant to my study. Furthermore, Carter suggests that choreographic engagements with time

42   Plate and Smelik, *Performing Memory in Art and Popular Culture*, 6.
43   Morrison, *Beloved: A Novel*.
44   Hirsch, *The Generation of Postmemory*.
45   Hirsch, 6.
46   Hirsch, 86.
47   Carter, "Embracing Transition, or Dancing in the Folds of Time," 132.

and space can help to illuminate gender transitioning as a permanent movement rather than a linear temporal progression. In embracing diasporic spatialities and non-linear spacetimes, the dances of perforMemory incite the audience to move away from Western hegemonic timelines, and invite them to re-formulate notions of time, space, self, history and identity. The absence-presence of historical figures, stories and perspectives is a recurring duet, or a rope onto which dancers hold when they perforMemory. (One could also say they *perforMemorialize*, to emphasize memorialization rather than memorization). In my development of the idea of perforMemory, I will also speak of ideas such as *choreobiography* and *memory2Go*, as part of my ongoing search for an evolving language that matches the dynamism of its subject matter. *Memory2Go* is also the title of the film which can be viewed as a complement to this book.

My research subscribes to Ananya Chatterjea's definition of choreography as "a mode whereby history can be imagined or interpreted yet again through the interstices of the present enactments."[48] To perforMemory is to enact this "mode," to perform the past from the standpoint of a body's whose essence is to move in the present. PerforMemory is a dancing presence that always looks back while being bound to move forward. The photography on the book cover illustrates this idea. It depicts Oxana Chi in the scene of "The Journey" in *Through Gardens*. Contrary to the conventional Western reading direction, the dancer on the photo moves from right to left, and by doing so, conveys a feeling of return. And simultaneously, her raised hands and feet, and especially the angle of her knees and elbows, unmistakably evoke motion, a march towards new spaces and times.

On this perforMemory odyssey, my inquiry progresses through the following questions-steps:

What is specific about dance as a form of perforMemory? How does perforMemory comment upon notions of home and diaspora? How does perforMemory negotiate Western constructs of time and space, and how does this impact counter-hegemonic memory-making? If perforMemory is about motion, what can the movements of perforMemory be?

Innovating, or Which Contributions I Wish to Make to Existing Scholarship

There is no such thing as a "neutral" state of research, argues academic-activist Lann Hornscheidt, because any assessment of existing scholarship inevitably involves a selection process that will value some sources and ignore others.[49] Horn-

---

48   Chatterjea, *Butting Out*, 21.
49   Hornscheidt, "Postkoloniale Gender-Forschung," 223.

scheidt further notes that these selections, especially when they claim to form an academic "canon," often invisibilize positionalities of race, gender and class. A *state of research* thus always also reflects what it leaves out. Similarly to Ha's notion of dis_remembering, Hornscheidt writes about "EntNennung" (dis_naming),[50] while Alanna Lockward, formerly curator of Black Europe *Body Politics* (BE.BOP), speaks of "EntErwähnen" (dis_mentioning).[51] I would also add that most academic states of research (in the West) obliterate academic productions from the Global South, and other forms of knowledge production such as artistic and activist research. Consequently, I do not find it useful to situate my work within a presumably "objective" state of research. Rather, I try – throughout the book – to highlight how my research may extend, expand and deepen existing scholarship which I have found useful to engage with.

In Germany, Aleida Assmann, who is less often cited than her spouse Jan Assmann, has made important contributions to the research on memory transmission and national-socialism. Memory studies sometimes suffer from an androcentric bias, which tend to grant mostly white male scholars a canonical status. While Assmann does not consider the art of dance, it would be interesting to ask how her inspiring distinction between "Ich-Gedächtnis" (I-memory) and "mich-Gedächtnis" (me-memory), or between the "Spur" (trace) and the "Bahn" (way) apply to performing arts.[52]

In a landscape of cultural memory studies populated with important works investigating the role of visual media and literature, my book aims to offer an important contribution at the intersection between dance studies, memory studies, gender studies, and postcolonial studies. My wish is to spotlight dance, an art form seldom at the forefront of the memory stage. I hope to contribute to the growing field of what I would call global feminist memory studies. Here I think for instance of Marianne Hirsch's work on postmemory, as well as her recently co-edited transnational anthology *Women Mobilizing Memory*, and of Claudia Bruns' research on the relation between the history of antisemitism and colonial-racism.[53] I was also inspired by the global connections devised by Michael Rothberg in thinking through the complexity of memory politics (although his work also centers male perspectives). In his articulation of "multidirectional memory," he points out the epistemic value of linking Holocaust and postcolonial studies. Rothberg discusses for example W.E.B. Du Bois' 1949 trip to the Warsaw ghetto, and his subsequent,

---

50   Nduka-Agwu and Hornscheidt, *Rassismus auf gut Deutsch*.

51   Lockward, "Diaspora."

52   Assmann, *Der lange Schatten der Vergangenheit*, 129.

53   Hirsch, *The Generation of Postmemory*; Bruns, "Antisemitism and Colonial Racism." More recently, see Altınay et al., *Women Mobilizing Memory* (2020); McCormick, *Staging Black Fugitivity* (2019), Baker, *Contemporary Black Women Filmmakers and the Art of Resistance* (2018)

relatively unknown publication in the magazine *Jewish life*.[54] Christina Sharpe also embraces a multidirectional approach, for instance in her "Memory for Forgetting" seminar at Tufts University where students investigate how visual artists, authors and filmmakers handle the trauma of Holocaust and slavery. What all the above mentioned works have in common is the will to create connections across conventional historical and geographic markers, without erasing the specificity of each traumatic event and art work. Here I also wish to note that I have been sharing drafts of my work informally in the research community since 2015, and to acknowledge that several brilliant publications have appeared since I completed the first iteration of my manuscript in 2017. I am particularly eager to witness the increased inclusion of spacetime as a category of research in the fields of performance, media and memory studies, and an increased critical engagement with linear time models and physics in performance and memory studies.[55]

The specificity of perforMemory resides in its capacity to address the multidirectionality of memory not only as a metaphor, but also as a reality, as dancers physically move in multiple directions on stage. Thus, my imagination of perforMemory is constituted by and contributes to conceptual multidirectionality. Most of the scholarship that brings dance and memory/history into constellation focuses on the role of re-enactments. The main concern is not so much dance as a device for performing memory, but rather the choreographic re-enactment of historical pieces and movements, or the performative re-enactment of historical events, for instance in Salamishah Tillet's discussion of Bill T. Jones's work.[56] One of the few scholars who has focused on dance and memory outside of the re-enactment paradigm is Ananya Kabir, a prolific scholar who published several important articles, albeit often with a focus on social dance.[57]

Considering all the gendered and racialized connotations and constructions of the body within hegemonic discourses that perpetuate Western capitalism, it is an urgent matter to look at dancing bodies as alternative knowledge production sites.

---

54   Rothberg, *Multidirectional Memory*; and Rothberg, "W. E. B. Du Bois in Warsaw: Holocaust Memory and the Color Line, 1949-1952"; See also Levy and Sznaider, *Erinnerung im globalen Zeitalter*.

55   Here I think for instance about the upcoming anthology on *Race and Performance after Repetition* at Duke University Press. At transcript publishing, see Mariama Diagne's new monograph *Schweres Schweben*, and the new anthologies *Music – Media – History*; *Postsocialist Landscapes*; *The »Spectral Turn«;*. Older anthologies on memory include *Moment to Monument* and *Peripheral Memories*.

56   Tillet, *Sites of Slavery*. See also Hardt, "Engagement with the Past in Contemporary Dance"; Lepecki, *Singularities*; Schneider, *Performing Remains*; Thurner and Wehren, *Original Und Revival*; Wehren, *Körper als Archiv in Bewegung*.

57   See Kabir, Ananya, "Oceans, cities, islands." and "Plantation, archive, stage." More recently, see "Creolization as balancing act in the transoceanic quadrille."

Therefore, my work draws on the strong legacy of innovative, feminist scholarship on memory, and shifts the center of gravity to the epistemological quality of dance.

I am also inspired by the tremendous work that queer scholars and artists produce(d) on archive, memory, and utopia. In a field of history characterized by the absence of perspectives of people of color, queer people and performing bodies, perforMemory does leave a trace. Subscribing to Jill Dolan's claim that the space and time of theater is a place of realization for "utopian performatives,"[58] perforMemory builds on the connected preoccupations and findings of gender, dance and memory studies, as well as on quantum physics and literature. However dance still remains a distant, rarely visited relative in the most known spheres of the gender studies world. Among relatively known Black feminist reflections on art as a form of resistance[59] and white feminist reflections on bodies and performativity,[60] the capacity of dancers to perform and transform power relations is less often a topic of inquiry. Scholars working at the intersection of gender and dance studies often focus on binary gender representations in dance, or on the impact of genderism on dance historiography.[61] My research fosters an innovative connection between transdisciplinary decolonial feminist research, dance, and the analysis of memory discourses and practices.

This book is also situated within the exponential development of critical dance and performance studies. My approach resonates with the works of Brenda Dixon Gottschild, Diana Taylor, Jacqueline Shea-Murphy, Rebecca Rossen, Nadine Georges-Graves, Ann Cooper Albright, SanSan Kwan, and Ramón Rivera-Servera.[62] These brilliant scholars often focus on cultural productions from the Americas, and on singular constructions of diaspora, such as "African-American," "Jewish," "Chinese," or "queer Latinidad" negotiations of identity. An inspirational transnational study was Ananya Chatterjea's discussion of "the production of culture in and through the body, itself produced through cultural constructions"[63] in the works of the African-American Urban Bush Women company and the Indian choreographer Chandralekha. In contrast, I focus on solo performances. Moreover, my research scope promotes a wide, diasporacentric approach that blurs conventional national and geohistorical divides. At the moment, I am not aware of a book that connects

---

58   Dolan, *Utopia in Performance*, 5.
59   For instance El-Tayeb, *European Others*; Lorde, "Foreword to the English Language Edition."
60   See Butler, *Bodies that matter*; Butler, *Gender Trouble*.
61   See Marquié, *Non, la danse n'est pas un truc de filles!*; Walkowicz, *Die Kampfkunst-Tänzerin. Der Gender Diskurs Im Interkulturellen Vergleich Des Tanzes*; Marquié, "Le genre, un outil épistémologique pour l'historiographie de la danse."
62   Cooper Albright, "Embodying History"; Dixon Gottschild, *The Black Dancing Body*; George-Graves, *Urban Bush Women*; Ramón H. Rivera-Servera, *Performing Queer Latinidad*; Rossen, *Dancing Jewish*; Kwan, *Kinesthetic City*; Shea Murphy, *The People Have Never Stopped Dancing*; Taylor, *The Archive and The Repertoire*.
63   Chatterjea, *Butting Out*, 75.

memorial approaches across the Black, Jewish and Asian diasporas in the field of dance.

The field of dance research suffers from the lack of transnational attention given to choreographers and scholars of color. If one leafs through the *Routledge Companion to Theatre and Performance*,[64] one will see that the "dance" entry, meant to provide a general overview for undergraduate students, does not mention any performer of color. In the German context, important works such as *New German Dance Studies* and *Körper als Archiv in Bewegung*[65] lack substantial engagements with the works of contemporary Afro-German, Jewish-German and Asian-German choreographers. These are only a few examples of the workings of "Ent_Nennung", and "EntErwähnen" in dance and performance. The exclusion of choreographers of color often goes hand-in-hand with the appreciation and reiteration of the same handful of established dance-makers. By publishing in the *Critical Dance Studies* series, I welcome a great opportunity to fill certain gaps in German scholarship and beyond.

Counter-trends come for instance from the above mentioned US-based scholars. Brilliant investigations live at the crossroads between area studies and dance studies, and work towards connecting dance, race and gender. Here I think of the recent anthologies *Oxford Handbook in Theatre and Dance*, *Black Performance Studies*, *Theatrical Jazz*, and *BlackTino Queer Performance*.[66] In terms of dance technique genealogy, a pathbreaking study was done by Brenda Dixon Gottschild, who demonstrated the role of Africanist dance in shaping the evolution of modern American ballet.[67] Her work remedies the elision of this major aspect of dance historiography. The absence of certain cultural productions in academia or dance historiography is even more glaring given that many Western choreographers owe their successful presence on stage to the rich influence of African, Asian, Indigenous, and Jewish inspirations.

In the spirit of Ann Cvetkovich's *Archive of Feelings*, which is simultaneously an academic analysis of archival matter as well as an archive in itself, my research aims not only to analyze choreographic repertoires, but also to contribute to the archiving of a new performative "repertoire" of cultural memory.[68] While Chi foregrounds the presence of Tatjana Barbakoff in the contemporary making of and writing about dance history, my work amplifies at a meta-level the presence of seven counterhegemonic performances in the landscape of contemporary cultural production. Thus, *Contemporary PerforMemory* traces a full circle between the re-emergence of

---

64   Allain and Harvie, *The Routledge Companion to Theatre and Performance*.
65   Wehren, *Körper als Archiv in Bewegung*.
66   George-Graves, *The Oxford Handbook of Dance and Theater*; DeFrantz and Gonzalez, *Black Performance Theory*; Johnson and Rivera-Servera, *Blacktino Queer Performance*; Jones, *Theatrical Jazz*.
67   Dixon Gottschild, *Digging the Africanist Presence in American Performance*.
68   Cvetkovich, *An Archive of Feelings*; Taylor, *The Archive and The Repertoire*.

Tatjana Barbakoff's precious, yet often silenced dance-historical legacy on stage in *Through Gardens*, and the re-surfacing of successful, yet often unacknowledged dance perspectives in contemporary academia.

Investigating, or Why Epistemology and Methodology Come into Play

Epistemological matters

Do you ever wonder how a squirrel finds the power to propel itself, how a spider wanders, how a cat tiptoes, or how a researcher moves through library catalogues and shelves? Sometimes, I stumble upon books in my library wanderings. I usually search the online catalogue, write down a reference, and make my way to finding the book... My eyes strive across the patterns, titles and shapes of books that surround the spot where THE book should be found. Besides working with catalogues and numbers corresponding to the library staff's order of knowledge, I always rely on intuition and kinesthetic senses.

Think about how Oxana Chi found out about Tatjana Barbakoff: through an exhibition catalogue in the fine arts department of the Amerika-Gedenkbibliothek (American Memorial Library, a major library built in Berlin after World War II as part of the US Marshall Plan). Had she stuck to the slim dance section, she would never have come across the catalogue which inspired her creation of *Through Gardens*. This story is told in our film *Dancing Through Gardens*, which can itself be found in the AGB library's collection, since it was showcased in the 2017 exhibition "Themenraum Tanz", in the realm of the *Tanz im August* festival.

The computer screen at the Humbolt-University library informs me that there is no entry recorded under the combined keywords "dance," "Holocaust," and "post-colonial." Feminist artists and academics are often aware of the bias induced by the overrepresentation of cis-male, white, Western, ableist perspectives in key positions in the arts and academia in Europe and the USA. A key preoccupation, particularly in Black feminist scholarship, has therefore always been to render visible the power dynamics dictating knowledge production, such as colonialism. Reflecting upon race, gender and epistemology, Grada Kilomba invites us to constantly ask:

> What knowledge is being acknowledged as such? And what knowledge is not? What knowledge has been made part of academic agendas? And what knowledge has not? Whose knowledge is this? Who is acknowledged to have the knowledge? And who is not?[69]

---

69   Kilomba, *Plantation Memories*, 27.

Kilomba's questions resonate with the earlier cited reflection of Chi on power and historiography in Germany, and with the reflections around dis_remembering, dis_naming, and dis_mentioning. Kilomba, Chi and Ha ask us to scratch the surface of knowledge, to uncover which social positionings affect its production. For instance in Germany, Jewish perspectives on the Holocaust, or Black women's perspectives on colonialism, are seldom part of German "academic agendas." And dance is rarely "acknowledged as knowledge" to repeat Kilomba's words. Yet dancer-choreographers such as the ones discussed here constantly negotiate epistemological issues, and anchor narratives of the past in the present subjectivities of their own selves.

The widespread absence of performance as a source of knowledge in European humanities is a legacy of colonial structures. I hope that my research will speak for a more widespread diffusion of diasporic dance as part of academic agendas, for instance at Humbolt-University. Because feminist knowledge production is dynamic, I have tried to apply transformation in my teaching as well. For instance, in my 2016 class "Performing Memory," I encouraged students to take part in Berlin's cultural life. I also invited dancers into the classroom, including a live excerpt performance by Oxana Chi. The fact that I received a teaching award for the seminar (Fakultätspreis für gute Lehre, First Prize), testifies to the university's openness to re-thinking access to knowledge, as much as it suggests the students' willingness to read not only books, but also dance as a valuable source of knowledge.

To hide one's positioning, or proximity to the research topic or the participants does not serve the quality of the research, but rather impedes critical reflection. I stand with Grada Kilomba's plea for "an epistemology that includes the personal and the subjective as part of academic discourse,"[70] and Patricia Hill Collins's emphasis on "experience as a criterion of meaning with practical images as its symbolic vehicles."[71] My experience of the performances, my experience of doing research, and the dancer's experiences merge into the quest for a truth that can be felt as much as it can be formulated. Situated within the lineage of Black feminist epistemologies, my writing interweaves personal narratives with academic theory, performance analysis and interviews.

From the "outsider within" to the insider without

One way of including the personal in the research is to rely upon autobiographical experience. An inspirational work in this regard was the anthology *Rites of Return*, co-edited by Nancy K. Miller and Marianne Hirsch.[72] Here authors explore dias-

---

70   Kilomba, 31.
71   Collins, *Black Feminist Thought*, 258.
72   Hirsch and Miller, *Rites of Return*.

poric memory in relation to their own biographies, with such diverse examples as Lila Abu-Lughod's return to her father's Palestine and Jay Prosser's search for a music of return in the Jewish Baghdadi diaspora. In an earlier publication, Nancy K. Miller had coined the term *autocritography* to name feminist writing born out of a mix of autobiography and critical reflection. Kimberly Benston later re-defined *autocritography* as a performative practice in relation to blackness.[73] I have certainly been practicing *autocritography* before naming it so. I am grateful that my multicultural and transnational heritage, which includes Jewish, Black, and Asian diasporic roots and rhizomes, has deeply enriched this book.

Autocritographical anthropology bears affinities with Patricia Hill Collins' sociological articulation of "outsiders within":

> The approach suggested by the experiences of outsiders within is one where intellectuals learn to trust their own personal and cultural biographies as significant sources of knowledge.[74]

I came to understand myself less as an "outsider within" than an *insider without*. I am partly an insider to the embodied memory of trauma carried forth by some of the dancers, such as the European Holocaust and slavery. In this sense, my reading of the performances encompasses personal connections to the trauma of forced displacement, racialized oppression and resistance. During the course of my study, I also became an insider to the world of performing arts. To become a Resident Artist with Oxana Chi's dance company, and to accompany her onstage with music and physical acting gave me a prime positioning (even closer than a first row seat) to witness dance. However, I am "without" the experience of a formal dance education, or of working as a professional dancer or choreographer, although I do dedicate a regular amount of time to dance training as part of my larger movement practice that includes martial arts. My research therefore benefits from what I call the position of an "insider without."

Black feminist epistemologies also allow research to be accessible to a larger audience, extending beyond a community of professors and graduate students. I do not think however, that this is limited solely to the perspective of Black feminism, but more generally applies to any researcher who takes feminism seriously. For instance, Doris Ingrisch, who works at the intersection of academic research, art, and gender, argues for the need to sensualize research ("sinnliche Wissenschaft"),[75] namely, to invite into scientific processes the emotional senses inherent to artistic

---

73   See Miller, Nancy K., *Getting Personal: Feminist Occasions and Other Autobiographical Acts* and Benston, Kimberly W. *Performing Blackness: Enactments of African-American Modernism.*

74   Collins, "Learning from the Outsider Within," 122; On Afro-German identity construction, see also Wright, "Others-from-Within from Without."

75   Ingrisch, *Wissenschaft, Kunst Und Gender*, 22.

endeavors. This is a laudable and arduous task. While subscribing to the conventional framework of academic research in the context of a Ph.D., I tried to subvert some of its most obstructive features by telling a story that might lead the reader to move fluidly through the book. This also explains why I sometimes address YOU, the reader, or make parsimonious use of the "us" pronoun.[76]

Decolonial feminist research?

I recall my first in-person encounter with Professor Nadine George-Graves, in her office at the Department of Theatre and Dance at the University of California, San Diego, in the spring of 2015. After a pleasant conversation about Afro-diasporic dance, I walked down the stairs to reach the Department's ground-floor office. There, outside the building, young Asian-American students were rehearsing hip-hop choreographies, using the wall's reflective textures as mirrors, and the open outdoor space as a dance studio. Their movements were obviously drawn from the iconography of mainstream African-American hip-hop culture. I wondered why they did not rehearse inside the dance studios, and found out that they were students registered in other departments, for instance engineering. Here, the outsider-insider dialectic had become tangible. Dance, bodies, and knowledge, are compartmentalized into categories constructed by society, and moving bodies often attempt to jump out of these boxes.

Feminist approaches and gender studies help us to reflect upon these categories of race, gender, sexuality, class and ability. I adhere to a constructivist approach, and strive towards a broad understanding of gender studies, stepping in Lann Hornscheidt's footsteps. Hornscheidt devotes much attention to the deconstruction of gender as a normative category, and the related discrimination form which they call "genderismus" (genderism).[77] They demonstrate how gender, and therefore gender studies, cannot be disconnected from the category of race, which is always at play, especially in the German context in which they write. Hornscheidt therefore suggests to re-name the field of "gender studies," and proposes the expression "postcolonial feminist studies." A corollary argument is that questioning the epistemological and ontological formation of historical knowledge formation is a legitimate field of inquiry for feminist research.[78] Similarly, Marianne Hirsch argues that feminist research on the topic of memory does not necessarily involve analyzing gender as a category, for investigating the construction of memory discourses and practices is inherently a feminist research task.[79]

---

76   Thank you Lann Hornscheidt, for inciting me to question the universalistic fallacy of "us".
77   See for instance the insightful constructivist critique of the various forms of gendered discrimination in Hornscheidt, *feministische w_orte*.
78   Hornscheidt, "Postkoloniale Gender-Forschung," 218.
79   Hirsch, *The Generation of Postmemory*, 18.

I understand my work as decolonial feminist research, which attempts to question hegemonic historical narratives, to foreground marginalized epistemologies, to inquire into the body as a site and source of knowledge production and transmission, and to connect feminist and decolonial perspectives.[80] The proactive term "research" breathes life and dynamism into the idea of "gender studies". And instead of the word "postcolonial," I prefer the prefix "de" to mark an active process of moving beyond or countering coloniality.[81] Decoloniality bears affinities with María do Mar Castro Varela and Nikita Dhawan's definition of postcolonialism as an attempt to move beyond the historical power structures of imperialism and racism that determine(d) the scientific disciplinarity of knowledge.[82] However, the very use of the words "colonialism" or "colonial" arises out of a fallacy, as I learned from Marianne Mballé Moudoumbou in the realm of a collective research project on intersectionality, for the word can be traced to Latin roots which mean "to take care." This explains why the word is hardly appropriate for referring to centuries of racialized violence. In the anthology *InterdepenDenken*, which I co-edited, Mballé Moudoumbou recommends the use of the word Maafa to name not only the subjugation of African bodies, souls and soils, but also any other form of genocide and violence against Afro-descendant people prior to, during, and after the Transatlantic Slave Trade, including South African apartheid and US segregation, or ongoing issues of police violence against Black bodies.[83] The word Maafa helps to un-think historical trauma out of a linear chronology, a point I discuss in the third chapter. The word Maafa however does not cover the full spectrum of historical trauma addressed in my book, since I also deal with the European Holocaust, and imperial violence affecting Indigenous and Asian-diasporic people, among others.

I coined the title of the anthology, *InterdepenDenken*[84] to name an intellectual process of interdependent thinking. The verb is a neologism, a German play on the words "Interdependenzen" (interdependencies) and "denken" (to think). The idea is to engage in an intersectional practice in which researchers continuously reflect upon their positionings in terms of constructed social categories, and how this impacts how they frame academic investigations.[85] In my case, this involves identifying as an able-bodied, Jewish, queer, nongender conforming womyn, academic

---

80   The term decoloniality is often attributed to Aníbal Quijano and Walter D. Mignolo, although it is not clear where it actually originated. See Quijano, "Coloniality and Modernity/ Rationality"; Mignolo, *Local Histories/Global Designs*.

81   On coloniality in Germany, see Kelly, *Afrokultur*.

82   Castro Varela and Dhawan, "Europa Provinzialisieren? Ja, Bitte! Aber Wie?," 9–10.

83   Ballé Moudoumbou, "Erste Annäherung zu Maafa," 127.

84   I coined the term at a working group that collectively co-edited an anthology on intersectionality. See AK Forschungshandeln, *InterdepenDenken*.

85   For suggestions on the InterdepenDenken paradigm as an epistemological and methodological tool, see Hornscheidt, "Aber wie soll ich das denn machen? Interdependenkend forschen: Methodologische und Methodische Handlungsvorschläge."

and artist of color socialized in the West, and recognizing how the intersection of these identities interacts with my epistemological choices, interview questions, and writing.

One of the major biases in an ableist Western perspective is to define vision as a superior sense when it comes to relating to the world, in contrast to other senses. Oyèrónkẹ Oyěwùmí argues that the Eurocentric idea of a "worldview" is restrictive, especially compared to the multidimensionality of an Africanist "world-sense."[86] In the process of interpreting meaning in live performance, this can be an incentive to pay attention to other elements, such as sound, and energy. Dancers certainly expect to be seen. However, to attend a live performance, and to (re-)view it as a video, is an entirely different experience. There is an abysmal gap between the emotions and reflections one goes through as an audience member, and the mediated experience of a dance video, suggesting that live performance works through more channels than the visual one. The third chapter of the book's negotiation of temporalities and movement in perforMemory reflects my efforts to go beyond a mere visual engagement with the pieces, and to search for a holistic, multisensorial experiencing of dance art.

Another fallacy induced by the coloniality of the knowledge systems in which I studied (and now teach), in 'higher' education is the misinterpretation, and consequently the repression of epistemic principles that have successfully generated knowledge for centuries. Here I think of the value of repetition, a strategy used by some performing artists, which I will discuss in chapter three in relation to cyclic time and Africanist dance. Repetition is a powerful storytelling tool that can also serve non-fiction writing. In this book, I occasionally use repetition as a tool, for instance when I cite a brief interview excerpt, which you will encounter again in the full interview transcript. Repetition, used ingeniously, can be(come) motion, and can (trans)form meaning. Just as coloniality works by repeating scenarios of dispossession, extraction, and oppression, people from the Global South have historically used repetition to create memory discourses and practices, and to plant seeds of knowledge at home and beyond.[87]

Diasporic networks

The research scope is intentionally wide in terms of geographic locations, choreographic styles, dance techniques, thematic contents and artistic intents. My goal

---

86   Oyěwùmí, *The Invention of Women*, 2–3.
87   The idea to acknowledge repetition as a valid academic writing tool comes to me from Simpson, *As We Have Always Done: Indigenous Freedom Through Radical Resistance*, 200-201. She offers brilliant Indigenous-based ways to unfold and scaffold academic storytelling, that interestingly bear similarity with my approach informed by my Afro-Indo-Caribbean lineage.

is not to compare the performances, but rather to contemplate kindred meanings among them, and to map out diasporic networks of perforMemory. I adhere to Hirsch's defense of a "connective rather than comparative approach"[88] to memory studies. In a sense, my inquiry responds to Ella Shohat's call for a "multichronotopic" research:

> [Transdisciplinary gender research] would require a *multichronotopic* form of analysis, particularly in terms of the ways space is *imagined* and knowledge is *mapped* within academic institutional practices. It would ask us to place the often ghettoized histories, geographies, and discourses in *politically and epistemologically synergetic relations*. It would require showing how variegated pasts and presents, 'locals' and 'globals' *parallel and intersect, overlap and contradict* while also analogizing and allegorizing one another.[89]

The juxtaposition of performances, topics and people not usually brought into convergence fosters precisely the "synergetic relations" pointed out by Shohat. By bringing together various geohistorical subject matters into one research field, I trace connections between the traumatic historical sites of the Holocaust and the Middle Passage, between past trajectories and contemporary journeys of resistance, between Afro-European, Taiwanese, Jewish, Caribbean, and Palestinian positionings. Most importantly, the geographic amplitude is paired with the large choreographic breadth of the works. The seven pieces step through multiple stylistic territories, from traditional Javanese dance to Afrofuturism, or from ballet to contact improvisation. Rather than sorting the works into airtight boxes, I search for converging threads of meaning, affect and narrative. The challenge resides in doing justice to the various choreographies, choreographers and themes in all their diversity, whilst also detecting convergences and resonances between them.[90] The key is to acknowledge differences (of sociocultural context, geographical location, political stakes, corporeal technique), rather than eliding them, to unearth how those differences may shape a multichronotopic, multidirectional, multilayered, and multidimensional picture of perforMemory.

I argue that the dance pieces are themselves "multichronotopic" works of perforMemory, thus necessitating a "multichronotopic" analytical approach to appropriately understand and address the performances. I would even suggest that Chi's current repertoire as a whole is a "multichronotopic" work, with geohistorical topoi stretching from the European Holocaust (*Through Gardens, Killjoy*) to the colonial looting of African cultural objects (*Neferet iti*) by way of the Afro-German feminist

---

88   Hirsch, *The Generation of Postmemory*, 8.
89   Shohat, *Taboo Memories, Diasporic Voices*, 15. [My emphasis]
90   Chatterjea, *Butting Out*, 12.

biography of May Ayim (*I Step On Air*) and Black transgenerational body memory (*Psyche*).

Drawing inspiration from Elliot Fox's idea of "diasporacentrism,"[91] I advocate for a diasporacentric approach, in which I bring together various performers who share a diasporic identity, albeit diaspora. I consciously expand Fox's Afro-diasporic concept, to account for a plurality of diasporic identities and solidarities, and to renew definitions of diaspora beyond the center-margin paradigm. Fox situates diasporacentrism in relation to African-American instrumental jazz, and infers its definition as a positive force:

> Diasporacentrism therefore is not a focus on loss or dilution; its emphasis is on struggle, survival, rebirth, the creation of new (albeit floating) 'centers.'[92]

In diasporacentrism, the diaspora paradigm thus shifts from the fragmentization of identity-formation to the rhizome-like creativity of identity-making. Diasporacentrism fosters an empowering definition of diasporic subjectivity. Arguably, taking the quotation seriously allows for a definition of diasporic identities which extends beyond specific racialized constructions.

Rather than naming the artists diasporic, I look at how they embody and enact diasporic resistance to hegemonic storytelling in terms of race and gender. I follow a diasporacentric orientation in the plurality of performances and theories, the variety of narratives, and the multiplicity of dance movements chosen for this book. Further, I argue that in challenging not only Eurocentric perspectives, but also Afrocentric or other forms of -centricity, the performers operate diasporacentric movements: for instance, when Wan-Chao Chang dances the complexity of migrations, when André Zachery re-shuffles the temporality and spatiality of the *Digital Middle Passage*, when Oxana Chi embodies a Chinese-Jewish-Russian biography from an Afropean perspective, and when Chantal Loïal creates a virtual and physical affiliation between her body and Sawtche's story. What I also find enticing in the idea of "diasporacentrism" is the emphasis on survival. *Through Gardens*, for example, emphasizes the struggle and performs the rebirth of Tatjana Barbakoff. *They Call You Venus* portrays the survival of Sawtche's spirit. *Digital Middle Passage* embodies the struggle and survival of Black bodies in the Americas. In these dancescapes, they perform tales of memory, of pain, of hope and of resistance.

The desire to address the contemporaneity and vitality of diasporic performance art compels me to search for new paradigms and perspectives. In a similar spirit, Ananya Chatterjea coined the term "alternative postmoderns" to describe

---

91   Fox, "Diasporacentrism and Black Aura Texts."
92   Fox, 369.

the choreographic "practices of mobile intersectionality and of resistance to inscription by and in the terms of the meta-narrative of Euro-Western dominance,
from a positioning in alterity."[93] She cites the example of postmodern choreographers of color who have not been acknowledged as postmodern, or were left in
the shadow of the monumental Judson Church. Today, the influential institution
is making efforts towards decolonization processes. Movement Research at Judson
Church curates a diverse range of performances, and possesses a dynamic Artists
of Color Council. In fact, two of the choreographers discussed here performed at
the Judson Church: André Zachery, and Oxana Chi (who performed at the Fall Season opening on September 18th, 2017). The Studies Project series regularly offers
sessions where matters of dance decolonization are discussed. On the specific topic
of lineage decolonization, I think of the panel curated by dancer Ambika Raina on
January 24, 2019 at The Museum of Modern Art, in conjunction with the exhibition *Judson Dance Theater: The Work Is Never Done*. I also think of issues 52-53 of the
Movement Research Performance Journal (MRPJ), guest edited by choreographer Rosy
Simas and writer Ahimsa Timoteo Bodhrán, on the topic of "Sovereign Movements:
Native Dance and Performance."[94]

Performing artists who move outside of mainstream productions and expectations are often described as *off*. To think of them as *off*, however, evokes a marginalization, an outsider-ness that hardly seems appropriate to qualify those trendsetting artists. It also does not reflect the scope of their careers in terms of awards
and tour history. Although they may perform *off-Broadway*, or *off-off-Broadway*, they
surf on the winds of artistic experimentation and innovation, producing avant-
garde works which are ahead of their times, and which inspire many other performers and institutions. I remember attending the piece *En Filigrane* in the vel-
vety cozy Théâtre Ranelagh in my Parisian hometown. It is an original creation
by dancer-choreographer Ibrahim Sissoko and cellist Ophélie Gaillard. The piece
uses an innovative blend of West African moves, hip-hop techniques, classical European and Roma music. After returning to Berlin, I discovered a few months later
that a mainstream public theater had mimicked the concept and aesthetics of the
hip-hop dancer moving around the cellist. The label *off* is obsolete. These dancers
do not play outside of cultural platforms, they are at the heart of them. They are
not off, they are on stage and on the move. In the 21st century, we should move
away from the term "postmodern" and its limiting linearity embedded in Western

---

93   Chatterjea, *Butting Out*, 104.
94   On April 9, 2019, I co-curated a Studies Project entitled "Memory Moves!" and my article on
     Black Queer Dance appears in issue 54 of MRPJ. Other events included a conversation on
     Black performance, spirituality, and epistemic absence hosted by Minister of the Arts André
     Daughtry on January 22, 2020. I also had the chance to attend the panel on "Decolonial De-
     sign, Indigenous Choreography, and Multicorporeal Sovereignties" held on February 18, 2018
     at Abrons Arts Center, documented as a podcast available on Apple Podcasts and Spotify.

colonial narratives of art history.[95] Like the earlier-cited shift from "worldview" to "world-sense," a new language can become a guiding light in the quest for new ways of writing and thinking about dance's past, present, and future.

Methodology

Along my multidisciplinary research path, I reaped from branches as various as cultural memory studies, dance and performance studies, gender studies, postcolonial studies, literature, critical race theory, queer studies/queer of color critique, historiography, theology and quantum physics. The book blends these various sources together in a transdisciplinary fashion, in which the borders between each discipline are marked by fluidity and flexibility.[96] The multichronotopic approach goes hand-in-hand, in my view, with multilingual meaning-making. Therefore, when quoting from French and German, I often offer the original text alongside my translation into English, in the spirit of scholars such as Gloria Anzaldúa, who has ingenuously juxtaposed languages to expand the multidimensionality of scholarship.[97]

At times, my work moves beyond inter- and transdisciplinarity, bearing affinities with postdisciplinary feminist research, defined by Nina Lykke as:

> [A] mode of organizing scholarly knowledge production that, on the one hand, can pass as a discipline and *claim the academic authority* that goes with that status but, on the other hand, which also maintains a *transversal openness* and a *dialogic approach towards all existing disciplines*, and which points beyond the traditional, monodisciplinarily organized university.[98]

Indeed, I managed to fulfill the requirements of a PhD program, while keeping a "transversal openness" conducive to a nuanced, differential knowledge production. I became aware of factors that impede a transdisciplinary or postdisciplinary approach, such as monodisciplinarity; the masking of the researcher's choices and positions; processes of canonization; the hierarchization of sources (e.g. primary vs. secondary); and the repression of poetics, politics and humor. To keep those at distance, I chose not to contain theory within a dedicated chapter. Instead, academic literature surfaces throughout the book, as I bring it into resonance with the performers' interviews, and with my own interpretation of the performances, which may or may not reflect the choreographer's intent.

---

95   For a critique of how "modern art" is historicized in Europe, and for an insight into modern art discourses and works produced in Taiwan, see the recent Bauer-Zhao, Lisa. *"Moderne Kunst": Betrachtung Eines Topos Im Kontext Der Globalisierung Des Kunstdiskurses.*

96   See Hornscheidt and Baer, "Transdisciplinary Gender Studies."

97   See for instance the use of bilingualism in Anzaldúa, *Borderlands.*

98   Lykke, "This Discipline Which Is Not One," 138. [My emphasis]

My readings of the dances are based on viewings of live performances in Germany, France, Martinique, Austria, and the USA, as well as on video footage made available to me by the artists. I also examined press reviews, publicity materials, such as artist statements, publications, flyers, and websites, and I recorded interviews with the choreographers. I do not try to read the dance performances in light of a specific theory, rather I understand the performances as theoretical sources. By "deriving theoretical insights from the creative works,"[99] one may re-define what theory is, and generate a critical conversation between multiple artistic and academic sources to show how the performances carry meaning in themselves.

Postpositivist research in dance

My approach is also dictated by the subject of my study, dance. In her own work as a dancer-choreographer, Oxana Chi evokes the affinities between dance-making and research:

> To me, dance is a very, very complex matter [...] akin to the soul. It is almost impossible to grasp. I wish to grasp it, of course, but it is impossible to grasp. And so it is important to constantly keep researching, like a scholar [...][100]

In an earlier publication on *Through Gardens*, I have discussed how her work generates knowledge in an active way (*Wissensschaffung*, or science-making), contrasting with a sedentary understanding of knowledge (Wissenschaft, or science).[101] Conversely, academics can use arts-based methodologies to stimulate academic knowledge production. With the moving matter of dance as an object of inquiry, I felt compelled to use creativity at various stages of my research: conception, reflection and formulation. I applied a "postpositivist research methodology in dance," as defined by Jill Green and Susan W. Stinson:

> [The research] must be created as the researcher goes along, in the context of this particular piece of research. In this sense, the researcher shares much in common with the choreographer, remaining open to emerging patterns and meanings and to forms that are appropriate for them. Just as in the case of the choreographer, the postpositivist researcher allows the form of the final product to arise from the process.[102]

---

99   Katrak, *Contemporary Indian Dance*, 2; See also the notion of "theory-in-practice" in Ramón H. Rivera-Servera, *Performing Queer Latinidad*.

100   Chi, Interview.

101   Zami, "Oxana Chis Tänzerische Wissensschaffung."

102   Green and Stinson, "Postpositivist Research in Dance," 95; On feminist methodology in dance studies, see also Desmond, "Engendering Dance: Feminist Inquiry and Dance Research."

This is less abstract than it sounds, as Green and Stinson propose concrete ways to apply post-positivist methodology in dance studies.[103] Connecting this methodology to Black feminist epistemologies evoked earlier, I devised my own research process characterized by a clear personal positioning, a search for "coherence" in selecting the performances, and the use of subjectivity to approach truth, for instance in interpreting the performances. I made sure to conduct open-ended interviews and to formulate specific questions for each choreographer. By interweaving interviews, academic theory, performances, and literature discussion, I aimed to identify resonances between a multiplicity of scholarly and artistic sources. Within their methodological framework, Green and Stinson identify three different research profiles: "interpretative," "emancipatory," and "deconstructionist."[104] If each one of them traced the side of a research triangle, my work would be situated right in the middle.

First, I adhere to the "interpretative" research mode through my strong relationship to the performances and performers; the use of participant observation; the use of autobiographical impressions and reflections, the conducting and transcribing of interviews; and the collection of personal materials from the dancers.

Second, my research aims to be "emancipatory" through its attempt to question the power relations surrounding the research and to highlight counter-hegemonic narratives. I circulated the interview transcripts among the dancers in order to give them a chance to revise them, and to make sure that they feel comfortable with them. In my view, however, the emancipatory research profile is also biased because of its assumption that the researcher can "help" the participants, which is not always the case. In any case, emancipatory research requires to be aware and respectful in the relation between the researcher and the communities involved in the research.

Finally, "deconstructivistist" researchers, according to Green and Stinson, acknowledge that their account is incomplete and biased, and are aware that their research may be oppressive to the persons at stake, no matter how critical they consider themselves to be. Nonetheless they strive to "create multiple interpretations of some dimension of the dance experience."[105] With each chapter, I intended to effect a shift, the way a theatrical light change alters the dramaturgical atmosphere of a performance. My interpretation moves through successive lenses of analytical focus, and spotlights multiple aspects of the dances: narratives, diasporic constellations, relation to temporality, spatiality, and physicality.

Green and Stinson even invite their readers to assess their own methodology, and to come up with a research profile of their own. The processual aspect of my

---

103   Green and Stinson, "Postpositivist Research in Dance."
104   Green and Stinson, 100–112.
105   Green and Stinson, 113.

research is best reflected in my writing. By including intermittently personal stories that situate me in my research environment, the writing reveals the journey that led to its constitution. It weaves together the "patterns" that have appeared since 2013: home, diaspora, displacement, trauma, power, movement, spacetime. Like the art of dance, this research required me to be flexible enough to move between phases of writing, phases of interviews, and phases of reading. Therefore I did not work in a linear timeline that separated reading, field research, and writing. Rather, I opted for a multimodal circular working process consisting of several spheres: reading, attending/viewing performances, interviewing, writing. The spheres were like circles which sometimes overlapped as I moved along them in a concentric way. Although it was often challenging, my research certainly benefited from a constellation in which each working sphere delivered input for the other spheres. This felt particularly appropriate to the dance world that surrounded me. If I had to name my academic style, I would call it *Conscious Re-Search Expression*.

Embodied research

Another aspect of my methodology involved not only the full engagement of the mind, but also of the body in the research process. Movement praxis provided me with a healthy counterbalance to time spent on the computer, expanding my body activity beyond eyes and finger muscles. But foremost, it enriched my research by allowing me to grasp the issues I was reflecting theoretically on another, corporeal, level of knowledge. Taking dance classes, attending rehearsals and performances, and especially working as a member of Chi's company since 2012, provided me with a way to engage myself fully in this research. Nadine George-Graves calls this "involved embodied research,"[106] and therefore I was not surprised to meet her at a dance studio I attended with Oxana Chi during my research time in the USA. There was my doctoral advisor in a class with the legendary Pat Hall, a former member of the Urban Bush Women (UBW) company, to whom George-Graves dedicated 15 years and a monograph of research. There we were, scholars-artists shaking body parts, releasing energy, jumping across space.

Decolonial feminist researchers should not be fearful of including their own selves within their research conception, implementation, production and communication. During my research, I met gifted dancers, for instance Maria Bauman-Morales, former Associate Artistic Director of UBW, who now runs her own dance company MBdance. I first met Maria at the Bronx Academy of Arts and Dance (BAAD!) in December 2015, when Oxana Chi and I performed *I Step On Air* on a split bill with MBdance. The company's motto is "Sweat your truth!" This precious dance incentive is as important as the need to trust one's sweat. An infinite number of emotional truth drops can form an ocean of corporeal writing.

---

106   George-Graves, *Urban Bush Women*, xi.

Challenges

When I interviewed André M. Zachery for this book, he mentioned how he appreciated my questions, and the impact of my perspective on the work:

> Who is the person that's doing it? Who is the person that's telling it? The story is going to sound totally different and have [a] totally different meaning from each person and experience that is allowed to get on the mic, or get on the dance floor, or get behind the computer and do the work.[107]

Echoing the epistemological reflections cited earlier in this introduction, Zachery interrogates the relation between knowledge and power. As a researcher, I also ask myself these questions. The fact that I am "telling" the research story impacts the outcomes in multiple ways. As stated earlier, my knowledge of each choreographer's repertoire varies greatly. Moreover, my personal relation to each dancer-choreographer varies greatly, since I have worked intimately with some and met others in person only once. Therefore, the dissertation necessarily reflects my elastic relations to the pieces and their makers. Additionally, ableism and class are not centered as categories of analysis, and most of the interviewed dancers identify as cis-gender.

I am aware that my research is strongly biased by a Western perspective because of my positioning and socialization in the West.[108] It was important to me to include the works of dancers-choreographers who are currently not based in the West, such as Farah Saleh (Palestine), Wan-Chao Chang (Taiwan) and Christiane Emmanuel (Martinique, a French department which is arguably still a French colony), however there is always more work to do to learn more about artists and academics from the Global South. My book also reflects the hegemonic influence of US-American academic productions, partly because the fields of feminist postcolonial research and critical dance studies are much larger in the USA than in Germany. I am grateful that my fluency in three languages helped me to include literature sources from the Francophone and Germanophone worlds.

The major challenge I encountered was: how to translate dance into words? One answer provided by Susan Foster is to choreograph the writing, in order to address "how the activity of writing is conceptualized in relationship to the activity of performing, and how that relationship will be represented in the text."[109] Departing from this reflection, I acknowledge the limits of the writing medium, no matter how well choreographed it may be, to reflect upon perforMemory. My

---

107 Zachery, Interview.
108 On feminism and the categories of "geography" and "nations", see Sirri, "Führt geografische und religiöse Positionierung zu Ausschluss?"; Küppers-Adebisi, "Nationalisierung interdepenDenken."
109 Foster, "Choreographies of Writing."

documentary film *Memory2Go*, created as a pendant to this book shall supplement the writing with an audiovisual expression and impression of the dance making at stake. What I hope to evoke through the writing are nuances, as in a concert where the sound of each instrument modulates the total listening experience. In my research arrangement, each performance, and each dancer refines the melody of perforMemory with subtle and sometimes unexpected tones.

Inventing, or Whence the Outline Comes From

"Dance is a barometer of culture – and a measure of society," says Brenda Dixon Gottschild.[110] As we know, a barometer is a tool that scientists use to measure atmospheric pressure, which helps in forecasting the weather. Today, even smartphones have built-in digital barometers. The idea of measuring the weight of the air in the atmosphere resonates with an ethereal imagination of dance. Whether dancers use a rather grounded or airy technique, the moving body always plays with weight and balance as it moves through the venue's atmosphere. Dixon Gottschild's metaphor of the barometer makes clear the powerful role of dance as a tool to assess and understand sociocultural politics. Just as we need tools to understand the movements of the weather, the moves of bodies dancing on stage can enlighten and deepen our knowledge of our social environment. And the dance barometer can indeed deliver precious information about sociopolitical pressure.

Here, each chapter begins with a literary quotation carrying a specific environmental metaphor, whose energy invigorates the chapter as a whole. Each chapter thus corresponds to a natural element, in a spirit reminiscent of the Chinese Five Elements theory (Wŭ Xing). These energies can be understood simultaneously as natural and supernatural forces, in the spirit of the Orishas deities. Energies move through the book separately, and together at once, in the spirit of the Kabbalah mysticism. In these and other spiritual systems, as in my writing, a main premise of thought is that past, present and future are interconnected, and that alignment matters.

The first chapter sets the grounds of inquiry by defining memory as a site of movement. Engaging with critical theory and literature, it opens up reflections on dance, choreography, and power, and introduces the pieces that constitute my repertoire of perforMemory. Here, I look at how selected performances negotiate the absence and presence of stories, perspectives, and bodies in hegemonic and counter-hegemonic narratives of the past. I develop the concept of perforMemory, and invent the notion of *choreobiography* to express the link between a choreographic and a historiographical process. Because perforMemory requires the effort to dig

---

110   Dixon Gottschild, "'Racing' in 'Place': Dance Studies and the Academy."

deep into the grounds of memory, to turn the self upside down, this chapter stands at the footstep of trauma volcanos. PerforMemory emerges out of the depths of the performances, reaching to the surface in eruptions. The magma of perforMemory is characterized by the earth element.

Diaspora, the motif of chapter two, is oceanic. In the Yoruba language, people from the diaspora are called "tokubo", meaning "the one who came/went over the sea."[111] It is not only in the Black Atlantic that diaspora is associated with watery metaphors. Diasporic journeys undertaken across the spaces of nations, stages and stories sometimes move in wave-like patterns. The diasporic condition can be envisioned and understood as an oceanic movement – be it inner or outer, of back and forth between real or imagined roots, between past and current positionings. The currents of diaspora flow with the water sign, as I connect three spaces where diaspora lives: in academia, on stage and on/in the body. The water element in this chapter signifies the fluidity of memory as it is constituted and transmitted individually and collectively. Water may be threatening, swallowing migrating bodies and sometimes drowning them in the void of white supremacist patriarchal capitalism. Water may also be the vivifying source of life, energizing, a carrying force, suggesting the vitality of an everflowing diaspora. By centering diaspora, this chapter asks how, given the legacy and contemporaneity of "colonial dismemberment,"[112] the stage, and eventually the body may become a space of diasporic remembrance.

The third chapter, "Dancing the Past in the Present Tense," explores how perforMemory moves through time and space. To perforMemory may help to pulverize stiff conceptions and conventions of time, and this in turn happens through motion. Air, is the element breathing through the third chapter. I call on whirlwind energies to explore time and the questioning of its shape within and beyond Western norms. In the first part of the chapter, I examine the performances through the lens of spacetime definitions, and ask how selected works *contemporize* the past. I explore how choreographic strategies of perforMemory bend linear conceptions of "history," time, space, and emotions on the diasporic stage. I argue for instance, that pieces perform time in ripples, cycles or waves. I embed the discussion of the works in a broader reflection on memory and time. The second part of the chapter spotlights a set of movements, and connects the physical and conceptual aspects of perforMemory. Spinning, jumping, crossing the grounds of memory, this chapter may recall wandering. It is a space of memorial blossoming, suggesting dance as the possible, imperative revival that may, that should occur after traumatic histories, or more recently the passing of a hurricane.

---

111   Küppers-Adebisi, "Nationalisierung interdepenDenken," 137.

112   Taylor, *The Archive and The Repertoire*, 209 Here Taylor analyzes the work of the theater group Yuyachkani as a strategy of "re-membering."

As you can see, each main chapter of analysis thus spotlights a keyword from the book title: historical trauma in chapter one, diaspora in chapter two, and space-time in chapter three. The fourth chapter is a book within the book, consisting of the full transcript of the seven interviews I recorded with each artist between 2013 and 2016. This chapter is a conversation, an encounter between a researcher's perceptions and the artists' intentions. Rather than a mere appendix, I envision the interviews as an integral part of the research, with many points of entry.[113] Here the artists reflect upon their solos and other works, including group pieces, offering insightful perspectives on dance-making and memory-making. This part of the book expands and extends the reflection about the performances, and situates the pieces in larger and/or longer trajectories and memories. While engaging with the book, you may wish to move through it in a linear way from the first to the last page, or you may also move in circles. For instance in between chapters one, two, and three, you could jump to chapter four to read some of the artists interviews. You can also find video excerpts of these interviews, along with dance performances excerpts, in the documentary *Memory2Go* produced as a companion to this book. In the film, you will also find a sense of movement, and a relation to the environment.

The environmental metaphors and elements connect to each other in a spiral-bound narrative: volcano, ocean, wind, and back to the earth, excavating the futurity of memory. The book thus comes full circle. With these geoastral, geohistorical and literary-physical threads, I hope to provide the readers with a rope to hold on to as they climb up and down through the dancescapes of perforMemory, where they may encounter story-hunters and dancing lions. Hence, the title of this introduction is a play on words referring to the famous quote:

> Until the lions have their own historians, the history of the hunt will always glorify the hunter.

This West African proverb suggests how power relations shape historiographical narrativization. It explains why the history of the Transatlantic Slave Trade is seldom told from the perspectives of the maroons who escaped plantations and lived in quilombos, and why Holocaust narratives rarely center efforts of organized resistance against fascism in the ghettos and concentration camps. It is often attributed to the Nigerian writer Chinua Achebe, and is also known as a proverb among the Igbo people of Nigeria. This old wisdom was passed on to me, orally, fifteen years ago, when I was working as an intern at the headquarters of the AfricAvenir Foundation in Douala, Cameroon. Whether I may have been a hunter and/or a lion in previous lives, I will now endorse the role of a storytelling scholar to tell you a tale

---

113   For an interesting combination of artist interviews, academic essays and performance scripts in the field of theater, see Johnson and Rivera-Servera, *Solo/Black/Woman*.

of historical resilience and presence. This story shall hopefully move you, if you join the dance.

1 MEMORY DANCESCAPES

Nous sommes sur un volcan, et nous sommes volcans.
En limites de frontières, nous sommes les sans frontières.
En questions sans réponses, nous sommes la question.
Nous sommes la réponse. [...]
Nous existons, nous demandons, nous réclamons, nous contestons,
interrogeons les questions de l'Histoire
et nous domptons les douleurs de l'Histoire.
(We are on a volcano, and we are volcanos.
On the margin of borders, we are those without borders.
In questions without answers, we are the question.
We are the answer. [...]
We exist, we ask, we reclaim, we contest,
we question history's questions
and we tame history's pain.)
Widad Amra[1]

Let's travel through memory as a *site of movement*. I love this passage by Palestinian-Martinican author Widad Amra, for it subverts conventional dichotomies. It expresses so deeply the paradoxical condition of humans who produce counter-hegemonic narratives. I recall deep conversations with Widad Amra at her home on the island of Martinique: about absence, about the entanglements of diasporas, and the entanglements of familiar and historical traumata and configurations. The phrase to "question history's questions" resonates with ears attuned to feminist voices, and it also carries the echoes of the choreographers' voices, as they ask, reclaim, contest why and how they arrived here. First and foremost, they exist on stage, working with explosive topics and forms, producing performances of political eruptions in volcanic settings. They move back and forth between the volcano as historical setting and the volcano as a well of stories from which they draw pain, doubt, hope, euphoria, fear, contemplation. PerforMemory is a dancescape, a site of political and

---

1   Amra, *Le Souffle Du Pays. Nabd El Jayzirah*, 34–35 [My translation].

emotional mobility. It may well be a sixth scape,[2] a dimension no less important that our commonly underestimated sixth sense.

Whether it is Oxana Chi spinning festively, Chantal Loïal sustaining and collapsing the spine, Wan-Chao Chang pulling energetically on a scarf, Zufit Simon rolling onto the stage, Farah Saleh walking on her hands, André Zachery flying high and low, Christiane Emmanuel racing in the air, all of the artists perform memory through movement, moving through historical figures and contemporary times. Their works invite us to move with them, without rising from our seats. PerforMemory can make the audience travel back in time while remaining in the present. What is deeply moving is the presence the performers radiate on stage. In solo or group constellations, they fill the stage with stellar energies, telling stories of quest and loss, inviting us to travel in stillness, yet also actively through memory.

With memory as a site of movement, perforMemory may be understood as a process and as a result. It enacts the will to acknowledge, and counter absence by embodying and performing presence. This understanding resonates with bell hooks' definition of memory as a "site of resistance."[3] PerforMemory connects memory, movement and resistance, contending that memory can become a site of moving resistance, or resistance through movement.

This chapter examines how the performances orbit around memory, and how they negotiate absence and presence in diasporic spheres connected with various sites of trauma such as the Holocaust, the Transatlantic Slave Trade, or the Nakba. Asking how memory is shaped through dance, I start by delineating the borders of memory dancescapes, in order to describe in successive chapters what it feels like to move through them. In a sense, this first chapter maps out perforMemory, sketching the silhouettes of stories, perspectives and bodies that are alternately and simultaneously absent and present. The first section is conceived as an archive, in which I sort through and introduce thematically my repertoire of perforMemory. I will provide information about the theme and structure of each piece. In the second section of the chapter, I return to reflections about memory as a site of movement, which I touched upon in the introduction, by interlacing creative and academic literature with concrete examples of perforMemory. (For biographical information on the dancers-choreographers, please refer to chapter four, where a note precedes each interview.)

The pieces, although they are fundamentally diverse in terms of choreographic vocabulary, movement techniques, dramaturgic construction, aesthetics and themes, share several features. First, they all relate more or less explicitly to a

---

2   Here I refer to Arjun Appadurai's five "scapes"(ethnoscapes, technoscapes, financescapes, mediascapes and ideoscapes) theorized in relation to the "global cultural flow" in the seminal *Modernity at Large*.

3   hooks and Mesa-Bains, *Homegrown*, 110.

diasporic journey, as discussed in chapter two. Second, they perform memory in a timespace that moves beyond past, present, and future distinctions, as discussed in chapter three. Third, one could say that the seven pieces express auto_biographical journeys, or at least a journey across the gap between auto and biography, between life and choreography. They constitute a kinetic knowledge through a process I call *choreobiography*,[4] to denote the intertwined processes of choreographing and (auto)biographical storytelling.[5]

Choreobiography allows dancers to put a name to the face of memory, to zoom in on an individual within the broader picture of history, to search for personal ancestors or artistic soulmates through choreography. To choreograph a biographical piece, centered on one individual who is named and embodied, is in itself a strong political statement. Choreobiography may additionally stir up the status quo of the past, in relation to the preoccupations of the present. Like a literary biography, a choreobiography tells a biography from a contemporary perspective, but through movements rather than words. Audre Lorde called her novel *Zami*, a "biomythography," to describe her genre that blends autobiographical narrative, myth/fiction and history[6]. The choreobiographing dancers also work through myth to inscribe their own(auto)biographical legends into history. Choreobiography thus is a pivotal genre of perforMemory. It emerges in the repertoire of Oxana Chi (for instance in the works *Through Gardens*, *Neferet iti* and *I Step On Air*). Chantal Loïal's *They Call You Venus*, as well as Wan-Chao Chang's *Impressions*, also intensely enmesh the choreographic process with the more or less abstract telling of an individual biography, be it historical (Sawtche for Loïal) or autobiographical (Chang).

Scholarship at the intersection of critical dance studies and cultural studies conceives of dance as *Meaning in Motion*.[7] Looking at signifying bodies moving through memory dancescapes, this chapter generates the idea of perforMemory as a form of *memory2go*: a tensile memory, whose content is transferable to others – if they are willing to connect. PerforMemory brings into existence a remembering anchored in the present. It reveals the powerful weight of dance as a "counterhegemonic cultural practice"[8] that may transform how we understand the past, stand in the present, and leap into the future.

Performative memory opens up worlds connected to, but divergent from, literary and visual engagements with memory. With a focus on embodied power as a key feature of performance, I draw connections between the material power of stage performance and the metaphorical power to re-write or challenge historical

---

4   Zami, "Oxana Chis Tänzerische Wissensschaffung."
5   On the connection between Black women's autobiography and dance, see Conyers, "Shedding Skin in Art-Making."
6   Lorde, *Zami: A New Spelling of My Name*.
7   Desmond, *Meaning in Motion: New Cultural Studies of Dance*.
8   hooks, "Choosing the Margin as a Space of Radical Openness," 153.

narratives. A question that guides this first step of the inquiry is: how do post-memorial artists choreograph interventions into hegemonic narratives?

Archiving a Repertoire of PerforMemory

Every long journey requires taking one step at a time. In Berlin, you can stumble over archival memory, as discussed earlier. Sometimes you can also fly over memory at a height of 39971 feet, and at a speed of 518 miles per hour. On the many journeys that I undertook for this research, I crossed and re-crossed the Atlantic's burial chamber, or the "grey vault"[9] on airplanes flying between Berlin and New York City. Memory feels as porous as the time zones separating the feeling of a Berlin evening from New York City's afternoon light, separating the city of the Reichskristallnacht from the city of the African Burial Ground. Over the years, I hopped from one place to another, and assembled pieces of dance into patterns of perforMemory scholarship. What the seven solo pieces have in common is their contribution to innovative forms of remembering, and to what Aïcha Diallo describes as a "living archive":

> The Living Archive understands itself as an imaginary archive that blurs the boundaries between past, present, and future; between written and alternative transmission forms; between the visible and the invisible; and interweaves them anew with each other.[10]

Diallo's definition attends to the critique of linear time conceptions, and to the multiplicity of the senses and realms of remembering, which will resurface in the next chapters. Interestingly, the imagery of interweaving threads evoked by Diallo's statement resonates with Oxana Chi's understanding of her choreographic process, which she compares to the task of "knitting" a rope, or a fisher's net.[11] Chi's description suggests that she uses her body to channel a connection between the memory of a historical biography (in this case May Ayim, in other cases Tatjana Barbakoff or Claude Cahun), and the contemporaneity of her dance.

Similarly, this book knits together a tapestry using threads from academic theory and from the "theory-in-practice"[12] of the dancers. The archive lives on in the moving bodies of these artists who transmit and perform memory in innovative and creative ways. How do the performances perform an imaginary archive, and

---

9   Walcott, "The Sea Is History," 137.

10   Diallo commissioned me to write an article about Oxana Chi's Neferet iti dance for this anthology. Diallo and MID Redaktion, *The Living Archive* [My translation].

11   Chi, "Von Hier Nach Dort - I Step On Air," 203.

12   Ramón H. Rivera-Servera, *Performing Queer Latinidad*. The author argues that performers also generate theory with their bodies.

how does my archiving of the pieces challenge conventional temporal, geographical, artistic and thematic boundaries? In this first section, I dwell on the repertory of seven innovative choreographers and introduce their dance pieces, which I
define as works of perforMemory. A dance repertoire that is also a memory repertoire in the sense of Diana Taylor,[13] perforMemory counterpoints the dispropor-
tionate attention granted to archival memory transmission. Reflecting upon the
workings of collective memory transmission, Taylor conceptualizes a tandem, non-
binary memory paradigm. She makes a convincing case for overcoming the usual
dichotomy between written and embodied cultural transmission, and between literary and performative knowledge. Besides other modes of transmission – such as
digital and visual modes – she prefers to distinguish between the archive and the
repertoire, which often go hand-in-hand. The author emphasizes the role of performance in general, not only theatrical but also social performance, in the processing
of historical traumata:

> How do the archive and the repertoire combine to make a political claim? How
> does performance participate in the transmission of traumatic memory?[14]

I argue that perforMemory demonstrates how integral dance performance is to
political remembering of traumata. PerforMemory counters the idea that dance is
the art of the ephemeral, in a similar move to Taylor's point, which calls attention to the dangers of admitting only written knowledge transmission as durable
and valuable.[15] Taylor highlights those dangers in the American context, revealing how the valorization of written knowledge transmission has served to oppress
and repress Native cultures and history. She smashes the myth of an enduring,
rock-like archive. Instead, she values the repertoire of "performances, gestures,
orality, movement, dance, singing – in short, all those acts usually thought of as
ephemeral, nonreproducible knowledge."[16] Her research demonstrates how in performance the body not only transmits, but actually enacts memory. Her argument
is strongly relevant within the context of gender studies, for it incites us to unveil
the bias induced by imperialism, white supremacy, capitalism, heteronormativity,
and patriarchy (to paraphrase bell hooks), and to consider how such bias affects
institutional archival processes. It also incites us to reappraise the strong, long-
lasting impact of performative memory production and transmission.[17] The seven

---

13   Taylor, *The Archive and The Repertoire*.
14   Taylor, 54.
15   Taylor, 193.
16   Taylor, 20.
17   However, Taylor suggests that the repertoire is not per se counter-hegemonic, since colonial-
      ism in her view also works through the performance of violence. See also Scolieri, *Dancing the
      New World: Aztecs, Spaniards, and the Choreography of Conquest*.

pieces of my repertoire attend to Taylor's deconstruction of the archive and its limits, and her appraisal of the repertoire as an enduring memory tool. Sometimes the dancers use both the archive and the repertoire to generate memory transmission. Here are some thoughts on how both Chi' *Through Gardens* and Loïal's *They Call You Venus* circumambulate archival matter, and perform "a history written with and against the archive."[18]

Oxana Chi's publication *Tanzende Erinnerungen*, as well as the documentary *Dancing Through Gardens*, reproduce some of the archived information on Tatjana Barbakoff, in the form of press excerpts and letters.[19] The publication and the movie are now part of the *archive* in several institutions such as Germany's National Dance in Cologne, the Israel Museum in Jerusalem, the Fondation pour la Mémoire de la Shoah (FMS, Paris) and several university libraries. Conversely, the piece *Through Gardens* is the *performative repertory* result of Oxana Chi's interest in and negotiation of the archive of Tatjana Barbakoff. Besides performing the solo at international venues and festivals, Chi has performed it at her yearly event series, "Salon Qi, a Femmage to Tatjana Barbakoff," in Berlin and Paris. By doing so, she perforMemoried marginalized aspects of dance history and the history of artist discrimination and resistance in 20th century Europe. The artist transforms the archival knowledge on Tatjana Barbakoff – which she accesses through regular communication and cooperation with the historian Günter Goebbels[20] and through her own research – into an embodied repertory piece, a repertoire of perforMemory. While archival material on Barbakoff is full of ellipses, inevitably filled with the imaginings of those who have collected it, and biased with their social positionings, the repertoire piece invites the audience to use their own imagination to generate meaning. Contrary to some archival claims, *Through Gardens* does not pretend to nail down a full, irrefutable account of Tatjana Barbakoff's biography. Rather, it choreobiographes her story, framing it in a historical context, and yet it remains open and abstract enough to offer a more differentiated story of what her life may have been from a contemporary perspective.[21]

Chantal Loïal also moves at the intersection of the archive and the repertoire. *They Call You Venus* is a performative intervention into the hegemonic narrative of Sawtche, as told in historical textbooks and archived in European institutions. The solo demonstrates how the perforMemory of Sawtche is no less resilient than the

---

18   Here the author refers to another Venus story. See Hartman, "Venus in Two Acts," 12.

19   Chi, *Tanzende Erinnerungen*, 2011; Chi and Zami, *Durch Gärten Tanzen (Dancing Through Gardens)*.

20   Drenker-Nagels, Goebbels, and Reinhardt, *Tatjana Barbakoff, Tänzerin und Muse*; Goebbels, *Tatjana Barbakoff*.

21   On the relation to the audience's interpretation, see Oxana Chi's e-mail to her musician Laszlo Moldvai (01.01.2010), in Chi, *Tanzende Erinnerungen*, 2011, 12.

presumed archival knowledge extracted out of her physical remains. The physical "archive" of Sawtche, by contrast, appears very malleable depending on whose hands hold her bones. Sawtche's actual bones did not resist temporal and spatial transfers throughout the 20th and 21st centuries. Pseudo-scientists objectified her body, experimenting upon it, alive and later dead, even going so far as to display the mold of her genitals at the Parisian Musée de l'Homme until 1974! Later, her bones were to become objects of ritual, buried in South Africa in a grave that is now a national heritage site. Thus the value and meaning of Sawtche's archive, depending on which hands hold it, reside in the context, and serve political purposes. The story of Sawtche's display, as a living and as a dead body, evokes a colonial display of power. Like a dance repertoire, the museum's archive is bound to its space-time of existence. The solid archive generates an evolving knowledge and is no more reliable or immutable than a performative, embodied one.

In this sense, I find that both *Through Gardens* and *They Call You Venus* resist what Marisa Fuentes calls the triple "physical, archival, and epistemic" violence that affects simultaneously "the body of the archive, the body in the archive and the material body."[22] Fuentes is critical of the risk for historical knowledge produced about enslaved women in the Caribbean to re-produce slavery's violence. The choreobiographies of Oxana Chi and Chantal Loïal counter the epistemic re-production of violence that occurs when dance historiography omits and/or dis_remembers the importance of Tatjana Barbakoff in the 1920s and 1930s; and when French coloniality re-asserts itself in the archiving of Sawtche's story and body. They are repertoires of memory that extend and expand archival knowledge. The pieces perform the possibility of an afterlife full of dignity, more so at a meta-level in the case of Oxana Chi, who revives Tatjana Barbakoff in the dancer's own field of expression, the stage, but also in the case of Chantal Loïal's use of display. A dancer's repertoire thus may "account for the palimpsest of material and meaning"[23] that go missing in the archive. It can perforMemory, generating memory as a repertoire colliding and colluding with the archive.

One of the aims of this research is to fill an archival gap on physical and digital academic shelves, and to make space for a new repertoire. The works demonstrate the enduring quality of performative memory, and its potential to subvert archival transmission and domination. The following repertoire, structured in thematic overviews, shall give you an impression of each piece. Seen and sewn together, through one lens of analysis, it constitutes a mosaic of memory as a site of movement. To facilitate the reader's access to each piece, I use headings that draw circles of meaning in which I place the performances. These are not intended to mark hermetically sealed epistemological boundaries, but rather serve as signposts

---

22   Fuentes, *Dispossessed Lives*, 6–7.
23   Fuentes, 6.

as you circumambulate the shifting tides of perforMemory. Moreover, the circles of meaning are not watertight. Rather, they are spheres with permeable borders, allowing fluid theorization and multiple positionings of the pieces. For instance, all of the pieces are choreographies of history in a way. They all deal with migration and displacement. And all of the pieces are rooted in autobiographical inspiration and imagination, as suggested by the interview transcripts. I could also have imagined other headings such as "gestures of war and love." Or I could have drawn distinctions between Afro-diasporic and Asian-diasporic perforMemories. You, the reader, are invited and incited – like audiences of perforMemory – to weave in your own shifting threads as you move through these memory dancescapes.

Dancing counterhegemonic choreobiographies

Through Gardens and *They Call You Venus* (re-)inscribe a historical female figure into collective memory by deploying performative knowledge. Not only do they "call names"[24] to resist erasure, they recall the bodies, and perform in their names, they embody their stories, they impersonate the women of color too often buried under tons of other names and stories. PerforMemory comes into being: powerful and challenging, it does not minimize historical tragedy but maximizes possibilities to deal with it. As the dancers stand firm on their feet, presence stands out in their choreobiographies. In their moves, terrestrial gravity exists side-by-side with ethereal grace.

THROUGH GARDENS – OXANA CHI

Through Gardens, the main inspirational piece for this book, is dedicated to the awe-inspiring story of Tatjana Barbakoff. She was a solo expressionist dancer and choreographer from Russia (now Latvia), of Chinese-Jewish descent, who was very successful in 1920s/30s Europe. Historical archives suggest that her work was often cited and discussed in the press. Because of the institutionalized persecutions of the Nazi regime, she fled from Germany to France, where she continued to dance in spite of all adversities. In 1944, she was arrested in French Nizza, deported three days later, and killed immediately upon arrival in Auschwitz. Much of the biographic information on Barbakoff comes from the restless research efforts of Günter Goebbels. The historian, who is in regular epistolary correspondence with Oxana Chi, has conducted extensive international research on Barbakoff and other artists for decades, and keeps historical memory alive through exhibitions and publications.[25]

---

24   hooks, *Yearning*, 116.
25   For more information on T. Barbakoff's biography, see Goebbels, *Tatjana Barbakoff*; Drenker-Nagels, Goebbels, and Reinhardt, *Tatjana Barbakoff, Tänzerin und Muse*.

Oxana Chi in Durch Gärten (Through Gardens); Werkstatt der
Kulturen Theater, Berlin, Germany, 2008, (photo by Annette
Hauschild, courtesy of Oxana Chi).

Her biography makes clear that Barbakoff was an influential muse. She inspired the creation of numerous paintings, photographies and sculptures by famous artists including Yva, Otto Dix, Kasia von Szadurska, Willy Maywald, Minya
Dührkoop, Gert Wollheim, Nini and Carry Hess, Waldemar Flaig, Sasha Stone, He-
len Dahm, and many more. Most artists were persecuted for being Jewish and/or
political protesters. Although many artworks were destroyed by the NS-regime,
and some of the artists such as YVA were also assassinated during WWII, the art
historical legacy that "survived" reveals the important role of Barbakoff and her

dance in 20th century art worlds. Interestingly, many of these artists were, like Barbakoff, independent working women*,[26] who defied the gendered restrictions of their times.[27]

Named after one of Tatjana Barbakoff's solos, the contemporary dance *Through Gardens* is not a re-enactment of her work. It is a gripping choreobiography, choreographed, interpreted and directed by Oxana Chi. The choreographic architecture has four spacetimes: Die Geburt (Birth), Das Fest (Celebration), Der Kampf (Struggle), and Der Neumond (New Moon). In between the main acts, the dancer performs short interlude scenes, such as the journey, depicted in the above picture. The mix of linear and circular dramaturgy, which I will return to later, generates a fascinating decoding of Western historical temporality and geographic spatiality.

The piece merges various techniques from European ballet, Chinese WuShu, Javanese dances and West African movements and expressions into the dancer's self-named "fusion" style. It also corresponds in my view to what Zenenga terms the "Africanist paradigm" of Total theater aesthetics,[28] with a harmonious aggregation of dance, live-music and theatrical expression. The choreography germinated from Chi's decades of training and performance in Europe, Southeast Asia and the USA. The technical precision of fast-paced pirouettes lives side-by-side with a proficiency in the slow-motion energetic flow of Qi-based arts. The movement quality is supported by the carefully designed costumes. Video projections round up the scenography. The photograph above, taken during one of the first iterations of the piece, shows the dancer in front of a bamboo folding screen, the backdrop against which she offers a live perforMemory of Tatjana Barbakoff. The dancer steps forward with movements reminiscent of Southeast Asian puppetry (Wayang Kulit), which Chi encountered during her formation in Indonesia. Barbakoff was also photographed holding a Wayang Kulit figure in her hands. As evoked in the introduction, I read the picture as a metaphor of perforMemory, with an interesting tension between the dancer's determination to move forward, and the walk orientation from right to left, that denotes a re-turning towards the past. Indeed, her repertoire consistently presents forgotten women biographies, inventively mixing abstract avant-garde aesthetics with tangible themes.

Like Barbakoff, Chi has received much acclaim from audiences and press alike, who particularly appreciate her unique choreographic creativity, her graceful and nuanced interpretation of movement, her narrative expressivity, and her interdisciplinary collaborations. Chi usually works as solo dancer-choreographer, and of-

---

26   Here I use a * behind the word "women" to account for the multitude of gender identities that these artists may have identified with – publicly or privately. The use of a * is common in German feminist writing.

27   For a feminist reading of Tatjana Barbakoff's biography see Zami, "Tanzkunst als lebendige Erinnerung"; and the movie Chi and Zami, *Durch Gärten Tanzen (Dancing Through Gardens)*.

28   Zenenga, "The Total Theater Aesthetic Paradigm in African Theater."

ten commissions musicians to compose and perform specifically for her dance as part of her evolving Ensemble Xinren. She regroups varying and varied musicians, brought together specifically for each piece. This is an emblematic feature of her work, which I have had the chance to participate in. The choreography stems from a movement research preceding the musical input. Once the musicians enter the rehearsal process, they compose and improvise in dialogue with the dance. The choreographic process continues, like a flexible frame within which the movements' pace and intensity may vary according to the musical elements. *Through Gardens* exists in various, innovative musical constellations: with piano and hang; with accordion, e-guitar, and hang; with cello and Chinese drum. Chi explains her will to keep the work in movement, like a life or an environmental process:

> The working process on *Through Gardens* equals a life. There is nothing sealed off and static that could not be changed during the performance timeframe. It is an ongoing process of experimenting and choreographing. It would be beautiful, if a luxuriant vegetation arose out of the manifold performance variations, always letting new bursts of buds.
>
> (Die Arbeitsweise an *Durch Gärten* gleicht einem Leben. Es gibt nichts Abgeschlossenes, Feststehendes, was nicht während der Aufführungsdauer verändert werden könnte. Es wird immer weiter experimentiert und choreographiert. Es wäre schön, wenn eine üppige Vegetation aus vielen verschiedenen Performance-Variationen entstehen würde und immer neue Knospen hervor sprießen ließe.)[29]

The first movement seed was planted in Oxana's memory garden in 2007, after she encountered a catalogue dedicated to Tatjana Barbakoff. The catalogue accompanied the 2002 exhibition held at the August Macke Haus in Bonn, curated by the museum's director Klara Drenker-Nagels, along with Hildegardt Reinbrandt and Günter Goebbels.[30] In spite of her presence in visual arts history, Barbakoff, however, is blatantly missing in contemporary dance historiography, in contrast with other historical figures.

Inspired by Barbakoff's memorial presence in the art world, Chi wishes to bring her memory back on stage...and her life back into movement. Journalist Sophie Lespiaux describes Oxana Chi's presence in *Through Gardens* as follows:

> Thus, Oxana Chi's presence on stage becomes at times solid and dense, almost telluric, in full control of inner energy and slow motion, and at times fluid and aerial, in a gracious moment.
>
> (Aussi la présence d'Oxana Chi sur la scène se fait-elle tantôt massive et compacte,

---

29   Chi, *Tanzende Erinnerungen*, 2011, 5 [My translation].
30   Goebbels, *Tatjana Barbakoff*.

presque tellurique, toute en maîtrise de l'énergie intérieure et du mouvement dans la lenteur, tantôt fluide et aérienne, lors d'un gracieux instant.)[31]

When Oxana encountered Tatjana's story, it was the first time she felt able to identify with a historical figure from European dance history. Indeed, their lives and styles reveal many salient parallels: diasporic origins; use of performance to criticize sociopolitical power relations;[32] solo interpretations of their own choreographies; collaboration with live musicians; expressive and poetic aesthetics and inspiration from several cultures, including Indonesian dance styles; and residence in Dusseldorf, Berlin, and Paris.[33] The piece tells Barbakoff's biography from a contemporary perspective, and travels through themes of migration, discrimination, resistance and performance. Through my personal, embodied engagement with the piece, I gained a lot of insight into the workings of dance and memory. Thus, *Through Gardens* is the choreobiographical keynote in my perforMemory composition. It epitomizes the shift between archival digging and repertoire dancing, between "history" and perforMemory.

THEY CALL YOU VENUS – CHANTAL LOÏAL

Another Afro-European choreographer, Chantal Loïal, performs a one-woman-biographical solo related to a different spacetime. Her trajectory and aesthetics diverge from Oxana Chi's. *They Call You Venus* is the first and only solo in Chantal Loïal's repertoire, who is mostly known as the director of the dance company Difé Kako. She choreographed it with the artistic support of Philippe Lafeuille and Paco Decina. The narrative is inspired by the biography of a Khoi woman originally named Sawtche or Ssehoura, also known as Saartjie or Sarah Baartman. Her story has been inscribed in historical archives under a variety of racist and exoticizing names. In the early 19th century, her family was massacred, and she was enslaved in Cape Town and deported to Europe, where she was forced to display her naked body at racist exhibitions and forced into prostitution. It is very difficult to find out the truth about Sawtche's biography, since what are officially recognized to be facts stem from the accounts of the persons who have brutalized her and her people, which leads back to the Igbo proverb cited at the end of my introduction.[34]

---

31   Lespiaux, "Durch Gaerten, une performance musicale et chorégraphique d'Oxana Chi." [My translation].

32   Already in 1925, Tatjana Barbakoff had to report to the police office after a show deemed too critical by the city's authorities in Königsberg. See Chi and Zami, *Durch Gärten Tanzen (Dancing Through Gardens)*.

33   On the parallels between T. Barbakoff and O. Chi, see Zami, "Mit Oxana Chi Durch Gärten."

34   Loïal, "On T'appelle Vénus - Dossier de Diffusion" I refute the assumptions that she travelled willfully to Europe, (and ask how "will" is defined when one is in the position of an enslaved human). Thus, I am cautious of the fact that even Chantal Loïal's discourse may sometimes re-produce the violence of racialized and gendered normativity constructions. For a reflec-

Chantal Loïal in On t'appelle Vénus (They Call You Venus); International Symposium-Festival Moving Memory, Berlin, Germany, 2016, photo by Layla Zami.

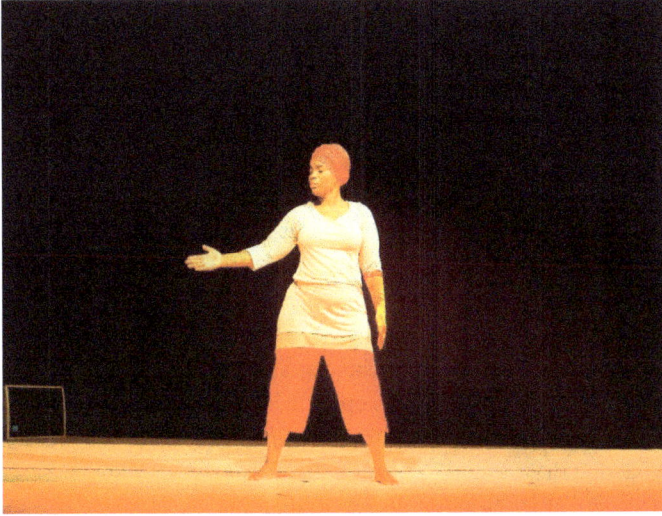

Her body and self were discursively constructed as representing the African "Other," and she was the target of racist-genderist violence: objectified, gazed at, despised, and forced to early death, as many other human beings from Africa, Asia, the Pacific and the Americas. Between her death and her burial, centuries passed. When Nelson Mandela was elected president of South Africa in 1994, he requested that the French government return what was left of Sawtche's remains, in an attempt to restore dignity to the body, to return it to its rightful place after centuries of displacement. South Africa had to wait until 2002 for the French Parliament to pass a law for Sawtche's remains to be transferred back "home."

Ever since attending the premiere at the Théâtre Aimé Césaire in Martinique in January 2011, I have followed the choreographer. I immediately published an article that was the first review of the piece at that time, to be followed by much press from multiple journalists. I described the feeling of witnessing how Loïal symbolically gave Sawtche her body back, through dance.[35] This visceral work of perforMemory

---

tion on the challenges embedded in the search for historical truth in academic contexts, and the possibility to acknowledge oral transmission in Indigenous and Black communities, see Simpson, *As We Have Always Done: Indigenous Freedom Through Radical Resistance*, p. 37.

35 Zami, "Rendre sur scène son corps à Sawtche."

felt like an intervention, a reclaiming of the embodiment so crucially lacking in most historiographical projects.

Dramaturgically, the solo is divided in two parts: the first one evokes Sawtche's persecution in Europe and the second one celebrates her posthumous return to South Africa. Even though this may seem like a chronologically linear divide, it can be interpreted as an emotional dramaturgical split, or as the reunion of pain and exile with a scene of home and celebration. The movements also carry traces of Loïal's experience both as a dancer in the European "contemporary" dance scene and as a dancer touring with West and East African companies. The dance also displays the dancer's personal repertory of Afro-Caribbean styles, and the quality of her isolation techniques.

Chantal Loïal's piece follows in a long lineage of artistic engagements with Sawtche's biography. For instance, the Urban Bush Women choreographed *Batty Moves* with the intent to "re-imagine her [Venus] as a whole self,"[36] centering the buttocks at the core of the dramaturgy. Conversely, after Chantal Loïal's preview performance in Lille in 2010, other choreographers based in Europe approached this particular biography. In the synopsis, Loïal emphasizes that she wishes to question Western processes of Othering which persist up to the present, rather than re-enacting the drama of her story ("rejouer le drame"). She wants to depart from the "official Black Venus" narrative in order to "offer her a victory over history."[37]

The piece choreobiographes Sawtche's story through Loïal's corporeal perception. Finding out about Sawtche through historical narratives, the dancer felt a connection to her personal experiences as a Black woman who had arrived in France at a young age and later toured with the company Montalvo-Hervieu.[38] In her artist's statement, Chantal Loïal explains how she reads the story from a personal perspective embedded in her socialization:

> Beginning with the theme of the Hottentot Venus is an occasion for me to dive into a work on the body, a body displayed, mutilated by the Western gaze, a body expressing more than any other, Otherness/Othering. Being myself a descendant of West Indian societies with pregnant cleavages, generated in historical violence on the bodies [...].
>
> (Partir du thème de la Vénus Hottentote est l'occasion pour moi de plonger dans un travail sur le corps, un corps exposé, mutilé par le regard de l'Occident, un corps exprimant mieux que tout autre l'altérité. Etant issue moi-même d'une société

---

36   George-Graves, *Urban Bush Women*, 59.
37   Loïal, "On T'appelle Vénus - Dossier de Diffusion" [My translation].
38   Cadeau, "Chantal Loïal - La diversité par la mise en danse du corps."

antillaise aux clivages prégnants, engendrée dans une violence historique et sur les corps [...].)[39]

The artist's statement expresses the impossibility of fully differentiating the historical protagonist from the artist's own autobiography in her dancing narrative. Yet, one must also note the challenge faced by the dancer as she navigates the troubled waters of epistemological violence. When she plays with the display of the Black female body, she constantly navigates the potential re-production of the historical genderist-racialized violence against the figure. In the performance, Loïal also speaks a text written by a white cis-man, Marc Verhaverbeke. The text is in the third person, conveying the outsider perspective of a voice which is trying to invest itself into the historical biography. The title of the piece is taken from the first sentence performed by the dancer. It underscores the fact that "Venus" was a derogatory name imposed upon Sawtche.

They Call You Venus, like *Through Gardens*, was produced with the clear intention of inscribing marginalized female perspectives into historiography. If these works perform what André Lepecki calls a "choreopoetic proposal for a political meditation on European historical amnesias,"[40] can they heal audiences? I actually witnessed audience members coming up to Oxana Chi and thanking her for "healing" them through her dance. It seems that Afropean perforMemory is sometimes perceived as a choreobiographic therapy: a powerful and "natural" remedy against a voluntarily agony that affects memory-making in Europe.

---

39   Loïal, "On T'appelle Vénus - Dossier de Diffusion" [My translation].
40   Lepecki, *Exhausting Dance*, 107.

Dancing after the ancestors: family, trauma and movement

The two following pieces were choreographed respectively by Zufit Simon, a European Jewish artist who does not however define her work as "Jewish,"[41] and André M. Zachery, an African-American artist whose artistic intents are strongly grounded in Black diasporic subjectivity.[42] In contrast to the two previous pieces, these do not evoke a specific historical biography, and use less theatrical dramaturgy, adopting instead a more experimental approach to performance. They revolve around the performers' current biographical itinerary through emotionality. In their solos, Zufit Simon and André M. Zachery orbit around their emotional selves, occasionally dwelling in the galaxies of their genealogy. Both performers draw from their family history, and research using body language, inquiring into how they may be injured, inspired, empowered, influenced by generational traumata. In my view, these postmemorial perforMemories traverse what Hirsch calls "a structure of inter- and transgenerational return of traumatic knowledge and embodied experience."[43] These solo dances seem to be less interested in what happened in the past than in the effect and affect of ancestral pasts on their descendants' present.

Zufit Simon in all about nothing; Moving Memory, Berlin, Germany, 2016, photo by Layla Zami.

---

41   Simon, Interview.
42   Zachery, "Futurity and the Containment of Blackness in Twenty-First-Century Performance."
43   Hirsch, *The Generation of Postmemory*, 6.

ALL ABOUT NOTHING – ZUFIT SIMON

Zufit Simon spent two years producing the trilogy *un-emotional*, through which she investigates the interrelation between body language and emotional expression. The piece *all about nothing* constitutes the second section of the trilogy. According to the artist's synopsis, the solo is a collage made up of her personal memories, which requires the audience to project their own emotions and memories onto it.[44] Emotions, traumata and movement seem to be the triangle within which Zufit Simon moves in this trilogy and in other works. As a matter of fact, she also choreographed a piece entitled *Meine Mischpuche* ('my family' in yiddish), in which she deals with the emotional "chain reaction" of memory transmission within family relationships. In the interview which you will find in chapter four, Simon expresses her concern for postmemorial beings, and the ways our lives are influenced by the decisions and movements of the generations before us, including voluntary and forced migrations. Simon's body of work clearly emerges from a self-questioning process that deals with family relationships: the relationship between individual family members, between her family and the geohistorical site known as 'Germany', and the relationship between her family's past and her own contemporary experience in Europe. These relationships materialize on stage in a corporeality marked by shifting positionings, fragility and humor.

I attended *all about nothing* twice: at the *schwere reiter* theater in Munich in 2014, where the dancer performed with the live-electronic mixing of musician Roberto Merdo, and at the Berlin Technical University for the closing of *Moving Memory*.[45] Sitting among the audience in Munich, I met Simon's parents, who had travelled from Israel to attend the premiere. After this intense and painful piece, and given their own history, I wondered how they felt about witnessing their daughter performing at a venue located on the street Dachauerstrasse, formerly the route leading from Munich to the concentration camp of Dachau. The tango that memory dances with emotion is omnipresent in Zufit Simon's work as a whole. She described memory as a burden, a heavy emotional weight:

> Memories are like a bag of emotions that we carry everywhere, no matter where we go, whether we are sleeping or awake…[Memory] is what we always take with us, that which influences our character, how we act, react. That is something one can never let go of, never get rid of.
> (Erinnerungen sind wie ein Sack von Emotionen, die wir überall tragen, egal wohin wir gehen, egal ob wir schlafen oder wach sind, das ist etwas das wir immer mit-

---

44   Simon, "All about Nothing."
45   *Moving Memory* was an international transdisciplinary academic symposium and performance festival held from October 20th to 22nd at the Technical University in Berlin, initiated and co-chaired by Oxana Chi and I. See "Moving Memory - International Symposium-Festival."

nehmen und das beeinflusst unser Charakter, wie wir agieren, reagieren. Das ist etwas, dass man nie loslassen kann, nie loswerden kann.)[46]

Zufit Simon's choreographic identity is marked by a dynamic appropriation of the stage space, a minimalist aesthetics and a physical body language drawing from European modern and contemporary dance. Thoroughly crafted, the choreography yet allows enough room for improvisation, in terms of how long and how intense each sequence becomes. *all about nothing* courageously embraces the asymmetry between "our own fragile corporeality and a constructive engagement with the fragile corporeality of others,"[47] as Naomi Mandel calls it in *Against the Unspeakable: Complicity, the Holocaust, and Slavery in America*. At the beginning and at the end of the piece, the performer makes use of a prop: a microphone on a stand. The contrast between the utterance of the words "I am so happy to be here," "I am so glad you all came," and the expression of the body (collapsing, crying, shaking), and constantly changing facial expression, demonstrates that the texture of emotions is indeed unspeakable. When she returns to the microphone at the end of the piece, about to speak, it is now clear that everything has been said, albeit not through words. Maybe the body can speak better than the voice? Surely Simon makes the unspeakable dance-able.

After attending the Munich premiere on June 26th, 2014, I wrote these lines in my research diary, which I share below in my own English translation along with the original German writing:

pain, pain, PAIN! is what Zufit danced tonight, in her solo all about nothing. The painful movements of the body: spasms, never-ending staccato that shake the solar plexus and the body as a whole, the tearless crying…What I saw was trauma, traces of trauma, archived on the body and directing the whole piece. How deep, how wide, how far, how close – in terms of time – were these trauma coming from?

The performance transmits the feeling of a disturbed society, which represses its disorder by brutalizing its bodies. Simon did not seem to repress her feelings, rather she perforMemories them to the outer edge. She reveals the dishonesty of our daily environment. The spasms on her face also remind me of the workings of medicine, and of a system that drowns its issues in anti-depression-cocktails. I see a face that can only smile for a fraction of a second, a smile that seems merely mechanical, like everything else in our automated era, a smile that is merely machinery, like the deportations in this very place a few decades ago.

At first the dancer sat on the side of the stage and watched us in the audience as we stepped into the performance space. She reversed the gaze by observing those that had come to observe. Suddenly, she took off her jacket and irrupted into the performance. She placed a microphone

---

46   Simon, Interview [My translation].
47   Mandel, *Against the Unspeakable*, 24.

on stage, which she would only use at the end of the piece. Was she expressing what Kien Nghi Ha calls the 'aufgedrückte Schweigen' (silence pressed onto) the German society? Or the limitation of words in relation to a deeper, clearer, moving, inner bodily expression through dance?

The dancer externalizes internalized emotions through her embodied perforMemory. In the program notes, she invites the audience to fill the space created by her dance with their own personal memories. Which memories come to my mind, my body sitting still while she is dancing at high-speed?

(schmerz, schmerz, SCHMERZ! tanzte Zufit heute abend, in dem solo all about nothing. Wie schmerzhaft die Bewegungen den Körper bewegten. Die Spasmen, die unaufhörlichen staccato, die mal die Brust mal den gesamten Body durchzuckten, tränengeschüttelt. Die Spasmen erinnerten/erinnern mich auch an Traumata, wie eine Kette von unkontrollierbaren Spuren, Trauma, die im Körper archiviert sind und die gesamte Handlung durchziehen. Wie tief, wie weit, wie fern, wie nah - zeitlich gesehen - liegen die Trauma zurück? Es ist unsagbar.

***

Der Tanz vermittelt mir Eindrücke einer gestörten Gesellschaft, die ihre Brutalität im Körper be_drückt. Diese Gefühle unterdrückt Zufit nichts, ganz im gegen teil, sie performt sie, stellt sie zur extremen dar. Sie offenbart ausserdem die Verlogenheit unserer Alltagswelt. Die Spasmen in Zufits Gesicht verraten auch eine Andeutung auf Medikament-süchtige Systeme, die ihre Probleme in Antidepressiven zu ertrinken versuchen. Ein Gesicht, welches nicht länger als eine Fraktion von Sekunden lächeln kann, ein Lächeln, welches nur noch mechanisch ist, wie alles in dieser automatisierten Zeitalter und wie damals auch die Abtransporte.

Am Anfang hat Zufit rasch ihre Jacke ausgezogen und explosiv losgetanzt nachdem sie von der Bühne aus sitzend beobachtete, wie das Publikum eingelassen wird und Platz nimmt. Sie stellt ein Mikro- auf, welches sie aber erst viel später im Stück verwendet. Drückt sie somit das 'aufgedrückte Schweigen' der deutschen Gesellschaft wie es Kien Nghi Ha nennt? Oder die Begrenztheit der wörtlichen Sprache gegenüber eine viel tiefere, klare, bewegende, innige Körpersprache?

Zufit verkörpert verinnerlichten Emotionen live, sie lädt laut Programmzettel das Publikum ein, ihre Darstellung mit eigenen Erinnerungen aufzufüllen. Welche Erinnerungen kommen in mir hervor, die so still sitze während Zufit im Höchsttempo tanzt?)[48]

DIGITAL MIDDLE PASSAGE - ANDRÉ M. ZACHERY

When Zachery dances with his Renegade Performance Group (RPG), the cast often consists of agile performers identifying as Black women*, such as Nehemoyia Young and Candace Thompson. In another piece, *Dapline!*, created in collaboration with visual artist LaMont Hamilton, Zachery worked with six Black cis-men of various backgrounds in terms of class, formation and age. The piece aimed "to show how at the root of dapping [a practice associated with Black masculinity], there is

---

48   Zami, "Research Diary - Unpublished Manuscript" Munich, 28.06.2014.

a constant response of intimate understanding and connection in the face of op-pression."[49] In both cases, Zachery challenges hegemonic gender representations, by departing from the gendered roles usually assigned to female* and male* bodies in the contemporary dance world. Instead, RPG's dances often convey the power of the Black female body, as much as they allow for a Black-male-identified body to embody vulnerability, or same-sex solidarity and affection.

André M. Zachery in Digital Middle Passage; Afrofuturism Series at Iron-dale Center, New York, USA, 2016, Photo by Kearra Gopee, Courtesy of the artist.

In his solo *Digital Middle Passage*, Zachery departs from his signature group choreographies, and travels alone through Black diasporic presence as a site of movement. The piece moves through watery metaphors across spacetime bound-aries, revolving around the malleable orbit of blackness. As the title suggests, the dance re-creates, re-imagines and re-traverses the Middle Passage between the African and the American continent. The adjective "Digital" signposts a location in the 21st century, reflected in the use of contemporary digital technology, for in-stance in Yvonne K. Paredes' musical composition, and in the media projections devised by the choreographer himself. André M. Zachery is both a dancer-chore-ographer and a multimedia artist. He conceived the piece as part of the *Afrofuturism Series*, which he developed with following questions in mind:

As an interdisciplinary artist, I have developed an interest in investigating the presence of the Black body as a medium of political and artistic expression

---

49   Zachery, "Renegade Performance Group."

through performance and technology. In what ways could one reimagine and recontextualize the images, legends, myths, symbols, lineages, practices, and stories of blackness (or, more specifically, Africanism) through dance and performance? Do we need permission to remix these materials? What new questions are we asking? In what new ways are we asking the questions? Are we excited to use technology? Can we use technology to express or reflect our spiritual and ancestral connection? What can be gained by using technology? What will be lost?[50]

When I attended the premiere, the solo was part of the *Untitled Distances* program, in between two group works choreographed by RPG. The music was performed by a cellist and an electronic sound designer. The performance indeed materialized a multidimensional and multisensorial dancescape. It felt rather surreal to watch the performer evolve through what seemed like an extraterrestrial aquatic dancescape inhabited by his multimedial projections projected onto the ancient walls of the Irondale Church in Brooklyn. What strongly came across to me as an audience member is the feeling that he was "going under" in order to re-emerge, which he confirmed in the interview.[51]

On stage, Zachery's body becomes the dancing surface where the submerged history of Afrodiasporic mobile resistance re-emerges, as it does in different settings from the dance studio to the church. Although RPG's contemporary dance aesthetics do not bear affinities with dancehall, parallels can be traced in terms of cross-temporal connections. In dancehall, single moves simulate shuffling with the arms or walking with chains, thus revealing a genealogy that can be traced back to the Transatlantic Slave Trade. The Caribbean "limbo" dance emerged from what is still known today as the "slave-ship dance." It testifies to the long history of moving resistance, and of the use of movement already on the unstable vessels crossing the ocean, a search for balance that becomes visible in Zachery's movements. Geneviève Fabre explains how the slave-ship dance combines improvisation and intention to physically imagine what it may mean to escape from the "prison of history."[52] In her account, this dance is imbued with agency and empowerment. The historical performance "was a creative and daring act that proclaimed, with the sovereignty of the body, the vibrant intensity of one's imagining power."[53]

This description bears affinities with the spirit of *Digital Middle Passage*. Zachery uses the power of imagination to re-imagine the power that his ancestors deployed to survive the slave ship journey, leading to his existence in the age of technology.

---

50   Zachery, "Futurity and the Containment of Blackness in Twenty-First-Century Performance,"
      64–65.
51   Zachery, Interview.
52   Fabre, "The Slave Ship Dance," 42.
53   Fabre, 44.

Digging up ancestral memory, he seems to gain an unyielding power to jump up, in this piece summarized in the press as follows:

> In twenty minutes, Zachery moved across the stage embodying the horror of the Middle Passage, displaying signs of power and agency and later, struggle and capture.[54]

The piece reflects the dancer-choreographer's taste for physical performance. It shows the artist's work through a conceptual dance score requiring strong technique and the will to improvise. With its abstract body language and the use of contemporary techniques such as Flying-Low,[55] and his own derived technique of Physical Propulsion, the performance is nevertheless anchored in representations of the Middle Passage. It flows against mainstream depictions of this era, producing an Afrofuturistic experience that is, in the dancer's own words:

> a self-exploratory work that was a true linking of past, present and future ideologies,[...] and concepts surrounding my own cultural heritage and my own experiences from traveling, researching, and interactions with experiences of blackness around the globe, and what that means moving forward.[56]

Rather than resting on a linear narrative, *Digital Middle Passage* moves through dramaturgical ebb and flow, alternating high energy sequences and slow moments of mindfulness. Zachery occupies the whole stage, while simultaneously effecting a 20 minutes crossing that starts off stage left and ends up stage right. Seen from the audience, he moves his way from the right (côté cour) to the left (côté jardin), thus progressing across the Western conventional sense of reading. So does dancer Oxana Chi on the cover of this book. Are they returning us to a Black future?

Dancing without borders: geopolitical and physical islands

The three remaining pieces in my study are paradoxically grounded in displacement. Here, the movements explore what it means to transgress geopolitical, physical and cultural borders. While displacement is a leitmotiv in *Digital Middle Passage*, and all other solos, it takes on a peculiar shape in the following pieces, in which the performers experience the alienation of living on an island, be it a geographic or a political one. In Wan-Chao Chang's words, these performances express "how physical displacement can transform people and their surroundings."[57] The displacement takes various forms: Wan-Chao Chang deals with her experience of being a more

---

54   Tighe, "Middle Passage in Twenty Minutes: The AFROFUTURISM Series."
55   Zambrano, "Flying-Low - Dance Technique."
56   Zachery, Interview.
57   Program Notes to the performance at Cowell Theatre San Francisco in October 2010. See Chang, "Wan-Chao Dance."

or less voluntary migrant, a nomad traveling from her place of birth, Taiwan (itself the home of displaced Chinese people) to Indonesia (to where her parents emigrated), and the USA (to where she emigrated as an adult). Christiane Emmanuel identifies her self and her dance with the creolized experience, with the desire to erase geocultural borders, and to blend her Caribbean-Indigenous-European-African cultural heritages into one tiny spot: the island of Martinique. Farah Saleh, a Palestinian citizen who has lived in Jordan, Syria, Italy, France, translates onto her body what it means to "be the border," in the words of Widad Amra quoted at the beginning of this chapter. Saleh asks how physical walls and checkpoints impact such fundamental human needs as love. The three soli are strongly affected by the political context of the places in which they were produced. They transform and are informed by geographic notions of space and place. In my interpretation, they embrace dance as a means of leapfrogging physical and mental feelings of containment.

IMPRESSIONS BY WAN-CHAO CHANG

Dancer-choreographer Wan-Chao Chang produced *Impressions* upon returning to her place of birth, Taiwan, after having spent 15 years in the San Francisco Bay Area. The piece is truly diasporacentric, reflecting Chang's personal approach to mixing Indonesian, Chinese, West Asian, Balkan and American dance vocabularies. As explained on her website, the solo "describes the inner and outer journey one has to make when seeking one's cross-continental roots."[58] The dancer wishes to translate into movement the multisensorial, disorientating experience of returning to one's home place. Landmarks shift, or vanish; and locational and temporal stability is missing, or shaking, as evoked in her artist's statement in English and Chinese:

> The crowds, noises, lights, the smog of Taipei! I am foraging my hometown for a quiet place to settle, but sequences from my past journeys keep coming back before my eyes...And then I find myself: once again I am walking toward the unknown...[59]

繁忙的台北街頭, 蜂擁車陣人潮, 不間斷的車聲人語。她, 獨自佇立街頭。
曾經懷抱夢想而離鄉探索, 走過舊金山, 行吟巴爾幹, 著迷於印尼的多面, 終在西亞
流連徘徊。不同的臉孔川流而過, 最後卻再也分不清誰是誰...
再回到故鄉, 已認不清身在何處。只想撥開層層吵雜的簾幕找塊安靜的地方落腳, 卻
壓不住腦海中一幕幕過往神遊的畫面, 起身再度漫遊...

58   Chang, "Impressions."
59   Chang.

Wan-Chao Chang; Cowell Theater, San Francisco, USA, 2010,
Photo by Shalom Ormsby, Courtesy of the artist.

Chang performed the piece to a combination of live-music and computer-gen-erated sounds, both composed and performed by Klaus Bru. Diasporic re-search, nomadic (in)stability and identity-formation form the core of her concert dance productions. The dancer conceived *Impressions* as a choreographic family album in which she recalls images from her past homes and migrating trajectories. Thus, it handles her own migrations to Java, her 15 years' stay as a migrant in the Bay Area (where she taught at the San Francisco State University), and her return to Taiwan. While in the group work *Keep Her Safe, Please!*, she blurred the boundaries between her own life and her parents' experience of migrations through Taiwan and Indonesia, in this solo she zooms in on her own life in and of movement.

The choreographer consciously grapples with her complex relationship towards Taiwan, where she no longer feels – or never felt – at home. Her work also registers her complex relationship to Java, a place of deep inspiration for her dance art, but a place she also associates with cultural isolation and her parents' troubled memories.[60]

As a solo dancer, Chang's stage presence is elegant, delicate and swift, as noted by journalist Renée Renouf:

> [...] the graceful arms and gestures of Wan Chao Chang illustrated the narration via silhouette, torso reclining, swaying in memory, compliant, yearning [...], Wan Chao emerged once or twice, moving with her characteristic slender grace.[61]

Chang uses these aesthetics to address the recurrent question that seems to haunt her work: "Where is my home?" When words cannot provide an answer, Chang dances the worlds opened up by this question, and inhabits the stage as a world worth lingering and living in.

CHOC(S) BY CHRISTIANE EMMANUEL

This solo work is a gem in the repertory of Christiane Emmanuel. Again, the leit-motiv is traveling through displacement. The piece "questions the memory of the body, its present and creates its evolution."[62] In her artist's statement, the chore-ographer reflects upon the relation between the tremors that shake the earth ma-terially and metaphorically. Her standpoint is the volcanic island of Martinique, where her practice is anchored:

> As our planet oscillates between economic turmoils, societal crisis and human clamors, these events make me question the evolution of our world and more specifically of Martinique, island enamored of the wind breeze and which no longer smells beautifully of vanilla. [...] I am crossing through my memory and thinking of all the big dates of history and to all of those who fought, so I am clinging on.
> (Alors que notre planète oscille entre bouleversements économiques, crise socié-tale et crise de l'humain, ces événements m'interpellent sur le devenir de notre monde et plus particulièrement celui de la Martinique, île amoureuse du vent et qui ne sent plus bon la vanille. [...] je traverse ma mémoire et je pense à toutes ces grandes dates de l'histoire et à tous ceux qui se sont battus, et je me raccroche.)[63]

What *Choc(s)* makes clear is that to perforMemory is to undertake an existential-ist task. The dancer literally clings onto a piece of cloth hanging from the ceiling, and later dances through and dwells in piles of shirts in a resourceful scenography

---

60   Chang, Interview.
61   Renée Renouf in Ballet.co Magazine, 2010, cited in Chang, "Wan-Chao Dance." [My emphasis]
62   Emmanuel, "Choc(s) - Artist Statement."
63   Emmanuel [My translation].

Christiane Emmanuel in Choc(s); Atrium Theater, Fort-de-France, Martinique, 2011, photo by Wilfrid Tereau, courtesy of the artist.

devised with the complicity of Martinican artist Valérie John. Using aerial work, Afro-Cuban and Martinican dance vocabulary, as well as contemporary imagery by David Gumbs, electronic music by Jeff Baillard, and live percussion by Daniel Dantin, Micky Télèphe and Marc Séraline, the piece condenses in a single event the plurality of economic, cultural, emotional, geotemporal shocks experienced by Emmanuel in the 21st century.

Choc(s) was created in the context of the general strikes of 2009, when the overseas departments of Martinique, Guadeloupe and Guyane literally shut down to protest against French settler colonialism and Euro-American imperial capitalism. The strikers protested against the astronomical prices of food and housing and the lack of professional prospects and agency for Caribbean citizens, especially Black people. They aspired to reclaim control of the land and other resources still mostly in the hands of the former slave owners' descendants. The strike, initiated in Guyana, soon to be followed by Guadeloupe and the neighboring island of Martinique, was violently repressed by French military forces sent out to ensure that the islands remained their private turf. In *Choc(s)*, the dancer begins the piece high up in the air, and ends in a firm relationship to the ground, executing Cuban rumba steps. In this evolution, I saw the tension between the will to move forward, to envision other possibilities and realities, and the necessity of remembering the past and knowing one's roots. Emmanuel's claiming of her African ancestry, and its legacy of resistance is evident here. Today, I also perceive the impulse of Emmanuel's Caribbean Indigenous ancestry in the piece's profound connection to the land, a point that I return to in the third chapter. Emmanuel's descent to the stage converges with Leanne Betasamosake Simpson, a Michi Saagiig Nishnaabeg academic activist, theory of "grounded normativity"[64] as an Indigenous movement of resistance against settler colonial dispossession and extractivism.

Awarded the regional Utopia Prize for Choreographic Creation in 2011, the piece reveals a visionary aspect of Emmanuel's dance art. Like Zachery and Loïal, Emmanuel is usually known for her group choreographies. A prolific artist, she has created several productions dealing with diverse topics, and sometimes entailing a memory aspect. For instance, *Jazz Dousss* is a piece dedicated to the jazz icon John Coltrane, in which a hip- hop dancer encounters two contemporary dancers. *An Kabel pou Lam* is an ode to the painter Wifredo Lam which sets his work into motion, and bears affinities with West African dance-theater. These pieces, like *Choc(s)*, live through a diasporacentric approach. In a context of physical and political confinement, the performances celebrate dance as the art of mobility. They affirm contemporary Caribbean identity as a diasporic reunion. African-American jazz dance, a Martinican folk dance tradition called bèlè, Cuban rhythms and contemporary European aesthetics coexist. In our personal conversation, Emmanuel summed up the essence of her practice as a choreographic negotiation of diasporic identity:

> At the end of the day, I think that I choreograph our way of being, our way of being in Martinique, ways of moving...I think that unconsciously, it is inscribed in my choreographic dreams and creations...well, maybe it used to be unconsciously, but now I am conscious of it, because it is recurrent! It all depends on the topic, if I am given a topic where one must dance an "i" letter, I think I would swing the "i," because we can not be a straight "i." We have too much to express! Our walk

---

64   Simpson, *As We Have Always Done*, 24-25.

is musical, our body is an orchestra, whether you look at the hips, the feet, the knees, the positions, the posture, the head nods, the gestures, the placing of the hands…we are a complete orchestra, it is all about putting it in symbiosis to make a choreography out of it.

(En fin de compte, je chorégraphie… je pense… sur notre façon d'être, sur notre façon d'être en Martinique, la façon de bouger, je pense qu'inconsciemment ce doit être inscrit dans mes rêves chorégraphiques, dans mes créations chorégraphiques… inconsciemment peut être avant, mais maintenant j'en suis consciente, parce que c'est quelque chose de récurrent ! Tout dépend du thème, si c'est un thème où il faut danser des « i », je pense que je rajouterai un balancement au « i », parce que l'on ne peut pas être un « i »droit. On a trop de choses à dire ! Notre démarche est musicale, notre corps est un orchestre, que l'on regarde les hanches, les pieds, les genoux, les positions, la posture, la tête qui tourne, la gestuelle, les poses de la main…nous sommes un orchestre total, le tout est de mettre tout cela en symbiose pour en faire une chorégraphie.)[65]

Whether or not Emmanuel's statement can be read as essentialist, it touches upon the potentially empowering relation between bodily expression and political expression, between body memory and intellectual aspirations. Eventually, there is a circular dynamic between the choreographing of bodies defined as Martinican, and the use of choreography to define what Martinican identity means.

PAROLE, PAROLE, PAROLE BY FARAH SALEH

Farah Saleh's art is animated by the belief that dance can be "a daily form of resistance," as suggested by the title of the lecture she gave at the Tanzquartier in Vienna on May 9th, 2014. The lecture was preceded by her "miniature" (meaning a very short piece) performance called *Parole, Parole, Parole.* Saleh uses dance to represent the Palestinian experience of geographical and psychological dislocation resulting from the Occupation. This piece, her first solo work, which originally premiered in Ramallah, is not performed in a conventional stage setting.

As the audience walked into the performance venue, I observed the dancer standing in a corner of the room, trying to make eye contact with some of the guests. The border between performer and audience is abolished. This brings us back to the words of Widad Amra which open this chapter, about borders and questions without answers. Maybe because the performer engages with an ongoing conflict, memory was not a keyword in the personal conversation I held with her. The historical trauma of the Nakba is still ongoing, and therefore the memory performed is a daily, present memory. According to Saleh, war in Palestine is a daily concern, never only a past memory but always simultaneously an ever-present

---

65   Emmanuel, Interview [My translation].

challenge. She also addresses this in other pieces, such as *Sandwich Labné*, evoking in a non-narrative way the story of two girls killed in the Gaza war, or *Ordinary Madness*. It is through my internet research, and my encounter with a press review about *Ordinary Madness*, that I encountered Saleh's work.

Farah Saleh in Parole, Parole, Parole; Miniatures Officinae Project, Ramallah, Palestine, 2013, photo by Nabil Darwish, courtesy of the artist.

The choreographies of Saleh emphasize gestures, theatrical expressions and what is usually called task choreography in performance studies.[66] She also ex-

---

66   Foster, *Reading Choreography: Bodies and Subjects in Contemporary American Dance.*

plores gestures in dance video installations such as *Cells of Illegal Education*.[67] Commenting on another piece, *Ordinary Madness*, she explains:

> So that's why we use a lot of gestures from greetings, and daily life moments and relationships that are very distorted sometimes. And of course we talk in a very subtle way also about political divisions, internal political division and also the Israeli Occupation [...][68]

Like *Ordinary Madness*, the solo *Parole, Parole, Parole* is situated in the spacetime of Palestine, and Palestinian experiences of displacement, repression, and oppression. The performance epitomizes and personifies the search for sanity and stability in the context of physical, psychological, intellectual and emotional pressure and fragmentation. Raja Shehadeh describes how "Saleh tried to express through movement how everything around us is changing and how we are becoming accustomed to it – or not."[69] This comment is relevant to both pieces in my view.

Indeed, movement seems an appropriate medium to express constant change. The atmosphere shifts quickly, for instance, as a gesture born out of love may turn into a frantic, aggressive one. Or as a gesture of war such as throwing something over a wall is turned into a tender act of love. On the wall, there is a reprint of a stencil graffiti in which a person wearing a Palestinian scarf throws flowers instead of stones. Saleh's movements play with synchronicity, dynamism and tenderness. Embodying what it means to move through Palestinian daily life, she stands on her head, looking at her surroundings from a new perspective.

The diversity of the seven artists' cultural heritages, from African-American to African-European to Palestinian, to Southeast Asian and Jewish, and foremost the diversity of their artistic reflections and practices, do not preclude connections between their performances. In order to generate new knowledge on the topic of memory, I have intentionally associated works and artists seldom brought together within hegemonic aesthetic, choreographic, geohistorical or political delimitations. Since dance requires the subtle coordination of the body-mind-soul triad, and works with specific attention to the self's movements through space and time, it is an art form particularly well-suited to handling displacement.

This first section reveals that, regardless of the diverging contexts and aesthetics of the works, each work of perforMemory grounds the past in the present, and literally brings to the body and stage surfaces narratives that may otherwise be buried in the archives. The performances share the capacity to perform fragmented

---

67   During the First Intifada, the Israeli military called "Cells of Illegal Education" the civil disobedient groups who were resisting the closure of all schools and universities, and gathering to learn and teach. See Saleh and Bindler, Free Advice and an Interview with Farah Saleh.

68   Saleh, "On Art Production as a Form of Daily Protest."

69   Shehadeh, "Palestinian Choreographer Finds Expression in Modern Dance."

identities and trajectories, and to address them through the ability of the individual body to dance, in solo. Fabre argues that the historical slave ship dance "reenacts the tragedy of dismemberment and dislocation, [and] it stages the possibility of transformation through recollection, reassembly and movement."[70] Similarly, perforMemory can be defined as a simultaneous embodiment of traumata and healing, of political oppression and rebellion. To perforMemory means to recollect within the single dancing body the fragments of recalled, imagined, and transformed memories, and to assemble divergent facts, emotions, and visions into the convergence of movement. One of the strongest impressions I was left with from my own experience of being on stage as part of Oxana Chi's work of perforMemory, was the electric sensation one feels in the shift from the closed intimacy of rehearsal to the exposure to the audience's presence, regardless of the size of the venue.

The repertoire of perforMemory can and should be archived. And in archival debates, presence matters. Let us return to the discussion of *The Archive and the Repertoire* which opened the first part of this chapter. For Taylor, presence is what singles out the repertoire and differentiates it from the archive:

> The repertoire requires presence: people participate in the production and reproduction of knowledge by 'being there', being part of the transmission. [...] The repertoire both keeps and transforms choreographies of meaning.[71]

Besides the metaphorical use of the word "choreography," I find the emphasis on presence particularly relevant to my analysis. What is presence? First, it is the presence of dancers filling the stage with their magnetic energy and complex choreography. Second, it is the presence of an audience which makes the performance possible. Presence does not travel on one-way roads, rather it moves in loops, back and forth between the perfomer(s) and the audience.[72] PerforMemory thus exists through presence and produces presence. In perforMemory, the dancer's repertoire overlaps with the historical repertoire of memory. A presence countering the absences of dis_remembering coexists with the contemporary presence of the dancer in their body, and on the stage. Presence is the common denominator to Wan-Chao Chang's danced displacements, André Zachery's crossing of a digital Transatlantic axis, Christiane Emmanuel's multifaceted shocks, Oxana Chi's post-memorial choreobiography, Farah Saleh's artistic activism, Chantal Loïal's decolonial pride, and Zufit Simon's memory-emotions. PerforMemory begins and ends with the presence of the performer and its experience thereof by the audience, be

---

70   Fabre, "The Slave Ship Dance," 43.
71   Taylor, *The Archive and The Repertoire*, 20.
72   See performance scholar Erika Fischer-Lichte on "autopoietische feedback-Schleife" in Fischer-Lichte, *Ästhetik Des Performativen*, 75.

it on stage or even off-stage, as in Farah Saleh's performance. Without the presence of the performer, there is no repertoire, neither a dance nor a memory.

Stage presence may unleash the magmatic force necessary to dig perforMemory out of absence. To dance is therefore to assert one's presence, an essential preoccupation for artists of color, especially queer ones. To conclude this archival section, I would like us to think with James Baldwin's emphasis on the links between (counter)hegemonic power, history and presence, in the conclusion of his bewitching novel *Just Above My Head*:

> To be forced to excavate a history is, also, to repudiate the concept of history, and the vocabulary in which history is written; for the written history is, and must be, merely the vocabulary of power, and power is history's most seductively attired false witness. And yet, the attempt, more, the necessity, to excavate a history, to find out the truth about oneself is motivated by the need to have the power to force others to recognize your presence, your right to be here.[73]

The word "excavate" evokes an earthy imagery that captures the spirit of this chapter, and returns us to the opening reflection on volcanos, borders, and memory. The quotation suggests the limits of archival, written history, to account for the past. It highlights the correspondence between power relations, mediums of memory transmission, and the search for historical and contemporary truth. The dancers-choreographers do not only offer audiences to see them, they offer them the possibility to experience performing arts and perforMemory through multidimensional and multisensorial gates. Rather than resorting (only) to conventional historiography, they use and create a kinesthetic vocabulary to perforMemory.

Memory as a Site of Movement

Performing memory in the age of Postmemory

Imagining perforMemory

Reading Baldwin's *Just Above My Head* as a young teenager, after having recently learned English, was a transformative experience. I had put it back on the shelf twice after getting through a couple of pages. One day – I cannot remember if it was a bright or a cloudy one – Baldwin's main protagonist, the gospel singer Arthur Montana, knocked at the door of my mind. His candid uncertainty brought our worlds – apparently so distant from one another – into proximity, obliterating spatial, temporal and social distances. Without Skype, we connected across the Queer Black Atlantic. Today, I may feel far more critical of or distant from the

---

73   Baldwin, *Just above My Head*, 512. [My emphasis]

novel, however in that time and context, reading an openly Black gay author felt liberating. Arthur's story is narrated through the memories of his brother and work partner Hall Montana. Towards the end, Hall, burdened by the loss of his beloved brother, questions the function of memory:

> I wonder, more and more, about what we call memory. The burden – the role – of memory is to clarify the event, to make it useful, even, to make it bearable. But memory is also what the imagination has made of the event.[74]

Postmemorial artists use their imagination on a daily basis to transform events into stories, traumata into accounts, to counter absence and to perform presence.[75] Restoring life to the past, they make every effort to render it accessible yet challenging, clear yet interlinked, bearable and possibly empowering. If imagination seems to be the ground on which postmemorial artists move, it is also the oxygen that animates perforMemory. PerforMemory is a site of movement that one can navigate by using the currents of imagination. During and after the performance, the audience will re-imagine what the dancer "has made" of the historical event. Imagination plays a particularly important role in choreographic process. In relation to corporeality and social transformation, dance is an inherently appropriate mode to imagine other selves, as noted by dancer-scholar Hélène Marquié:

> To imagine is not to dream, but to feel/sense and experiment, to give oneself the possibility to be. [...] To dance, thus, is to become whom you imagine.
> (Imaginer n'est pas rêver mais ressentir et expérimenter, se donner la possibilité d'être. [...] Danser, c'est donc devenir ce que l'on imagine.)[76]

Consequently, dance can be a spacetime in which performers realize utopian futurities, a point I will develop in chapter three. Furthermore, Marquié notes that performing artists have resorted to dance to transform and transcend categories of identity, including gender, independently from and in parallel to the growth of queer studies and critical theory scholarship in general.[77] Considering that memory transmission, including transmission of historical memories, can best be understood as a construction of the imaginary, I find it particularly fascinating to look at dance performances that connect the imagination of other selves to the investigation of the past. Believing that the body is the site where traumatic memory is archived, it becomes even more compelling to look at the dancing body as a resourceful channel to re-imagine chronicled and prospective realities, what was, what is, and what can be.

---

74   Baldwin, 567.
75   Hirsch, *The Generation of Postmemory*, 18.
76   Marquié, *Non, la danse n'est pas un truc de filles!*, 100 [My translation].
77   Marquié, 101.

PerforMemory shares common ground with postmemory as defined by Marianne Hirsch. Like postmemory, the notion of perforMemory conceptualizes artistic embodiments of traumatic histories from a connective and affiliative perspective. It also encapsulates the possibility to bring together, without equating, such varied historical traumas as the European Holocaust, the Transatlantic Slave Trade or Maafa, the Nakba and other catastrophic experiences of (dis)humanity in order to better explain the workings of memory. Hirsch is interested in the memories transmitted intergenerationally within the family or through society at large:

> Postmemory's connection to the past is thus actually mediated not by recall but by imaginative investment, projection, and creation.[78]

My analysis of perforMemory does not distinguish between "recalled" and inherited or appropriated memories. For instance, Farah Saleh's *Parole, Parole, Parole* solo does not necessarily stem from a remote spacetime, but could just as well represent memory of everyday life in Palestine. Wan-Chao Chang performs her personal diasporic trajectories from Taiwan to the USA via Indonesia and back to Taiwan as well as the traumatic experiences of her parent's migrations as inherited through storytelling. André M. Zachery activates his Haitian-African-American ancestral memory of the Middle Passage while re-mixing it in the digital age and thus invites us into the process of his own contemporary experiences.

Through Gardens and *They Call You Venus* are luminous examples of performances that re-imagine historical biographies along with the transformation of the performers' selves. Both choreographers identify autobiographically with the figure they embody on stage, as you can sense from their interviews. Loïal identifies with the story of a Black woman who was excluded and discriminated against through Western body norms, and with her struggle for corporeal and political freedom. Chi identifies with the art and story of a solo expressionist dancer, and with her struggles and success as a female artist of color, striving for visibility, recognition, and professional development in a difficult political context. She describes her dancing encounter with Barbakoff as follows:

> What I noticed, and had already noticed earlier, was that dance historiography only accounts for certain persons, however humans with whom I can not identify. With this work *Through Gardens*, I could identify with a [historical dance] figure for the first time, namely Tatjana Barbakoff.
>
> (Was mir aufgefallen ist, und mir aber auch schon früher aufgefallen ist, dass auch in der Tanzgeschichte es immer nur bestimmte Personen gibt, Menschen mit denen ich mich aber nicht identifizieren kann. Mit dieser Arbeit zu *Durch Gärten*

---

78   Hirsch, *The Generation of Postmemory*, 3.

konnte ich mich zum ersten Mal mit einer Figur identifizieren, nämlich mit Tatjana Barbakoff.)[79]

What is at stake here is the role of sociopolitical power relations in general historiography, and more specifically in the formation of "dance history." Chi's work intentionally counters dis_remembering ("Ent_innerung")[80] of Tatjana Barbakoff, as Loïal does for Sawtche. Although both pieces deal with a traumatic historical subject matter, their perforMemory is celebratory. Through her work of perforMemory, Chi shapes for herself the role model that institutional memory denied her. Crossing the line between autobiography, genealogy and historical memory, *Through Gardens* and *They Call You Venus* exemplify and generate what Marianne Hirsch calls "non appropriative identifications," which Hirsch identifies as a major challenge for "postmemorial artists":

> [T]o find the balance that allows the spectator to enter the image and to imagine the disaster, but that simultaneously disallows an overly appropriative identification that would make distances disappear and thus create too available, too easy an access to this particular past.[81]

Both Loïal and Chi, for example, blur boundaries between their own and portrayed selves, and leap across the auto/biographical slash, yet trace distance with clear references to historical biographies in the program notes, the dramaturgy and their pre- or post-show discourses. Distance is also materialized in the theatrical settings and in the demarcation between audience and stage. "Balance," as Hirsch calls it, is also the physical and metaphorical feat devised by all dancers. (Dis-)equilibrium pervades both Christiane Emmanuel's *Choc(s)* and André Zachery's *Digital Middle Passage*, whose dances seem to search for a ground to stand on. Emmanuel does so by descending down from several feet above the stage. Zachery's spiral kinesthetics pierce across the stage, assembling the energies of capoeira-like movements to his very own technique of jumping.

Visual art and literature offer cultural lenses that may be applied to performance. For instance, Hirsch's discussion of the materiality and tactility of photographic family albums would also be relevant to Zufit Simon's search for her *Mischpuche* as she dances on fragile, imploding clay eggs, or to Wan-Chao Chang's piece, which creates the impression of family albums in movement.[82] The notions of displacement, cropping, ellipses and repetition also exist in choreographic practices, as we will see in the chapter on spacetime narratives. In dance – per essence the art

---

79   Chi, Interview. [My translation]
80   Ha, "Die Fragile Erinnerung Des Entinnerten."
81   Hirsch, *The Generation of Postmemory*, 161.
82   Chang, "Impressions."

of dis/placing bodies through space and time – choreographic dramaturgy nourishes itself through ellipses and repetitions.[83] Pieces like *Through Gardens* condense centuries of history and gigantic memory dancescapes into one or several moving bodies. PerforMemory exists in this realm, and challenges one to reconsider magmatic explosions of memory. At this point two questions arise, which will be addressed throughout the book: if perforMemory is a form of postmemory, what is then specific to perforMemory? How does the focus on concert dance influence perforMemory?

Moving center stage

Memory is above our heads, behind our backs, at our feet and in front of us. I share with Jill Dolan the belief that the theater is a space where performance brings utopia into existence.[84] The dancers discussed in this study diverge from dominant norms in terms of either/or gender, race, sexual identity and class. Their artistic processes and products also do not aspire to replicate dominant models. While utopia and performance can (co-)exist outside of the theater (as astutely suggested, for instance, by Queer Latinx scholars such as *Muñoz and Rivera-Servera*),[85] what happens to the moving research matter of concert dance on the stage space? The stage is no ordinary space to occupy, as I know from my own experience as a live performer. Dance can display and enact tension, release, balance, accents, pace, coherence, fragmentation, emotionality and multiplicity in ways that diverge from other art worlds through its visceral embodiment. Hence, dance on stage potentially performs memory in a very distinctive mode, a corporeal one. What is striking and decisive is the interaction between the "expressive" and "liberating" potential of moving bodies on stage,[86] and what it implies for the writing of historical narratives.

For bodies that carry long and ongoing legacies of enforced invisibility that persists in the present spacetime,[87] the negotiation of visibility procured by stage dance is particularly interesting. The dancers in this book intentionally move center stage, often contesting how the past is being written and how the present is being ruled. In her work on the Urban Bush Women dance company, George-Graves, reflects upon this power to shift representations through performance:

---

83   On patterns, archive and African diaspora, see Campt, *Image Matters*, 2012.

84   See Dolan, *Utopia in Performance*, Introduction.

85   Muñoz, *DISIDENTIFICATIONS. Queers of Color and the Performance of Politics*; Ramón H. Rivera-Servera, *Performing Queer Latinidad*.

86   Zenenga, "Power and the Body," 66.

87   See also Chatterjea, *Butting Out*.

I argue that by creating characters who exist in alternate realities and characters who represent entire populations, the company is attempting to rewrite master narratives.[88]

This argument can be made for the performances discussed here as well. For instance, in their respective works, *Impressions* and *Digital Middle Passage*, Chang and Zachery create an alternate reality constituted by their ancestral and/or family memories. In this reality, they are the only presence on stage. As leading-roles, they guide us through the story that unfolds as they dance it. Zachery re-inscribes American history from a Black, cis-male perspective, and his single performing body crossing the stage expresses the condition of millions of diasporic subjects. Farah Saleh dances a character who represents the Palestinian people, and the impossibility of living a normal life. In another work, *Ordinary Madness*, Saleh and her performers perform the checkpoint situation, transforming it into an emotional roller coaster, where gestures expand *ad absurdum*. In *Choc(s)*, Christiane Emmanuel performs an endless circular trajectory (tourner en rond), materializing physically her vision of the island's political situation.

In the field of theater, Harry Elam developed the concept of "(w)righting history" in reference to German-African-American playwright August Wilson and his cycle of plays on several eras of African-American history.[89] To (w)right history is to refute "master" narratives, and to imagine other ways of assessing and telling history. PerforMemory "(w)rights" history "within the space and through the agency of performance"[90] at the prime level of its making: the human body and its motion. In *Through Gardens* and *They Call You Venus*, the protagonist's body dances beyond its own death, thus generating an alternate reality in which there is an afterlife of motion after oppression. In the German context, *Through Gardens* contests the "master narrative" of the Holocaust – which minimizes or negates the agency of both perpetrators and victims, and objectifies the people who were deported. The choreographer re-inscribes women of color out of erasure.

In all of her recent repertoire, Chi embodies a leading protagonist who exists in an alternate reality but is connected to existing power relations. In *Neferet iti* for instance, Chi plays with the codes of museum display, shifting the audience's gaze to itself, returning the gaze, blurring the boundaries between the objects and subjects of the gaze. Her beginning pose evokes for a moment the ubiquitous display of non-Western art and culture in museums in the West. The pose sets itself in motion, and the statue begins to trace a solar trajectory with outstretched arms. It could be the hours of a day or a century passing as visitors pass by the statue of *Neferet iti*. The statue comes to life, the representation of the pharaoh becomes

---

88   George-Graves, *Urban Bush Women*, 72.
89   Harry J. Jr Elam, *The Past as Present in the Drama of August Wilson*, 3–4.
90   Harry J. Jr Elam, 14.

the pharaoh, the dancer becomes *Neferet iti*. The usual one-sidedness of museum displays is transformed into an encounter, the usual immobility of the displayed is infused with movement and the figure even sets down her crown on the head of one of the audience members. Constantly embodying a story moving away from "history," she becomes a center stage character full of agency, verve, fragile yet energetic, resourceful and open. All of the performances embody personal stories related to collective histories. Moving beyond the mere representation of history, they create memory on stage, mourning absence and illuminating presence, refusing to let their characters – and thus their selves, drown in mainstream narratives of history.

Embodying history, HERstory, theirstories

Other artists outside of this research scope have also tackled the relations between dance, history, and memory, for instance Opiyo Okach in his dance production called *Cleansing*. Choreographed for his Compagnie Gaarà, the piece premiered in Nairobi in 1997 and was performed by Okach with German-Ethiopian dancer Afrah Tenambergen and Congolese dancer Faustin Linyekula, 23 years young at that time. Today, Linyekula is rather famous within the European dance scene, yet many people ignore this foundational moment in his career. Okach's intent was to perform and question three realms of "cleansing": cleansing as a daily practice, as a spiritual ritual, and "as a quest for "purity" in such various contexts as the genocides in "Nazi Germany, Rwanda and Bosnia."[91] The piece's innovative mix of contemporary and traditional African performance art generated widespread interest from audiences and the media, and yet it remains absent from what is understood as the world dance history canon in the West. By bridging the distance between genocides usually thought of as remote from one another, *Cleansing* performMemoried a new relation to the spacetimes of historical trauma.

Okach's whole repertoire, including his recent solo works such as *Body Evidence* and *Border Border Express*, articulate his consistent exploration of relationships between identity, space and world politics. I attended *Border Border Express* at the Hebbel am Ufer (HAU) Theater in Berlin in 2013, shortly after having begun work on this research project. The dancer slowly wrapped himself, in a circular motion, in a red-white plastic banner similar to those used in road construction to set boundaries. The gradual, almost indiscernible transformation of a stage prop into a spiritually infused costume revealed the capacity to use the body-in-movement to tell tales of migration, to cross imaginative and real borderlines and borderlands, to transport the audience into a spacetime that is located so intensely in the "now," beyond chronology and topography. This image has stayed with me as a vivid

---

91   Okach, "Cleansing."

metaphor for the intertwining of presence, memory, and choreography that occurs in perforMemory. In Okach's, and in other dancers' movements, perforMemory interlaces the threads of corporeal meaning, emotions, reflections, stories through movement.

Defining choreography

The idea of an enlacing choreography echoes Aimée Meredith Cox's definition of choreography as:

> [...] embodied meaning making, physical storytelling, affective physicality, and an intellectualized response to the question of how movement might narrate texts that are not otherwise legible.[92]

In her study about the *Choreography of Citizenship* in Detroit, Cox discusses choreography as a metaphorical, sociological or anthropological analytical tool to read social contexts outside of the performing arts. Yet, her definition is also relevant to the actual process of dance choreography, perhaps because she herself is a trained dancer. Her definition appeals to the essence of perforMemory, and more specifically the pieces discussed here, in their capacity to address and redress dominant historical narratives and memory discourses and practices. In this definition, embodiment, physicality and movement are at the core of the choreographic process. By anchoring the story in the body and at the same time subverting bodily boundaries, choreographed movement expands the frame of interpretation by allowing for multiple meanings. Choreography makes it possible to embody history, telling unspeakable trauma without speaking, inscribing unwritten memories without writing, contesting points of view without being contentious.

In an interview that Lou Straus-Ernst conducted with Tatjana Barbakoff in 1933, soon after she had fled from Germany to France, the artists reflected upon the ability of dance(rs) to perform feelings, realities, and imaginations that may otherwise not be expressed. Straus-Ernst admired Barbakoff's ability to perform "a dancing expression for an inner truth which could not be told in other ways."[93] Today, Chi's perforMemory of Tatjana Barbakoff enacts this embodiment in the present. Embodying the story on stage, she sets history into motion, actually enacting the story as she performs it. When I interviewed Oxana Chi in 2013, she expressed her will to challenge what I would call the casting in the (hi)storytelling movie:

> I deemed it important to keep on researching and to find out: how does 'history' work in Germany? Who tells 'history'? How, when, and where is 'history' told?[94]

---

92 Cox, *Shapeshifters*, 28.
93 Straus-Ernst, "Bei Tatjana Barbakoff"; printed in Chi, *Tanzende Erinnerungen*, 2011, 16–19.
94 Chi, Interview.

Through Gardens is a tribute, or a "femmage," a term which Chi uses to disrupt the androcentrism of the word "hommage." Indeed, Oxana Chi's femmage-tribute to Tatjana Barbakoff tells a story outside of dominant history and performs the memory of a forgotten figure of dance historiography. The contextualizing information plays an important role in understanding a story without words. When I accompanied Chi on her travel to Indonesia in 2010, documenting her tour with a video camera, I was touched by the lively reactions of the audience and the strong interest from the press. She performed *Through Gardens* to an audience of 5000 at the open air festival Solo International Performing Arts, held on the volcanic island of Java. The hosts introduced the show in English and in Bahasa Indonesia with a succinct summary of the story of Tatjana Barbakoff. Although the Javanese audience surely knows about German history, they may frame it differently than people located in Europe, especially in Germany. Despite the apparent distance from their own histories, the audience's intense attention suggested their strong connection to the performance. Even if the plot might seem remote from their own history, body language leaps over spoken language barriers. The celebratory, meditative and dramatic aspects of the performance resonated for audiences at home with performed storytelling. As I was later to experience, dance occupies a pivotal position in Javanese culture, in which the stage is a popular setting for collective history and sociopolitical critique.

Whether in Java, Paris or Berlin, I witnessed people stirred by the core of choreography as defined earlier: *Through Gardens* used movement to transmit meaning beyond language, and beyond factual storytelling. The meaning embodied by the choreographer took on added dimensions as it reached each audience member and moved them to project onto the story their own meanings and memories. Thus, perforMemory invites a new perspective on the past, and incites a transformative experience of and in the present. Just as the shift of tectonic plates has repercussions on the earth's surface, the digging up of forgotten or silenced memories may impact the outer borders of memory itself, namely the social relations that shape it.

Between telling history and performing memory

Women stand firmly on the ground, bent slightly forward. Standing upright with obliquely curved spines, chins parallel to the floor and gazing towards the horizon, they seem to be frozen in their march or movement. This choreographic sequence, *Sri*, by Chandralekha, has received very different interpretations from scholars Ananya Chatterjea and Uttara Coorlawala. While Chatterjea reads the scene as a portrayal of gendered submission, Coorlawala sees powerful women demonstrating "an extreme exercise of strength, flexibility and willpower."[95] The

---

95   Coorlawala, "Ananya and Chandralekha," 399.

capacity of this scene to raise such divergent interpretations suggests the role of subjectivity in movement analysis. Both interpretations can be found in the dance studies reader *Moving History / Dancing Cultures*. Co-editor Ann Cooper Albright asks in her own essay, what it would "mean to reinscribe history through one's body?"[96]

This question opens up reflections on diaspora, space, and time. Dance carries the weight of agency. The seven soli inscribe history onto the dance floor where they leave the trace of their bodies' movements. With this premise in mind, I argue that when choreographers tell stories inspired by the past (as known or imagined from books, orally shared stories, collective representations, and individual memories), they do not merely represent a so-called history, they enact memory. This is where perforMemory lives: its very existence is bound to movement. Memory in this case does not exist outside of its performance. Echoing Albright, Lepecki asks:

> Where does history rest, if at all? And how is history reawakened and put into motion? How is it that it finds its grounding, its pacing, its anatomy?[97]

The imagery of historical anatomy is relevant to the idea of perforMemory, and topics of pace and motion will be addressed in chapter three. For now, I wish to emphasize a choreohistoriographic approach to dance and memory. History as a word or concept, is at risk if it is equated solely with a Western patriarchal capitalist heteronormative melody, which sometimes sounds a grating tune. Its tonic sound is the attempt to be "objective" that has characterized the field for so long. In contrast, the word "memory" is in deeper harmony with the body and allows for a range of complex, multilayered and non-competitive stories and positionings. Hence Oxana Chi's intention to expand history beyond its oftentimes narrow radius. Other feminists criticize the possessive "his" in history, replacing it sometimes with terms such as "herstory" (which troubles androcentrism but still reproduces binary genderism).[98]

On this battlefield of history, Black feminists have constantly contested the white supremacist monopoly on the writing of history, just as Afro-centric activists have invited us to listen not only to the hunters, but also to the lions' stories. They have searched for the narratives that were buried, erased, or submerged. The task of perforMemory is to invest the body as the site of recuperation of these stories, and the site of production of new stories.

---

96   Cooper Albright, "Embodying History," 439.
97   Lepecki, *Exhausting Dance*, 106.
98   For a detailed critique of genderism, see Hornscheidt, *feministische w_orte*.

Emotions in motion

Queer theory recognizes the role played by emotions in allowing us to access personal memories and to engage with memory on a societal level, especially in relation to traumatic pasts. bell hooks, for instance, speaks of "the intertwinings of psychohistory,"[99] a term that accounts for the coexistence of facts and emotions. Working on embodiment and emotions, Sarah Ahmed scrutinizes – in the language of her title – the "cultural politics of emotions" such as fear, love and pain, and colors the "canonized" white pages of phenomenology with a queer of color critique.[100] In her *Archive of Feelings*, Ann Cvetkovich redefines archival practices and materials, advocating for the inclusion of emotionality and ephemerality. By claiming that trauma "raises questions about what counts as an archive [and] what counts as a public culture,"[101] Cvetkovich's paradigm opens the door to new forms of documenting and understanding the past, and to new ways of rendering it meaningful for the present.

Artists, and indeed dancer-choreographers, queer or not, have been working this out on stage before academics arrived at theorizing it on paper. What is particularly striking about Oxana Chi's embodiment of Tatjana Barbakoff is the emotional quality with which she invests movements and facial expressions, in the tradition of German *Ausdruckstanz* (expressionist dance). Zufit Simon blatantly asks the audience to face fake, or contradictory emotions. When Chantal Loïal performs the pain experienced by Sawtche and the postmortal joy of her remains returning to her ancestral land, she sets emotions into motion even while allowing space for interpretation. All these soli perforMemory other stories, what I prefer to call *theirstories* rather than history, namely by embodying historical women figures in works in which "subversion and critique are braided with celebration and creativity."[102]

In her study of contemporary Indigenous American stage dance, Jacqueline Shea Murphy describes a similar embodied research process, in which the dance moves beyond the re-presentation of historical events and becomes itself a historiographical process:

> Rather than only recounting history through dance, this choreographing and choreography also presented itself as historical research tool and document. [...] a way of researching, an epistemological 'way of knowing', with theoretical insight and historical legitimacy, and as itself embodied documentation, with archival value.[103]

---

99   hooks and Mesa-Bains, *Homegrown*, 110.
100   Ahmed, *The Cultural Politics of Emotion*.
101   Cvetkovich, *An Archive of Feelings*, 10.
102   Chatterjea, *Butting Out*, 187.
103   Shea Murphy, *The People Have Never Stopped Dancing*, 10.

This description supports my claim that perforMemory can take the form of a choreobiography or choreohistoriography. The understanding of dance as a precious form of knowledge is deep-rooted among Indigenous populations whose cultures have always been embedded in the correlation between life, art and knowledge transmission, as Shea Murphy notes.

When I speak of perforMemory as a choreohistoriographic device, entwining choreography and historiography, scientific and artistic research,[104] I aim to highlight how dancers invite the past to flow into our present, in a way that is specific to their live art. Dancers themselves emphasize the "insight" and "legitimacy" of their practice, and challenge the assumption that only scholars theorize. They are also keen to translate body knowledge back into words, and deploy kinesthetic knowledge, as well as an acute awareness of the historical and emotional forces at play in their work, as the riveting interview transcripts demonstrate. André M. Zachery commented upon the link between choreographic imagination and bodily epistemology in his *Digital Middle Passage*:

> I was actually more imagining that I had to re-submerge to almost get permission from the ancestors that were lost, on the voyage, in the sense that I had to literally almost drown myself, to find their spirits under the water, to then get permission to move forward. And so that's literally what the piece is about in a nutshell...and how literally we, I, collectively are preparing, getting ready to now move, to move forward.[105]

This statement by dancer-choreographer André (Zachery) can offer a response to the dance scholar André (Lepecki) cited earlier. When history rests in movement, the choreographer reminds us, it is never at rest. Put into motion by dancers, it catalyzes a mixture of intricate choreographic composition and preparation and danced improvisation on stage. As Zachery articulates with such clarity, embodied epistemology sets shifting and interlocking (volcanic) layers of being into motion, enacting connections rather than divisions. Thus, the choreography-spirituality-history triad weave together inextricably in the works and words of so many of the choreographers in this study. Loss, and journeys of spiritual recovery, are leitmotivs in all seven pieces.[106] Here, we spiral back to the beginning of this section. As bodies move on stage, they not only represent, but also perform contemporary and historical stories, spiritual connections and political feelings. Beyond interpreting

---

104 Wehren, inspired herself by prior works, speaks of choreography as a historiographical practice, however she focuses here on dance historiography, not on memory in general: on the re-enactment of ancient choreographies through contemporary choreography. See Wehren, *Körper als Archiv in Bewegung*.

105 Zachery, Interview.

106 On spirituality in the work of Ronald K. Brown, see Paris, "Reading 'Spirit' and the Dancing Body."

how selected dancers embody "history," we can ask how they perform memory and how this may in turn impact current power relations.

Memory2go

Escaping and shaping memory

Survivors of traumatic events, such as Child Survivors of the European Holocaust, often seem to travel through memory as a site of movement, and to envision it as a moving and movable "being." In their accounts, I often read about the distance required to re-member and translate their traumatic memories into an artwork, such as a literary novel, or a work in another medium that may be understood as art in the present time. For instance in *Je me souviens*, Boris Cyrulnik, who hid in France during the Nazi period, talks about the artistic process as a "détour," a roundabout way to produce "a representation that may now be shared" so that "we may now inhabit the same world."[107] The *détour* is also a key concept in the work of Edouard Glissant on post-slavery Caribbean societies,[108] in which the détour is an alternative to the impossibility of retour (return). This vision of memory as a world that may be inhabited is also inherent to Ruth Klüger's concept of "Zeitschaften" (timescape):

> Ortschaft, Landschaft, landscape, seascape – there should be the word timescape to transmit what a place is within time, to a certain time, neither before nor after. (Ortschaft, Landschaft, landscape, seascape - das Wort Zeitschaft sollte es geben, um zu vermitteln, was ein Ort in der Zeit ist, zu einer gewissen Zeit, weder vorher noch nachher.)[109]

PerforMemory is located afterwards and afterwords. Performance takes place in a specific timescape as much as it creates one. In 1992, Klüger coined the word 'Zeitschaft' (*timescape*) – which did not yet exist as such in the German language – to assert the impossibility of conceiving of the concentration camp as a "place," as well as the impossibility of putting this traumatic experience into words afterwards. The dancescapes of perforMemory are timescapes through which the audience moves, and the dancer-choreographers can become guides on this journey. Like Ruth Klüger's "Zeitschaft," they connect spatial and temporal realms.

Dancescapes function metaphorically and materially. Zufit Simon fills the stage with clay eggs, building a landscape of fragility populated with shapes that may be seen as obstacles or supporting figures. Her bodily research investigates how the past trauma of her Jewish parents impacts her present. *Digital Middle Passage*

---

107   Cyrulnik, *Je Me Souviens*, 80 [My translation].
108   Glissant, *Le Discours Antillais*.
109   Klüger, *weiter leben*, 78.

transforms the stage into a wide seascape that Zachery traverses within the span of twenty to thirty minutes. Pulled irresistibly towards the ground – or the depths of the ocean – he dives into a maritime timescape, trying to "update" centuries of American slavery into his body moving in the Digital Age. In her *Impressions*, Wan-Chao Chang creates a physical border out of a red cloth, a boundary that she moves with, against and around as she recalls her own and her parents' geographic and cultural migrations. Farah Saleh choreographs the timescapes of a love relation in a virtual world, when a Skype chat presents the only possibility of meeting, and overcoming checkpoints.

Coming back to the topoi of the concentration camp, which appears in one scene of *Through Gardens...* I I I I I I I The blinking mouse on my laptop screen arrests my attention. As the clock ticks, I realize that I, too, am struggling to find words to write about this topos. After going out for a breath of fresh air, I come back to the writing, realizing that the words *concentration camp, KZ*, prevent me from moving forward. Recalling the agility Oxana Chi deploys in *Through Gardens*, I am struck once again by the contrast between the physical immobility of the writing activity, and the dynamism of perforMemory.[110] I start conceiving of this memory in movement as a *memory2Go* that I as a spectator can in turn take home with me. In this iteration of perforMemory, the dancer reaches the very limits of breath, swings her arms energetically in a circular motion, and employs strategic kung fu kicks as she faces invisible enemies arriving from all directions at unexpected moments. As a descendent of people who had to flee Germany in 1933, with Jewish, Black, Indian, and Indigenous family members who have been deported and murdered during the Shoah, the Transatlantic Slave Trade and other times of settler colonialism, I am grateful for the emphasis that her movements place on resistance. Across specific body memories, her life experience nevertheless connects to the experience of oppression, and resistance to it.

The idea of memory2go can prompt the image of disconnection. The disconnection may also be the cultural production of memory remote from one's personal or family past. Alison Landsberg addresses this type of memory, which she calls *prosthetic memory*. She defines it as the "production and dissemination of memories that have no direct connection to a person's lived past, and yet are essential to the production and articulation of subjectivity."[111] Her analysis focuses on multiple sites of memory in the USA, including Holocaust memory and slavery memory as represented in comics, film and interactive museums. For Landsberg, prosthetic memory is characterized by mediation, (bodily) experience, commodification and usefulness. Although controversial, her thesis produces an innovative understanding

---

110   On mobility and disability, view the swimming pool example in Hornscheidt, *feministische w_orte*, transdisziplinäre genderstudien:189.

111   Landsberg, *Prosthetic Memory*, 20.

of cultural meaning-making. Landsberg's central argument – which is also helpful in understanding perforMemory – is that some forms of memory may raise empathy across lines of race, class and gender, in spite of every individual's varying subjectivity. She hopes that such forms of memory may awaken political consciousness and stimulate counter-hegemonic alliances, and emphasizes the value of learning about the past through experience and interpretation, rather than through learning the "facts."

Interestingly, Landsberg did not include dance in her research scope, although it is a mode of expression that provides just such a possibility as it transmits memory through experience and interpretation. In her solo *Through Gardens*, Afro-German artist Oxana Chi handles the memory of Tatjana Barbakoff, to whom she does not have a genealogical or ethnic connection. What Chi does is to find in Barbakoff's biography stories of success, struggle and hope which resonate with her present. Working out a narrative which is much more nuanced and complex than a factual history lesson, she breathes life into an individual trajectory otherwise invisibilized in a historiographical mass of nameless numbers. *Through Gardens* reveals the possibility to perforMemory mediated, embodied experiences, and to share them with audiences, who can in turn take the memory2go and connect it to their personal memory universe. Like a USB-stick's[112] connection to a computer, perforMemory generates a memory2go in the interstitial encounter between the dancer's body as a medium of storytelling, and the audience's receptive capacity. What distinguishes a memory device from a dancer's corporeality however is the agency that the artist puts into the production of liminal spacetimes where memory, historical trauma, and diaspora co-exist.

PerforMemory thus also moves beyond the distinction between cultural and communicative forms of remembrance (*kulturelles Gedächtnis* and *kommunikatives Gedächtnis*),[113] for it allows them to coexist in one space – the stage. To erase memory, as Brenda Dixon Gottschild reminds us, would "act as a roadblock to empowerment" for Afro-descendent and Jewish people, because for them "facts of history" are "facts of life."[114] Therefore, perforMemory is potentially empowering – and this is precisely where its analytical power resides.

From the choreography of power to the power to choreograph

It is not only people's rulers who know that historical and contemporary power relations are (also) a matter of performance. Scholars in gender studies and performance studies, as well as those working at their intersections, have demonstrated extensively that historical and contemporary power relations are (also) a matter of

---

112   And it is indeed a brand for USB-devices as I just found out!

113   Assmann, *Erinnerungsräume*.

114   Dixon Gottschild, *Digging the Africanist Presence in American Performance*, 6.

performance.[115] The reverse is also true: dancers perform power, and dance historiography tells much about the history of power. Negotiating Black women's power for instance, is a key aspect of Urban Bush Women's choreographies, as shown in Nadine George-Graves's extensive research about the company. She extends Judith Butler's notion of performativity by superimposing a "meta-theatrical" level, where "an aesthetic use of performativity in a performance site implies *awareness* and *agency*."[116] Stage, body and memory are each layers that constitute a site of performativity.

Power is at stake here, rebounding power, always landing on both feet: political memory. The power residing in the act of performing contains the power that molds social relations, and therefore memory. To politicize memory therefore means to acknowledge memory as a location where power struggles take place. These struggles can happen on the stage, where power may be wrapped in various costumes. Praise Zenenga comments upon power and performance as follows:

> [...] mainstream theatre and dance depend on the power of the body to express different kinds of power, such as political power, intellectual power, spiritual power, physical power, social power, and even economic power. The speaking, dancing, and acting body not only expresses but also wields these forms of power.[117]

While he specifies that he is referring to the context of his home country, this quotation can certainly extend its reach beyond the Zimbabwean borders. Western academia often resists acknowledging the body, and even more so the dancing body, as a source and generator of power. The performances, as do their makers' reflections upon them, convey the idea and materiality of corporeal power, more so because in this case, the performers dance their own creations. An awareness of all forms of power that dancing bodies can represent and enact on stage is also clearly articulated in the conversations reproduced in chapter four.

Farah Saleh, for example, advocates dance as a form of daily resistance, in her art as well as in her educational practice. This is materialized in the solo *Parole, Parole, Parole*, which I witnessed at the Tanzquartier Vienna in 2014. Her lecture-performance shifted immaterial borders between daily movements, audience interaction and informative talk. "Parole," the French word for "speech," is absent at first. The dancer watches the audience walking into the theater space. The dancer and the audience coexist within a silent space where conventional borders have been erased. Saleh transforms embodied memories of what she calls *Ordinary*

---

115   For a comparative analysis of performativity in gender and performance studies see for example Gebske, "Performativität zwischen Zitation und Ereignis."

116   George-Graves, *Urban Bush Women*, 40–41. [My emphasis]

117   Zenenga, "Power and the Body," 65.

Madness of daily life in Palestine into choreographed and improvised movement. In a geopolitical context such as Palestine, where mobility cannot be taken for granted, dance may bring with it a sense of overcoming boundaries and it can foreground political and economic power and autonomy. Clearly, Saleh and all the other dancers discussed here are political performers. They are what Ananya Chatterjea calls *artists as cultural activists*, who articulate through choreography "complex critiques of hegemonic sociopolitical phenomena marking the contexts in which they live and work."[118] PerforMemory proves that artists can perform cultural memories, challenging historical narratives and contemporary settings, swimming against the mainstream, and thus eschewing racist and genderist cliches while keeping a broad audience in sight.

In this first chapter, I asked how memory is shaped through dance. I started mapping an alternative cartography, where memory is a dancescape, and perforMemory a compass. I sketched out the outer borders of memory dancescapes, and established my own archival repertoire of perforMemorial artists. The thematic focus of the performers works towards inscribing memory in political ink. If we embrace dance as an enduring form of transmission, eschewing the ephemerality paradigm, we may envision memory dancescapes as worlds inhabited by moving beings. Whether they contain hermetic or permeable borders, these dancescapes constitute sites of memory that are full of movement. Choreographing memory using postmemorial aesthetics, the dance-makers intervene in hegemonic narratives of history both as choreographers and as dancers. Not only do they embody history, they perforMemory a form of memory that is a memory2go, full of presence and power. Their performative engagements with storytelling is just as valid and vital as the efforts made by artists in the realms of literary and visual arts to remember traumatic pasts. In spite of each field's presence on the library shelves, I argue that perforMemory is as powerful as any other form of artistic memory. I have set the décor of memory dancescapes, which will be set into relief as you move deeper into the book. Now that we know where perforMemory lives, let's wander a step further, and wonder how diasporic forces shape its dancescapes.

---

118   Chatterjea, *Butting Out*, 35.

2 DIASPORIC MOVES

> *You may shoot me with your words*
> *You may cut me with your eyes [...]*
> *But still, like air, I'll rise.*
> *Out of the huts of history's shame*
> *I rise*
> *Up from a past rooted in pain*
> *I rise*
> *I'm a black ocean, leaping and wide,*
> *Welling and swelling I bear in the tide.*
> *[...]*
> *Bringing the gifts that my ancestors gave*
> *I am the dream and the hope of the slave*
> *I rise, I rise, I rise*
> Maya Angelou [1]

I have travelled across the Atlantic many times, within a child and within an adult body. Moving to the Americas seems to be in the family, and my ancestors arrived here over centuries, across the generations, from Russia, from Africa, from India...displaced voluntarily or involuntarily. Some stayed, some went back. In 2015, I arrived in the United States as a Visiting Research Scholar. In the diasporic space of the USA, I wrote many of the sentences that were to become the first steps of this book. After an initial stay at the University of California San Diego (in the Department of Theatre and Dance), I transferred to Columbia University, where I became a scholar at the Institute for Research on Women, Gender and Sexuality. This change in coastal location provided me with direct access to the diasporic hub and dance metropole of New York City. I had to move several times, and in the summer, my home became the Arts And Healing Center, where I resided with Oxana Chi. The center belongs to Bessie Award-winner choreographer Marlies Yearby, who lives on the third floor. How far was I from anticipating that five years later,

---

1   Angelou, *And Still I Rise*, 42.

I would be completing this manuscript for a distribution by Columbia University Press, and become a member of the Bessies (aka NY Dance & Performance Awards) here in New York?

Oxana and I stayed and rehearsed onsite, on the first floor, sharing a flat with Laurie Carlos, a senior writer, playwright and actress. Carlos had become famous through her innovative work in theatrical jazz[2], and as an early and influential member of the dance company Urban Bush Women. It was somehow surreal how my academic readings took shape in real life, through encounters, rehearsals, performances. I had met Laurie Carlos on paper in the anthology *Solo/Black/Women*.[3] Now she was a three-dimensional housemate, who liked to ask me, if I "need anything from the bodega?"[4] before stepping out for her daily walk. We bonded over the fact that we both grew up in Black-Jewish-mixed households, and Carlos shared stories about Crown Heights, itself a historic landmark where Black and Jewish Americans have lived side-by-side for decades, though with little communication or interaction. The Black social landscape of the neighborhood is made up of African-American inhabitants, and more recent Caribbean migrants and their US-born children.

Crown Heights, and more generally New York City, is a diasporic space through which people of variegated cultural heritages, inspirations and aspirations pass. Each group carries its own baggage, filled with different histories, and leaves its own footprints on the US-soil. It seemed to me that no one – except Indigenous people – could claim New York to be home, and yet everyone inhabited the space as though it were a home. The Lenape peoples, however, who originally walked Broadway before Manahatta became Manhattan, seemed absent.[5] And yet, when we began to pay attention, Oxana Chi and I would encounter cultural signposts and Indigenous presence. We learned about Indigenous People Day, which commemorates resistance to European conquest, as an alternative to celebrating the conquest of America on the so-called Columbus Day. We travelled to Randalls Island to witness the festivities organized by the Redhawk Native American Arts Council. We attended the annual Thunderbird American Indian Dancers Annual Dance Concert and Pow-Wow at the Theater for the New City, where we met the powerful

---

2   For a brilliant, in-depth analysis of the legacy of Laurie Carlos and others see Jones, *Theatrical Jazz*.

3   See Sharon Bridgforth's interview in Johnson and Rivera-Servera, *Solo/Black/Woman*.

4   "Bodega" is a Spanglish diasporic word for the corner shops run by Spanish-speaking migrants.

5   Teju Cole refers to this in his novel *Open City*. For more information on Lenape past and present, see Native Resistance Network. "Mother Earth – Manna-Hata – A Native Perspective." and The Lenape Center https://thelenapecenter.com/

Two-Spirit[6] award-winning grass dancer and multidisciplinary artist Sheldon Ray-more, a New York based member of the Cheyenne River Sioux Nation. We did more horizon-opening homework. So I began asking myself whether Natives were truly absent from the cityscape, or whether our socialization and education determined what and how we acknowledge presence. And I kept wondering about the absence-presence of my own Indigenous ancestry within the diasporic space of Martinique.

Real life experiences in turn shaped how I read theory and interpreted perfor-mances. In that academic year of intense travel between the USA, the Caribbean, and Taiwan, my understanding of diaspora became indistinguishable from mo-tion. My working schedule in New York consisted of a productive and agreeable balance between library time for research and writing, training time with dance icons such as Pat Hall – former Artistic Director of the Cumbe Center for African and Diaspora Dance – and rehearsal time with Oxana Chi. At that time also, Can-dace Thompson, a Trinidadian contemporary dancer and soca teacher, invited me to join the freshly launched Dance Caribbean Collective (DCC) Scholarship Team. At the DCC meeting, and subsequent festival, diasporic connections were again omnipresent. A broad understanding of what Caribbean identity may mean, and how it can be preserved, performed or imagined through movement, seemed to constitute the common ground, the ocean harboring individual and collective is-lands of creativity.

Stepping through these New York dance spaces was a memorable, challenging and refreshing experience. It was even more fascinating to become myself part of its dancescapes. In July 2015, DCC member André M. Zachery invited Oxana Chi to perform her piece *Neferet iti* as part of his three-day festival at the University Settlement Theatre on the Lower East Side. Oxana Chi's dance, and my brief musi-cal contribution, opened the festival. Later, when we toured the piece in Indonesia and Taiwan, my physical participation expanded. Besides playing saxophone and ocean drum, I performed a few capoeira movements, including a headstand. When I think of it today, I am reminded of the insider-outsider's perspective evoked in my introduction.

In that piece, Oxana Chi embodies the Egyptian statue known as the Nefertiti Bust, stolen from Egypt in 1912. Today, it is displayed in the *Neues Museum* located on Berlin's museum island, as a huge tourist draw. Since Germany first displayed

---

6   The term Two-Spirit stems from Indigenous American cultures to account for what is usually
     called LGBT*Q identities in the West. Across Native tribes, Indigenous words exist to refer to
     two-spirited persons and/or transgender persons. Prior to colonization, persons positioned as
     two-spirited often played a special role (e.g. healers, visionaries) in society, and were already
     in their childhood acknowledged and respected as cross- or transgender humans. I take this
     historical and contemporary information on the role of Two-Spirit in American First Nations
     from personal conversations and from the blog post Laframboise and Anhorn, "The Way Of
     The Two Spirited People."

the bust to the public in 1924, Egypt has been reclaiming it back, without success. Chi's dance raises awareness about the colonial looting of cultural objects, as well as about the discrepancy between hegemonic racist discourses about migrants, and their instrumentalization for marketing purposes, as exemplified in the Berlin campaign that praises the Pharaoh Queen as "beautiful migrant."[7] A diasporic quest for origins, the dance entails a multitude of cultural influences. After the 2015 show in New York, legendary dance critic Eva Yaa Asantewaa summarized her first impressions of Oxana Chi's fusion dance as follows:

> A chart of her dance background would look like a spinning globe – from ballet and Cunningham and jazz to Javanese and Egyptian dance. Her Solo *Neferet iti* [...] dares to draw visual and kinetic elements from different cultures, too, in a quilt-like, multi-textured performance. Her Central American plumed headdress, her yellow-gold harem pants, her hip thrusts and shimmies, her archer's bow draws, Masai jumps, capoeira maneuvers, vogue hands and dervish spins add up to a heady mixture. She believes it all works – you can see that – and makes it work. A somewhat delicate presence, she is, nevertheless, a woman writ large, claiming concert dance space for a diverse and teeming world, blessing that space.[8]

The journalist appreciates the dancer's unique dance aesthetics, characterized by the borrowing from and mixing of multiple kinesthetic idioms from Europe, Africa, Indonesia, and Brazil. As Asantewaa suggests, it is through the process of fusion that these elements come to "work," – a term borrowed from voguing vocabulary – because the performer "makes it work." The writer recognizes the specific "shimmy" technique of the Egyptian Raks Sharki dance style, often misnamed and misunderstood as "belly dance."

In the anthology, *Taboo Memories, Diasporic Voices*, Ella Shohat explains how this appellation, stemming from the French "danse du ventre," originates from and participates in a colonial fragmentation of the body, and how the label misses and minimizes the feat of a sophisticated, full-body performance technique. Shohat also refers to colonial exhibitions and how the so-called belly dancers were used in the colonial project rather than being praised as artists.[9] Today, Chi re-frames this technique in order to de-construct the colonial mis-use of Neferetiti's bust.

---

7   See Chi, "Neferet iti - Reloaded"; and Zami, "Oxana Chi von Zopf bis Fluss: Transkulturelle Tanzkunst und alternative Geschichtsschreibung."

8   Asantewaa, "Hamilton and Zachery at University Settlement's Performance Project". We actually toured this version of the piece on the diasporic spinning globe, and during my time as Visiting Research Scholar, I enjoyed being part of the performance at Dixon Place Theatre in NYC, upon invitation by curator Sangeeta Yesley. I also had the privilege to travel to accompany Oxana's solo at the Youth Government Auditorium in Taipei in August and September 2016.

9   Shohat, *Taboo Memories, Diasporic Voices*, 50.

By juxtaposing ancient pharaoh iconography, colonial history and Raks Sharki, her performance complicates and contradicts Western narratives.[10] Shohat goes on, criticizing teleological world conceptions that "segregate" temporality and spatiality, and put the global "South" historically "behind." She argues for a vision that sees all "worlds" as coeval:

> The spatiality and temporality of cultures as scrambled, palimpsestic in all the worlds, with the premodern, the modern, and the postmodern coexisting and interlinked globally.[11]

Oxana Chi's performance brings about these coeval worlds, as she challenges the conventional inscription and restriction of culture within markers of space and time. The "spinning globe" evoked by Eva Yaa Asantewaa mirrors a dynamic understanding of diaspora in interaction with dance. To be "claiming concert dance space for a diverse and teeming world" is to perform diaspora and to diasporize performance. Interestingly, the critic read the piece through the lens of her own African-American cultural heritage, by referring to the practices of voguing and quilt-making. The making of quilts is inherently a palimpsestic handicraft. It was historically used by African-American women to literally compose stories, to record and to transmit memory of the past to the next generations.[12] Thus, when the journalist compares Oxana Chi's dance-making to quilt-making, she strikingly touches upon what I see as the power of perforMemory: a diasporic assemblage of diverse choreographic materials, gathered in expressive patterns of storytelling. Chi's "fusion dance," as much as what Shohat calls "polycentric aesthetics" are fundamentally diasporic. Shohat further notes how diasporic strategies contest the European monopoly over artistic creation, and counter the meta-narrative of art history:

> While a Euro-diffusionist narrative makes Europe a perpetual fountain of artistic innovation, one could argue for a multidirectional flow of aesthetic ideas, with crisscrossing ripples and eddies of influence.[13]

I hope to give visibility to such a "multidirectional flow" in this book. Oxana Chi's current repertoire certainly flows in multiple directions, and takes as its source a plurality of cultural influences and techniques, as gracefully described by Asantewaa. The multiple textures of her dance are the result of several decades of training

---

10   Chi's intervention corresponds for instance to the strategy discussed in Karentzos, "Postkoloniale Kunstgeschichte" "Die postkoloniale Kritik richtet ihr Augenmerk nicht nur darauf, wie diese Objekte als Trophäen des Kolonialismus fungierten, sondern insbesondere auch auf die Grenzziehungen und Ausschlussmechanismen, mit denen solche Exponate als 'andere', von der 'eigenen', europäischen Kunstproduktion getrennt markiert wurden."
11   Shohat, *Taboo Memories, Diasporic Voices*, 15.
12   hooks, *Yearning*, 116.
13   Shohat, *Taboo Memories, Diasporic Voices*, 79.

and inspiration gathered in over 40 countries. What is born of this fusion is a multilayered vocabulary of perforMemory. The "black ocean" sung by Maya Angelou, and quoted at the opening of this chapter, could function as a metaphor for the possibility for dance to incorporate many continents.

Diasporic dancespaces are now taking shape, be they volcanic, or oceanic. Diasporic artists dance in multiple directions in search of alternative artistic currents. The "diasporacentric" quality of the dances fuels my "diasporacentric" research, to return to the notion first mentioned in the introduction. If diaspora is indeed, to follow Fox, a "permanent intervention,"[14] dance as a medium that is mobile per se seems to be an optimal site of creation for diasporic identities and practices. The magma of perforMemory resides in its painful archeology, and the dancers use their very bodies as tools to excavate stories that have been buried, overseen, forgotten, ignored. PerforMemory can be described as a movement in which the dancer combines the backward looking twist of the Sankofa bird's head, with the feet strongly grounded in the present, as in ballet's first position, and with the torso's anticipation of the next movement to come, such as a jump into the future.

In the previous chapter, I have asked how postmemorial choreographers use imagination to perform counter-hegemonic interventions. The idea of a memory2go that was discussed in the previous chapter takes on new significations and implications when wrapped in diasporic layers. I will now explore how selected performances negotiate the interrelation between diaspora and memory. The physicality of memory's movement becomes amplified by conceptual movement inherent to diasporic transformations. Advancing further on this path, I will now invite you to engage with Jewish, Black and feminist definitions of diaspora, while distinguishing between "diaspora" as an entity and "diasporic" as a process. I reflect on the existence of diaspora in multiple spaces: the theoretical space of academia, the physical space of the stage, and eventually the corporeal space of the body.[15] I wonder: Which meaning(s) does perforMemory take on when dressed in a diasporic costume?

Moving Through Diaspora

Inhabiting diaspora

Carefully picking up a green Chinese silk dress, cradling it in her arms, Oxana Chi gently drags herself into it, and begins a magical, nostalgia-imbued dance. This scene in *Through Gardens* is reminiscent of dancer Tatjana Barbakoff's own

---

14   Fox, "Diasporacentrism and Black Aura Texts," 368–69.
15   See also Zami, "Dancing the Past in the Present Tense."

memories of her childhood, and how she enjoyed letting the cloth textures lead her movements.[16] On another level, this moving tableau in *Through Gardens* suggests the absence of Tatjana Barbakoff in today's dance historiography, and reflects the mindful ways in which Chi embraces Barbakoff's cultural legacy. The absent body of the past dancer becomes present in the performative timespace, blurring the historical and physical boundaries between Barbakoff's diasporic search in the 19[th]century and Chi's diasporic dance and political message in the 21[st]century. I particularly enjoy the versions in which Chi performs to a hang instrument. The venue fills with serene soundscapes, and the dancer moves through the vibrations as if they were silk. Her hands caress the air, inspired by the Chinese kinesthetics of Tai Chi Chuan, and borrow from Javanese classical dance, with its elaborate finger choreography and mindful poses. Yet, the slow flow is sometimes punctuated by tragic staccato, as exemplified in the interludes of shaking hands. Chi's diasporic perforMemory of Barbakoff embeds the appreciation of her Chinese genealogy within her own fascination for and training in Javanese dance. At the end of the scene, Oxana Chi returns to the back right corner of the stage, steps out of the dress and places it back in its original place, as if waking up from a dream...or dropping off a memory.

The choreobiographic *Through Gardens* performs "the diasporic world we now inhabit," to use the words of Hirsch and Miller. In this world of *Diaspora Poetics*, intimate and public relations coexist and inform one another, and diasporic actors perform *Rites of Return*:

> For some, return is an act of undoing – a counterfactual effort to imagine a world before disaster and displacement. That act of imagination can also become an act of repair, however tenuous. [...][17]

Through Gardens, especially its first half, performs a rite of return to pre-World War II Europe. Indeed, we are projected into a time before Tatjana Barbakoff's flight and exile. Pieces of knowledge about the 1920s and 1930s are woven together, as Oxana Chi imagines and remedies the loss of historical figures, and presents them through performative presence. This dancescape materializes the diasporic movements required to travel through space, time, and dance historiography. Chi shifts from Barbakaoff's geographical origins to her cultural journeys. The audience experiences memory as a space to be inhabited and traversed.

---

16   Straus-Ernst, "Bei Tatjana Barbakoff"; printed in Chi, *Tanzende Erinnerungen*, 2011, 16–19. See
      my discussion of this point at the beginning of the introduction.
17   Hirsch and Miller, *Rites of Return*, 18.

The bridges of diaspora

In *Kinesthetic City*, Chinese-American academic and choreographer SanSan Kwan explores the relationship between urban space and concert dance in five sites of Chinese diasporas: Taipei, Hong-Kong, Los Angeles, Shanghai and New York City's Chinatown. She evokes how diasporic Chinese born outside of Mainland China are called "huaquiao,"[18] in which "hua" stands for "Chinese" and "quiao" means "bridge":

> When indeed [would I return], considering I have never really known the other side of the bridge? Still, for the *huaqiao* the bridge is always there; there is always the assumption of return. It is never a matter of simply leaving but always of going and coming, shuttling across the bridge, continually circling back – even if only in the imagination.[19]

What strikes me here is the dynamic quality of the diasporic condition, and its connection to a permanent state of transition through the verbs "going," "coming," "shuttling," "circling." Also, the idea of a bridge, and to a greater extent, the linguistic translation of the space of diaspora, is appealing because of its malleability. It can also be found in the writing of feminists of color, who metaphorically describe their back, or their home as a *bridge*.[20] I am inclined towards a materialization of diaspora in space through the structure of the bridge, which by essence is a constructed site, a place of mobility between worlds, where stagnation is not allowed.

In our conversation, dancer Farah Saleh also spoke of a bridge metaphor: the border between Palestine and Jordan, called "the bridge."[21] But also, the idea of "building cultural bridges" between Palestinian and Israeli people, an idea which Saleh is suspicious of, because she argues that an uneven bridge connecting two unequal levels is counterproductive. However, her dance *Parole, Parole, Parole* creates choreographic bridges that might otherwise be lacking between Europe and Asia, Africa and America, daily sanity and constant oppression, as does André Zachery's *Digital Middle Passage*, and Christiane Emmanuel's *Choc(s)*. For instance, when Zachery takes the thirty minutes of his solo to traverse the stage, he transforms the waters of the Black Atlantic into a walkable route, a cultural itinerary of oceanic memories, a dance-able bridge. More so, because he traverses from right to left, he moves against the tide of the conventional reading direction of Western languages, thus conveying a feeling of return. Similarly, Christiane Emmanuel trans-

---

18   Kwan, *Kinesthetic City*, 3; See also Lin, "Kinesthetic City."
19   Kwan, *Kinesthetic City*, 3.
20   Anzaldúa and Moraga, *This Bridge Called My Back*; Anzaldúa and Keating, *This Bridge We Call Home*. For an interesting analysis of the importance of travel in the life of Afro-German feminist activists, see also Wojczewski. "À la recherche d'un enracinement. De l'importance des voyages au sein des itinéraires de féministes activistes afro-allemandes."
21   Saleh, Interview.

formed her family home into a diasporic hub for Afro-diasporic dance production and transmission.

Chantal Loïal performs the body as a bridge – between South African and French history and politics, between Afro-Caribbean and European movements, between the factual and the emotional storytelling of Sawtche. Choreographer Wan-Chao Chang is a "huaqiao" diasporic Chinese, whose work constantly transpires the imaginative and physical coming and going between the Asian and American continents. From *I Thought Here Is My Home* to her *Impressions* solo, she walks along a diasporic path, striving to connect her multiple diasporic experiences in Indonesia, Taiwan and the USA. In the interview, Chang spoke extensively about her personal questioning of the idea of (not) belonging, and of return.

The conversation, and the performances reflect what I would call *nomadic melancholia*, inspired by the cultural theory of Nathalie Etoke and José Esteban Muñoz on "melancholia" in reference to diaspora. Both authors claim melancholia as integral to diasporic subjectivity. In *Melancholia Africana*, Etoke praises a "flexible" diasporic consciousness. For her, the pain of not belonging, rather than impeding diasporic beings, empowers them to be free:

> Diasporic consciousness is a feeling of belonging that contributes to existential fulfillment. It keeps memory alive by putting it through a blues-riddled archeology. The past grinds the present. The past forces the present to face its responsibilities. A present which is itself built on the ruins and steles of that which survived destruction, that which is born out of destruction.
> (La conscience diasporique est un sentiment d'appartenance qui contribue à une plénitude existentielle. Elle entretient la mémoire en la soumettant à une archéologie criblée de blues. Le passé triture le présent. Le passé place le présent devant ses responsabilités. Présent lui-même établi sur les ruines et les stèles de ce qui a survécu à la destruction, de ce qui est né de la destruction.)[22]

For Etoke, this applies to the specific context of African and Afro-descendent people. Her definition of melancholia africana echoes bell hooks' work on "yearning"[23] as a feature of blackness: the aspiration to counter the silencing of one's voice or history. Indeed, the Afro-diasporic dancers Chi, Loïal, Zachery, and Emmanuel, do perform soli of deep melancholia. The violence inflicted upon Black people throughout the centuries, be it the deportation of Sawtche/Venus to Europe, of Africans to the Americas, or the European Holocaust, appears in their pieces not (only) as a source of mourning over the past, but also as a well of creativity for the present. As in the volcano metaphor discussed in the previous chapter, the dancers perform a choreographic archeology, transforming each stratum of the past into a

---

22   Etoke, *Melancholia Africana: L'indispensable dépassement de la condition noire*, 33 [My translation].
23   hooks, *Yearning*.

movement's sequence. Memory2go lives in this melancholic, nomadic, diasporic interstice between history, geography, memory and futurity. Melancholia is also at the core of Muñoz's articulation of queer of color subjectivity:

> I am proposing that melancholia, for blacks, queers, or any queers of color, is not a pathology but an integral part of everyday lives. [...] It is this melancholia that is part of our process of dealing with all the catastrophes that occur in the lives of people of color, lesbians, and gay men.[24]

Like Etoke, Muñoz defines diaspora as a feeling, or rather a state-of-being that should not be rejected or repressed, but embraced, for it constitutes the ground on which people of color, and more specifically queer people of color may perform, or dance their daily remembrance and resistance. It is thus not surprising that what I call *nomadic melancholia* suffuses the work of queer Afropean dancer Oxana Chi, as described in the above-mentioned scene of the Chinese dress. A strongly melancholic mood also pervades Christiane Emmanuel's going-in-circles in *Choc(s)* and Farah Saleh's search for a place to stand on her hands among the audience in *Parole, Parole, Parole*. A diasporacentric approach allows us to extend the scope of melancholia beyond the territory of race.

Retuning to Chang's diasporic search through the lens of my own personal background, as a queer person born in France of Jewish-Caribbean descent and living in the Euro-American space, I realized that Chang was putting into words and movements a feeling I experience in my own meanderings. Her choreography seems to seek what Hirsch calls a "mutual imbrication [...] between a desire for roots and an embrace of diasporic existence."[25] Furthermore, we can see this in the juxtaposition of dance styles which work towards finding a place in relation to each other, like the coexisting aspects of her identity. In *Impressions*, she uses dance techniques from Indonesia, China, the Balkans, and West Asia. Wan-Chao Chang calls her dance "ethno-contemporary," a word locating the work in a contemporary, global spacetime. Although the term ethnic seems loaded, she aims to signify a search for the contemporaneity of traditional techniques. Her choreographic practice reflects the desire to knit together through movement the diasporic pieces of herself:

> Also when we go abroad, people ask us "Show your cultural dance. Show your culture," and then I start to struggle. My culture? Should I show Chinese dance? Well, I'm ethnic Chinese. But I'm not really coming from China, right? Should I show the Taiwanese Aboriginal? Well I'm coming from Taiwan but I'm not Aboriginal! Where's my culture? So it was a struggle at that time for me, because I'm still

---

24   Muñoz, *DISIDENTIFICATIONS. Queers of Color and the Performance of Politics*, 74.
25   Hirsch and Miller, *Rites of Return*, 2.

searching for the root, and there is a stage where I recognized that, well – how do you define culture, actually? It's the environment I grew up with. [...]

There is my home is the beginning of the process, because I feel that I've always been an "alien". At that time I was searching, where is *my* home?[26]

I Thought Here Is My Home exemplifies the issues at stake in Chang's work and in our conversation, we kept returning to the theme of cultural belonging and geographical (dis-)orientation. Chang's dancescapes englobe a multitude of worlds. The *Home* solo was the embryo from which the group piece *Keep Her Safe, Please!* was born. Depending on the reading, one may draw a different interpretation from them. On the surface, the dance is about the conflicts between Chinese migrants and Javanese residents, as experienced by the choreographer's parents in the sixties and as reproduced in 1998. Because her Chinese parents emigrated from Indonesia to Taiwan after the main wave of migration from mainland China (which happened in the 1950s), they were called "new migrants" in Taiwan. Chang also deals with her own migration stories, and the uncanny experience of being called and treated as an "alien" in the USA. The original title, *Keep Her Safe, Please!* was later complemented with the space-time marker *Jakarta 1998*, which may have to do with the influence of the US-based festivals that programmed the piece. In any case, the choreographer consciously grapples with her complex relationship to Java, a place where her family experienced rejection, but which is simultaneously also a place of deep inspiration for her art. This inspiration is particularly visible in this piece, in which Javanese dance movements and gamelan music alternate with Chinese drums.

The multiple layers of diaspora space

Wan-Chao Chang performed *I Thought Here Is My Home* at the "Festival of the Silk Road" in San José, California.[27] Dancers[28] form a circle around an individual. Disappearing as swiftly as they appear, they resemble the roaming limbs of an itinerant family that assembles, disassembles, reassembles. The movements alternate between Javanese techniques – bending the legs, shaking the isolated shoulders – and European "modern" dance vocabulary – hands rising up and down in mimicry of waves. The group surrounds one dancer, who soon steps out of the circle, walking across the stage to the front right corner. Later the dancers will form a line of gracefully aligned, standing bodies, whose heads fall to the side as if pulled by a puppet string, and whose upper bodies regularly seem to collapse to the beat, through a rolling of the spine. The circle of women may epitomize protection, a

---

26   Chang, Interview.
27   See the video Chang, *I Thought Here Is My Home*.
28   Wan-Chao Chang, Aliah Najmabadi, Tara Pandeya, Jade Raybin, Hannah Romanowsky, and Kristen Sague.

temporary shelter that dissolves into the whirling movements of the white clothes held by the dancers. They may also personify a threatening force restricting one's mobility, while the dancer in the middle seems to attempt to grab something in the air, as if trying to find something to hold on to.

Cloth is also a leitmotiv in Wan-Chao Chang's 2012 solo *Impressions*. In the prelude, a wide red ribbon is tied to a pillar. The dancer holds it behind her, and appears to be tied to the ribbon, which prevents her from stepping forward. Suddenly, she releases herself, or is she released by the ribbon? Simultaneously, the music starts abruptly, and the piece begins. Is Wan-Chao holding onto Chinese culture, symbolized by the particular color of red? Is the diasporic relation to her Chinese heritage impeding her, or giving her the impetus to dance and to move forward?

When I first viewed this scene of displacement, I could not help but to think of the beginning of *Through Gardens* as I first experienced it live in 2009 at the Werkstatt der Kulturen in Berlin. Although they differ greatly in terms of aesthetics and techniques, both scenes share the use of a red cloth, reminiscent of the navel string to which the dancer/protagonist is attached. In the scene of "The Birth," Oxana Chi rests on the ground, a solitary figure wrapped in velvet red. Her shape does not reveal a human figure, until she starts moving, accelerating and intensifying her moves to the sound of the quickening heartbeat of the electric guitar, played by Hannes Buder. She repeatedly moves between the floor and the air, a flexible spine allowing her to reach down and rise up with outstretched arms at a very quick speed. Then she bursts out of the velvet cloth, revealing her human face, the mouth open, gasping for air, her arms spread out as if to welcome life's embrace, and the beat stops. Tatjana is born, and reborn in Oxana's dance. Throughout this scene, the dancer will move within the velvet cloth, which is now a mysterious costume. When she slowly leaves the stage, she pulls the rest of it behind her, attempting to drag with her what seems like a heavy weight. With patience and endurance, she manages to carry it away, as if rolling the navel string back up. Even when she is already out of sight, we continue to watch the cloth follow after her, a diasporic node tied to her movements. The intensity of this scene is emblematic of the expressionist aspect of Chi's dance style. She persistently pulls her own costume's extension after herself. Is this cloth a "bag of emotions," as understood by Zufit Simon, which Chi gracefully pulls to her? Explaining why she prefers to work as a solo artist, Chi says:

> My body is African, and my energy comes from many places. It's African, but also Eastern European, Asian...many energies come together, and build up, generate my individual energy. I also need to care for this energy in a certain way. I call this 'housekeeping.' [...] So, I have always noticed that these energies absolutely do not fit within the mainstream, and also do not fit within a white, Western, male-

dominated society. It simply does not fit. Therefore, I work at my own rhythm and at my own pace.[29]

Pace is an aspect I will return to in the next chapter. Chi moves diaspora to a different level of consciousness, progressing fluidly through geographic markers of spaces. By envisioning a distinction between body genealogy and body energy or performative energy, between inherited identity and "affiliative self-fashioning,"[30] the dancer creates diaspora spaces which she may inhabit and in which she can perform. The diaspora spaces are also within her and exteriorized out towards an audience through the performance. This "theory-in-practice"[31] brings us back to the idea of inhabiting diaspora as a world. As suggested earlier, dancescapes are also worlds of habitat, and perforMemory is a possible mode to live within them, by constantly shifting and re-imagining their boundaries.

Both Chang's and Chi's articulation of diaspora through perforMemory can help us to understand Avtar Brah's theorization of diaspora space, a critical conceptualization and conceptual critique of diaspora. For Brah, a diaspora space is characterized by "relational positioning" and "multi-locationality across geographical, cultural and psychic boundaries."[32] Applying Brah's concept of diaspora space to the stage means considering which boundaries surround the stage physically and metaphorically: geographical boundaries between in/outside, or between the stage and the audience; cultural and psychic boundaries between an imaginative performer and a more or less receptive, open-minded audience; financial and technical opportunities which provide support as much as they can constitute limitations. What does it mean to enact multilocationality on the stage?

The multilocationality of diaspora takes on a new meaning in the digital age, which in turn influences memory cultures. In a blog post on "Archive and Aspiration," Arjun Appadurai reflects upon the new possibilities for migrant "minorities" to connect "neuro-memory and social memory" online, and to find or build virtually the space they may be denied in the physical world, and asks how this in turn may shape the "materialities and architectures" of memory.[33] One does not necessarily need to disconnect digital memory from corporeal memory. In this matter, André Zachery's choreographic work connects a raw type of physicality to a multilayered use of projection and sound technology in *Digital Middle Passage*, a point discussed at length in the interview.

The dances I regroup here under a widely extended diasporacentric umbrella, have in common the will to move in spite of and beyond the white, Western, (cis)-

29   Chi, Interview.
30   Nelson, "The Factness of Diaspora," 25.
31   Ramón H. Rivera-Servera, *Performing Queer Latinidad*.
32   Brah, "Diaspora, Border and Transnational Identities," 625.
33   Appadurai, "Archive and Aspiration."

masculine patriarchal capitalism which takes on different names. Regardless of their various positionings within geographic, racialized, social and physical worlds, and regardless of their public recognition within worlds of dance, the choreographers challenge hegemonic identifications. Their performances live at the crossroads of dance, memory and diaspora. They create a space for diaspora to exist, to be performed and re-imagined. When Oxana Chi holds onto the velvet costume of her own design, or when Wan-Chao Chang holds onto the Javanese Gambyong dance cloth, they inspire me to ask: what is this diasporic condition humans strive to hold on to? How can it be defined?

Jewish/Black/Feminist diasporas

In the postscript to *Other Germans: Black Germans and the Politics of Race, Gender, and Memory in the Third Reich*, Tina Campt reflects upon Avtar Brah's work and offers a retrospective theorization of diaspora in cultural studies. Campt invites us however to "engage this concept [of diaspora] with an awareness and articulation of its limits [...],"[34] and to also pay attention to Black identity formations that may not correspond to US-based diasporic definitions, for instance in the Afro-German context. Herself an African-American scholar, Campt resists the idea of using African-American contexts as prototypes of Black diasporic experiences and maps out the tense relationship between memory and diaspora for Afro-German populations. I would add that the idea of diaspora should also not serve to flat iron identities such as Jewish, queer and other notions that constitute the diversity and *diversality*[35] of diaspora. What is particularly interesting in Campt's articulation of a "crowded space of diaspora," inspired by her encounter with Afro-German survivors of the Holocaust, is the role of memory in the formation of diaspora:

> This complex technology of memory as an act of both remembrance and commemoration engages strategic forms of *forgetting imposed institutionally from without as well as individually and collectively within* specific communities. In this way, it is important to recognize that *memory provides the source of the defining tension of diaspora* and diasporic identity: the *dynamic play* of originary and imaginary homes, and the complex networks of relation forged across national, spatial, and temporal boundaries.[36]

If we read this quotation in light of the repertoire of Afro-German choreographer Oxana Chi, and more specifically *Through Gardens*, we may understand perforMem-

---

34   Campt, *Other Germans*, 174.
35   On the neologism "diversalité", diaspora, memory, history, and colonial power see for example Bernabé, Chamoiseau, and Confiant, *Eloge de La Créolité*, 37–39; Glissant, *Le Discours Antillais*, 126–61.
36   Campt, "The Crowded Space of Diaspora," 101. [My emphasis]

ory as the site of creation of this "dynamic play." Moreover, if we agree with Campt that forms of collective memory transmission usually found among Black diasporic populations may be absent in the Afro-German sociocultural context, then perforMemory appears particularly crucial. Although Campt does not refer to dance art, her reflection is relevant to all solos described and examined here. As suggested earlier, these performances of dis_placement interweave notions of memory and imagination, roots and utopias, and create new spacetimes which are no longer bound to geohistorical boundaries. *Impressions, Digital Middle Passage*, and *Through Gardens* not only cross these boundaries, but actually challenge how they are traced. And if memory is indeed the "defining tension of diaspora," perforMemory works through the physical tension of muscles dancing in and through diaspora.

Diaspora, where do you come from?

It is useful at this point to reflect upon Black, Jewish and feminist diasporic genealogies and positionings in relation to memory, while it is beyond the realm of my research to mention all coexisting and conflicting definitions of diaspora.[37] The term diaspora has become a landmark in cultural and postcolonial studies, irrespective of whether it is deemed relevant or obsolete. Diaspora's etymology is often constructed in reference to persecution, displacement and geohistorical origin-destination dynamics. In the Greek language, *speirein* means "to disperse, to scatter," and dia means "through." In the introduction to *Diaspora and Transnationalism: Scapes, Scales, and Scopes*, Ato Quayson narrates "the polysemy of the historical context from which [the term diaspora] first emerged,"[38] in relation to Jewish history. Judith Butler offers a contemporary definition of diasporic Jewishness, in which the self cannot be thought independently from the "Other" in Jewish philosophy, theology and ontology. Departing from this, Butler contests Zionist definitions of Jewishness and more importantly argues for the right to define Jewishness as distinct from, against or beyond Zionism.[39] Other Jewish diasporic definitions are proposed by Daniel and Jonathan Boyarin, who challenge normative conceptions of nation, religion and lineage and acknowledge the *Powers of Diaspora*.[40] Like Butler, they are skeptical of a presumed Western universalism and suggest a definition of diaspora which is broad, has space for multilayered identities, and is critical of

---

37 For a good overview of current debates in the field, see the new anthology Cohen and Fischer (eds.), *Routledge Handbook of Diaspora Studies*. Here I also think of the important, but androcentric contributions of theories of Stuart Hall, Homi K. Bhaba, James Clifford, among others. See for instance Hall, "Cultural Identity and Diaspora."

38 Quayson and Daswani, "Introduction – Diaspora and Transnationalism: Scapes, Scales, and Scopes," 8.

39 Butler, *Parting Ways*.

40 Boyarin and Boyarin, *Powers of Diaspora*.

genderism and Zionism, because according to them both subvert what they understand as Jewish ethics. In both Butler and Boyarin's work,[41] diaspora is not (only)
related to territory or land, it is a more or less chosen genealogy and a way of being
in the world. The idea that diaspora is not only fraught with risks, but is also a
source of power, is particularly fitting for performance analysis:

> This is the paradoxical power of diaspora. On the one hand, everything that de-
> fines us is compounded of all the questions of our ancestors. On the other hand,
> everything is permanently at risk. Thus contingency and genealogy are the two
> central components of diasporic consciousness.[42]

Interestingly, the idea of envisioning diaspora as power also prevails in Africanist theorizations of diaspora, as suggested earlier in the discussion of diasporacentrism. In the above-mentioned essay, for instance, Tina Campt refers to Audre Lorde and her foreword to *Showing Our Colors: Afro-German Women Speak Out*,
an anthology co-edited by May Ayim, among others.[43] For Audre Lorde, Afro-descendant citizens share an African cultural heritage that is a source of strength.
Whether Jewish or Black, this understanding of diaspora echoes André Zachery's
perception of Afrodiasporic ancestral connections, as described in his commentary
on *Digital Middle Passage*. And at a metalevel, my research itself regularly jumps between Jewish and Black diasporic consciousness. Or maybe they are interwoven
into a vast net of interconnected performative meanings. Whether or not they explicitly evoke the term "diaspora," I find that a powerful diasporic consciousness
pervades all the performances. As reflected in the interviews, the choreographers
dig into cultural legacies of struggle and strength to create a work that can speak
to any audience. Here, risk is intrinsic to the choreographic process: the risk of
disclosing one's diasporic self and the risky opportunity to challenge social power
relations.

The Boyarins warn against the risks of using diaspora as an umbrella-word to
regroup contexts that are to diverse to share one name (e.g. Black diaspora, Chinese diaspora,...). Although I understand where these worries come from, I argue
for a renewed conception of diaspora, which allows for multiplicity without masking diversity. While the authors consider "the repeated experience of *rediasporization*"[44] to be a specific feature of Jewish identities and itineraries, I contend that
all diasporic communities may experience constant and/or continuous *diasporiza-
tion*. Palestinian dancer Farah Saleh's account of her biography and the shuffling

---

41   For a nuanced comparative critique of Butler and the Boyarins, see Cooper, "A Diasporic Cri-
      tique of Diasporism."
42   Boyarin and Boyarin, *Powers of Diaspora*, 4.
43   Lorde, "Foreword to the English Language Edition." The original German title of this book is
      Farbe bekennen: Afro-deutsche Frauen auf den Spuren ihrer Geschichte.
44   Boyarin and Boyarin, *Powers of Diaspora*, 11.

across countries offers such an example of permanent "rediasporization." Wan-Chao Chang for instance, deals with the multiple diasporic experiences of being a Chinese in Indonesia, a Taiwanese in the USA, and a newcomer in her birth country Taiwan, as reflected in her words and works. This to-and-fro materializes in her use of space in *Impressions*, and the (eventually released) tension of the cloth that binds her to the pillar, always pulling her back like a magnet, or like the memory tension that forms and informs her diasporic identity, to come back to Campt.

I hope it is clear by now that I understand "diasporic dance art" as a form of connection, a tool of analysis that supersedes the plurality of geographical locations or sources of diasporic or racialized identity, be they Caribbean, Afro-German, Afro-American, Palestinian, Chinese, or South East Asian. This is also reflected in the plurality of words that the choreographers use to define their work: Oxana Chi's "fusion" of diverse influences, Wan-Chao Chang's "ethno-contemporary,"[45] Chantal Loïal's "laboratory." Moving alongside the choreographers, I often witnessed how, when they identify as dance makers, they are always asked "what kind of dance" they "make", and it seems that people expected a definition restricted to the perimeter of one or two words, and a spacetime of one or two minutes. The question, rather, may be what researchers and audience members make out of the dances which the choreographers make. Labeling a dance, especially in an academic context, is an ongoing concern. Muñoz contends that a process of "world-making" is at work in pieces produced by performers of color.[46] Scholars writing about performance indeed also create worlds, they trace boundaries and create maps in their writing, delineate performances and performers in space and time and assign interpretations, which may be in resonance or dissonance with the artists' intentions regarding the dances. Researchers should therefore ask themselves, as does Susan Foster: "What kind of worlds do we as scholars create for a given dance when we undertake to describe and analyze it?"[47] The word/world I "create" for now is a diasporic one, where diaspora is the texture out of which I weave my analysis of perforMemory. And when I choose to write or speak of "diasporic dance," rather than "Black Dance,"[48] I open diasporic worlds, characterized by the mobility of dance as a vec-

---

45 With this term, Chang refers to a contemporaneous renewal and transformation of various traditional forms of dance. For a critique of the label "ethnic", see Foster, "Worlding Dance," 2. "The substitution of 'world' for 'ethnic' at UCLA and in various labeling practices, such as the music industry and arts programming, has worked euphemistically to gloss over the colonial legacy of racialized and class-based hierarchizations. [...] Yet through this relabeling, the colonial history that produced the ethnic continues to operate."

46 Muñoz, *DISIDENTIFICATIONS. Queers of Color and the Performance of Politics*.

47 Foster, "Worlding Dance," 3.

48 On the question of (not) defining Black dance, see: Allen, "What Is Black Dance?"; Dixon Gottschild, *The Black Dancing Body*; and George-Graves, *Urban Bush Women*.

tor for shifting identities and diasporacentric performances, rather than diasporic dancing subjects.

Queer [in] diaspora

One of my most memorable places to experience and co-create New York's diasporic dancescapes is the Bronx Academy of Arts and Dance (BAAD!). Oxana Chi performed there twice, in a lovely theater run by dancer Arthur Aviles and writer Charles Rice-Gonzalez, two gay Latino artists and community leaders with seemingly endless ingenuity and generosity. The first time, in 2015, I sat in the last row among an enthusiastic and attentive crowd, and videotaped the premiere of Oxana Chi's solo *Psyche* at the BlackTinX Performance Festival. When I entered the space, my doctoral self discovered a couple of shelves of dance theory and magazines and I could buy the book *Performing Queer Latinidad*. The second time, in 2016, I found myself on stage in Chi's piece *I Step On Air*. In the context of the yearly women's month festival, we shared the evening with Black lesbian dancer-choreographer Maria Bauman, whose company motto I mentioned in the first chapter: "Sweat your truth!". To me, it expresses with such humor and accuracy the physicality of the knowledge generated by dancers, the materiality of their work and the corporeality of their social engagement. This incentive has stayed with me ever since, as I sit typing these words, as far as I could possibly be from sweating, sipping some more yogi tea to restore the body heat swallowed by the machine, looking back at my yoga set of the morning and looking forward to going to dance class tonight. With every drop of the dancer's truths, the stage becomes a flowing river of knowledge about the past and what it means to our present.

Acting and playing music in *I Step On Air* that night at BAAD!, in conversation with Oxana's dance solo, I felt how in the space of performance, we were creating a queer diasporic space of remembering for May Ayim that was simultaneously accessible to the US-based audience, their aspirations and imaginations. The venue felt like a queer diasporic home because of the staff and artists, their energies and performances.[49] Later at home, I was to start reading the book I had bought there, enjoying Ramón H. Rivera-Servera's discussion of choreographies of queer latina/o resistance at BAAD!, and other "counterpublicspaces" where identities of queer latinidad are realized in and through performance. The author argues that:

> [...] performance functions as a site where marginalized communities, such as queer Latinas/os, make home by participating in embodied experiences with others in the midst of travel to collectively devise strategies of being and being together.[50]

---

49   On the topic of Black performance, queerness, and spatiality, see also Zami, "Of Circles and Cycles: Remembering, Ritual, and Rhythm in Black Queer Female Dances."

50   Ramón H. Rivera-Servera, *Performing Queer Latinidad*, 29.

That night we performed at BAAD!, I felt indeed a sense of togetherness through movement. I was also touched by the programmers and audience's expression of gratitude for a performance that made them feel empowered – as Black lesbians, as artists, as people of color – but also people bonding in humanity across boundaries of race, age or gender. #grateful was also the hashtag used by dancer Maria Bauman in a Facebook post from March 29, 2016, in which she thanks her crew, BAAD!, and ends with the words "Oxana Chi and Layla Zami were inspirational. Watch out for more split bills from us!" Indeed, a few months later, she invited us to be a part of her program at NYU Jack Crystal Theater, in which Oxana Chi participated, while teaching obligations for my "Performing Memory" class kept me in Berlin. In my experience, the performance *I Step On Air* co-shaped a diasporic space of collective remembrance and resistance. The audience strongly identified with May Ayim's biography – evoked by Oxana Chi's movements – and May Ayim's poem "Gegen Leberwurstgrau für eine bunte Republik,"[51] which I performed in its English translation. Chi, as an Afro-German performer commemorating and celebrating the Afro-German historical feminist Ayim, fashioned through dance a diasporic storytelling that made sense across definitions and populations of diaspora. Performing *Psyche* and *I Step On Air*, she inscribed her perforMemory into the dancescape of New York City. Not only did BAAD! become a temporary space for Oxana Chi's perforMemory, but her own act of dancing became the dynamic site of a memory2go that a plurality of individuals could take home that night.

The idea of diaspora is inextricably embedded in paradigms of migration and gender, and an expanding field of queer diasporic studies challenges diaspora studies to move beyond heteronormative understandings of migration movements, family and exile.[52] For example, Fatima el-Tayeb uses diaspora "to describe a population that does not share a common origin – however imaginary it might be – but a contemporary condition."[53] Moreover, she defines "queering ethnicity" as a strategy of diasporic citizens, the "strategy of claiming a space within the nation by moving beyond it."[54] Reminiscent of strategic essentialism's adherence to the nation framework, the definition simultaneously takes a deconstructionist step out of the nation-state category. Again, I am reminded of dancer Chang's dialectical holding onto the red ribbon, which pulls and pushes her. I also think of Saleh's

---

51 Ayim, *Blues in Schwarz-Weiss*, 62-65.

52 See, for example, Ellis, *Territories of the Soul*; Hayes, "Queering Roots, Queering Diaspora"; Johnson and Rivera-Servera, *Blacktino Queer Performance*; Gopinath, *Impossible Desires*; Boyarin, Itzkovitz, and Pellegrini, *Queer Theory and The Jewish Question*.

53 El-Tayeb, *European Others*, xxxv; See also more recently her analysis of Othering processes of Roma/Sinti, Muslim, and Black citizens, in relation to antisemitism and Holocaust memory in: El-Tayeb, *Undeutsch*.

54 El-Tayeb, *European Others*, xxxiv.

performance of *Parole, Parole, Parole* at the Tanzquartier in Vienna. The dancer progressively claimed a space within the room: when she moved around and between the audience members, who were scattered around the room, the attendees created a half circle, which I interpreted both as a desire to grant her enough space to move, and as spatial distancing from the performer's body before times of social distancing. There she was, a Palestinian citizen reclaiming space within an Austrian cultural venue, and eventually coming close to the Vienna audience, attempting to ignite a connection to people who navigated through their own relation to space, distance, and proximity.

Oceanic forces sometimes carry diasporic entities, in the spirit of Maya Angelou's opening words to this chapter. In *Black Atlantic, Queer Atlantic*, Natasha Tinsley Omise'eke criticizes the androcentric bias of Black studies scholars and their failure to account for queerness, while she regrets the absence of blackness in Western feminist theory. By "reading for Black queer history and theory in the traumatic dislocation of the Middle Passage,"[55] she anchors Black queerness in Afro-diasporic history and rejects polarized accounts of queer and diasporic themes in academia. Omise'eke's vision of Queer Africana studies emphasizes the potential role of metaphors to "provide conceptual bridges between the lived and the possible that use language queerly to map other roads of becoming."[56] She wants her essay "to perform the oceanness that it thematizes."[57] In Zachery's dance, the work also performs the oceanic migrations and interrogations it addresses. In perforMemory, the dances per se perform and transform the topic, issue, question, or mood they handle. The performances are imbued with energies that can guide new ways of becoming.

Michelle M. Wright identifies the use of the autobiographical genre in literature, artistic and activist activities as a "diasporic strategy"[58] used by Afro-Germans. I believe that this "diasporic strategy" can be extended beyond the Afro-German context. However, beyond the search for the diasporic roots of the choreographers, I am rather interested in examining the resonances between their work. As noted earlier, the seven solos proceed to what I call choreobiography, embedding autobiographical sources with historiographic quests and choreographic creativity. This may echo with the above cited diasporic works of Fatima el-Tayeb, Michelle M. Wright, and Natasha Tinsley Omise'eke and their theorizing of artistic expressions. Yet, dance is always absent in these precious contributions, as well as in other landmark works analyzing the power dynamics of identity constructions

---

55   Omise'eke, "Black Atlantic, Queer Atlantic," 193 I found about out this article through Vanessa Agard-Jones'.

56   Omise'eke, 212. I see parallels with the previously cited works by Lann Hornscheidt on language as epistemic violence.

57   Omise'eke, 212.

58   Wright, "Others-from-Within from Without."

such as *Mythen, Masken, Subjekte*.[59] Given the gendered, racialized, capitalized, ableist connotations of the body within hegemonic discourses of Western heteronormative patriarchal capitalism, it is particularly interesting to look at how choreographers perforMemory in ways that sometimes queer conventional representations of memory. I argue that the stage is a site where hegemonic spaces are referred to, while the dancers imaginatively and actually move beyond them. So, diasporic and queer strategies converge with performance strategies in the desire to "move beyond,"[60] the negotiation of the steps ahead that will eventually lead to a new path.

Another intersection between Black and Jewish diasporas is their relation to forced dispersal and trauma. I reflected upon this in an autobiographical experimental piece of creative writing "Ein all_zu_täglicher Tag*,"[61] published in the academic anthology *InterdepenDenken* dedicated to intersectionality. My narrative condensed years of German experience into the spacetime of a single day, to render a sense of constant mobility that paradoxically is the only way to obtain stability and safety as a diasporic subject in the West. Scholarship located at the interstice between performance studies, queer studies and critical race theory demonstrates that positionalities of race, gender and sexuality are not only displayed by, but also performed by the body.[62] For instance, in my view, *Through Gardens* offers a queer-feminist reading of Tatjana Barbakoff's diasporic trajectory from the perspective of Oxana Chi. The works allows space to embody Barbakoff as a strong diasporic female subject, and for an interpretation that questions conventional art historical assumptions of heteronormativity. This performance of diaspora could be understood as queer, without representing queer sexuality.[63]

In the context of performance, dance art as an ontologically mobile expression permits new relations to trauma and diaspora. In her discussion of diaspora in relation to queer archives, trauma and feelings – not in relation to dance – Ann Cvetkovich writes:

> The presence of geographic dislocation in a range of trauma histories suggests the intersections of trauma and migration. For example, the trains to the concentration camps play a significant role in Holocaust testimony and memorial, and have additional resonance in the context of the Jewish diaspora. Ships figure prominently in the production of cultural memory about the Middle Passage, the traumatic process of transport from Africa to Americas.[64]

---

59   Ha, "Macht (T)raum(a) Berlin."
60   El-Tayeb, *European Others*, xxxiv.
61   Zami, "Ein all_zu_täglicher Tag*."
62   See, for example, Ramón H. Rivera-Servera, *Performing Queer Latinidad*.
63   Zami, "Oxana Chis Tänzerische Wissensschaffung."
64   Cvetkovich, *An Archive of Feelings*, 120.

Interestingly, *Through Gardens* and *Digital Middle Passage* deal with deportation without representing trains nor ships. The performances deliberately renounce these iconic objects, yet this uncanny mobility is ever present, and the bodies are the vectors. It seems that the dancers have the power to physically and emotionally relocate what has been "dislocated": memories, feelings, ambitions.

From diaspora to diasporic

The point where these Black, Jewish, and feminist definitions of diaspora and diasporic dances meet is in the affirmation of diaspora as an empowering force. Although fraught with obstacles, diasporic identity-formation entails the power needed to exist, subsist and resist in the "crowded space of diaspora."[65] This space is not a clear blue sky. It may be a multi-textured horizon, constantly shifting according to the current position of the clouds of race, class and gender, and depending on one's standpoint. As one dives deeper into diasporic realms, more layers appear, constantly changing tone, as in the transformations of a long sunset. As mentioned earlier, diaspora has been extended far beyond its etymological origin to become a key concept, for instance in the fields of Africana studies. Martinican thinker Edouard Glissant, who joined the theoretical movement of *Créolité*, reminds us that the African diaspora is by no means only the transatlantic one. Mobility on and outside of the African continent began long before the arrival of Europeans, and continues until today. In an interview with Mantha Diawara, Glissant speaks about memory and defines diaspora as follows:

> It's the moment when one consents not to be a single being and attempts to be many beings at the same time. In other words, for me every diaspora is the passage from unity to multiplicity.[66]

The conversation was actually recorded on a boat traveling across the Atlantic...Glissant argues for the use of diaspora beyond the Jewish trope, reclaiming the term for the description of dispersal and mobility in other cultural and geo-historical contexts. The ability to perform – and to be – several beings within one performance is the key to the most powerful performances. To dance you may even need to become many beings at once, to endorse multiple identities on stage. Dancer-choreographers train on a daily basis to realize this feat. They can render the complexity of historical figures, of contemporary inner and political conflicts within one performance or throughout their repertoire. Chantal Loïal performs a historical narrative of Sawtche as much as she embodies her own story. Oxana Chi embodies Tatjana Barbakoff, May Ayim or Neferet iti...yet even as she inhabits them, she fills their narratives with her own self. Farah Saleh is all of her

---

65   Campt, "The Crowded Space of Diaspora."

66   Diawara, "Conversation with Edouard Glissant Aboard the Queen Mary II (August 2009)," 59.

generational selves, and is any enamored Palestinian living in the situation she narrates. Wan-Chao Chang is herself, is her parents on a diasporic journey, is the migrant person that watches her piece and identifies with her tale. Zufit Simon pushes to the extreme the coexistence of beings, shifting, changing, transforming within seconds from a welcoming smile to a breaking down in shivers. Therefore, I prefer to speak of a diasporic process than of diaspora as an entity. Particularly when it comes to the performing arts, the adjective offers more flexibility than the noun.

In this regard, Nadine George-Graves offers a definition which is more flexible than the roots narratives originally preponderant in theorizations of diaspora. She defines "diasporic spidering" as:

> [...] the multidirectional process by which people of African descent define their lives. The lifelong ontological gathering of information by going out into the world and coming back to the self.[67]

What strikes me in George-Graves' formulation is the corporeality of the diasporic process at stake. Her rendition of "diasporic spidering" evokes a protagonist physically stepping in multiple directions on the stage, gathering and generating knowledge through movement. Knowing that a performance scholar coined this concept allows me to ask what it means if the metaphor is twinned with a material reality like the corporeality of dance. Moreover, this quotation suggests that the *rediasporization* invoked by the Boyarins may be as true for Jewish as for Black diasporic subjects. While Marianne Hirsch asks "what postmemorial practices, what alternate histories, are enabled by the tremendous capacities offered by the World Wide Web as an archival space?",[68] Nadine George-Graves asks how spidering as a paradigm can pertain to performative and digital diasporic processes. This resonates with a pattern I found in all seven personal conversations I held with the artists. Each one of them reflected upon the way they connect the information found on their journey "out into the world" and how they process it within themselves. Yet, the shuffling between self and world is a circular, uninterrupted dynamic, and when the dancers perforMemory, they re-send information, diasporically processed, I may say, out to the world in the form of movement.

After I left the Department of Theatre and Dance at the University of California San Diego, where Professor George-Graves was based at that time, I met again with her on the East Coast, where she occasionally has professional engagements in the performing arts world. By some diasporic spidering magic, we met at the Bushwick Starr Theatre in Brooklyn, at the festival "Imagining Justice for the Dark

---

67 George-Graves, "Diasporic Spidering," 33.
68 Hirsch, *The Generation of Postmemory*, 228.

Divine," curated by Jaamil Olawale Kosoko and Kate Watson-Wallace. On that opening night, the event ended with the performers gently throwing a big roll of thread
to the audience. As they unrolled it, they invited each of us to pass it around. The
thread connecting the audience members symbolized and materialized the "diasporic spidering" and its ongoing connective trajectories between diasporic subjects.
There I was, holding onto a slim but nevertheless strong diasporic string that linked
me to to my doctoral sponsor Dr. George-Graves sitting behind me, to Oxana Chi
sitting next to me, to other audience members, and to the dancers on stage. All of
us were holding onto the diasporic condition.

Is this the feeling that Katja Petrowskaja strives to describe in her essay *Vielleicht
Esther (Maybe Esther)*, in which she narrates the quest for truth at the intersection
between her family's story and institutional narratives of Shoah history?[69] The nar-
rator describes her physical, geographic search for more information, the constant
back and forth between the information collected from others and the implications
of her own reflections. Petrowskaja wants to know the story of her grandmother, in
a troubling territory where she cannot even ascertain her grandmother's first name,
hence the book title. When the author uses the word "spinnen," evoking the German for spider, she refers to the activity of spinning yarn. She aims to find the lost
threads ("verlorene Fäden") and stories that resist linearity,[70] yet she lacks the appropriate tools to knit the story backwards. The spinning metaphor is reminiscent
of the African-American women's quilt memory evoked earlier. What Petrowskaja's
storytelling suggests is the fragility of the diasporic condition and the challenges
encountered in any attempt to reconstruct the past.

Digital communication plays a role both in Petrowskaja's search for a Jewish
past and George-Graves' theorization of Black diasporic practices. In the digital
age, when not only diasporic threads, but also wireless networks connect us
through the air, diasporic spidering moves at the junction between the motif
of crawling found in the traditional African myth of "Anansi," and the modern
technology of web networks. Across the differences of their cultural settings,
the European essayist-journalist and the US scholar-dramaturg share a sense
of diasporic identity as a process that is performed at multiple levels, rather
than a fixed identity. Moreover, both quests revolve around the present in which
diasporic memory is being fashioned. For George-Graves, "African diaspora (and
Black identity) in this sense becomes also a contemporary active process – an act,
a performative."[71] This proactive aspect of identity-formation becomes particularly
interesting in relation to the performing arts. For instance, in developing *They Call
You Venus*, Chantal Loïal collected "Black Venus narratives" while building on her

---

69   Petrowskaja, *Vielleicht Esther*.
70   Petrowskaja, 134.
71   George-Graves, "Diasporic Spidering," 37.

own personal assumptions about what Sawtche's biography may have felt like. When she dances around the accessory of the skull, or liberates herself from a cloth bound around her chest, she accesses the performative truth that lies in-between what has been written about Sawtche and her own biography. Similarly, in *Through Gardens*, Oxana Chi switches back-and-forth between historical archives detailing Tatjana Barbakoff's story and her own process of *choreobiographing* Tatjana Barbakoff – accessing a story of her, a possibility of a story – through choreographic investigation and imagination. Wan-Chao Chang's dance threads around three islands from Java to California and Taiwan. Farah Saleh anchors her work in the dialogical relation between a permanent nomadism and a strong connection to the space of Palestine as a homeland.

I argue that the notion of "diasporic spidering" outlined above is relevant not only to the four Afro-descendant dancers, but to all seven artists discussed here. All of them share a contemporary condition as artists dwelling on their multilocational cultural heritages to perform alternative visions of present-relevant memories, and this is how I wish to bring them together, regardless of the nationalist and geohistorical factors that might separate them. While in the next chapter, I will specifically come back to the relation between performativity, time and identity, for now I want to highlight the interconnections between diaspora as a conceptual umbrella, the stage as a diaspora space in Avtar Brah's sense, and performance as a mode by which diasporic motion or diaspora as motion can come into being.

Here I define the dances as diasporic, because I contend that through their dance performances, the dancers fill diaspora with meaning. The result is not diaspora as an essence inherited through genealogy or geography, but diasporic motion as constantly re-imagined on stage, through the body. At the beginning of this section, I asked: "What is this diasporic condition we hold onto?" A possible answer can be found in conceiving of the diasporic condition as a string indeed, created in the dance for the dancers and their audience to hold onto. If the diasporic condition is a string, PerforMemory is also a texture, generated by living and moving bodies. PerforMemory, like silk, is originally bound to the body that creates it, yet it can be collected and processed without harming its creator. When dancers release diasporacentric dances to gift us with their silky perforMemory, they offer us a chance to transform it, to receive a piece of cultural cloth that we can try on at home.

The Stage as a Diasporic Space

I sit in the Pratt Library, Brooklyn campus, my eyes temporarily resting from the blue light emanating from the laptop screen, looking out the window onto the green. I remember flying over the Transatlantic axis, and physically shifting my working environment from Europe to the USA. I reflect upon other beings who crossed the Atlantic, at other times, by other means, think about the strenuous Middle Passage and the diasporic webs it unfolded. Obviously and luckily, my flight is in no way comparable to the shipping of bodies several centuries ago, some of whom may have been my African and Indian ancestors arriving in Martinique. I keep thinking about what binds diasporic descendants of the Middle Passage to each other, knowing that it is so much more complex than it often seems.

My thoughts rewind to a few days earlier when, after completing my writing routine at Pratt, I took a walk to the Irondale Center where the Renegade Performance Group (RPG) was to debut its performative "Afrofuturism series." I was excited to finally view the work live after having followed their virtual evolution online. Now I even feel like a remote part of their galaxy because I responded to their call for donations to support the series. RPG Founder and Artistic Director, André M. Zachery is a choreographer, dancer, and multimedia artist, whose passion incites respect. He performed a powerful solo entitled Digital Middle Passage. The ebbing and flowing movements executed to a restless live-music were often propulsive, sometimes tender. The video technology designed by himself, as well as his choreography, disclose cyclic patterns. Circumambulating on stage, sometimes on the floor, sometimes in aerial jumps, the dancer's body draws the picture of an ever-present Middle Passage, not bound to spatial or temporal limits. The mostly Black audience seemed to travel with him to a realm where they could re-imagine the past in the hope of a future.[72]

This excerpt from my research diary connects the diasporic condition evoked in this chapter to memory and movement. While perforMemory may not be solely a diasporic matter, diasporic stories can sometimes only be transmitted and archived through perforMemory.

Diasporic space is the place

Passing through the stage space

Digital Middle Passage epitomizes the driving force behind diasporic movements of memory. In my view, it thematizes contemporaneous forms of violence against Black bodies in the public space as much as it addresses the historical mistreatment of African bodies and their forcible displacement to the American continent. It connects ancestral spidering to digital web networks in the contemporary diaspora. Performing Digital Middle Passage, Zachery imagines and experiences what it may be like to return to a place and time to which you have never been. This piece, a part of his Afrofuturism Series, is nevertheless embedded in ancestral memories

---

72   Zami, "Research Diary - Unpublished Manuscript" Brooklyn 10.11.2015.

of a Caribbean-African heritage, as you can tell from his interview. The performance confers a physical reality to the paradigm of "culture as a site of travel."[73] PerforMemory lies and lives at the crossroads of memory as a site of movement and diasporic motion.

For the *Generation of Postmemory*[74] that blossomed on the graves of their ancestors' trauma, the body becomes a site and source of historical archive in the diaspora. Embodying diaspora, history, home and trauma, and performing them on stage, may convey a sense of historicity and meaning-making in the present. Diasporic dance performances in the 21st century can stage alternate narratives of and perspectives on the past, offering perforMemory as a tool to understand and transform the present. The performing-spidering, not only in the space of the World Wide Web, but in a wide array of worlds brought onto and created on the stage space, transforms the stage into a diasporic space.

Drawn to Afrofuturism, Zachery is animated by the will to find alternative definitions and forms of existence for living in a Black body carrying past experiences of the Middle Passage and present experiences of migration:

> So I am now asking: well, how do we remix that experience [of the Middle Passage] to reconsider that moment of transformation for this idea of Afrofuturism? In the sense of relating it to Sun Ra's *Space is the Place* (the movie where he leaves Earth and he finds another planet to exist in liberation), this solo is about a speculative experience for blackness in the present moment. What is it that, where is it that we can metaphorically go from this state of constant, you know, resistance and revolution within our bodies and in our psyche, to a space where we can define a landscape, or planet, galaxy, atmosphere of an existence independent from whatever circumstances that we had prior, meaning on Earth, or in the United States or wherever you're from in this realm of the diaspora.[75]

If for Zachery and others, diasporic space is the place, diaspora may be the solar center around which the dancescapes orbit in a *diasporacentric* fashion. Circling is a key movement of perforMemory, as I will show in the next chapter. The stage may well be the place where choreographers are in control of the atmosphere. It seems to me that Oxana Chi, André Zachery, Wan-Chao Chang and others perform a kinetic search for belonging within the spaces of diaspora – rather than performing Blackness, Jewishness, Europeanness or Chineseness. Because they sculpt diaspora within rugged dancescapes, their performances epitomize physical mobility and personify emotional and political mobility.

---

73   Clifford et al., "Travelling Cultures," 3.
74   Hirsch, *The Generation of Postmemory*.
75   Zachery, Interview. For Zachery's latest production in the *Afrofuturism Series* , see King and Zachery, "Untamed Space: What Can Black Creativity Look Like?"

The Anansi-spider story is also constructed as a story about the spider deity leaving Earth, reaching beyond the realm of human knowledge, and coming back to it. The Trickster God, sometimes held to be the creator of the world, and commonly known as Anansi in the West African geocultural space, lives in the storytelling that brought her/him/them all the way to the American continent. Somewhere in the diasporic spacetime travel, Anansi's name and identity changed. Today, African-American and Caribbean stories tell of the superpowers of Aunt Nancy or Brother Nansi. What the dancers share with these diasporic spiders is the power to create diasporic worlds. While Anansi is seen as having the power to reach the realm of God, dancers connect with ancestors, with spiritual forces, to create, choreograph and dance, as expressed by Chi and Zachery in their interviews. No matter how futuristic their pieces may be, they resonate with a centuries-old tradition among Black, Jewish or Chinese diasporas, of passing down memory through arts and storytelling. Today, as Anansi is embodied in a modern animation blockbuster, Zachery offers an alternative tale without words, performing his version of the Middle Passage and transition. To do so, he may be using traumata recorded in his body cells as much as his creativity and computer skills. The result is a modern tale, accessible across generations without the necessity of mastering a specific language, such as English or French. It transmits not the statistical memory of the Middle Passage, but the impressions of it as they may have left their imprint within bodies. On stage, dancers may acquire the capacity to "define the landscape" and "the atmosphere," as evoked by Zachery. Regardless of the analysis that may be produced on their works thereafter, they create worlds of their own, and let the audience travel with them.

Sometimes dancers work together with scenographers to actually shape the use of space. For instance, Christiane Emmanuel collaborated with Valérie John to achieve the spectacular scenographic décor of the piece *Choc(s)*. Valérie John, also a Martinican artist, usually works with visual arts. Much of her work is centered on themes of "déplacement" (displacement) and "dépaysement" (which can be translated as a disorientation produced by a change of country – le pays – or place). Speaking of displacement in art, John describes a patchwork approach to art as both an action and a result:

> The artist does patchwork in order not to get lost. [...] The artist transports what s/he accumulated over the journeys which s/he compels her/himself to undertake out- and inside the art work. The artist wants to be the sea for its multiple transformations, and more so, the *backwash*, the undertow of waves on themselves after they hit an obstacle or the riverside.
> (L'artiste rapièce pour ne pas se perdre. [...] L'artiste transporte ce qu'il a accumulé lors des voyages qu'il s'impose hors et à l'intérieur de l'oeuvre. L'artiste veut être

la mer à cause de ses multiples transformations et plus encore le ressac, ce retour des vagues sur elles-mêmes après avoir frappé un obstacle ou un rivage.)[76]

I find striking similarities between John's vision of her visual work and Zachery's commentary about and the reality of his choreography, in which he spins on himself, and seems to constantly have to face the backwash that rolls him backwards to the right of the stage. In this Afrofuturist Middle Passage, I witness all of these elements, the patchwork, the backwash, the ocean and Maya Angelou's exhortation to "rise" above a painful and painfully biased historiography. In Zachery's journey through watery perforMemory, I see and experience sometimes sequentially, sometimes simultaneously, the transtemporal flesh of Christina Sharpe's multiple definitions of the "wake."[77] The wake can be "the track left on the water's surface by a ship; the disturbance caused by a body swimming or moved, in water" or a "state of wakefulness." It can also be the memorial spacetime of "grief" and "celebration" in which a ritual is held for the death.[78] Therefore Zachery's perforMemory of the *Middle Passage* across space and time bears affinities with Sharpe's ontological reflections on Black beings.

Patchwork is also the leitmotiv used by Valérie John in her design of the scenography for Christiane Emmanuel's *Choc(s)*. Hundreds of white shirts cover the back wall of the theater, while dozens of others are piled up in a big bundle occupying the center of the stage. Later, the dancer will search through this pile, and find pieces of colorful clothing, which she will put on, resulting in a surrealist patchwork costume. The initial disorientation, effected by the white shirts, disembogues into a re-structuring of the space, and now Emmanuel moves with confidence. The solo actually starts with the dancer hanging high up in the air, stepping, running, reaching for an invisible goal, later she will run around on the floor stage, actually traveling through the piece. Both *Choc(s)* and *Digital Middle Passage* share a generous occupation of the whole stage as a space to be traversed, be it from above as Emmanuel, or rolling over the floor as Zachery. In both soli situated in the de-layed wake of slavery, the performer's quest, sometimes in slow-motion, sometimes in high-speed tempo, is a quest for space, a will to occupy multiple locations and find stability on moving grounds.

The stage as a home

In the dreamlike beginning sequence of *Choc(s)*, Christiane Emmanuel's airwalk, five meters above the stage, makes me think of a surreal nightwalker. When it comes to dreams and space, Christiane Emmanuel fulfilled what she calls "the biggest dream of her life," which was to turn her ancestral family home into a dance

---

76   John, "De lieu en lieu(x)," 131. [My translation]
77   See Chapter 1 in Sharpe, *In the Wake: On Blackness and Being*.
78   Sharpe, 21–36.

center. In the interview, she explains how she created a performance space on the rooftop of the house:

> By the way when I created this place, and when I started doing projects in this space, I chose the title "setting dreams into motion," simply because for over 20 years it has been my dream to build, to turn the roof deck into a dance space... Things went quickly, and now the deck of the Red House, the House of Arts is actually the family house that I was born and grew up in.[79]

Space matters to Christiane Emmanuel. Her work strives to expand notions of spatiality and to shape space through movement – an approach which is in turn influenced by the space the dancers occupy. Diving into her work (process), space seemed omnipresent: while viewing her performances, while conversing with her at her studio in La Maison Rouge/Maison des Arts, and while listening to her presentation at the Habitation Clément (a former rhum plantation turned into a museum and cultural center). In the interview, Emmanuel emphasized how working with space is at the core of her practice as a choreographer, and compared the dance practice to architecture. She is herself indeed an architect of dance and a dancing architect, especially since she initiated the architectural transformation of her parent's house to accommodate her dance practice center. Visiting her dance studio, one experiences kinesthetically the intricacy of personal and professional spheres. On the ground floor, one observes that the reception hall and office are steps away from the home's kitchen. And to reach the studio on the highest floor, you pass the floor on which her mother lives, a mother appeasing the space with the energy of a woman taking rest after having raised ten children. The choreographer puts the Maison Rouge at the center of her working process, thus reversing the process by which the so-called "ultra-marins" (overseen citizens from the French oversea departments) are pushed out to the periphery of France. The space of France, where she experienced both success and racial marginalization during her tours, is no longer a center for Christiane Emmanuel, but a periphery, faraway from her home/dance/island center, and therefore no longer central to her work.

When I interviewed her, she was just returning from a festival in Ouagadougou, Burkina Faso, where she had performed upon invitation by curator dancer Irène Tassembédo. She explained how Francophone festival structures often impede the exchange between Caribbean and African choreographers on the continent, who are neither financially nor structurally encouraged to work with each other. Traveling to the "root" continent meant for her to counter this hegemonic relation and to create a new relational space, where Martinican dancers performed for an international audience in Burkina Faso, among other African artists and audiences. In addition, through her residency program (to which Oxana Chi participated in

---

79   Emmanuel, Interview [My translation].

2014 and in 2019), Emmanuel herself regularly invites artists from the Global South and/or Western artists of color, to work in the studio space.

The transformation of her childhood home into a home for dance gives Emmanuel access to a space where she is in charge of the landscape, the timescape, and the dancescape. This does not prevent her from working in various spaces with her dancers, when the choreography requires it. For instance, when she created the piece *Mangrove*, commissioned by the Regional Office, and inspired by Wifredo Lam's iconic "Jungle" painting, the choreographer asked her dancers to rehearse and experiment in the open air to help them integrate a feeling for the Caribbean environment into their motion. In order to work with dancers on the bodies-as-cane-reeds depicted in the painting, she felt the need to improvise with them outdoors, on the theme of verticality, in the Martinican forest.[80]

"Defining the landscape," to borrow from André Zachery's expression, can also be shaping the home, and occupying the stage as one's home. Let us move from forest to gardens, to explore the relation between stage, environment and spatiality. Especially when I witnessed *Through Gardens* "from within," as one of the cast's musicians in Dresden and Berlin, I felt that Oxana Chi also occupied the stage space as a home. Not only does Oxana Chi inhabit the biography of Tatjana Barbakoff, she also seems to transform the dance space into a house where she lets the audience in. When she choreobiographes the story of Tatjana Barbakoff, it is as if she is decorating the house of memory, hanging the painting of memory2go on the walls. This happens regardless of the venue size, from the gigantic open-air stage at the *Solo International Performing Arts Festival* (SIPA) in Solo, Indonesia, to the intimate space of the Societätstheater that housed the *Jewish Music- and Theater Week* in Dresden. When the dancer-choreographer must adapt the choreography to the spatiality, it has impact on the timing of the music, the pace and the sequencing. For instance, crossing the stage from the back left corner to the front left corner will take much less time if the piece is performed on a smaller stage. Just like diaspora space and the multiple positionings it requires, the choreography evolves with the context, as the dancer sculpts space by moving through it. In the scene of the Chinese Dress described earlier in this chapter, the stage also becomes a diasporic home where multiple identities, imaginings and belongings can coexist without entering into conflict or collision. When Chi picks up the dress and inhabits it, slowly bringing it back to life through her movements, she creates a melancholic atmosphere, inviting us to enter the memory of Barbakoff through the memory of Tatjana's appreciation of her mother's silk clothes.[81] In this space of multiple diasporic identities, the stage offers the possibility to re-play history and to perform a new memory.

---

80   Emmanuel, "Rencontre."
81   Chi, *Tanzende Erinnerungen*, 2011.

In *Parole, Parole, Parole*, Farah Saleh actually transforms the stage into a home-like place, especially when she invites the audience to witness a private Skype conversation. Is the stage also a home to Farah Saleh, or to Wan-Chao Chang, who relate of their nomadic condition and diasporic routine? Or for Chantal Loïal, who grew up between Guadeloupe and metropolitan France? What is the relation between occupying the stage as a physical home – a center where one is grounded – and turning this stage-home into a home for perforMemory – a place where the dancers and/or audiences can attain a sense of being at home because of their own existence in the space?

PerforMemory unfolds itself in real spaces which themselves function as the scenery of the imagined spaces arising in the interaction between kinesthetic storytelling and the audience's interpretations. In a context in which independent dancers have limited access to resources for scenographic design, choreographers devise resourceful ways to produce intense pieces relying solely on the dancers, and which can be adapted to various stage sizes. Thus, the narrative, message or energy conveyed is not bound to specific physical surroundings. The stage spaces invested by the dancers do not necessarily tell stories in themselves, but they can be transformed by the performances and become a projection area for the embodiment of memory.

Finding a home space in the dance place?

The dancing body as a home

The question of (not) belonging to a cultural, geotemporal and artistic framework appears in all the seven conversations I held with the dancers, regardless of their geographical and genealogical positionings. Despite the fact that each artist has a very distinct choreographic style and repertoire, parallels in terms of intentions, preoccupations and processes emerge from the dancers' voices captured on paper in the final chapter. Particularly in relation to diaspora, one may see convergences between them, for example between André Zachery's investigation of Black diasporic experiences in the USA, and Wan-Chao Chang's migrant citizenship in search for a place and a culture to feel at home with. Let's return to Chang's *I Thought Here Is My Home*. When she performed it on October 11th, 2009, at the COUNTERpulse Festival in San Francisco, she also participated in a public discussion about "dancing diaspora." The title of the performance already conveys the intricacy of diasporic trajectories and identities, deliberately leaving blurry the location called "here." Is it Indonesia, a place her parents grew up in, and left? Or the USA, where despite all her successes, she could not shed her "immigrant status"? Is it Taiwan, to where she returned, yet which also did not feel like "home"?

Maybe home is all, or none of these places. Can the diasporic space of the stage become a space where the dancer will feel at home no matter where she goes? Or is the home bound to the dancing body and its movement in the performative here and now? In my understanding of Chang's words and works, the perforMemory space seems to offer the dancer a temporary relief, a shelter from and for questionings about identity and belonging. To perforMemory is not always to answer these questions, rather it may be to express the questions differently, like moving from discordance to concordance in a musical harmony. In the solo *I Thought Here Is My Home*, the body is at home in the scarf-like cloth wrapping the dancer's waist. But the cloth slips away from her, as swift as a letter may drop from a word. The absence of a single letter, or of a prop, inflects the meaning of the sentence. If I let the "t" slip away,

The body is at home.

becomes

The body is a home.

And there is no more space to call a home, to inhabit as a home but one's body.[82]

Similarly, in the seven works of perforMemory, there is an epistemic proximity between occupying the stage as a home for the dancing body, and inhabiting the body itself as a diasporacentric home. This spirals the argument back to the metaphor used by DeFrantz and Gonzalez, and evoked earlier in the introduction, according to which diaspora is akin to a "flexible and self-repairing" skin that both makes us vulnerable and safe.[83] To inhabit the body as a home may be a rare constant parameter in a diasporic dance environment marked by movement, transition, and transformation.

Searching for a place to call home can be a collective endeavor. In the group piece *Keep Her Safe, Please!*, which also draws from *I Thought Here is My Home*, Wan-Chao Chang blends Chinese-Taiwanese and Indonesian cultures and movements. Yet amidst the group choreography, Chang sometimes remains alone with her movements. At one point a circle of dancers breaks apart, and she becomes a soloist on stage. A long white cloth bound around her waist supports the dramaturgy. Twice, the dancer attempts to cover herself with it. She picks it up from the floor and delicately covers her shoulder, as if it were a scarf. But as soon as she starts to move in it, as if to enjoy the soft touch of it, it drops to the floor. She picks it up again, this time with a different energy, faster paced, almost anxious, she spins on herself and then throws the cloth on her upper body. But once again, she fails to find a long-lasting way to move with(in) the cloth, for it immediately falls to the ground against her will. Akin to the earlier mentioned diasporic skin, the cloth seems to represent the nerve-racking fragility and ephemerality of "home" in the diaspora. A simple accessory frames the movements of a diasporic identity, exteriorizing the unstable and precarious layer we carry within us, the fleeting and

---

82   Here I am also inspired by Cox, *Shapeshifters*.
83   DeFrantz and Gonzalez, *Black Performance Theory*, 11.

changing notion of belonging. The dancer then engages in multiple twists and finally leaves the stage with the cloth on the floor. This very focused moment of the performance is followed by a group choreography in which the dancers constantly change positionalities, crossing the material and metaphorical diaspora space of the stage with movements both vertical and horizontal. The multilocationality of diaspora theorized by Avtar Brah, and the process of "homing diaspora and diasporising home"[84] can be achieved on stage.

Moreover, in this diasporic space of the stage, the performing body becomes a locational space in itself, which is able to "continually challenge the minoritising and peripheralising impulses of dominance"[85] by moving center stage. Avtar Brah also asks:

> When does a location become home? What is the difference between "feeling at home" and staking claim to a place as one's home?[86]

When choreographers and dancers coming from marginalized sociopolitical locations transpose the space of the margins to the center of the stage, they potentially enact a huge effect on hegemonic relations. At least in the time-space frame of the event in which they perform, they move from the margin to the center, not only transposing themselves to the center (of the stage, the narrative, the performance) but actually transforming what a center is. Dancers travel through space and time, materially on stage and metaphorically. So maybe their diasporic journeys are about settling down their imagined and imagining selves in the instantaneity of the performed moment, and furthermore inscribing their narratives into history, through perforMemory.

Dancing allows for a shifting conception of home, which can be claimed in any space as long as the dancer is alive. Dancers share with vocalists the singularity of an art that resides within the embodiment of their selves, independently from any accessory such as a canvas or an instrument. Defining dance (space) as home means challenging conventional inscriptions of home in terms of geographical boundaries and ascriptions of bodies according to historical-cultural norms. When scholar Chandra Talpade Mohanty asks if home is "a geographical space, a historical space, an emotional, sensory space?"[87] my answer, in this case, is yes, yes, yes and yes. The confluence or overlapping coexistence of geography, history, emotions and kinesthetics within the dancing body is a strong argument that emerges from my interpretation of the works and from the conversations I held with the choreographers.

---

84   Brah, "Diaspora, Border and Transnational Identities," 623.
85   Brah, 633.
86   Brah, 623.
87   Mohanty, "Crafting Feminist Genealogies," 487.

The focus on solo performances invigorates the sense of the body as a home. While most of the choreographers discussed here often work in groups, Oxana Chi has been creating mostly solo dances. She explains why she prefers to work and perform alone:

> [...] when I dance, I try to pour myself more and more into the dance, and my body...to give everything that is possible to give. And if I must work with other dancers, I won't be able to give on stage what I would like to show. And I won't be able to develop myself the way I want to develop myself, because...I am a seeking person. I seek much in my own self. I can not manage that when I work with other dancers.[88]

In this conversation, the dancer comments upon the interrelation between artistic, financial and personal choices. Although or because she has worked with bigger ensembles, and with a few exceptions, Oxana Chi seems best able to channel her message and energy when she occupies the stage alone. Interestingly, she attributes this personal approach to solo performance to a process of individual development, whether artistic, spiritual or another form of growth. The image of the dancer "pouring" herself into the dancing body, rejoins the metaphor and kinetic reality of the body as a home. When Oxana dances-becomes Tatjana, she seems to actually bring her home on stage. Knowing that Barbakoff's body was destroyed, pulverized in Auschwitz concentration camp, the task taken on by Chi takes on a poignant meaning: to return to her (Barbakoff), or to her_story, a performative home through the stage presence of a performing body.

Brenda Dixon-Gottschild, who founded the Coalition of Diasporan Scholars Moving (CDSM), argues that "dance is a message in a cultural envelope,"[89] namely the body, which can take on different appearances. Sometimes dancers transcend the physical markers of the body to express another story, sometimes they actually play on identification and similarity (as when Oxana Chi embodies Tatjana Barbakoff).[90] It is also true in the case of Chantal Loïal, when she performs what she calls the story of the Black Venus. Here, the performance lives through Chantal's identification with the bodily features of Sawtche, and their oppression in Western normative discourses and practices of exclusion. In the second part of *They Call You Venus*, the celebratory Africanist jumps, taking their strength from the ground, and performed to South African gumboots music, epitomize the diasporic, posthumous return "home" through the body of the contemporary dancer and her diasporic dance. The performance represents a powerful intervention in the context of France, a location characterized by a geohistory of colonial imperialism.

---

88   Chi, Interview.
89   Dixon Gottschild, "Dance Is a Message in a Cultural Envelope."
90   See Zami, "Mit Oxana Chi Durch Gärten."

Discussing French hip-hop dance culture, Felicia McCarren argues that "dancing simultaneously gives us an identity and a location yet allows us to bypass or out-strip these."[91] She finds that precisely this tension between displaying and moving the body within markers of race, class and gender, and moving the body beyond it, constitutes the attraction of dance as a form capable of commenting upon and challenging sociocultural and political norms:

> While hip hop dancers are broadly thought to represent themselves, in a social-re-alist dance form linked to its political-social program, in fact dance allows dancers to present their bodies, in all their embodiments, as something other than them-selves. While staging the question of visible difference, dance performance re-mains an art of the visual rather than the entirely visible; it poses a challenge to reductive categories.[92]

Dances of perforMemory illuminate this strong counter-hegemonic power of dance. Experiencing and traveling through the works, one is invited to focus on a single dancing body, and its capacity to transcend restrictions or assumptions of racialized, gendered, and class-based identity. The visual is not always visible, and the visible suggests through motion, rather than words, what home, diaspora, resistance, and memory may mean.

When the choreographers deal with racism, genderism and other factors that influence how history is made, such as classism and ableism in their works, they politicize the performance of memory. However, they transmit a corporeal message that, precisely by being physical, can make the body's outer self not so relevant anymore. Journeying through their dancescapes of perforMemory, the audience gets the chance to encounter history, and eventually to encounter, via the perform-ing body, an individuals made of emotions which everyone may relate to through personal experience: hope, fear, loss, panic, mourning, courage, joy…The diasporic dancescapes shape home as a space in movement, constantly reinventing itself at the intersection of body, geography, culture, history and emotion.

The dancing body as a diasporic memory

DeFrantz and Gonzalez estimate that in diaspora, "we wear memory on our bod-ies."[93] In dance, perforMemory is more than an outer surface, it is an inner organ, sometimes even a full-body movement. Dancers of perforMemory create memory as a living entity, almost a living being. They infuse narratives of the past with a sense of contemporaneity anchored in the presence and present of the dancing body. In their works, I read subversions of hegemonic narratives in the alternative

---

91   McCarren, *French Moves: The Cultural Politics of Le Hip Hop*, 85.
92   McCarren, 85.
93   DeFrantz and Gonzalez, *Black Performance Theory*, 11.

embodiments of the past into the present. In a context when diasporic subjects are usually pushed to the margins of society, literally moving on the stage center confers visibility and reality to bodies and their perspectives on trauma and empowerment. The notion of diaspora and the action of dance as outlined in this chapter shape the realization of perforMemory.

Sometimes the interaction between diaspora, dance, and representation is spatially visual. I remember arriving in Dresden for a show in 2014, and finding the streets filled with posters of the large annual *Jewish Music and Theater Week (Jüdische Theater- und Musikwoche)*. The Afro-European choreographer Oxana Chi was portrayed next to Jewish cultural icons, in a city so often portrayed in the media as a Neo-Nazi haven hosting racist demonstrations. Already in the physical space surrounding the performance venue, the geographic location of the performance, the programming of Oxana Chi and her work impacted the city, its spatiality and its relation to history. It expanded how the city could be perceived and navigated. Dance shaped the material and metaphorical topography of a city – and country – struggling with its antisemitic past and present.

To understand the need, still vital, to modernize the representation of "culture" in Germany, we can learn from Afro-German scholars. Nicola Lauré al-Samarai, for instance, analyzed how Afro-descendant artists from Germany root their search for memory. Describing the work of Afro-German poets, sculptors and musicians, she speaks of an "inSpirited topography" which she defines as:

> [...] a moving cartography [...] which, through the amalgamating and merging of seemingly disparate contexts, enables [one] to trace the hidden ruptures of history, and to look into them through [one's] own geopolitical views.
> ([...] eine bewegliche Kartographie [...] in der das Ineinandersetzen und Verschmelzen scheinbar nicht zusammengehöriger Kontexte es erlaubt, den versteckten Rissen der Geschichte nachzuspüren und diese mittels eigenständiger geopolitischer Lesarten in den Blick zu rücken.)[94]

While dance is not included in her analysis of variegated art practices, her concept is relevant to diasporic choreographic practices, especially since it brings the motion factor into focus. Using perforMemory as a compass, I have started to sketch diasporic dancescapes as they comment upon, challenge, inform and transform the transmission of cultural memory in their respective geopolitical contexts. At a meta-level, my research in itself traces such a "moving cartography" that juxtaposes contexts not usually brought into proximity.

In this sense, my aim is also to contribute to what Natasha Kelly has defined as a necessary "program change" for German culture and media representations. Kelly

---

94   Lauré al-Samarai, "Inspirited Topography," 126–27 [My translation].

argues that Germany finds itself in a "permanent cognitive coloniality."[95] Referring to the concepts of "Ent_Nennung" and "Ent_Wahrnehmung,"[96] Kelly deconstructs the formation of historical discourses that exclude Black stories and perspectives from the dominant collective memory as inscribed in history books and cultural agendas. In her dissertation, later published under the title *Afrokultur als Wissenskultur – ein Programmwechsel*, (Afroculture as knowledge culture – a program change), Kelly argues that in order to acknowledge the fundamental role of Black culture as knowledge, Germany needs to "change the program."[97] Her monograph connects the legacies of W.E.B. Du Bois, Audre Lorde and May Ayim, whom she calls a "change agent." The program change – which also evokes an association with the realm of technology – means allowing for minoritized discourses to find space in the transmission of memory. Self-positioned as Black Feminist academic-activist, Kelly actually strived to contribute to this program change by giving a platform to Black German artists, among others Oxana Chi, who she commissioned to create the piece *I Step On Air* in 2012. By touring through many universities since then, both in Germany and abroad, the piece in fact has contributed to bringing dance into academic spaces such as Bielefeld University, the City University of New York, Yeditepe University Istanbul, and Rutgers University, thus activating the program change called for by Kelly.

All the performances discussed here contribute more or less to a "program change," and share the will to encounter history through feminism and/or decoloniality, in my interpretation. In contrast to the "cognitive coloniality" criticized by Kelly, they counter absence and perform memory as presence, demonstrating that emotions and motion are viable sources and forms of knowledge. PerforMemory breathes through these interstices, allowing the audience to sense them by witnessing the body as home, located in the present but reaching into to the past. The living body, moving through space, becomes a diasporic memory transmitted to the audience, at the intertwinings of history, corporeality, geography and culture. Not only is the dancing body a home, it is the materiality of perforMemory and the tool or kinesthetic software used by the artists to change the "program" of hegemonic memory.

Oxana Chi's whole repertoire has contributed to changing the memory program, both at the level of the use of dance as a form of knowledge, and through the content of the performances as discussed in the first chapter. Besides impacting the visual cityscape as described earlier, her continuous efforts to perform alternative storytelling of the past, to counter the absence of perspectives of women,

---

95   Kelly, *Afrokultur*, 161 [My translation].
96   Here Kelly refers to Nduka-Agwu and Hornscheidt, *Rassismus auf gut Deutsch.*; Lockward, "Diaspora." See my discussion of these terms in the introduction.
97   Kelly, *Afrokultur*.

especially women of color, happens in several spaces: theaters, universities, conferences. For instance, *Through Gardens* inscribes a Chinese-Jewish-Russian expressionist dancer into dance history, and into the current programming, reclaims her heritage and demonstrates how she impacted both the dance and visual art worlds of Europe in the 1920s and 1930s. I also see a memory program change in Zufit Simon's repertoire, which brings *Mischpuche* into German theaters and re-vitalizes the role of contemporary Jewish artists in Germany's cultural landscape. Simon also changes the programming of gender norms through a non-gender conforming body and performance. Chantal Loïal also performs a new program that diverts from the institutional French one: she re-tells the story of Sawtche, challenging the racialized and gendered projections that have been imposed on her body, and replacing the absence of a Black female body with the strong, energetic presence of a contemporary Black female performer. Her perforMemory shifts the cliché which frames a large Black woman's body as a sexualized object, to a body as subject and in charge of its own story. Farah Saleh circumvents the impossibility of contact between Palestinian citizens across the Israeli territory. She performs the possibility of reaching out, and also changes the program of a Western dance space by including the audience in the performance, making it borderless. Christiane Emmanuel changes the political program of the Martinican island, representing the "tourner en rond" (going in circles) of the status quo, but resolving to dance her liberated, Caribbean-Black-Indigenous body. Wan-Chao Chang performs the bridge across Asia and America, changes the program of nationality as constructed in Taiwan, the USA and Indonesia. She dances diaspora as a presence, and evokes other imaginings of being across geocultural spaces. André M. Zachery actually uses digital programming to record and project his own movements, resulting in an Afrofuturist program change. The Digital Middle Passage surely is a new way of confronting the traumatic colonial past, differing from the conventional program as taught in school.

When the dancing body becomes a diasporic perforMemory, the memory program changes. Memory2go is a response to the need for a program change. Just as an actual change of software impacts the work place and work processes in the economy, the program change that perforMemory brings about can revolutionize the cultural ecology of Western memory spaces. Staying with the watery metaphors of this chapter, I am reminded of what Christina Sharpe calls "the weather," namely the afterlife of slavery that is omnipresent in our present environment. Yet Sharpe notes how Black beings respond to a difficult climate, by creating "new ecologies."[98] The conclusion of my reflection on diaspora is to offer perforMemory as an alternative ecology, in which the dancing body not only transforms the location of the

---

98   Sharpe, *In the Wake: On Blackness and Being*, 205.

stage into a home, but actually creates a new shelter and stakes claim to the body as a home.

We have seen that the stage can become a diasporic space, the shelter for a moving home that is dance. I invited the reader to come a step closer to perforMemory, to feel what moving through diasporic dancescapes may be like. If memory is a site of movement, it exists through a constant wind of change. Diasporic motion is the core of perforMemory. Just as wind shapes sand sculptures in the desert, or traces wave patterns on the ocean, diaspora as a concept shapes and shifts memory's movements. The political and emotional mobilities evoked earlier work through, and orbit around diasporic constellations. Thus, contemporary perforMemory as I define and approach it here, is molded by diaspora. This is not to say that perforMemory does not exist outside of diasporic relations. However to frame memory performances within diaspora, or to pinpoint diaspora within memory dancescapes, compels us to search for the connections between memory discourses, counterhegemonic storytelling, and movement.

To understand what it means to find a home space in the dance place, I find it relevant to reflect upon this quotation by Sara Ahmed:

> Being grounded is not necessarily about being fixed; being mobile is not necessarily about being detached.[99]

To dance is to be grounded and mobile, dynamic and centered. Diaspora is movement, be it the "welling and swelling ocean" sung by Maya Angelou, or Kazim Ali's poetic "breath that swirls around and returns."[100] In the poem "Still I Rise"[101] cited at the opening of this chapter, Angelou evokes the treasure in one's backyard, in her case: the pride she takes from her cultural heritage, the capacity to rise above a painful, traumatic past. All the solos eventually seem to reveal that dance may help to retrieve something. It may be that one comes back from a world journey only to find that the treasure so dearly searched for lies in one's own backyard, or that the way is the destination, as is the core belief of Taoism. All these texts connect the space of home to the being of one's self. Although I do not dance on stage, I relate strongly, through performing experience, personal genealogy, and academic research, to the understanding of the dance space as a home place. Traveling through diasporic dancescapes is as challenging as it is promising, according to Wan-Chao Chang:

---

99   Ahmed et al., *Uprootings/Regroundings*, 1.
100   Ali, *Orange Alert*, 68.
101   Angelou, *And Still I Rise*.

I force myself to come out – to keep my memory for a certain stage and move on to find different things. It's...not an easy journey, but when you find something different that belongs to yourself, I think it's a treasure.[102]

PerforMemory harbors a treasure trove waiting to be uprooted and unearthed, or waiting to emerge out of oceanic depths. Writing this book led me to explore a new direction within my own diasporic journey, to spider and spiral in search of my ancestry. An invitation to perform *I Step on Air* in New Delhi with Oxana Chi has given me the opportunity to travel to Tamil Nadu, where I am searching for the East Indian roots of my West Indian genealogy. This journey is full of diasporic surprises and treasures, such as the fact that "Zami," a rare family name found on my mother's island of birth, Martinique and in the Caribbean (a name many know from Audre Lorde's eponym book), is also found in ancient historical texts to refer to a women community in India. Remembering the hours of travel that took me from the performance venue in North India to a mountain top in South India, I sense the complex intersection of diaspora, memory and movement. I perceive how as a diasporic subject, I am bound to a nomadic melancholia and a melancholic nomadism. Besides circling around spatiality, diaspora and memory are embedded in definitions and questions of time. In a constructivist approach, the movement of time and space are not given entities. Rather, they are variables in the search for the interrelation between remembering the past, and aspiring to understand, and change the present and to make the future a possibility. Consequently, the next chapter shall explore the dimension of time as it relates to perforMemory, in order to apprehend how time conceptions inform expressions of cultural memory, and to appreciate the swift and subtle ways in which memory moves through spacetime.

---

102 Chang, Interview.

3 DANCING THE PAST IN THE PRESENT TENSE

Il y a des millions de lieux autour de nous
Il y a des millions d'années avant et après nous
Il y a des millions de croisements
sur le carrefour de la réincarnation
Et ici, à cette table,
en ce moment précis,
nous partageons
un thé
Sommes-nous venus à un rendez-vous
pris dans nos vies antérieures ?
(There are millions of places around us
There are millions of years before and after us
There are millions of crossroads
at the crossing of reincarnation
And here, at this table,
in this exact moment,
we share
a tea
Did we come to attend an appointment
scheduled in our prior lives?)
Chung Hing[1]

I enjoy morning tea time: slowly dropping a teabag into a cup, observing the spreading color and aroma, waiting for the water temperature to cool, feeling warmth flowing down my throat with each sip. My tea routine is flexible, it varies according to seasons and emotions, and includes a broad range of teas, from herbal mixed teabags to a specific loose green tea from Taiwan. My time management during this routine is also flexible, and varies from gulping the tea down quickly while checking e-mail, to savoring it at a zen pace. Today, my daily

---

1   Chung-hing, *Chants de Thé*, 17 [My translation].

tea routine involved an echinacea tea from the "Yogi Tea" brand. The company prints a quotation on each bag (it is not clear to me whether these quotations originate with Yogi Bhajan, whose face is also printed on the package, or from the packaging factory staff, or from a computer-managed anthology of poetry). My appreciation of the quotations is as variable as my tea ceremony. This morning, the words struck me with their poetry and accuracy. They felt so deeply in tune with my concern of the day, namely, how to structure this chapter on time within a poetic stance on dance, and in tune with my readings of the day on the 'dance' of quantic matter.[2]

As the teabag evanesced into the hot water, the other end of the string, waving outside of the cup, carried a tiny piece of paper with the inscription: "Each single heartbeat dances to the rhythm of the soul." I was magically transported back to thinking about the interconnection between corporeality, time, and movement. I remembered and reflected on the way the dancers move their bodies not (only) to a paced tempo of recorded or live music, but also to their own rhythm, their own sense of being in the moment, their own pace of remembering. The imagery of a heart dancing, rather than beating, suggests a body that moves outside, beyond normative conventions of time and space. If the heartbeat dances "to the rhythm of the soul," its movement may vary in pace according to the emotional and intellectual fluctuations of the soul. The teabag also transported me back to the first time I attended *Through Gardens* in 2009, and to the experience of the first scene. At the very beginning of the piece, under a dim light, a shape wrapped in a red velvet cloth laid on the ground. Her movements seemed propelled by the sound of a heartbeat, generated live by guitarist Hannes Buder on stage, at first low and slow, then increasingly quick and loud. The heartbeat emitted a signal to the audience: you are about to witness the birth of an individual, a performance, a story, a perforMemory. The heart and its magical triad also punctuate Oxana Chi's interview about dance and memory:

> Dance really is simply body, soul, heart. All of those are needed, otherwise one can't dance.[3]

This is how perforMemory re-emerged through the shimmering surface of my morning tea. The tea became, as in Chung-Hing's above quoted poem, a place at the crossroads of time, space, memory and humanity, where the common teatime opens the possibility to embrace the multiplicity of temporalities and positionings that surround and inhabit us. PerforMemory reaches out through geohistorical timelines, and transforms the stage into a network of overlapping history, geography, emotion, and memory threads.

---

2   Rovelli, *Reality Is Not What It Seems.*
3   Chi, Interview.

On this research odyssey that you are joining by reading, we encountered multiple universes. We ambulated within the volcano, excavating traumatic memory as a site of movement (in chapter one). Swimming with oceanic energies, we traversed the stage as a diasporic space where dancing bodies find and create a home by performing memory (in chapter two). In this third chapter, we will move to and fro with the storm that swirls through these dancescapes. A hurricane of displacement carrying past traumata into the present, but also a regenerating breeze, a whirlwind that lets dancers and audiences breathe across space and time. In fact, there may be an inherent intimacy between temporality and whirlwind energy. The word *tourbillon*, French for *whirlwind*, also refers (in English and in French) to a system engineered to increase accuracy in the mechanics of watchmaking. A tourbillon's function is to compensate for the impact of gravity on time-keeping. Balance, slowness, and regularity are key in this spinning process that works with, and against gravity. Horology meets choreography!

I will now look into perforMemory through the lenses of spacetime, physical and metaphorical movement. This chapter explores how the selected performances challenge Western conceptions of history, time, and space. Here, I ask how dance "contemporizes" the past, and how dance-makers connect the physical and conceptual realms of perforMemory together. I start by returning to the repertoire outlined in the first chapter, and propose a reading in which each dance conveys a different temporality. For each one of the seven solo performances, I offer a specific interpretation of time, as a narrative structure and as a device of perforMemory. Then I reflect upon the interconnection between performance, time and memory, and weave together multi-textured threads pulled from dance and performance studies, critical race theory, quantum physics, gender studies, and historiography. In the second part of this chapter, I engage with the movements of perforMemory in a material-literal and metaphorical sense. Selecting three sets of movement, I decipher their corporealities, and argue that they not only reflect, but also enact conceptual moves. I look at *spinning* as the process of turning around perspectives, *jumping* as the endeavor to bridge gaps, and *crossing* as the possibility to transgress boundaries. I invite you to now advance further through shapeshifting dancescapes, to reflect upon temporal and spatial ecologies of perforMemory.

The Timescapes of PerforMemory

Time breathes and breezes, time runs and roams, time flies, flees and foams, time sweats and sneezes, time crawls and curls, time evaporates and evacuates, time leans and leads, time rests and ripples, time spins and swirls, time tiptoes and tips, time ticks and twists, time ticks…time moves. The word timescape is an anagram of spacetime. Like the word *dancescape*, it evokes the intricacy of time paces and places. In a timescape, time unfolds into space, time unfolds as space. Here you may hear the echo, carried by the wind, of Ruth Klüger's *Zeitschaft* (see chapter one). Klüger wrote about the concentration camp as a non-place, or a place that only exists in relation to time and history. Time and space are not distinct from each other, rather they move in relation to one another, shaping a landscape that may be the décor for memory. The timescapes of perforMemory may be conceived as times in place, or places moving in time.

Discussing the specificity of theatrical time and space, Jill Dolan emphasizes the role of the present time in the space of the theater, and how it brings about what she calls "utopian performatives":

> The very present-tenseness of performance lets audiences imagine utopia not as some idea of future perfection that might never arrive, but as brief enactments of the possibilities of a process that starts now, in this moment at the theater.[4]

Interestingly, the word utopia is anchored in spatiality, for it also means a non-place or a place not yet existing. Yet, what I read in Dolan is an understanding of u-topia as a spacetime, a performative moment that exists within the venue of the theater and within the temporality of the performance. Although the performances mentioned here do not necessarily attempt to perform "future perfection," they do enact narratives that move away from linear time, and embody narratives that challenge the production of historical spacetime. Subscribing to the idea of present-tenseness allows us to understand how perforMemory may "illuminate and transform the present,"[5] to come back to the words of bell hooks discussed in the introduction.

Stretching time: bending hegemonic timelines

In this section, I revisit the repertoire of perforMemory through the lens of time, and ask: how do the seven solos perform time? How do their sense and uses of time collide and collude with Western notions of linear temporality? I argue that choreographers *stretch* time, and thus generate a perforMemory that moves aside, away from, and beyond the traditional idea of "history." When encountering historical matter, the performers often circumvent chronology, and perform memory within other processes of narration. This non-chronological epistemological endeavor bears affinities with Alexandro Murguía's reflection on historiography. The Californian poet and scholar writes:

> I am not writing history per se; instead I am unraveling the strands of time/space/memory that define my presence here. I propose a history based not on 'objective'

---

4   Dolan, *Utopia in Performance*, 17.

5   hooks, "Choosing the Margin as a Space of Radical Openness," 155.

Western epistemologies, which are not objective anyway, but on intuition, memory and landscape; not on linear chronological time, but on circling the events till they become understandable to me.[6]

Unraveling "the strands of time/space/memory" resonates with the imagery of a quilt evoked in the previous chapter, and equally signifies the multiple layers of intuition, memory and landscape merging in the dancescapes of perforMemory. At a meta-level, this book's structure is analogous to the vision cited above, for I strive to circle the performances as the performers circle past, present and future events. Dancers ground a performing presence in the "present-tenseness" of the show*time*, connecting time, space, and memory to find new ways to engage with the past, outside of conventional chronologic and geographic boundaries. In the coming sections, I conceptualize each performance through a specific representation of and relation to time. These interpretations are merely the fruit of my own reflections, although they may at times correspond to the choreographers' intents.

Paying attention to the multisensorial qualities of the performances, I propose an interpretation focusing on dimensions of time as I experience them in the works. Dancing the past in the present tense, the performers all move at the crossroads of time, space and emotion. These elements are no longer distinctive categories, rather they (e)merge on stage, generating a new spacetime dimension for a *memory2go*. By stretching the definitions, functions and motions of time, the dancer-choreographers resist the very temporalities that simplify, silence or suppress their stories. They perforMemory a present presence, and generate a spacetime made of multiple textures, shapes, and paces. Through dance, they (re-)invent how the moving body may metaphorically and materially intervene into and transform postmemorial discourses and practices, physically, epistemologically, ontologically, and phenomenologically.

Pulses of time in *all about nothing*

Doors open, the audience calmly walks into the performance space. Performer Zufit Simon is already there, watching. She sits towards the back of the stage, in front of an emergency exit door. In contrast with the classic scenario – in which the artist enters the stage to an already seated audience – the performer is waiting for the audience to come in. Certain spectators become aware of it, some are briefly confused (is the performer ready or should I step back out?), others appreciate the dramaturgical irony, still others focus on choosing a seat to occupy for the hour to come. When the audience quiets down, the dancer rises, but does not start to dance immediately, again (en)countering some expectations projected upon her body. She walks in an energetic, resolute manner towards the audience, reaches the

---

6   Murguía, *The Medicine of Memory*, x.

left side of the stage where she grabs equipment, as if she were one of the technical staff. Zufit Simon is determined but takes her time, like someone who refuses to surrender her body to the hurry she is in. She sets up a microphone stand and a microphone at the front edge of the stage, then takes her jacket off, and hangs it to the side of the stage. Now she walks resolutely towards the microphone, ready to speak...but instead of words, a swift popping moves her body, a slight but intense contraction of the torso. She moves away from the microphone and starts to dance, choosing movements over words, the corporeal over the verbal expression. Later on in the piece however, she will use the microphone, speak, and perform the gap between a statement expressed in words and facial expression (e.g., "I am so glad you are all here") and the deep emotional state transpiring through the body, which I perceive as sadness, despair, anger.

I attended the premiere in Munich on June 28th, 2014, when Simon performed as part of her artist residency at Blauer Reiter. Simon's dance had been recommended to me by Oxana Chi who curated her performance *Adom* for the TANZnews series in 2010. Two years later, on October 21st, 2016, when Oxana Chi and I co-curated the *Moving Memory Symposium Festival*, we invited Simon to perform *all about nothing* in Berlin. This time, she began by speaking into the microphone. At the very end of the piece, as her energy filled up the wide space of the Freiraum Theatre at Technical University, Zufit Simon returned to the mic, gathering herself to speak...only to abruptly turn around and leave the stage, conveying the feeling that everything necessary had already been uttered. Both versions of the piece stretch dramaturgic rhythm, mold temporality, and bend linear timelines. By setting up the stage after the audience has been let in, and further playing with timing throughout the piece, the performer shifts conventional time markers of concert dance.

In this piece, the choreographer expects audience members to project their own, personal memories onto her performance. Thus, she hopes to create a collage that melds her memory with the audience's. This takes us back to Diana Taylor's definition of the *repertoire* in relation to traumatic memory (see chapter two), in which the presence of an audience is fundamental to the transmission of memory. Performance activates memory within the performative spacetime, as the audience attends and experiences the event, albeit internally. Taylor further writes that the "body responds to and communicates a violent occurrence that may be hard to locate temporally and spatially."[7] Almost throughout the whole dance solo, the dancer shakes incessantly, moved by an uncontainable shuddering. The movements are impressive, since they require a complex technique of control over body muscles at a microscopic scale. As a narrative tool, the shuddering, shaking, palpitating body evokes a sense of timelessness. The body seems to communicate both a memory

---

7   Taylor, *The Archive and The Repertoire*, 203.

of violence, and the violence of memory as it pervades the present. As an audience member, I wanted it to stop, I waited for it to stop, and yet the shaking went on and on, whether the performer stood, or lay on the floor, sat curled up, held her knees in her arms, or was in the process of getting up and going down, continuously shaking. Not the heartbeat, but the fast, intense shuddering marked the passing of time. The shudder became a timeframe, a time measure, like a heart or a drumbeat. Her sequences extended in length, to the point of exhaustion for the performer – and the audience. And yet the courageous decision, and the precision of the constant shuddering never felt boring, rather it transmitted the electrifying sensation of time, when each second seems to implode the very notion of time.

Moving her body in a constant state of contraction – that's what shuddering is, dance-technically speaking – Simon lets the audience understand, or imagine, or re-imagine the traumatic memory stored in the body and expressed on the stage. Shuddering, or *tremblement*, in French, can be an intellectual act of tremor, as we will see at the opening of the next chapter. Linear time is not relevant in this performance, neither are distinctions between a pre- and post-traumatic moment. Here I also think of my earlier analysis of home in relation to Mohanty's emphasis on the emotional, sensory, historical and geographic realms of a *home*. In performemory, these attributes become true for time, which feels deeply emotional, sensory, marked by the motion of the body from one emotional state into another, from one physical movement to another. We move from "present-tenseness" to a tensed present, and a presence full of tension. Experiencing *all about nothing*, I felt immersed in the sensation of time passing, and with each second of shudder, I could sense a year, or a generation passing through the artist's body. Pulses of time stretch throughout the piece, and challenges the sense of how time passes in a theater, sometimes making two minutes feel like an eternity. The shuddering inflected the dramaturgy with a feeling of conflict: Zufit Simon tried to move, perform, express something that was being overlapped, overrun by the motion of contraction, of shuddering. In this here and now, time felt dolorous, like a pain that is neither increased nor reduced by the passage of time.

Time in suspension in *Digital Middle Passage*

If diasporic space is the place, how does it interact with diasporic times? The solo *Digital Middle Passage* attends to the relationship between Black identity and notions of time and space. It investigates what can be gained from condensing the memory of the Middle Passage to a spacetime of twenty minutes.[8] The Renegade Performance Group's website explains how the piece focuses on spacetime: "Time and space in regards to Black existence is suspended between two realms: one familiar

---

8   Tighe, "Middle Passage in Twenty Minutes: The AFROFUTURISM Series."

and the other foreign."[9] This description reflects André Zachery's efforts throughout his repertoire: the will to explore Black diasporic subjectivity through performance, and more generally to envision and enact new ways of moving through time
and space, eventually moving around the very categories of time and space. By juxtaposing millennial technology and the historical name marker of the Transatlantic
Slave Trade, the title already intervenes in the linear progression of time as constructed in the West. Suggesting that the digital realm can be used to access the
history of the Middle Passage is innovative. Indeed, the artist uses both his skills
as a dancer-choreographer and his expertise in 3D-technology to explore the past
from a contemporary position. When his physical body dances across the stage,
simultaneously with its digital reproduction, and transformation (projected onto
the screen), he performs a multidimensional Black existence, that seems to exist
in several layers of spacetime simultaneously. In a fascinating essay entitled "Futurity and the Containment of Blackness in Twenty-First-Century Performance,"
published by Zachery two years after I interviewed him for this book, he reflected
on his use of projections:

> By creating a visual landscape with projections responding via delay to onstage
> movements, I was attempting to acknowledge, rather than fixate on, gaze: the
> image of my body bent and warped as if being pulled through dimensions while
> leaving traces of my real self in fragmented form.[10]

The synchronicity of moving bodies hints at the complexity of diaspora, inviting us
to transcend the usual divide between time and space. The dancer lives and moves
in these multiple realms. Is he a contemporary citizen connected through digital
communication? Or just any human traversing the Atlantic? A Black diasporic subject moving between the African past and the American present...or all at once?
Zachery's performance occupies many diasporic spaces at the same time, as he
moves and lives, simultaneously on stage and on screen.

In this, he reminds us of the complexity of what searching for memories of
the Middle Passage means. Let's take the historical case of Olaudah Equiano as
discussed by Michelle Wright. While historians debate(d) whether or not Equiano
was a Middle Passage survivor, Wright argues for the possibility of multiple narratives to coexist. Drawing on a principle in particle physics, according to which
a particle may be in several places at the same time, Wright states that Equiano
may live simultaneously in the various epistemologies of his self. Thus, for Wright,
the narratives of his story should no longer be seen as contradicting one another,

---

9   Zachery, "Untitled Distances."
10   Zachery, "Futurity and the Containment of Blackness in Twenty-First-Century Performance,"
      75.

but rather understood as juxtaposed truths.[11] I would add that this knowledge does not only stem from particle physics, but is very much in tune with a broad array of cosmologies, for instance in some West African cultures.[12] André Zachery, like Oxana Chi, Ronald K. Brown and Christiane Emmanuel, strongly emphasized the role of spirituality in their choreographic practice. All of them hinted more or less explicitly at the presence of spiritual powers – ancestors, spirits, natural forces – guiding and influencing their dance. Zachery explained that he felt the need to "literally dive," to reach out to the ancestors, to receive their permission to move further across the stage.[13] This translates visually in his intense use of floor work, when his body, lying parallel to the ground, slowly spins on its own axis with the help of a swift rotation of the outstretched arms that induces a full rotation of the torso. Even when he leaves the ground, he seems to be pulled back towards it, as his hands adhere to the smooth surface of the marley. We can read his *Black Dancing Body*[14] not only through the prism of history, but also as a geography. The dancer coexists with his digital self, as well as with his genealogy. He moves within, and co-creates an extensive spacetime eventually liberated from historical chronology and geographic boundaries, with an intentionally flexible approach to their coordinates:

> Time and space for me are truly malleable, and it's not something where I'm interested in giving exact counts or placement of movement.[15]

When Zachery moves to the music, he indeed departs from a classical synchronization between movement and sound. He collaborates with an electronic musician who uses a lot of improvisation. He also seems informed by contact improvisation, and allows the dance and the music to be realms of their own making. The choreography does not necessarily determine the length of a musical sequence, rather at times it may be the contrary, in a practice often departing from Black rhythmic traditions of matching the dance steps to the beats.

While Simon's time pulses, Zachery's time seems to hold its own breath, to be air-suspended between what he terms the familiar and the foreign, between the

---

11   Here Wright refers to the "principle of superposition" in particle physics and to the differing versions of Equiano's biography. While he wrote in his autobiography that he was born an Igbo (in what is today Nigeria), some historians have later attempted to locate his birth in the USA, thus contradicting his narrative about surviving the Middle Passage. Wright, *Physics of Blackness*, 24.

12   When I lived in Douala, Cameroon, working as a trainee with the AfricAvenir Foundation, we had conversations on possibilities for souls to travel out of the house at night, without their bodies leaving home.

13   Zachery, Interview.

14   Dixon Gottschild, *The Black Dancing Body*.

15   Zachery.

embodied traumata of slavery and the incarnation of Black survival. He shuffles
time around, from diasporic journeys into the past to present political concerns;
from a rocket-speed spiraling of the torso to the gradual, barely perceptible movement of a hand touching the ground. After approximately ten minutes, music elon-
gates, and the dancer lies on the floor. He stretches his spine backwards, hands and
feet reaching towards the ceiling – or the sky. Time is in slow motion, as the projection of the performer on the wall lets his bodies dissolve into each other, vanishing,
in an imagery evoking death. There is another moment, at about 18 minutes, when
he freezes, and then jumps in a deftly executed tour-en-l'air, evoking a complex ballet technique. He seems to perform and enact liberation from physical, emotional
and any other type of constraint.

The solo actually epitomizes the artist's proficiency in his own technique of
"Physical Propulsion," itself inspired by the Flying-Low work codified by David
Zambrano. Zachery describes his technique as "dynamically engaging the cranial-
sacrum connection for seamless floor vocabulary, intelligent shifts in body weight,
and fierce aerial movement."[16] There is an interesting parallel between the *post-
injury* context, at the small-scale of the *body*, in which Zambrano developed his
Flying-Low technique (inspired by a Brazilian jump roper and a kung fu practi-
tioner),[17] and the *post-traumatic* spatio-temporal surfaces, at the large scale of American *spacetime*, in which Zachery uses his "Physical Propulsion" to traverse the *Digital
Middle Passage* on stage. *Digital Middle Passage* rests on the performer's intense connection to the ground from which he briefly departs and to which he returns, with
seamless motion across the floor.

In this installment of RPG's *Afrofuturism Series*, I witness Alondra Nelson's understanding of Afrofuturism as "narratives in which time collapses into a single
plane [that] are not necessarily unconcerned with history"[18]. The choreographer's
strong concern for history as a field to be explored and re-mixed, shapes this
solo in which time seems suspended. With knowledge of the contemporary violence against Black bodies in the United States, the solo makes clear that its scope
reaches beyond the memory of slavery as a past trauma, but actually encompasses
the present tensions inherent to being present in a Black body in the Americas. We
may also think of Stephanie Batiste's analysis of "the capturing, collapsing, and extension of time such that the past, present and future exist in the same moments,
words, gestures" in Sharon Bridgforth's theatrical jazz performance *Delta Dandi*.[19]
The capacity to capture and generate multidimensional time within one body, and

---

16   Zachery, "Physical Propulsion."
17   Zambrano, "Flying-Low - Dance Technique."
18   Nelson, "AfroFuturism."
19   Batiste, "Aquanova," 238.

one breath, is a gem that brings us to the next artist. While André Zachery's performance holds past, present, and future in a spacetime of suspension, Oxana Chi's dance beholds time within a sense of infinite motion.

Cyclic time in *Through Gardens*

In her dance *Through Gardens*, Oxana Chi structures the narrative in a theatrical dramaturgy consisting of four main acts: the "Birth" (die Geburt), the "Celebration" (das Fest), the "Struggle" (der Kampf), and the "New Moon" (der Neumond). Each act or scene paints a tableau of Tatjana Barbakoff's life. The dance bears affinities with four seasons, with a festive, colorful, warm summer mood in the Celebration; a blue, white, winter void in the Struggle, a spring energy in The Birth and the New Moon, and an interlude of autumnal nostalgia. At first, the narrative appears embedded in a chronological temporality that takes the audience linearly along Barbakoff's biographic timeline. Yet in my view, at closer review, the piece implodes linear time, most clearly through the final scene of the New Moon, which comes after the audiences has witnessed abstract renderings of the birth, successes, resistance, deportation, and death of Tatjana Barbakoff. Oxana-Tatjana now lies motionless on the floor. One may think that the piece has ended – as would be the case in a conventional narration of Holocaust biographies – but the live-music continues. After a few minutes, the dancer gets up, and starts to move extremely slowly, as if awakening into an afterlife. She takes off the blue costume used in the last combat scene. Left with a minimalist black outfit, the aesthetics contrast sharply with the elaborate costumes of the previous scenes. Although Tatjana just "died" on stage, she now lives and moves on in Oxana's dancing solo.

Dancing the past in the present tense, Chi re-imagines what Barbakoff's past may have been and thus transcends the historiographic sources from which she drew information about Barbakoff. The choreography allows for multiple interpretations: is this a dream, a glimpse of the fourth dimension, a vision? The scene embodies what Dolan calls "utopian performatives,"[20] for Chi enacts into the performative spacetime of *now* the possibility of Barbakoff's survival and/or afterlife, and inscribes her memory as a dynamic process to be acknowledged and appreciated collectively and individually. In this scene, Oxana Chi repeats certain patterns of movements, assembling fragments from earlier sequences in a new, seamless choreography. This time however, she dances in slow motion, inducing a dream-like feeling, giving the audience the chance to re-experience her movements at a different pace. Even the kick and fight movements which were executed so swiftly in the Struggle scene, are now in slow motion. The gracefulness of the swaying torso, the Javanese hand postures, and the smooth floating of the arms, evoking

---

20   Dolan, *Utopia in Performance*, 5.

the Tai Chi figure known as *caressing the clouds* diffuse a soft haze over the tragic ending of narrative.

Just as a clock slows down time when it is set in motion – as physics experiments have shown[21] – so does the temporality shaped by the choreographic motion of the dancer. A *mise en abyme*, the final scene performs a postmemorial choreobiography of memory, and becomes a perforMemory of perforMemory. In the contemporary artist's corporeal search for historical traces, it almost feels as if perforMemory could fold itself over. The deceleration of the pace leaves a mnemonic imprint of the whole choreography on the audience. Oxana reaches out to Tatjana through a memory that is continuously reinvented anew, created in performance, a memory2go, a diasporic spidering fabricating *as it goes* the thread of memory.

What does Oxana Chi's play with pace express about hegemonic timelines and counter-hegemonic storytelling? In a way, she is "citing" herself, her own movements. The choreographer lets phrases recur, as if memorized, yet at an altered pace, and shows how a slight alteration of tempo may impact the whole narrative. In most of the Western historiography on the Holocaust, or let's say in the biography of Tatjana Barbakoff, a dead dancer cannot rise again. Motionless beings do not come back to motion or life, and movements from the past can not be reiterated. The process of inviting chronology into her choreobiography, to finally transcend it, also bears affinities with Indigenous tools of storytelling. Jacqueline Shea Murphy has noted, for instance, how the dramaturgy of the piece *No Home but the Heart* refers to historical chronology and dates, while simultaneously questioning linear time, and overlapping time periods in order to alter knowledge transmission on the topic of colonization in the Americas.[22] Similarly, Oxana Chi's dramaturgy refers to historical markers of the 20th century while re-mixing them.

The title of the scene, "New Moon," hints at a cyclic type of temporality, and invites one to reconsider the whole piece through a new lens, a cyclic, seasonal, non-linear temporality. To witness this scene is to leave the linear thread that seemed to hold the performance together. Instead, the dancer unravels a multi-textured sense of time, and allows the audience to re-assess each scene as part of a cycle, and as a cycle itself. Time here becomes circular. Time relativity is demonstrated in the cyclic temporalities of *Through Gardens*. Chi, who is inspired strongly by her visits to the Asian continent, expresses how her relation to time was impacted as a young German leaving the West for the first time:

> India was quite an important experience for me, because I found a particular freedom for my choreography and dance which really matters to my choreography. Namely, that I can treat time as I wish to. My movements need a wealth of time,

---

21   Capra, *The Tao of Physics*, 170.
22   Shea Murphy, *The People Have Never Stopped Dancing*.

and I want to deeply savor each movement – and this is what India taught me – something which may have gone lost in Europe, or which may never have existed in the first place.[23]

Inspired by the experience of another relation to spacetime, especially in the performance realm, Chi is strongly interested in a flexible approach to time, which becomes a process-based parameter in the hands of the choreographer. Cyclic relations to time pervaded most Hindu and Chinese cosmologies a long time before reaching Western physics. Cyclic time connects the self to its environment, to the cosmos. For example, Ananya Chatterjea has analyzed Indian choreographer Chandralekha's relation to time as follows:

> [Movements] are not fixed in the physical time that binds us to routine, but happen in metaphysical time, cosmic, memory time, when in one blink, a whole era, millions of years can be said to have passed by.[24]

This is the feeling emanating from the "New Moon" sequence, and from *Through Gardens* as a whole. In the scene of the Chinese Dress described in the last chapter, Oxana-Tatjana puts on a Chinese costume to evoke Barbakoff's relation to her mother's silks. The memory or re-imagination of the mother may echo contemporary quests for a mother figure. Both beings co-exist in the dancing body: the 20th century Barbakoff and the 21st century Chi. Physical time, cosmic time and memory time juxtapose against perforMemory a biography that dominant dance historiography often fails to account for. A pirouette, or a turn of a hand becomes a timeframe in which either a few minutes or several years of Tatjana Barbakoff's life have passed. Thus, cyclic time contests Western linear time, and its corollary of (past) cause and (present) effect.

Oxana Chi's signature use of live-music, and the elaborate collaboration with artists who compose and improvise for her choreographies (as I had the wonderful opportunity to do) also play a role in shaping cyclic time. In conversation with one or more instruments, the dance shapes the manufacturing of time: the choreography determines when a sequence starts and when it ends. Within these cues given to the various musicians of her Ensemble Xinren, cycles of dance and music evolve according to the energy of the moment. This happens for instance in the version of the Birth evoked at the beginning of the chapter, where the musician mimics the sounds of a heartbeat. The increasing velocity of the hearbeat-guitar must happen in a fine-tuned concordance with the intensity and pace of the dancer's movements. Although the movements do not have to exactly match the music or vice-versa, the sense of time passing for the dancer within her costume is in tune

23   Chi, Interview [My translation].
24   Chatterjea, *Butting Out*, 62.

with the musician's percussive playing. The artists find synchronicity outside of a conventional 1-8 count. When the dancer bursts out of the cloth, the guitarist immediately pauses. A new cycle of motion and music may begin, and so does time move throughout the piece.

In an e-mail addressed by Oxana Chi to hang and piano musician Laszlo Moldvai, dated January 1st 2010, the choreographer poetically worded the interrelation between circularity, time, choreography and music in *Through Gardens*:

> Since the dance sequences continuously repeat themselves, and spin almost like a whirligig, there remains much freedom of interpretation for the audience.
> (Da sich die Tanzsequenzen immer wiederholen, wie ein Kreisel sich quasi im Kreis drehen, bleibt den Theaterbesuchern viel Raum für eigene Interpretationen.)[25]

Furthermore she mentions the idea of circular time, or a time circle ("zeitlicher Kreis"), revealing her desire to dance in a non-linear dramaturgy, which should be sustained by the music composition-improvisation. Indeed, the circular motion of time is reflected in the circular movements embedded in the cyclic conception. Interestingly, the relation between circles and cycles recurs throughout her repertoire.[26]

Deploying her strong skills in ballet techniques such as *pirouettes* and *tour fouettés*, her dance is also embedded in Africanist techniques and aesthetics.[27] Her storytelling mixture of dance, live-music, and dramatic expression corresponds to what Zenenga calls African Total Theater.[28] Her reflections on time suggests that in her dance, "[t]ime is a factor, but enough time rather than a set amount of time," a feature of Africanist dance, according to dance scholar Kariamu Welsh-Asante.[29] Welsh-Asante theorized seven common features, or "senses" that characterize Africanist dance (which for her also encompasses certain forms of ballet, jazz and modern dance). One of these senses is "repetition." Asante suggests that an Africanist use of repetition works through an intensification of movements. Thus,

---

25   Chi, "E-Mail an Laszlo Moldvai, 01.01.2010"; Oxana Chi published the e-mail herself in the catalogue Chi, *Tanzende Erinnerungen*, 2011.

26   See also Zami, "Of Circles and Cycles."

27   For an elaborate analysis of Africanist influences in American ballet, see Dixon Gottschild, *Digging the Africanist Presence in American Performance*.

28   Here I refer to the aesthetic paradigm defined in Zenenga, "The Total Theater Aesthetic Paradigm in African Theater.'"

29   Asante's search for common features does not mask the complex diversity that marks the multitude of dance styles produced on the African continent, nor their own distinctions between traditional and contemporary forms. See Welsh Asante, "Commonalities in African Dance," 150.

the repetition of a movement carries its transformation through the modulation of its pace, or emotional quality, or execution.[30]

The use of repetition in *Through Gardens* struck me as particularly powerful and fascinating. When the dancer repeats a phrase of movements, the repetition is always in itself a transformation and an intensification, moving towards a climactic resolve, especially in the scene of the Celebration and of the Struggle. Here, the repetition turns hypnotic, and pulls the audience into it. The repetition of the celebratory pirouettes and jumps, and of the resistive kicks and swings of the arms, render the circularity of memory palpably visible. The accelerated precision and the increased emotionality of the patterns emit a rushing flow of time, a storm which the dancer navigates kinesthetically.

Through Gardens performs a cyclic *memory2go* in which conventional delimitations between past, present, and future are disrupted. The dancer perforMemories a dynamic engagement with the epistemology of a historical figure, she generates a corporeal spacetime in which notions of historical time and geographical space coalesce into the performing body. The performance epitomizes a cyclic approach to *choreobiography*, and allows the audience to circle (around) the perforMemory of Tatjana Barbakoff, second by second and step by step.

Immediate time in *Parole, Parole, Parole*

When I first came across Farah Saleh's work, reading about her piece *Ordinary Madness* in the Internet, I wondered if this would qualify as perforMemory, since it obviously dealt with the present reality of daily life in Palestine. I came to the conclusion that if my research aims to move beyond the temporal frame of linear progress, her work, certainly works with the past, as near as it may be, from a present position. When I interviewed Farah Saleh, she did not use the historical term of "Nakba," maybe because she views it as an ongoing preoccupation in Palestine rather than a far-away memory? The solo *Parole, Parole, Parole*, as well as the group work *Ordinary Madness*, do perforMemory, although they do not engage with only with the past. Memory here becomes the present: it can be the memory of today, yesterday, the last hour, the last second...

Here, time feels immediate. Saleh's dance sculpts a time that is imperative, instantaneous, detached from its fore- and after. In *Parole, Parole, Parole*, dancer and audience occupy one spacetime. When I witnessed it, Saleh did not dance on the stage, rather she danced across the whole room occupied by the spread out audience. I felt a bitter irony in watching European citizens "displaced" across the room by a Palestinian dancer, in a more or less voluntary interaction. Some audi-

---

30   For more reflections on repetition in the work of Oxana Chi and Chantal Loïal, see Zami, "Danser le passé au présent."

ence members had to make space for her, as she walked on her hands closer and closer to them. Others stuck to their spot and took in her kinesthetic message.

Because of the extreme proximity between performer and viewers, I felt that time flowed differently, almost like conversational time, but a conversation in which one party – the audience – sometimes remains silent or motionless. At the Tanzquartier Vienna, Saleh felt it difficult to connect with her audience. However, in other contexts, she has stated that the solo makes her feel like "being with the people and feeling things with them, and making them feel things."[31] This suggests the abolition of spatial and temporal separations between the audience and the performer. She uses proximity to be in intimacy with the audience, wrapping each spectactor into her spacetime, and reminding us that performance does not really exist independently from its witnesses. The gracefulness of the body reflected years of practice in contemporary and traditional Western and Eastern dance styles. She produced smooth waves of motion, sometimes interrupted, when the body collapsed, as if falling into a timeless gap.

The piece also involves the simulation of a Skype conversation between Farah Saleh and a distant lover. The Wall and checkpoints split up Palestinian citizens physically and psychologically, a reality transcended only in the virtual spacetime of a loving relationship. Skype becomes a means to communicate across geopolitical frontiers. In the piece, the fact that Saleh's supposed lover, close to her heart, is out of reach, is amplified by her physical presence among strangers, and her movements within this spatial intimacy. Reminiscent of contact improvisation, her way of interacting with the audience underlines the distance between her and the physically absent lover. Looking back at Saleh's work in times of social distancing measures and recommendations deemed to mitigate the spread of COVID-19, I think about the invisible walls that we are asked to erect around ourselves, about the virtual reality we find ourselves relying on, and about France, a country that so vehemently opposed to the Muslim veil, now is itself wearing a mask. Without equating the diversity of these realities, I ask myself in which *Ordinary Madness* we find ourselves in, and if it may afford us a new understanding of Palestine.

Illustrating the tension of memory politics in Palestine, Hanan Ashrawi wrote in her foreword to *Birthing the Nation*:

> As I sit in my home in Ramallah, the sights, sounds, and smells of the Israeli attack bombard my senses: helicopters, bombs, bullets, gas. The conflict that shapes this book is sadly alive and indeed booming louder than ever. News broadcasts around the world almost daily report the rising death toll. This sinister numerical game, whereby Palestinian victims of Israeli fire are daily given as *x numbers* killed and

---

y numbers wounded, reduce our humanity to a series of abstractions. The victims' names, identities, dashed hopes and shattered dreams are nowhere mentioned.[32]

This resonates with my own memory of learning about the Shoah in school, and missing my relatives' names and images in the vast narrative, and feeling like history was a missile thrown at me. The more zeros added to the books' count, the deeper I would feel that "history" nullified the humans behind the numbers.

PerforMemory counters the dehumanization of historical abstraction. To perforMemory allows us to reunite various spacetimes within the moment of the performance, to interweave information about what may have preceded the traumatic event, and the protagonists' daily issues and realities. Farah Saleh's dance reclaims individual agency from the anonymity of hegemonic narratives. Yet, her politically loaded dance is also about... love, as she pinpointed in the interview:

> For this miniature in general my intent is to make people feel this possibility of love, that very human simple thing that can happen when people are close. And how easily I can do it with people that are very close to me, me personally and the person I love...[across] this huge gap and distance, not really physical distance but political distance, where I cannot reach this person.[33]

Farah Saleh dances conflict, but also and maybe mostly gestures of love in times of war. The distance she speaks of is not only a spatial one, but also a temporal one, a distance shaped by waiting, longing and lingering – as performed in the piece. Although this piece is the shortest of the soli discussed here, it stretches time outwards from the hegemonic clocks of news and geopolitical chronologies. She shows that perforMemory can be sensuous, and sensuality may help to retrieve an imagined past, heal the wounds of the present, and dream the possibility of a more tender future.

Ripples of time in *They Call You Venus*

When Chantal Loïal dances the pain and joys of Black women, is she Venus? Is she Chantal? Is she both, as she says in the interview? Performance allows for those boundaries to be blurred, and for this actual blurring not to confuse, but rather produce a new meaning, and to make a statement about the continuities between present and past racism in France. *They Call You Venus* traces the true story of Sawtche, also known as Sarah Baartmann or the Black Venus. In contrast with Chi's search for traces (Spurensuche) of an erased figure, and her reclamation of Barbakoff's vital role in cultural memory, Loïal centers a historical figure who is often cited in black and postcolonial studies. The story of Sawtche's deportation and

---

32   Kanaaneh, *Birthing the Nation*, xi.
33   Saleh, Interview.

enslavement found its way into literary and artistic engagements in the later 20th century, yet these often work(ed) with images and texts written by the very people who oppressed them. The story seems emblematic of the violent intersection of racism, sexism and capitalism produced against bodies positioned as Black and female. In an analysis of Elizabeth Alexander's 1990 *Venus* poem collection, Samantha Pinto writes that "Baartman is large, in Elizabeth Alexander's text; she is her own world, her own system of reference, even as she is limited by another set of meanings."[34]

Loïal also creates her own world, on stage, and moves at the critical border between referring to a history of racism and the racism of history, and tracing her own epistemology. The solo form highlights the centrality of the performer as "her own system of reference." This materializes in a choreography that comes across as waves of movements and time. Within this aquatic choreography, I identified three parts: the humiliation, the resilience and the return.

Here, time floats. The dancer's body often moves slowly, allowing the audience to be drawn into the story and into the folds of time. At the beginning of the piece, the light design conveys the feel of exhibition and display. Loïal appears, like a living display, in squares of light. She takes her time. Motion is sometimes extremely slow: for instance her hands cover her body protectively at the height of her chest and genitals, she moves them, delicately, raises them in front of her, until the outstretched arms point diagonally to the upper sides, then reaches back behind her, as she interlocks her fingers, bends her knees and leans her upper body towards the ground. Still in the same stream of conscious slow motion, she raises herself, turns, side-facing the audience, until the de-centering of the pelvis releases the locking of the hands. This floating quality recurs in various sequences, and reflects the artist's search for fluidity:

> With a work on slowness, the Venus dance took a streaming character, showcasing the fluidity of movement, as if in progressing through an aquatic environment. Below, implicit as a watermark, African[ist] dance is always around, folds into, melts into the movement, rediscovers itself in a contemporaneous aesthetic.
>
> (Avec un travail sur la lenteur, la danse de la Vénus a pris un caractère coulé, mettant en valeur la fluidité du mouvement, comme une évolution dans un espace aquatique. Derrière en filigrane, la danse africaine jamais bien loin, se plie, se fond dans le mouvement, se redécouvre dans une esthétique contemporaine.)[35]

Does this oceanic process stem from Loïal's personal positioning (through genealogy) in and professional interest (through her dance styles) for the Black Atlantic? In any case, the fluidity of her motion influences the temporality, which also feels

---

34   Pinto, *Difficult Diasporas*, 60.
35   Loïal, "On T'appelle Vénus - Dossier de Diffusion." [My translation]

aquatic, channeling a sense of rippling time as the story unfolds. Her body keeps undulating, while the choreography stitches elements of Afro-Caribbean styles, traditional Western alignment and floor work techniques known as "modern dance" and ballet. Episodes of rising energy, such as the scene when she shivers more and more intensely – again, the figure of the tremor – resolve into a release of tension, as if multiple times were bending over themselves.

"I am woman, I am Black, I am myself!"…with this loud statement, Chantal Loïal punctuates the representation of Venus' humiliation and oppression with an affirmation of subjectivity and political autonomy, and enters into a spirit of joyful resilience. The soundtrack is now South African, and Loïal proudly and strongly swings the arms, stomps the feet and moves in a contemporary blend of African and Caribbean dance styles. As a former company member of the Ballet national du Congo and Ballet Théâtre Lemba, she brings to the stage a proficiency in both Central and West African dance styles. The hands that were often bound in the last scenes are now released, free to flex. When she performs the Africanist motif of the finger tracing a vertical descending line along the body, each finger suddenly possesses agency.

In her artist statement,[36] Loïal mentions her will to produce an entire life within a unit of time, place and space. This reference to the classical "rules of theatrical dramaturgy" reminded me of my literature teachers in French primary school education. However, Loïal defiantly deviates from these rules, or maybe uses "the master's tools" to tell a story that I do not remember hearing in school. Waves of motion and emotion let the audience travel across centuries and places, from the 18th century to the 21st century, from South Africa to France by way of the Caribbean. Time ripples, and her performing body becomes the only relevant unity of spacetime.

Fugitive time in *Choc(s)*

According to an Indigenous oral tradition, the world began with a woman falling from the "skyworld." The story is told as follows by Robin Wall Kimmerer, an enrolled member of the Citizen Potawatomi Nation and environmental professor on Turtle Island:

> She fell like a maple seed, pirouetting on an autumn breeze. A column of light streamed from a hole in the Skyworld, marking her path where only darkness had been before. It took her a long time to fall. In fear, or maybe hope, she clutched a bundle tightly in her hand. [...][37]

In *Choc(s)*, Christiane Emmanuel seems to fall from the sky, in a rather neoteric fashion, immersed in a science-fiction soundtrack. She evokes the imagery of a

---

36   Loïal.
37   Kimmerer, *Braiding Sweetgrass*, 3.

time out of time. At the beginning of the piece, she hangs high up in the air above the stage, in a vertically oriented fetal curl. Slowly, she stretches her body out and opens her eyes, as if coming (back) to consciousness, and soon begins a dynamic walk that transforms into a sprint. Her expansive leg and arm movements make her airwalk sometimes seem like she is rolling, swimming or flying through the air. In the artist statement, Emmanuel refers to the piece as the scanning of her memory, in search of referentiality:

> I am crossing through my memory and thinking of all the big dates of history and to all of those who fought, so I am clinging on.[38]

Is she also clinging onto the diasporic condition? Her words suggest the intricacy of historical time and a contemporary location. Not only does she cling to a rope but she often clings to pieces of cloth, or to the ground on which she crawls and rolls. In this solo, the performer often seems to encounter obstacles. Maybe her dancing limbs embody the suffering, loss and alienation generated by an ongoing colonial regime on the island of Martinique.

Choc(s) dissolves chronological demarcations between the past of slavery and the present struggle against oppression. The dancer-choreographer binds together elements from task-based choreography, contemporary idioms and traditional steps of Cuban rumba and Martinican bèlè, in a corporeal quest for a memory that may sustain the body into the present. The piece deals with the burning matter of the protest that led millions of people to protest and boycott the economy in 2009 and 2011. Running through the streets of Martinique, citizens protested against an economic structure in which the descendants of slave owners (known as 'Békés') continue to hold a monopoly over the majority of the island's resources, from the food industry to the land. The population expressed outrage against ongoing racial inequities, and the astronomic costs of living (food, rent,...). The history of social protest in Martinique bears many stories erased in hegemonic memory transmission, yet sometimes retrieved through oral memory. For instance, Christiane Chivallon collected oral testimony about the 1870 revolt against slave owners in southern Martinique. In an important work reflecting on the construction of the memory of slavery in Martinique, she centers the role of embodied memory which "cannot be detached from the body," in her words, a "mémoire incorporée" (incorporated memory):

---

38   Emmanuel, "Choc(s) - Artist Statement."

[...] this memory becoming body renews the circuits of being "against": against command, against the plantation-system, against power, against inequalities, against official narratives [...].[39]

On stage, Christiane Emmanuel also seems to constantly bump *against* a force that stops her, to move in protest against the societal structure of capitalism, in an attempt to run against time. The scenography supports the choreographic message and evokes the white collar world order. At first we see a wall of large, white shirts. At center stage, a pile of white shirts form a circle. Once the dancer lands on stage, a video projection transforms the whole stage environment into a cityscape, marked by a strong riff. The pile of shirts now resembles a volcanic crater, which makes me think of the volcano of Mount Pelée in the North of the island. Now within a grayish network-like scenery, Christiane Emmanuel keeps running and searching. Although she dances a rush and run, she often takes her time. Gestures extend into a long stretch of time.

The temporality of this solo makes me think of the realms of futurity and fugitivity, such as those found in Tina Campt's analysis of an "alternative visual archive of the black diaspora." Campt speaks of the "performance of a future that hasn't yet happened, but must" and looks out for "strategies of diasporic survival" in unexpected places such as passport pictures.[40] Emmanuel performs these strategies in *Choc(s)*, when she spends much time running, in the air or on the ground, as if time was an aspirated fluid, moving in the fragile spacetime. Her visual archive is also performative. Her embodied strategy of survival is firmly anchored in her relation to the island's geography, geophysics, and geopolitics. In a choreographic quest for balance, for something to hold onto, for a space or timeframe to stand on/into, she performs the harsh search for stability and safety. Her use of aerial work epitomizes an ambivalent relation to conventional markers of time and space. "Images of Skywoman speak not just of where we came from, but also of how we can go forward,"[41] says Kimmerer, and so does Emmanuel: she dances in the Earth- and the Skyworld, bending linear spacetime to move from one to another. *Choc(s)* collapses the hegemonic narrative of a post-slavery society. Moreover, it grips onto what is behind, and attempts to attain, through performance, a timespace ahead of her own subject located in the equation of the 21st century Caribbean.

---

39   Chivallon, *L'esclavage, du souvenir à la mémoire - Contribution à une anthropologie de la Caraïbe*, 532 [My translation]. The word *incorporée* can be translated as *embodied*. Like *incorporated*, the etymology is Latin, coming from *in* and *corpus* (Latin for *body*, in French: *corps*).

40   Campt, "Black Feminist Futures and the Practice of Fugitivity."

41   Kimmerer, *Braiding Sweetgrass*, 5.

Swirling time in *Impressions*

If time were a musical figure, in this piece it would be a staccato. The solo engages with the impact of Wan-Chao Chang's memory from the years when *home* was away from home. Upon returning to Taiwan, she questions how these memories affect her daily reality. The title, *Impressions*, suggests that Wan-Chao Chang digs into the imprints left by memory within her body to render a sense of time that is physically past but mentally and bodily present, thus influencing her motion in contemporaneity. Her choreography seems to slowly unfold layers of spacetime. Here, time is a surface, and the dancer's hands float over it.

The sequences follow each other in staccato-like fashion, but the dance movements remain mostly fluid. Hands flow gently through the air, in a remix of Javanese dance techniques. They often reach out, trying to grab something, as if there was an invisible support to hold onto within the motion of time, or as if the dancing hands could hold onto time itself, and stop it from fleeing. Towards the end of the piece, hands also appear as a video projection, and the dancer plays with the image, projecting the shadow of her hands onto the video representation of her hands, reminiscent of the Javanese *wayang kulit* art. The self moving in the now thus enters into touch with the hands moving in another dimension, be it past or present, reaching for each other. As in *Choc(s)*, time is fragile, and equilibrium is the remedy to this temporal fragility.

Time can also be a precious memory, a location in space and time that the dancer tries to hold in her hands. So is the prop, the scarf that may be a thread of diasporic memory that she moves with, within and without. In one brief sequence, the scarf will even capture the saxophone of the accompanying musician. The scarf entangles the instrument, the body, the movements and sounds, almost arresting time.

Do you remember the "millions of years before and after us" and "millions of places" in Chung-Hing's poem, cited at the beginning of this chapter? Here they are, in Chang's performance, in movement, and overlapping. Rhythm plays an important role, especially when the music carries the movements in a lively manner. Stepping, sometimes leaning the arched back behind herself, isolating the shoulders, even running, all these movements harmonize with the dynamism of the solo. Nevertheless, at times the dancer takes the time to pause, to decelerate the pace, as the music goes on. In these sequences, her movements evoke a movie still. The stretching time indeed feels cinematic, with Chang's coming and going through the performance venue.

She could be wandering in flashbacks of her past, or debating in which spacetime she wants to stay, can stay. The body seems to be struggling between leaving something behind (a place, a situation, a memory) and running back after it. With only two or three steps, the dancer could be jumping back and forth from the USA to

Taiwan, from Taiwan to Indonesia, from one layer of her life to another, trying to reunite these moments in a performative way and moment. At one point, Wan-Chao Chang starts spinning on her own axis, using the technique of dervish dancers. In Beijing Opera tradition, performers walk in a large circle to indicate narratively that they are traveling a long distance. Here Chang sticks to the small circle of her self, and yet her dance leaves a swirling trace in the air, and conveys the impression of an intense journey, be it a geohistorical, emotional or mental one. She dances the motion of time at a microscopic scale. Wan-Chao Chang's perforMemory combines calm, fluid body energy with dynamic, agile motion and control over each and every muscle.

Scientist Carlo Rovelli has compared the apparently peaceful and clear water surface of a lake to "the rapid dance of myriad of minuscule water molecules."[42] He further uses the metaphor of dance to explain the movement of time, space and the nature of spacetime according to quantum physics:

> Every cubic centimeter of space, and every second that passes, is the result of this *dancing foam* of extremely small quanta.[43]

Chang's *Impressions* can help us understand kinesthetically what this "dancing foam" may look and feel like. Quanta matter moves beyond the notion that time and space move in a linear fashion, or exist independently from each other. The dramaturgy resists the linearity that often structures Western narrative projects of historiographical hegemony.

Time – and its measurement, as we know, is a social construct which varies from society to society. Chang dances *Impressions* of time as it inhabits her being. She clings onto the imprints left over time on her body. She performs within a swirling temporality, connecting through movement, her *Impressions* of the past as they swirl into her present. Her perforMemory bridges the gaps between space-times capsules of being (somewhere else), wishing (to go back), and remembering (another space and time).

The quantic dance of memory: moving through and beyond past, present and future

I have tried to show how each solo performs and is informed by a different notion of time.[44] (En)countering hegemonic narratives requires a re-imagination of the conceptions of time in which they exist. Scratching beneath the surface of Western

---

42   Rovelli, *Reality Is Not What It Seems*, 183.
43   Rovelli, 192. [My emphasis]
44   Here I may have been inspired (more or less consciously) by having read, as a teenager, *Ein-stein's Dreams* by writer and physicist Alan Lightman. Did you know that his mother was a dance teacher?

historiography, one finds recurrent norms of time and space. Dancers may comment on, and transcend these notions, which in turn may impact discourses and practices of memory transmission. I argue that each dancer works within, and/or creates a specific spacetime, and thus offers new ways to approach memory. Paradoxically, I find myself undertaking what Jill Dolan describes as the difficult task of the performance scholar, namely "to document a complicated process of engagement with a live event whose presence I can only trace as I remember it in the future."[45] Although these pieces live from their liveness, it is only afterwards that I try to translate them into words. The remembering "in the future" inevitably diverts from the multi-sensory experience in the spacetime of the performance. Tina Campt encourages us to "expand our sensorial engagement" with photography, for instance by trying to listen to images of black diasporic refusal and survival.[46] My conceptualization of perforMemory is also an invitation to move beyond the mere visual realm of dance studies. To move through the world of performing arts is to experience a whirlwind made of multiple paces and textures of time.

To perforMemory is to question what time actually means. On stage, it becomes particularly clear and intense to wonder what experiencing time means. I remember the evening of February 16th, 2017. Oxana Chi and I co-curated a performance night called *Black Herstory Night* at Dixon Place Theater in Manhattan. One of our goals was to promote visibility for Black women perspectives and narratives during Black History Month. We had included ourselves in the line-up, and I was looking forward to performing with Oxana, as always. I was also particularly excited to present the New York premiere of my *Homesong*, a short spoken words and saxophone solo. I remember waiting in the spacetime called "backstage before the show". Our first guest performer, Rosamond S. King, a poet, performer and tenured humanities professor is about to open the evening. As nervousness and concentration bubbles start to inflate and fill up the air, she evokes how every minute "feels like an eternity" *before a performance*. I agree, feeling the same way: lingering on these small islands in the waiting sea, a few minutes ahead of showtime, each passing second seems to stretch into a long, infinite moment. This feeling always makes me reflect upon how subjective time is, how a second is not a mathematical, intangible unit of time, but rather a bubble that floats and carries one along different paths, at varying paces, depending on the winds of personal emotion, situation and position. The stretched time of waiting backstage contrasts so sharply with the intense, sky-rocketing time feeling on stage *during the performance*. Once I step onto the stage, performing a text or playing an instrument, I feel swallowed in a time hurricane, now suddenly time rushes and I focus on performing at an appropriate pace. It is a conscious effort to modulate time, while the intensified

---

45   Dolan, *Utopia in Performance*, 15.
46   Campt, "Black Feminist Futures and the Practice of Fugitivity"; Campt, *Image Matters*, 2017.

bodily production of adrenalin, serotonin, dopamine, tends to accelerate speech or play rhythm. The seconds that seemed eternal a few minutes ago in the backstage time/space, now ripple so fast...and I try to catch them with each pause of breath. I perform my text, my song, alone, or accompanying Oxana Chi, and I leave the stage feeling detached from my usual time senses.

When we toured *I Step On Air*, I realized how 45 minutes of performance space-time have an entirely different feel from a 45 minute rehearsal. Strangely, with each show, the performance felt shorter, although we timed it, and did not alter the duration. It felt as though time was shrinking. This surely had to do with experience, with the ease that comes with repeating a work, with traveling through the performance several times. Like the familiarity that comes with having walked an itinerary several times, I could now wander through the piece at a different pace. This is still one of the most challenging aspects of performances to me, and can only be refined through repeated practice and accumulated experience: surfing on the non-linear time feel on stage, while staying precisely in tune with the measured clock time without using neither clock nor metronome. Let's say the choreographer determined that sequence A should be about five minutes. You do not want to shorten it to two minutes or extend it to ten minutes. As a musician, I constantly work on timing, and I am grateful that Oxana Chi's clear vision and precise coaching during rehearsals trained me to advance further in the art and science of timing. I always strive to not let myself be pulled away through the whirlwind, and to stick with our commonly agreed route, while still allowing plenty of time for improvisation, and plenty of room for alignment with potential fluctuations according to the energy of the evening.

In my work as an Interdisciplinary Artist-in-Residence with Oxana Chi Dance & Art (and formerly with Ensemble Xinren), I am fascinated by the complexity and polysemy of synchronicity, because the choreographer does not always expect a simple, flat synchronicity between the dance moves and the music sounds. Yet, audiences have repeatedly commented on how well we perform *together*. By *spending* much *time* working *together*, in and out of the rehearsal space, we co-create our own spacetime universe in which synchronicity takes multiple shapes. These experiences helped me to understand how we do not only move 'forward' in time, from past to present to future, but how we rather shift in time from one cognitive state to another. Time is a matter that we can craft. While humans seem to move through set units of seconds, minutes, hours and days, they actually move through waves of emotion, through varying positionings in space, through evolving environments, and through various levels of consciousness. All of this is at stake in how dancers perform in time, and how humans perceive time.

Dancing right here right now: from ephemeral to epiphenomenal time

If time has a scent, can dance fill the stage with the fragrance of memory? In Ancient China, the "hsiang yin" was a clock that indicated the passing of time through the burning of incense, the ashes of which eventually revealed a philosophical or poetic text or koan.[47] I read about it in the work of Korean-born philosopher Byung-Chul Han, who explains how the incense-clock measured time by filling the air with fragrance, thus materializing how time can become space.[48] The performances discussed here reunite the notion of time and space within a performing body. In perforMemory, time becomes space, and memory becomes the motion of time in space, as the dancers imagine and embody alternative ways of relating to time and memory.

A plurality of other examples could be cited to illustrate non-Western conceptions of time and memory transmission, for instance American Indigenous practices of sand painting and their temporary temporality, which Teshome Gabriel takes as a starting point to reflect upon erasure as a practice of memory.[49] I mentioned in the introduction that many performance and dance scholars have defended the ephemerality paradigm, while others defend the idea of the body as an archive. Scholars such as Julia Wehren in Germany or Rebecca Schneider in the USA make clear that performance cannot be restricted to its presumed disappearance and ephemerality. However, these engagements with the relation between performance and history/memory often relate to practices of choreographic or theatrical re-enactments. While my analysis focuses on the actual enactment of memorial discourses and practices through performance, I share Schneider's enthusiasm for the resilience of performance as an alternative to the ephemerality paradigm:

> When we approach performance not as that which disappears (as the archive expects), but as both the act of remaining and a means of re-appearance and "reparticipation" (though not a metaphysic of presence) we are almost immediately forced to admit that remains do not have to be isolated to the document, to the object, to bone versus flesh.[50]

Schneider refutes the assumption that performance disappears, choosing to focus instead on what remains. The various temporalities described above, born out of my own reading of the choreographies, resist the disappearance of the performing body in the narrow corridor of linear time. They show how the dancing body leaves traces across spacetimes, and how to perforMemory amounts to creating a multiplicity of spacetimes for memories to unfold. If we agree that the body stores

---

47   The author develops an interesting reflection about time as a fragrance. See Han, *Duft der Zeit*.
48   Han.
49   Gabriel, "Ruin and The Other."
50   Schneider, *Performing Remains*, 101.

memory – across millenniums of generations and millions of kilometers – then it becomes urgent to think corporeal practices beyond the realm of ephemerality.

The dancers' understanding of their body as a channel for a memory retrieved from other generations, locations and dimensions is underlined by the conversations presented in the next chapter. Dancers also use their bodies as a channel for contemporary interventions within historical definitions, in order to affect sociopolitical change. For example, Farah Saleh worked on a project entitled "Archive of Gestures," which she presented during a residency at The Center for Humanities at Brown University in 2016. In an interview given around that time period, she explains:

> I'm investigating the idea of artist as archivist. The body contains counter-archives or counter-narratives to the official narrative. [...] My question is: how can artists contribute to change by problematizing social and political memories? I'm interested in latent stories or invisible stories of Palestinian history that were never officially archived or deliberately obscured. I'm archiving the gestures of the actors of these stories using historical archives that were documented, personal testimonies, and imagination.[51]

Her words return us to my leitmotiv, namely that bodily performance, and particularly dance, does not only represent, but actually contributes to the process of accessing and creating knowledge about the past from a present standpoint. I have tried to trace how this extends to other contexts, from Palestine to the USA, from the memory of slavery to the Holocaust. I could cite other reflections by the dancers, such as Oxana Chi's argument that past and present times cannot be thought of as strictly separated.[52] For instance, the idea of the artist as archivist is inherent to Chi's entire repertoire, in her use of dance to perforMemory silenced narratives.

When I accompanied her perforMemory from Germany to the USA by way of Finland, Turkey, and India, in such various settings as a Jewish feminist conference in Belgrade, the Delhi International Queer Theatre and Film Festival, or the Black German Heritage and Research Association Conference's plenary session at the University of Toronto, I was humbled to hear the audience's gratitude. Many people expressed how deeply the contribution impacted them, for it enriched, supplemented, and at times contradicted conventional forms of knowledge transmission which they were familiar with. Upon Oxana's request, I often contextualized the performances before we slipped in the roles of performers. This juxtaposing of biographical storytelling and choreobiographic process marks most of her current repertoire. Oxana Chi's choreobiographic process works through an epistemology that relies both on the linear, chronological knowledge of history, and on the non-

---

51   Saleh and Bindler, Free Advice and an Interview with Farah Saleh.
52   Chi, Interview.

linear, performative spacetime of her own sense of a dancing being in contemporary Germany. Success, struggle and search (for inspiration or liberation) are sites of corporeal investigation in her research into dance historiography as well as in her negotiation of 21st century realities.

Another point of entry for understanding how dance bends hegemonic timelines is to reflect upon non-Western structures of time, as transmitted through embodied memory. Here, I am not only thinking about Black or Africanist knowledge systems. Earlier I suggested that *Through Gardens* rests on cyclic time – which may have to do with Chi's interest in and knowledge of Indian and South East Asian arts and cultures. I also find that the cyclic dramaturgy of *Through Gardens* bears affinities with the structure of the dance of Shiva. This dance is described in Capra's *Exploration of the Parallels between Modern Physics and Eastern Mysticism*:

> The Dance of Shiva symbolizes not only the cosmic cycles of creation and destruction, but also the daily rhythm of birth and death which is seen in Indian mysticism as the basis of all existence. At the same time, Shiva reminds us that the manifold forms in the world are maya – not fundamental, but illusory and ever-changing – as [s/]he keeps creating and dissolving them in the ceaseless flow of dance.[53]

Through the performative cycles of Tatjana Barbakoff's successes and struggles, and the framing of birth and death within a circular narrative pattern of dance, *Through Gardens* displays the "ceaseless flow of dance," and lets Tatjana Barbakoff (re-)appear and (dis-)appear. The dramaturgy flows, as do the movements, seamlessly connecting a rich source of techniques originating in various geographies and histories: Chinese Wu Shu, German expressionist dance (Ausdruckstanz), Javanese classical dance, Afro-European ballet… Here again, I am reminded of the wind element, of a breeze that carries this chapter on time. In a cycle, there is not necessarily a beginning or an end. This is why the scene of the New Moon – which by its very title evokes the lunar cycle – is so powerful: it infuses Barbakoff's death with an afterlife, a dramaturgic move seldom found in Holocaust representations.

Another insightful example of alternative spacetime is André M. Zachery's Afrofuturist perforMemory. In the work *Hidden Tracks* from the series *Untitled Distances*, the artist "looks at the African diaspora practice of the 'Ring Shout' as a spiritual time vessel – holding past, present, and future simultaneously in a single gesture."[54] In a way, the idea of a time vessel is always relevant to PerforMemory, a vessel challenging us to re-think how we relate to time, to space, and to their interrelation with the self. If we return to the above discussed *Digital Middle Passage*, I find it particularly striking to look at the dance through the lens of

---

53   Capra, *The Tao of Physics*, 242.
54   Zachery, "Untitled Distances."

Wright's scholarship on the *Physics of Blackness*, which offers a visual metaphor of spacetime. She writes:

> If the spacetime of the Middle Passage Epistemology can be represented by a line (or an arrow), then the postwar epistemology [...] should be represented as a circle with many arrows pointing outward in all directions. This nicely sums up the argument of Physics of Blackness: in any moment in which we are reading/analyzing Blackness, we should assume that its valences will likely vary from those of a previous moment. The circle denotes the "now" of the present moment, and the arrows represent all the spacetimes that intersect with that "now."[55]

A good vantage point from which to witness the constant transformation of Blackness is an audience seat at Zachery's RPG performances. Zachery kinesthetically renders what it means to disrupt the "Middle Passage Epistemology" and to let linear time implode to make space for new ways of thinking, living and performing African diasporic identities. The term "valence," used by Wright, originates in the realm of physics to describe the motion of electrons, but it is also used in psychology in relation to emotions. Zachery's dance opens up existential questions about the valences of Black perforMemory. It incites us to ask how Black bodies interact with the past, and with each other in the present, and how they find the physical and emotional power to move towards the future. Moreover, I find the metaphor of the line and the circle of utmost relevance to the work of RPG. In *Digital Middle Passage*, the dancer actually traces a line by traversing the middle space of the stage (starting from the right and ending to the left, from the audience's perspective), while also embracing circularity throughout the choreography. In the soloist body, I see an arrow flying high and low, out and back, to the circular motion of spacetime. Circular motion is the infinity of a journey in which the performer consistently reaches out to ancestral legacies and millennial fantasies, however irresistibly anchored in the performative *now*. And *now* is the reference point of what Wright calls "Epiphenomenal time,"[56] the present spacetime in which Blackness is situated. Wright derives her theorization of Epiphenomenal time from an ingenuous interweaving of literary criticism, phenomenological philosophy, quantum physics and diasporic critique centered on Black memory.

What is most appealing about Wright's inclusion of Epiphenomenal time is her emphasis on the *agency* of a contemporary subject, whose existence is determined by the interrelation of the multiple dimensions of Black identity. Wright does not reject linear time conceptions, rather she argues for a combination of chronological linearity – which acknowledges a traumatic history – and Epiphenomenal time – which allows for complex, colliding and colluding definitions of subjectivity –

55   Wright, *Physics of Blackness*, 20.
56   Wright, *Physics of Blackness*.

to be able to define, or understand ontologies of Blackness. Her work focuses on literary examples. On her fascinating theoretical odyssey into Blackness, she does not visit the performing arts world. Yet, I find that Epiphenomenal time may be clearly understood through stage performance, in the dancing bodies' execution of movements in the time and space of now. I argue that performance, and more specifically dance, are primordial sites of realization for Epiphenomenal time, and that the dancescapes of perforMemory can shape our understanding of the various textures of temporality, such as those I presented earlier. The multiple "strands"[57] of perforMemory's time are not only a metaphor for identity, they also speak to a material breadth of dance styles and movements. Not only is Wright's theory particularly attuned to Zachery's work, it is also relevant to other works: I see in the immediate time of *Parole, Parole, Parole* a salient example of Epiphenomenal time, and I sense in the swirling time of *Impressions* the circle pointing in many directions. Therefore the validity of her theory, as the validity of perforMemory can be extended to other realms of identity outside of the scope of Black diaspora. PerforMemory *right here and right now* is less ephemeral than it is Epiphenomenal.

Intensity as the spacetime of perforMemory

If we connect the reflections on space and the dancing body as a home from the previous chapter to the timescapes of perforMemory imagined in this chapter, we can apprehend dance as the practice of moving *beyond* ideas of past, present and future, or what Ella Shohat calls a "teleological" world conception that "segregates" temporality and spatiality.[58] PerforMemory can combine both linear and Epiphenomenal time. The dancers do refer to historical events, traumata and facts such as the Holocaust and the Maafa or Transatlantic Slave Trade. Yet, they associate these referential markers to a self-referentiality embedded in their performing body.

These reflections on time lead me to propose intensity as the epistemological and ontological framework of spacetime in the context of perforMemory. In this changing spacetime atmosphere, intensity seems to be the constant that holds the dance of quantic memory together. If the dancing body is a home, intensity is the wind that breezes through its spatiotemporal, emotional, kinesthetic windows. Intensity is a key feature of live performance. In times of pandemic, the absence of live performances, and the attempt to fill the gap with virtual events (ironically called 'live' on Facebook and Instagram!) have reminded us that when dancers move on the screen rather than on the stage, what is most at risk to fade away is the intensity of the performance experience.

---

57   Wright, 83.
58   Shohat, *Taboo Memories, Diasporic Voices*, 15.

As we have seen, some physicists describe the motion of spacetime as a dance. The earlier mentioned "dancing foam"[59] in Carlo Rovelli's scientific writing suggests that time and space do not exist independently from one another, or as abstract entities or measure units. This is why Rovelli and other scientists like to say or write that there is actually no such thing as time, or the passing of time as Western theory and socialization teaches it.

> At the extremely small scale of the quanta of space, the dance of nature does not develop to the rhythm kept by the baton of a single orchestral conductor: every process dances independently with its neighbors, following its own rhythms. The passing of time is intrinsic to the world; it is born of the world itself, out of the relations between quantum events that are the world and that themselves generate their own time.[60]

While Rovelli speaks of dance, Frank Capra also describes the dance of the matter as a cosmic dance and takes the example of Shiva's dance:

> Different particles develop different patterns in their dance, requiring different amounts of energy, and hence have different masses. [...] Thus, not only matter, but also the void, participates in the cosmic dance, creating and destroying energy patterns without end. For the modern physicists then, Shiva's dance is the dance of subatomic matter.[61]

So it is all dance! Does this suggest that our environment is *per se* the ephemeral, an ever-renewing interaction of particles of microscopic spacetime? Or that ephemerality does not really exist, and therefore it is absurd to call the art of dance ephemeral? Refuting the ephemerality of dance is important to make the case for performance's capacity to tell history, and to acknowledge the role of the (moving) body in the production and transmission of cultural memory. Beyond the metaphoric eye blink and the poetic imagery of dance, I find a deeper connection between the movement of spacetime and dance. In my interpretation of multidimensional temporality emerging out of seven soli, intensity, rather than ephemerality, is the core. As suggested above, I read in the works of the seven dancers various manifestations of non-linear time. I sense the motion of time in cycles, waves, pulses, ripples. I see instantaneous, fugitive, suspended time. These motions do not travel along a past-present-future continuum. Through performance, the dancers contemporize the past.

To perforMemory amounts to producing memory2go, a memory-as-you-go, intimately and intensely bound to the moving body. In the interaction of muscles,

---

59   Rovelli, *Reality Is Not What It Seems*, 192.
60   Rovelli, 178.
61   Capra, *The Tao of Physics*, 245.

time, and space, the dancers generate their own spacetime of intensity in which cultural memory can become visible and experienced. These spacetimes are what Dipesh Chakrabarty would call a time knot. Referring to the vocabulary of time in his first language (Bengali), he offers a compelling imagery of linear time as straightened time knots:

> Time, as the expression goes in my language, situates us within the structure of a granthi; hence the bengali word shomoy-granthi, shomoy meaning "time" and granthi referring to joints of various kinds, from the complex formation of knuckles on our fingers to the joints on a bamboo stick.[62]

In perforMemory, the *shomoy-granthi* or time joints physically connect kinesthetics and history. When memory is located and performed within the body and its movement, perforMemory moves at the physical junction between time knots and body articulations. Therefore, new concepts of spacetimes become possible, in the very spacetime of dance performance.

Because the body is political, connecting corporeal presence to the contemporaneous agency of the moving subject is inherently a political move. By anchoring memory to the body, perforMemory strongly politicizes memory. When the bodies moving and the stories they are telling stem from diasporic perspectives and processes, dance can become a mode of resistance countering hegemonic historiography. Dancing the past in the present tense not only allows for the "politicization of memory,"[63] it is a fundamental way to achieve it. PerforMemory thus counters erasure of the bodies and their stories, as the dancing bodies leave a swift trace, visual yet invisible, temporary yet unalterable. Dance as resistance operates from the resilience of intensity, and accomplishes an epistemic transformation of our cognition of time and space, actually renewing cognition itself by creating performative timescapes, and performance as a spacetime of intensity. As noted earlier, intensity bears affinity with intensification. Repetition as intensification transforms the repetition of a movement into the intensity of an emotion, an intentional and intensive knowledge transmission. This can be seen in Oxana Chi's use of modulation of pace in spinning and fighting (back), Zufit Simon's and Chantal Loïal's shuddering, Farah Saleh's alteration of daily gestures and intimacy, André M. Zachery's repetitive spiraling and diving, Wan-Chao Chang's searching and twisting. In the second part of this chapter, I will now engage with the material and metaphorical physicality of perforMemory. If dancing the past in the present tense is intense, it has much to do with the physical movements that belong to the dance repertoire of perforMemory.

---

62   Chakrabarty, *Provincializing Europe*, 112.
63   hooks, "Choosing the Margin as a Space of Radical Openness," 155.

The Moves of PerforMemory: Shaping the Dancescapes

After my diasporic journey through the USA, Martinique, and Taiwan, I returned to Berlin, Germany, to complete my doctoral program. In the spring of 2016, while working on my manuscript, I also designed and taught the award-winning seminar "Performing Memory: race, gender and diaspora in cultural discourses and practices" at Humboldt-University. The students fed a copious blog on Tumblr with their written and audiovisual contributions on the topics of memory.[64] Meanwhile, digital social media kept me connected to the distant New York City's dancescapes. They gave me a regular glimpse, albeit on screen, into the work of the dancers. In that spacetime, away from New York, I began to appreciate Instagram. I had started to use it in 2015 for a professional development training at the New York Foundation for the Arts (NYFA), undertaken on behalf of Oxana Chi's dance company. Browsing Instagram felt like stepping onto a platform where "diasporic spidering"[65] came to life. Some pictures performed the memory of the dance world I was starting to miss, both as a protagonist and as a spectator. One day, I paused on a post by Candace Thompson, founder of the Dance Caribbean Collective (DCC). The photo of her solo *Of Circles and Bright Colors* transported me back to the live experience of the performance, in the summer of 2015, during the first edition of the DCC Festival *New Traditions*. I was pulled into the flow of smooth movement calibrating a graceful alignment, into a whirlwind of colorful energy. The Instagram post caption read:

> Floating. Dance can be so much about creative illusions but we have a real ability to shift energy, harness power and realize new collective existences. How will you use that gift today?[66]

To perforMemory is to "use the gift." Dancers who are choreographers do not merely execute a set of movements imagined by someone else. They interpret movements which they have carefully selected themselves, through conceptual processes, and/or through creation and improvisation in the recurrent rehearsal spacetime. They present their self-in-presence to the audience, performing movements with the intent of expressing an aesthetic creation, a political message, an emotional evolution. Foremost, they are acutely aware of the interrelation between physical performance, societal environment and social transformation. Thompson's words carry the belief that dance should not merely be seen as a space of representation, but also as a spacetime of action. When dealing with historical

---

64   "Performing Memory."
65   George-Graves, "Diasporic Spidering."
66   Thompson, "Of Circles and Bright Colors."

trauma, dancers can "shift energy" in order to address and transmit cultural memory without inducing the re-traumatizing of themselves or the audience.[67]

These seven works of perforMemory demonstrate the ability to "harness power" through dance. They combine a search for aesthetic quality with a critical inquiry into sociopolitical concerns. Topics of women's history, diasporic migration, coloniality, survival, healing, social change, and personal transformation build a repertoire of perforMemory. Ananya Chatterjea's understanding of dance is helpful to reflect on the ways that perforMemories can intervene into power structures of memory-making:

> Dance images [...] despite their impermanence, have energy and the power of liveness, spirit, and the fiery passion of their creators' politics. They shore up in other but vital ways the project of decolonization, creating aesthetic frameworks that are permeated with an interventionary politics, working not solely in reaction to hegemonic structures, but generating beauty and power that, while creating specific kinds of pleasure and value, resists reinscription into reigning dominant constitutions.[68]

The idea of dance as intervention described above is key to all these solos, which embody the duality of beauty and power without subscribing to mainstream definitions of them.[69] Their empowering figures, stories and forces live within the moving presence of the performer. Beyond the visuality of dance, I would now like to ground the interpretation of dancing bodies in their materiality.[70] Here I rejoin a conception of critical dance studies, defined by Jacqueline Shea-Murphy as "a dance studies model, with it attention to corporeality and the energies and agencies engaged by bodies moving, within particular frames and contexts, in time and space."[71] In her emphasis on the body's agency in dance, I also see a meeting point between gender and performance studies.

I will now focus on three sets of corporeal practices that performers use to move through the dancescapes of memory: turning, jumping and crossing. This choice is largely inspired by my analysis of *Through Gardens* as a thread of inquiry throughout the research. Interestingly, when Oxana Chi dynamically embodies the successes of Tatjana Barbakoff, she engages in all three, turning, jumping and crossing, sometimes simultaneously. I obviously do not mean to say that these are the only movements of perforMemory, neither in *Through Gardens* nor elsewhere, given the diverse

---

67   Hirsch, *The Generation of Postmemory*, 161. See discussion of this in my chapter "Memory Dancescapes."

68   Chatterjea, *Butting Out*, 135.

69   Although André M. Zachery claims that he is not interested in the beauty of movement. See Zachery, Interview.

70   On this, see also Martin, *Critical Moves*.

71   Shea Murphy, *The People Have Never Stopped Dancing*, 8.

array of forms performed by the dancers. Rather, I propose to concentrate on three forms which I find to be particularly meaningful in the conceptual connections they make possible. In these various and complex manifestations of turning, jumping and crossing, I find that the physical movements generate knowledge about their makers' relation to the production and transmission of cultural memory. In contrast with the last section on temporality, here I do not move successively from one solo to the next. Instead I structure the exploration around the spatiality of the movements, which I put in relation to relevant examples from the performances. The questions spurring my reflection are:

What are the movements of perforMemory? Which corporeal tools do the dancers use? How do they physically and metaphorically intervene into memory-making discourses and practices?

Turning

Spinning selves

In a frenzied, festive atmosphere, Oxana Chi *perforMemorializes* a whole-bodied celebration of Tatjana Barbakoff, where turning plays a structuring role, which I find emblematic of perforMemory's corporeality. Spinning on her own axis, the dancer nimbly executes turns. Some of them are drawn from ballet, such as the pirouettes en retiré – meaning that a thigh is withdrawn high in *second position*. On the blog "Ballet Bag," which provides an insight into ballet techniques, the *pirouette* spin is described as follows:

> A complete turn of the body on one foot. The supporting foot can be either on pointe or demi-pointe, with the working leg positioned sur le cou-de-pied, in arabesque, à la seconde, in attitude, etc. Legs give the impulse from a deep plié in preparatory position, arms control the turning speed and the head is the last part of the body to turn away from an imaginary "spotting" point and the first to hit the point again once the body completes the turn.[72]

This suggests the complexity of a spinning technique usually performed by (cis-)men, according to blog founders Emilia Spitz and Linda Uruchurtu. Hence, Chi's performance also destabilizes the gender roles associated with this *pirouette*. Sometimes she spins on her own axis while reaching from one corner of the stage to the other, as if propelled by an energizing force that allows her to move in spins, rather than progressing in a straight linear fashion. Often, she breaks conventions by softening the rigidity of ballet lines, thus "giving ballet a fresh spin," as goes the motto of the above cited blog.

---

72   Spitz and Uruchurtu, "Bag of Steps: Turns."

The dancer sometimes uses, as a starting or ending point of the spin, a figure reminiscent of the ballet pose known as *attitude*. Sometimes her body wraps itself in the turn, as if embracing itself. In this position, the dancer stands on one leg, her foot flat à terre, the other leg lifted back with the knee bent. One arm on the side of the lifted leg is curved over the head, the other arm is extended to the side. According to the educational glossary of the American Ballet Theatre, the attitude was originally derived from a 16th century bronze statue representing a dynamic, flying, Mercury with wings on its feet.[73] The Mercury deity stands for gatekeeping between the worlds, and is known to be a patron of the arts, success, and commerce. Therefore it is interesting that Chi reframes the ballet attitude in her choreobiography of Tatjana Barbakoff, and uses a figure connected to success to express and celebrate the historical dancer's achievements. The performative turns and spins of Oxana-Tatjana chart a whirlwind of emotions, rendering what this stage of her life may have felt like. As mentioned earlier, Barbakoff gained increasing recognition as a dance-maker in the 1920s and 1930s. She performed at the Schauspielhaus Düsseldorf theater in 1921, and soon started dancing in other prestigious venues across Europe, including opera theaters and city halls. After her show on October 26th, 1924 at the Königsberg City Hall, the newspaper Ostpreußische Zeitung reported as follows:

> Deepest internalizing in sharpest cultural state is what we found in Tatjana Barbakoff. Spirit and energy at the peak of their possibilities. What is ravishing in Tatjana Barbakoff's dance, is her being's release, the peaceful abstraction from the world of demands and laws that accost us from afar. One stands as hypnotized under the irresistible influence of this dancer.
>
> (Tiefste Verinnerlichung in schärfster Kulturfassung fanden wir bei Tatjana Barbakoff. Geist und Energie auf dem Gipfel ihrer Möglichkeiten. Was an Tatjana Barbakoff entzückt, das ist das Erlöste ihres Daseins, die selige Entrücktheit über die Welt der fremd an uns herantretenden Forderungen und Gesetze. Wie hypnotisiert steht man unter dem unwiderstehlichen Einfluss dieser Tänzerin.)[74]

The journalist emphasizes the energetic realm surrounding Barbakoff's expressionist dance, a quality I also found in Chi's piece *Through Gardens*. The contemporary dancer also emits an hypnotic energy, especially in the circular dynamic of the Celebration scene. Without representing specific times and places, or other markers of memory related to the 20th century, the choreography suggests how Tatjana Barbakoff became an influential dancer, and a source of inspiration for many well-known artists. The sequence seems itself like a painting set into motion, a warm feast for the senses in the tones of red, green and yellow.

---

73   "Attitude."
74   Cited in Goebbels, *Tatjana Barbakoff*, 13. [My translation]

The dancer also uses half-turns to re-turn her body frontally towards the audience, which could be interpreted as a connection between reaching back into the past and looking forward, or what metaphorically lies ahead. Here one may also think of the Sankofa, the Akan symbol of a bird looking back to draw the knowledge necessary to move forward. The spinning movement of perforMemory is also the starting point for a narrative turn away from hegemonic discourses on the Holocaust. This highly dynamic scene of *Through Gardens* embodies the movement of turning as an act of life, of overcoming obstacles, of advancing towards a goal. In this sense it inscribes a precious step in the choreobiography of Barbakoff. Interestingly, Oxana Chi uses diverse forms of turns throughout her current repertoire. In the piece *Neferet iti* (briefly addressed in the last chapter), Chi ends the piece with several minutes of continuous spinning, reminiscent of dervish rituals. Here, turning feels meditative and healing. It concludes the performative quest for the pharaoh's roots and routes. The turn bears the texture of a wave flowing across the timescapes of memory, disrupting the coloniality of hegemonic spacetimes.

My reading of spinning can also be applied to André M. Zachery's *Digital Middle Passage*. Turns are omnipresent in Zachery's corporeal language. When he spins and turns on stage, he collapses the conventions of Middle Passage narratives, bridges their fallacies, and amplifies their scopes and dimensionality. He grounds his work in the knowledge of Afrodiasporic history, yet deconstructs what has been written about it, and reconstructs it as cathartic experience only bound to the body moving live on stage. Spinning may be a tool of empowerment, an energy that carries the body across past, present and future. Sometimes, Zachery spins in a capoeira-like fashion, a wave seems to go through his torso as he spirals repeatedly on his own axis, in a very flexible use of the back and hips. Other times the spinning goes with a sinking to or rising from the floor, and unearths the vertical dynamic of his turns. At one point, Zachery starts on his knees and turns on his own axis as he gets up with arms reaching towards the ceiling. This brief moment of rapid turn, entailing a hint of ballet or so called "modern" dance technique, however, resolves immediately in Africanist aesthetics. The body collapses on a flexible spine, the knees and upper body are closer to the floor, as if bending under a heavy load, or leaning over a barrel. The turn also marks an interruption in the slow motion pace preceding and following it. At times the dancer rotates in both directions within a luminous circle, a moon-like image projected onto the floor center stage. His hand affixed to the ground is the axis on which he pivots, as if his body was the arrow of a time traveling clock. In both *Through Gardens* and *Digital Middle Passage*, perforMemory is embedded in a spiraling motion, whether it is momentous for Oxana Chi, or recurrent for André Zachery. Turning here stands for the idea of intensity as a performative spacetime.

Circling memory

Circularity is also a strong motif in Christiane Emmanuel's *Choc(s)*. The circle inhabits her whole repertoire, for she often draws from the Martinican "traditional" dance named bèlè, which is structured as a circle, as she explains in her interview (see next chapter). In relation to *Choc(s)*, she also emphasizes the circle:

> And [in] this piece we are actually in a dynamic of 'going around in circles,' I run always in the same position, always facing forward, never facing back, I reroute, I return myself, I turn around to run, still forward, in the opposite direction, but it is always a race going in circles. So I ask: am I bored, am I going around in circles, am I searching for something else? It all depends on the audience and how they understand it.
>
> (Et dans la pièce justement nous sommes dans une dynamique de tourner en rond, je cours toujours dans le même sens toujours face et jamais de dos, je détourne, je me détourne, je me retourne pour courir face dans l'autre sens, mais c'est toujours une course en rond. La question que je pose: est-ce que je m'ennuie, est-ce que je tourne en rond, est-ce que je cherche quelques chose ? Tout dépendra du public, comment il recevra la chose.)[75]

The race in circles varies in pace and intensity. At first, Emmanuel is running around the piles of shirts stacked center stage in a circular shape resembling a volcanic crater. Her race circles us me back to Amra's metaphor according to which "We are on a volcano and we are a volcano."[76] The dancer blurs borders, she is racing on the volcanic island of Martinique, while performing herself in a magmatic flow. At times she seems lost, conveying a feeling of disorientation that recollects Sara Ahmed's phenomenological definition: a feeling that "shatter[s] one's sense of confidence in the ground or one's belief that the ground on which we reside can support the actions that make a life feel liveable."[77] The actions at stake here are the efforts necessary to come to terms with the colonial legacy that pervades and poisons the island's socioeconomic structures up to the present. Emmanuel explains that she choreographed the piece in the context of the political uprisings of 2011, when people protested on the streets against the economic-social-racial inequalities.[78] To fully understand her dancing race, one also needs to know that street demonstrations in Martinique, such as the carnival-bound street marches and dances, which sometimes follow a circular itinerary, often entail running. As I experienced it, not the slow marching, but the actual racing up and down the hilly landscapes of the city's capital binds its participants together, in a synergetic

---

75   Emmanuel, Interview. [My translation]
76   Amra, *Le Souffle Du Pays. Nabd El Jayzirah*, 13. [My translation]
77   Ahmed, *Queer Phenomenology*, 157.
78   Emmanuel, Interview.

dynamic of autonomy and liberation. In light of my earlier description of the *fugitive time* at work in her solo *Choc(s)*, the run also carries the legacy of the imagery of slaves running away from the plantation. This is particularly visible when the dancer runs vigorously, progressing in large strides across the stage, occasionally turning around as she faces invisible obstacles that prevent her from running further.

It is also interesting to note how Emmanuel's choreography echoes patterns found in Caribbean visual arts. Here I think for instance of the strategies of "erring, opacity, circumvention, diversion, regeneration, provocation, metaphor-mosis"[79] described by Emmanuelle Bermude in her analysis of Martinican visual artist Patricia Donatien-Yssa. Dancer Christiane Emmanuel impersonates those processes on stage.[80] Her performance works through these strategies of resisting the coloniality of capitalism in a negotiation of the curvilinear element. The dancer runs in circles, meaning that her race has neither a beginning nor an end. The circle is a leitmotiv in Africanist performance traditions, explains for instance Nadine George-Graves:

> In these traditions, dancers stand in a circle to symbolize the communal experience. With no front or back or head or rear, the circle is inherently non-hierarchical. Everyone can see and be seen. It also creates a sacred liminal space in which transformations can occur. When one or two people step into the center of the circle she/he/they take on the energy from the others. They shine as individuals by stepping out of the group while remaining a part of it, supported by it. Often when a semicircle or arch is presented on stage, it is to include the audience as the completion of the circle.[81]

In my research, the performers are alone on stage, yet they still rely on the circle's multiplicity. And Christiane Emmanuel indeed experiences transformation within the circle. When she digs into what seems like a pile of white shirts, she unearths colorful pieces of clothes that she puts on successively on top of one another. The result is an expressionist tableau, an unusual collage on her own body. Her new costume mixes up a Western "male" suit with the popular and colorful aesthetics of the female market workers. The costume transformation induces a movement transformation: now Christiane Emmanuel sways the hips, and tentatively switches to the register of Caribbean traditional dances. The circle, place of clothing mutation, becomes the space of a corporeal metamorphosis.

---

79   "errance, opacité, contournement, détournement, régénération, provocation, métar-mophose," Yung-Hing, *Art Contemporain de La Caraïbe*, 175. [My translation]
80   See Emmanuel, Interview for the discussion of choreographying the painting "La Jungle" by Wifredo Lam.
81   George-Graves, *Urban Bush Women*, 142.

Curvilinearity is also one of the main features of Kariamu Welsh-Asante's theorization of Africanist dance. In the words of Asante, "[t]here is power in the circle, the curve, the round, supernatural power if you will."[82] The rotation described earlier, in *Through Gardens* and *Digital Middle Passage*, is a vessel of energy. In addition to rotating on themselves, the choreographers also make use of the circle. The movements are set at specific moments of the choreography, suggesting a sense of dynamism, power, progression. Circling and circulating energy, Oxana Chi for instance traces half-moon crescents with her arms. Within her *cyclic time* dramaturgy, some scenes form a circle within the circle. Often times, Chi also runs in circles, but also backwards, and her circular race is not disorientated at all, on the contrary, it is a clear, decisive progression (although sometimes backwards) through the stages of Tatjana Barbakoff's achievements. The circle is materialized solely by her movements, thus when she dances a full circle, she creates an abstract open space where her imagination and the fantasy of the audience can meet. André M. Zachery also performs curvilinearity. His circle too is one of power, even more so when he dances within a round moonlight projection spotlight. The circle is truly ritual here, even if, in the Digital Age, the ritual is performed by a lone dancer remote from the group. Maybe the group is present-absent, in the invisible spirits surrounding the dancer. Chantal Loïal also associates rotation and celebration. She concludes the scene representing the posthumous return of Sawtche's spirit to South Africa with a double circle: she sweeps through the stage spinning on her own axis, tracing circles with her hands and pelvis in the air, as well as marking a curvilinear trajectory. When she reaches the point at which she started the circle, she disrupts the circularity at the sudden appearance of the skull prop. This makes clear that the circle stood for positivity. The dancer embodies the quantic dance of memory, a joyful choreobiography in which not only the body's skeletal remains return to the homeland, but also a lively body returns to its self, a black woman body-home moving live on stage.

Celebratory atmospheres can be channelled through movements, and theatricality of dance works well without words. The circle shape disrupts and smoothes the edges of the conventional rectangularity of concert stages. Scenographic and choreographic circles transform the spaces into imagined locations. It is through the power of imagination that we see the circle that they trace as they spin and loop around. This connects to circling as an epistemological tool: dancers can approach and reach memory through circularity and curvilinearity. To rotate the self on its own axis, or around the stage, is a vital movement of perforMemory. Through rotating torsos and rotating shapes, the performers imagine and materially inscribe curvilinearity into the spacetime of the stage. The circular quality of the performa-

---

82   Welsh Asante, "Commonalities in African Dance," 146.

tive "now" or Epiphenomenal time discussed earlier in reference to Wright[83] is a three-dimensional reality in these works of perforMemory. Performative turns let memory become a shifting, malleable, transportable memory2go.

Jumping

Jumping requires power. The power to contract and release specific muscles. Jumping also enacts power, when a jumping body conveys force and liberation. When Chantal Loïal represents the confined Sawtche, the jump is a movement through which the body frees itself from bondage – maybe symbolized by the tight use of her head wrap to bind her chest. Here the jump is less a matter of reaching a spectacular height, as in classical ballet, but rather a search for a connection to the ground, in the spirit of Africanist dance techniques. It is a stomping-jumping, when the feet successively hit the ground and march on the spot, as torso and head drop and rise with increasing power and speed. This figure requires a precise synchronicity of all body parts. The dancer also makes a festive use of the jump. Still in the celebratory spirit mentioned above, she performs various types of jumps in the sequence depicting the restitution of France to South Africa, or the return of Venus to Sawtche. Loïal's dance reflects training in both West and Central African styles, with the jumps originating in West African techniques, in which the body lengthens through the arms and legs. Sometimes she aligns one jump after the other, deploying a variety of jumps that all serve the theatricality of joyfulness and celebration.

Jumping is also festive in Oxana Chi's Celebration sequence discussed earlier in relation to spinning. A complex jump consists of the dancer jumping backwards, throwing the waist back and simultaneously reaching forward with the hands, all of this without interrupting the flow of the circular choreography. Here the jumps are integrated into the curvilinear trajectory. The constant changeover between spinning and jumping creates a very dynamic and intense atmosphere. Chi also deploys an Africanist jump inspired by the imagery of a Senegalese bird, in which the body reaches out through all its extremities. Chi actually uses jump techniques throughout her current repertoire. In *Neferet iti*, in *I Step On Air*, and most recently in *Psyche*, she undertakes jumps at key moments of the performance, often inducing empowerment. Jumping across the stage, Chi's moves consciously break down rigid linear narratives and build up new possibilities of relating to history. She may also be jumping over the obstacles of traumatic memory, bridging silenced narratives to inspire a transformative spirit, spurring on political awareness and stimulating social healing. For both Loïal and Chi, the jumps enact the willpower, strength and

---

83   Wright, *Physics of Blackness*.

determination of the protagonist to be in charge of her own story and body, and of the body as a story.

Jumping is intensity. It is a movement of perforMemory in the sense that it epitomizes the body's capacity to be present, and the idea of present as a constant tension (and release) of the body. When Zufit Simon jumps in *all about nothing*, she makes use of a very strong core, and channels the energy from the torso upwards in a rushing movement of rising. Jumping is a repetitive figure here too, sometimes occupying only a brief spacetime. Sequences of jumps are repeated, with arm variations, the arms sometimes reaching back, sometimes extended to the ceiling. Simon uses quick, intense jumps to move forward, for instance when she is on the floor, her upper body leaning backwards, supported by the hands and legs raised forward above the ground. Sometimes she hops in a *pas-de-chat* like fashion, traversing the stage like a joyous being animated with youthful energy. Or she jumps laterally, bending the elbows and knees simultaneously, or she jumps and releases by catching an imaginary force in the air. She can also jump and throw her bent legs backwards. All of these jumps stem from a personal impulse, and her choreography conveys the impression of spontaneity, of the transitory nature of emotions. Here, jumping queers one's relation to body and self.

Jumping defies gravity. In jumping, dancers (en)counter gravity, and spend a brief spacetime at the edge of its range. The jumps in *Digital Middle Passage* turn the stage into a place of departure and return. Rather than returning to Africa to search for traces of history (as Saidiya Hartman does in the novel *Lose your Mother*[84]), the dancer departs and returns to the dance floor, the soil, at his own pace and within the performative spacetime. A poetic summary of gravity is offered in a TEDx talk by scientist Kelly Holley-Bockelmann:

> And so what gravity is at its core, is just the response of moving matter to all those dimples in the universe. [...] We are in spacetime. If a gravitational wave passes by, we are going along with it, we are waving too, because we are a part of the universe.[85]

As André Zachery jumps up and down, tuning his body to the sound and gravitational waves of the space, he seems to rebound on the dimples of spacetime. Physics are inherent to his physicality. His own technique of Physical Propulsion, as he calls it, was devised out of his proficiency in the Flying-Low technique codified by David Zambrano, which uses spiraling as the base for jumping:

> The class utilizes simple movement patterns that involve breathing, speed and the release of energy throughout the body in order to activate the relationship

---

84   Hartman, *Lose Your Mother*.
85   Holley-Bockelmann, "TEDx Talk: The Spacetime Symphony of Gravitational Waves." For a literary perspective on gravity in dance, see Brandstetter, "Dis/Balances. Dance and Theory."

between the center and the joints, moving in and out of the ground more effi-
ciently by maintaining a centered state. There is a focus on the skeletal structure
that will help improve the dancers' physical perception and alertness.[86]

In his class description, Zambrano further mentions the physical principles of co-
hesion and expansion, which can clearly be seen in Zachery's coherent core and
expanding energy. His relationship to the floor is intensely mobile. Jumping, or
propelling himself to and from the floor, he enacts power, performing the ability
of dancers to "harness" power as evoked in the earlier cited Instagram post by his
wife Candace Thompson-Zachery. She, like Zambrano, speaks of shifting energies,
and this is precisely what is at stake in Zachery's jumping tools. Zachery departs
from Zambrano's Flying-Low, to fly high and low. In his classes descriptions, he describes the process as "intelligent shifts in body weight" along the "transverse plane
of the Z axis." The personal appropriation of the technique devised by a contemporary dancer on his own post-traumatic body becomes a means of impersonating
the movements of post-slavery Blackness.

What does Zachery's use of a flying technique express about the perforMemory
of chattel slavery? *Digital Middle Passage*, and more specifically the jumps, may be
interpreted in light of the tale of the Flying Africans. Prevalent in African-American
popular culture, the tale describes how enslaved Africans used metaphysical powers to fly back to Africa. Depending on the context, the flight has sometimes been
interpreted as a metaphor, in which the slaves' spirits fly back, be it through physical death, or through a metaphysical, spiritual, extraordinary reality. Considering
this ambiguous relationship to death and liberation, Soyica Diggs Colbert defines
the flight as a paradigmatic black movement. In her essay on the myth of "Flying
Africans," she

> considers the depictions of Flying Africans as black performances and more partic-
> ularly black movements, paying particular attention to the way the depictions of
> flight enact a performance and imply other meanings of movement, including po-
> litical and geographical. [...] Although the implications shift over time and across
> geographic locations, the negotiations with the freedom drive and the death drive
> persist in depictions of Flying Africans.[87]

In order to examine how the tale of Flying Africans affects and reflects Black culture, the author analyzes literary and oral works, such as Toni Morrison's *Song of
Solomon* and music by Kanye West and the Parliament Funkadelic. Her brilliant essay printed in the anthology *Black Performance Theory* does not however look at dance
productions. *The Digital Middle Passage* dance is paradigmatic of the performance of

---

86   Zambrano, "Flying-Low - Dance Technique."
87   Diggs Colbert, "Black Movements," 130. See also Commander, *Afro-Atlantic Flight*.

"flight" as Black diasporic mobility, as a tool to attain physical and psychic liberation, and beyond. The audience experiences spacetime through a jumping body, re-framed in the context of a performative engagement with the memory of the Middle Passage. Here there is no slave ship, no space ship, only the body as a vessel of memory. When Zachery jumps and flies high and low, he physically enacts the possibility for the body to defy laws of geophysical and geopolitical gravity. Thus, I interpret his dancing jump-flight not merely as a Black movement, but as a paradigmatic movement of perforMemory. His jumps, like those of Chantal Loïal and Oxana Chi, draw energy from ancestral grounds, and float above any attempt to reduce and narrow one's identity.

The role of jumping in these works makes me wonder if there is a Black diasporic jumping cultural motif that stands for celebration and liberation across time and space. Upon reading my analysis of jumping, dance expert Judy Pritchett (Frankie Manning Foundation) brought to my attention the work of Gena Caponi-Tabery, who explored the role of jumping in 1930s African-American culture.[88] This incited me to wonder if parallels could be traced between Afro-European Oxana Chi's use of jumps (albeit based in ballet techniques) to chorebiograph the successes of Tatjana Barbakoff (in a context of hostility against Jews in 1920s and 30s Europe), and the flourishing jump element in 1930s Black culture in the USA? Looking at "jumping" jazz, athletics and basketball, Caponi-Tabery writes that in the 1930s, African-Americans "transformed the jump, a historical gesture of celebration and defiance, into a cultural exclamation point."[89] To me, this also rings true for André Zachery's contemporary (meta)physical search for elevation in the 21st century. Also, as the author notes, the relation between jumping and African-American culture does not begin in the 1930s, as it can be found, for instance, in ringshout dance worship of the 19th century.[90] In any case, the dances of perforMemory, and particularly the Black diasporic ones, travel across multiverses of cultural practices to rejoin Caponi-Tabery's argument, namely that reaching up through the air in public can correspond with (aspiring to) accessing social and political elevation.[91] In other words, in jumping lies the possibility of emancipation from laws that are meant to put one down. If we take her argument a step higher, we can even propose that jumping in the intense spacetime of concert dance demarcates bodies not only from material ground and sociopolitical constraints, but also signifies reaching for a realm beyond conventions of calendar time and geographical space.

The performances addressed here testify to the body's capacity to become not only a tool of representation but an actual site of subversion, to challenge dominant

---

88   Caponi-Tabery, *Jumping for Joy*.
89   Caponi-Tabery, 144.
90   Caponi-Tabery, 154.
91   Caponi-Tabery, xv.

sociopolitical relations and mainstream configurations. Through my participation in dance and movement classes, be it Afro-Haitian or Kukuwa styles, kung fu or capoeira, I learned to sense through my own body the intense training required in order to become proficient in certain forms of corporeality. Yesterday for instance, in synchronicity with my writing on jumping, the Kukuwa[92] class involved a lot of jumping. The dynamic cycle helped me release the tension accumulated over several hours of computer-writing. I reveled in the jumps, trying to improve my movement quality. I simultaneously strove to improve the verticality of the jump – thus involving more energy from the lower body and abdominals – and its materiality, to make it look and feel as "light" as possible – requiring a flexible engagement of the knees and other joints. In the brief spacetime I spent in the air, seeing my flying self in the mirror, time and space felt so intense that it was not relevant whether I jumped high, or long. In jumping, I always sense and enact a complex relation to gravity, a spacetime of intensity, and a form of power.

In jumping, or moving oneself, the self may connect to a deeply located intelligence generated within the body. This recognition is fundamental to understanding how the body can be not only the conduit, but also the source of sociopolitical intervention, as argued by choreographer-scholar Ananya Chatterjea:

> I want to insist on perceiving the body as intelligent and multivalent, which subverts the traditional distrust of the body in much of European or Western discourse. I also want to assert the body's proactive role in political and cultural commentary, locate intellect within the body, and recognize how the articulations of the intelligent body are chiseled through the fine and intense training modes used by these choreographers.[93]

Power, intensity and gravity are main protagonists in the production of perforMemory. In the context of hegemonic ascriptions of bodies to racial and gendered categories, and the consequent negation of their power, jumping encompasses the body into agency. It places diasporic subjectivities in different relations to time and space. This perforMemory indicates how performers use kinesthetics as a refined medium to embody and express social critique and to imagine and enact other realities or ways of moving through it. Jumping is a liberating movement of perforMemory. It liberates the body from the constraints of spacetime as traditionally defined within Western sciences. It liberates the dancing body from hegemonic narrations. Moving to and fro from one story to

---

92 Kukuwa is a movement class developed by a Ghanaian dancer, Ellen Kukuwa, now taught and trademarked in the fashion of techniques such as Pilates and Limon. Her daughter Cassandra Nuamah teaches it in New York City: a lively variation of movement sequences, combining traditional and contemporary dances from all over the African continent. See the website Kukuwa, "Kukuwa."

93 Chatterjea, *Butting Out*, 25.

another, hopping back and forth from present self to past selves, dance jumps bridge abyssal gaps of absence in Western historiography, digging out millennial possibilities, realities and energies.

Crossing

Snow storms sometimes sweep across New York, forcing it to slow down and relax, and to temporarily freeze materially and economically. As I begin writing this section, a blizzard blankets the city. Rolling and growling sounds rush out of the alleys through which the air makes its way. The powerful winds transform the space they traverse, reminding humans that their interaction with the environment is bound to forces that can never be entirely controlled or countered. Blizzards, like diasporic moves, are forces of displacement. I think of Wan-Chao Chang's dance, which at times reminds me of a tree balancing in the wind. Her body seems to swing to the rhythm of the memories that come and go within her. In the swirling spacetime of her solo *Impressions*, she moves as if shaken by the wind, sometimes gently, sometimes fiercely. The head deftly counterbalances the body's weight, leaning from one direction to the other. The arms trace a circle around her head that ends in a dropping of the lower body and flexed elbows. The hands reach out to the ceiling, as if gathering imaginary threads. The scarf worn around her neck, flowing around her hands, echoes the fluidity of her movements. In these *Impressions*, as in other works of hers, the stage becomes a meeting place for the plurality of dance styles she learned and stored in her body memory. When she crosses the stage, she uses a range of techniques, although altered. Reflecting her training in Javanese classical dance, the dancer at times meanders gently through the stage. The body shifts weight, the upper body twists, the knees bend alternately, one foot stepping backwards after the other while the opposite arm reaches forward. Waves of qi move downward from the shoulders to the delicate hand poses. The pulling of the scarf, like other movements are rooted in the Indonesian Gambyong dance style.[94] Sometimes her ballroom years re-surface, in the jiggling shoulders and the hopping way she crosses the stage laterally, and her training in Chinese folk dance also re-emerges at times. Her experience as a dancer in the Ballet Afsaneh company flows into the piece too, when she picks single dance elements from the countries located on the historical Silk Road. Other times she sweeps across the floor, constantly shuffling back and forth, turning the intimate stage into a large space to be wandered through.

Wan-Chao Chang's solo of perforMemory collects the places where she lived, and translates the embodied memory of these places into a dynamic relation to the current spatiality of the stage. Activating each cell of her dancing body, the artist

---

94   Cahyaningtyas, "The Gambyong Dance."

re-connects to her memory and renders corporeal impressions of it. She brings to life Gloria Anzaldúa's vision of the body as a "geography of self," mapped in her drawings by overlapping the veins of a body and the streets of a territory.[95] This visual overlapping also echoes Christiane Emmanuel's dance against the backdrop of a digital scenography, a projected map in which the streets eventually overfill with a red fluid. In Chang's choreography however, national borders are transcended. Instead, cultural influences merge within the dynamic assemblage of the dancing body.[96]

In contrast to Wan-Chao Chang, Farah Saleh handles the borders within one territory or nation. Her work is preoccupied with the physical borders that divide the Palestinian territory as much as with the impact of these borders on emotional subjectivity. *Parole, Parole, Parole* is a solo of transitions between places and emotions. The dancer constantly evolves from one spot to another, dis/placing and displaying the body. The first transition is smooth, for the dancer enters the performance space with the audience. She briefly goes through the room as more audience members enter. Holding a bundle of flowers in her hand, her walk is abruptly interrupted when she bumps into one of the venue's walls. She remains there, standing at a physical obstacle separating her from her imaginary lover. The audience sees her from behind, in a tragic pose that may also suggest the body searches that Palestinian citizens must regularly undergo at checkpoints, when they wish to travel across the country. The body drops, hesitantly searches for balance, and is animated by a wave going through each body part. In the artist statement found on the website of the Miniatures Officinae institution which supported the first iteration of the piece, she reflects upon geopolitical obstacles to love:

> In Palestine, love and the act of loving are not always that easy. And it is even more complicated when a Palestinian from Gaza falls in love with someone who is not from the strip. Someone from Ramallah for instance, sister city, not (yet) twin. Is the love story between Gaza and Ramallah im/possible?[97]

This "im/possibility" translates into her site-related performance in which she interacts with the audience and with the venue. When she bumps against the wall, she embodies the geopolitical constellation and the physical borders restricting the freedom of movement – and of loving. When she cannot cross the space, the flowers become the ones who travel, as she turns her back to the audience and throws them across the room, in a tragicomic mix of marriage ritual and resistance. Here

---

95 Anzaldúa, *Light in the Dark/Luz En Lo Oscuro*, 30.
96 For an interesting discussion of Anzaldúa's concept of geographies of selves in relation to choreography and identity-making, see the recent thesis Dava D. Hernández, "Dancing Mestizaje: The Choreodramas of The Guadalupe Dance Company."
97 Saleh, "Note D'intention. Parole, Parole, Parole." [My translation]

she also cites the street art star known as Banksy, whose stencil on the Israeli wall was reproduced in the performance venue. It depicts a street protester, who in contrast with the stone-throwing imagery associated with the Intifada, is ready to throw a flower bundle over the wall. There is such a striking irony in this image, which in the context of the performance seems to amplify the power of love as a means of resistance. Saleh's interest in the interrelation between love, physical distance, and political resistance, also makes me think of the work of the Post Natyam collective,[98] which deploys dance across geocultural boundaries to *queer* borders, gender and dance practices. Borderlands are marked by the intricacy of physical and emotional boundaries, as Anzaldúa reminds us in a text that could be applied to the Gaza strip:

> A border is a dividing line, a narrow strip along a steep edge. A borderland is a vague and undetermined place created by the emotional residue of an unnatural boundary. It is in a constant state of transition.[99]

In Saleh's performance, the wall of the TanzQuartier Vienna becomes the narrow strip along which Saleh strives to move…on her hands. By reversing the verticality of her body, she conveys a feeling of difficulty, of struggle in expressing the "emotional residue" of her love relationship. Her performance seems to engage with the confluence of geographical borders and psychic boundaries, crossing the minds of those living under Occupation. When the body cannot move freely across the border, it finds other ways of transgressing it. Saleh's work takes on an acute urgency in times of (post-) pandemic, when gathering and travel restrictions have spread across the globe, and affected bodies and territories not otherwise privy to these realities.

While in *Ordinary Madness*, Saleh choreographed the interrelationships of individuals within the group, this time she performs alone, even the beloved "other" is absent, and the only beings in proximity are the audience. The dancer plays on this proximity, for instance she walks on her hands towards audience members who then feel the need to move away from her to give her space. However she returns in the opposite direction, which leads them to move back to their original spot. She approaches certain attendees extremely closely, mimicking the gesture of someone assessing its fellow human beings. Apart from certain cues, there does not seem to be a predefined plan for the trajectory of the dancer. Rather, she engages with the site, and with the audience. Dancer-scholar Aimée Cox maintains that through choreography a body may inform, or transform the spatiality of its surroundings:

---

98   Chatterjee et al., "Post Natyam Collective"; See also: Chatterjee and Lee, "'Our Love Was Not Enough': Queering Gender, Cultural Belonging, and Desire in Contemporary Abhinaya."

99   Anzaldúa, *Borderlands*, 25.

> Choreography suggests that there is a map of movement or plan for how the body interacts with its environment, but it also suggests that by the body placement in a space, the nature of that space changes.[100]

Saleh's work raises the question of positioning in material and metaphorical spaces. Her choreography influences how the viewers place themselves in the venue, despite or because it works through site-specific and audience-specific improvisation. Like in contact improvisation, her dance is all about intimacy, and about crossing: people, borders, space. She transforms the space from a regular theatrical setting into a place where performer and viewers inhabit a common location. Attending the performance in Vienna, I sensed that Saleh did not easily connect to the audience.[101] However, the performance expressed the will to transition, to be open to affinity in a hostile environment. *Parole, Parole, Parole* translates daily preoccupations of Palestinian citizens into the embodied memory of a performer's dancing body. PerforMemory here is a source of knowledge and meaning-making, just like the theoretical references used to make sense of performances.

In the movements of perforMemory, dancers connect the strands of identity bound by memory, emotion, space and time. Diagonal moves across the stage challenge the convention of Western reading that moves from left to right or from front to back. A performer moving in diagonals traverses the whole stage without fully facing, nor turning one's back, to the audience. The diagonal may trace counter-hegemonic directions urgently needed by all those who want to move away from oppressive society structures. In the context of perforMemory, the diagonals also materially enact what "multidirectional memory"[102] may look like.

In *Through Gardens*, Oxana Chi makes a broad use of the space. In the scene of the Journey, she uses diagonal trajectories, or diagonal movements to cross the stage-world. A video projection shows Wayang Kulit figures, puppets used on stage in Indonesia to depict historical events and comment upon sociopolitical issues. As the video ends and the stage lights dim, the dancer returns to the stage in a new costume. The puppets on the screen are mirrored by her silhouette detaching from the dark. Standing at the back left corner of the stage, she follows the paths of light as they appear and disappear diagonally, in zigzag shapes. Her steps are reminiscent of Tai Chi walking exercises, in which one slowly steps one foot after the other in order to regulate the yin-yang balance in the body. She adds another dimension to this technique, by letting an almost imperceptible energy circulate through her body, a flow which animates her arms. Thus, she seems to be a puppet hanging in the air which is being moved by external forces. In this fashion, she travels across the whole stage in diagonal lines, finally reaching the top right corner.

---

100   Cox, *Shapeshifters*, 29.
101   Saleh, Interview.
102   Rothberg, *Multidirectional Memory*. [See my introduction]

The performer crosses world borders in a few steps and a few minutes, but conveys the feel of a prolonged journey, because of the diagonal use of space, and because of her use of time, namely movement in extremely slow motion.

This trip may represent Tatjana Barbakoff's migration from Latvia to Germany at the beginning of her career. However if the scene is understood in a non-linear interpretation of spacetime, as suggested earlier in this chapter, it may also stand for all of Barbakoff's voluntary journeys and forced displacements. Consequently, I also see it as Barbakoff fleeing from Germany in 1933 and eventually criss-crossing France, going from one hiding place to another, attempting to escape the fascist persecution she was exposed to as a Chinese-Jewish-Latvian dancer performing sociopolitical critique. It may also tell of the dancer's dreamed travels from China to Europe. The scene may therefore be interpreted as a linear reading of the piece's dramaturgy, as much as a disruption of it. Each time she reaches the end of a light path, a newly lit diagonal appears for her to step into. To zigzag across the stage is to reach the borders of the stage. Here we can return to the bridge motif discussed in my chapter on diaspora. Tatjana Barbakoff's dance art itself was described in relation to bridges, as suggested by this German press article published in *Die Deutsche Zeitung* on October 17th, 1925:

> Barbakoff's dances were dreams. Her face, her play of features, moving within its own self, without the intention to enter in contact with us in the audience. Dreamlike. Her dances [were] also magic bridges, tying one silent moment to the other. And standing on this bridge, there was she, the dancer: what was her life expression in relation to the infinity stretching behind her?
>
> (Die Tänze der Barbakoff waren Träume. Ihr Gesicht, ihr Minenspiel, so ganz in sich selbst bewegend, so ganz ohne jeden Willen mit uns im Zuschauerraum in Verbindung zu treten. Traumhaft. Ihre Tänze auch zauberische Brücken, von Stille zu Stille geschlagen. Und auf dieser Brücke stand die Tänzerin: was war ihr Lebensausdruck vor der Unendlichkeit, die hinter ihr sich spannte?)[103]

This poetic reflection on Barbakoff's dance also rings true for Chi's contemporary perforMemory of her, and especially her strong use of dance expressionist qualities in *Through Gardens*. Although neither Barbakoff's nor Chi's dance seems to be always calm, they share a surrealist approach to dance, an endeavor to paint society in dreamlike colors, no matter whether the dream is a sweet one – or not. Dreams are also characterized by the differential spacetime feel that we experience in them. Maybe what all seven dances of perforMemory discussed here have in common is the use of their dances as bridges, between past, present, future, between time and space, between forgetting and reclaiming the past, between understanding and transforming it. Crossing the stage, they bridge the many gaps

---

103   Cited in: Goebbels, *Tatjana Barbakoff*, 19. [My translation]

between the centuries and miles of displacement, and create a crossroad, as in Chung-hing's poem opening this chapter, where historical trauma is met with the infinite possibilities of diaspora.

Power is the common thread tying the three movement categories of spinning, jumping and crossing on stage. All these movements do not merely represent power, they wield multidimensional forms of power through embodiment. The dancing body may be a confluence of the intellectual, corporeal, social and economic realms of power.[104] I find that all these performances work towards the simultaneous negotiation and expression of power, regardless of their geographical origins.

In my search for a connection between the material and the conceptual implications of the dancers' art of occupying the stage, I demonstrated how they use their bodies as living tools to sculpt dancescapes as their décors for an endeavor to produce and transmit cultural memory. The complex ways in which they process notions of and relations to spacetime through performance, suggests that they exert the power to stretch hegemonic time linearity, to mold space, and to ultimately shape the context in which they deal with the past. Dances can provide a live personification of "psychohistory."[105] Spinning, jumping or turning can become a process which takes into account how "historical facts" – such as the trauma of the Holocaust or Transatlantic Slave Trade – have an "impact on our emotional world." The movements of perforMemory thus serve the project of a performative narrativization of cultural memory, in which factual information matters less than embodied emotion. Memory is a site of movement, where the dancing body can turn into a diasporic home by being intensely present within the present spacetime.

Some works of perforMemory bear similarities with what Ann Cooper Albright defines as "New Epic Dance" in the work of African-American choreographers who "refuse the static doneness of historical documentation, lifting the black and white printing off the page and imbuing it with the ability to move, shift, and, finally, to transform itself."[106] The timescapes and the movements of perforMemory meet in the realization of this aspiration. The dancers physically engage their body joints and articulations in relation to the performative spacetime, giving flesh to Chakrabarty's metaphoric time-knot or "granthi."[107] Eventually, perforMemory may well render futile our perceived distinctions between the movement of a body and the movement of time. Infusing the stage with the power to represent oneself and to share this representation with the audience, the dancers invite us to move

---

104 Zenenga, "Power and the Body," 65. See also chapter one.
105 hooks and Mesa-Bains, *Homegrown*, 100.
106 Cooper Albright, "Embodying History," 440.
107 Chakrabarty, *Provincializing Europe*, 112.

beyond the very idea of representation. What remains is the idea of intensity as a self-generated spacetime of perforMemory, in which dancers activate multiple tools such as turning, spinning and crossing to dance the past in the present tense.

4 DANCE DIALOGUES
IN CONVERSATION WITH...

La pensée du tremblement
éclate partout avec les musiques
et les formes enfantées par les peuples.
Elle nous préserve des pensées de systèmes de pensée et des systèmes de pensée.[...]
Elle nous réunit dans l'absolue
diversité, en un tourbillon de rencontres :
elle est l'Utopie
qui jamais ne s'arrête et qui ouvre
demain comme un fruit partagé.
(Tremor thinking
erupts everywhere with the music
and the forms birthed by the people.
She preserves us from the thoughts of systemic thinking and from systemic thinking.[...]
She reunites us in absolute
diversity, in a whirlwind of encounters:
she is the Utopia
that never ceases and that opens
tomorrow as a shared fruit.)[1]
Édouard Glissant & Sylvie Sémavoine Glissant

Thinking of, through, and in *tremor*, as described by the Glissant duo, is an epistemological, and at times ontological, mode explored by artists and intellectuals in Caribbean environments. This quotation evokes all the elements of my last three

---

1   Glissant and Glissant, "La pensée du tremblement." [My translation] I draw this quotation from a collaborative article by Sylvie and Édouard Glissant. The word 'pensée' can be translated as *thinking* or *thought*, which is a feminine word in French grammar. I believe that the authors deliberately emphasize the "she" which also evokes an analogy to the idea of 'Mother Earth'. On the metaphor of a fruit-identity, see also the work of Daniel Maximin (Guadeloupe).]

chapters: the volcano (chapter one), the whirlwind (chapter three), and I may say the ocean (chapter two), since Glissant's archipelagic thinking is inextricably anchored to the shores of Martinique. In December 2014, Oxana Chi was invited to work in Martinique as an artist-in-residence at the dance center *La Maison Rouge/Maison des Arts*. In collaboration with local dancer-choreographer Christiane Emmanuel, who directs the center, Chi choreographed a duo called *The Journey*. The short piece engages with the dancers' respective experiences as choreographers of color working within the whirlpool of the European cultural production industry. It is a sad, sensual, energetic, humorous work-in-progress. The dancers, full of verve, sometimes stumble, but eventually always land on their own feet and selves, as they journey through more or less difficult memories of their dancing career.

The Journey with Christiane Emmanuel (left), Oxana Chi (right), and Layla Zami, (musician). La Maison des Arts, Martinique 2014, photo: Emilie Alves de Puga, courtesy of the artists.

The photograph above depicts the two performers trying to reach for each other's hands. Yet, they will not get to shake hands, because each dancer hypnotically follows the lead of her own hand. The photographer captured the moment when they still seem able to reach for each other, before their bodies shift into the spiraling motion of perforMemory. At the forefront of the picture, you can see me holding a drum, and paying close attention to the dancers' movements. The picture mirrors the research positioning I have come to call an *insider without* (see introduction). Having had the delight of accompanying the performance on stage with live drum and saxophone sounds, I sat in the optimal position of a participant observer. Although I have not accompanied all seven performers live, I feel a connection to each choreographer interviewed. I was able to conduct and record deep conversations on their intents, aesthetics, trajectories. Thus, the picture is emblematic of the committed, corporeal engagement that carried me through this research journey, a journey full of revelations, challenges and achievements.

This final chapter is a journey within the journey, a journey of personal encounters. It could be taken as an art book within the academic book. It includes the transcripts of the conversations I had with each dancer-choreographer, traveling to the countries where the dancers were living or performing at the time. The conversations were held between September 2013 and December 2015 in Germany, France, Taiwan, Martinique, Austria and the USA. Here I have placed the interviews in chronological order, not so much to return the reader to linear time, but more to give a sense of the research process, and its evolution.

This conversational chapter represents a diasporic spidering in itself, it occupies multiple spacetimes and encompasses, in a way, the multidimensional temporality and spatiality of the research. It is indeed the result of a "whirlwind of encounters", in which I repetitively found diversity to be a key opening the house of unity on the island of utopia, to paraphrase Glissant. Most importantly, as announced in the introduction, this section of the book offers you to simultaneously zoom into and zoom out of the dances of perforMemory. Zoom in, because here you will find detailed reflections on particular aspects of the performers' works. Zoom out, because the performers locate the works within a broader artistic vision.

In addition to commenting upon a solo piece, each dance-maker also discusses the processes of creating other works of perforMemory. It is my hope that this broader conversational scope expands upon the reflections in prior chapters, illuminating the performances in light of the choreographers' artistic intents. The interviews express themes which I have partly addressed in my analysis: inspiration, spirituality, energy, quest, passion and motivation. What all interviews have in common is the expression of the dancer-choreographer's envisioning of their very own universe where memory matters, movement matters, and movement moves the matter of memory.

In recording this oral material, I also thought of Patricia Hill Collins' emphasis on "the use of dialogue in assessing knowledge claims,"[2] a fundamental posture of Black feminist epistemology. The interviews offer the reader the chance to re-engage with the performances from the perspective of, and in the words of, the dancers. Yet, in my desire to foreground the artists' perspectives on their own work,

---

2   Collins, *Black Feminist Thought*, 260.

I am crisply aware of the fact that the interviews are framed by my own questions. The reader should also bear in mind that the interview format, like the writing format, channels the meaning within a narrow words corridor, sometimes limiting the transmission of corporeal experiences.

In the context of the book, rendering the interviews as written transcripts inevitably leaves out a vital dimension in the ways people, especially performing artists, transmit meaning. The transcripts hardly give a sense of the body and vocal gestures that the interviewees use to enrich their oral answers with emotional meaning. This difference between "meaning" and "information" in interview situations is inherent to practices of interview, as discussed by the Routledge Memory & Narrative series' main editor:

> The oral expressions that interviews document, however, contain more than words arranged into sentences arranged into narratives of varying lengths, an illusion that transcripts foster. Spoken expression is inseparable from emotion and gesture. A context of direct interaction with other people also suffused by emotions shapes what is said as well. Every interview occurs in a process of a physical performance for an interlocutor.[3]

Thus a double-level translation happens here, namely translating body movements into oral words, and translating those into words. However, I videotaped every conversation, and am delighted that my documentary *Memory2Go* (2021) entails precious audiovisual material in which such a "physical performance" can be seen, heard, and perceived.

A note on languages and translations: I wished to interview four choreographers in their first language, respectively German for Oxana Chi; French for Christiane Emmanuel and Chantal Loïal; and English for André M. Zachery. Zufit Simon spoke with me in her third language, German. (Her first language is Hebrew, and my bat mitzvah notions of ancient Hebrew were not be appropriate for our conversation.) With the support of the individuals listed in my acknowledgments, I translated the conversations with Chi, Emmanuel, Loïal, and Simon into English. Farah Saleh and Wan-Chao Chang conversed with me in English, their first language being respectively Arabic and Chinese. As we moved in this diasporic linguistic interstice, we found a meeting place in a language that is as dynamic and flexible as their dance movements. Therefore I hope to have found a balance between some artists speaking in their first tongues – but inevitably translated in the writing, and artists translating their thoughts directly within the interview process. Each dance-maker had the chance to review and approve the interviews, with edits if needed.

---

3   Cándida Smith, *Art and the Performance of Memory: Sounds and Gestures of Recollection*, 2.

Each conversation is different, as you will see I did not have a fixed set of questions to apply to everyone, everywhere, everywhen. Rather, I prepared each session in relation to my background research, knowledge of the work and the artist. During the course of the conversations, I adapted the questions I had prepared (and sent beforehand to the artists), in order to be flexible enough to respond to what they shared. This dynamic and fluid interview practice corresponds to the application of the epistemological and methodological orientations outlined in my introduction. It also resonates with the interview principles and best practices recommended by the Oral History Association, especially the necessity to "seek an in-depth account of personal experience and reflections, with sufficient time allowed for the narrators to give their story the fullness they desire."[4]

A biographical note precedes each interview, presenting key aspects of each artist's career. Because each interviewee connected their repertoire to their own biographies, they confirmed my hypothesis of *choreobiography*, namely of choreographic practices inextricably enmeshed within their makers' life paths. The interviews also reinforce the idea of an Epiphenomenal time, addressed in the previous chapter, for the conversations often draw from a linear engagement with repertoire development, along with a situational reflection situated in the "now."

I read throughout the interviews a desire to navigate perforMemory away from main streams of concert dance, exploring, sampling, re-creating alternative currents of resistance, history, oppression and liberation. The performances seem to all have in common their creators' will to re-member and understand painful pasts in order to overcome present inequalities and imagine future realities. I hope that you enjoy reading these conversations as much as I enjoyed having them.

---

4   Oral Historian Association, "Principles and Best Practices." I was inspired to use these principles by Conyers, "Shedding Skin in Art-Making."

Oxana Chi in Tanz auf der Stelle; Impressions from Through Gardens, Nacht & Nebel Festival (Nikodemus Church), Berlin, 2012, photo by Layla Zami.

Oxana Chi is a German-Nigerian choreographer, dancer, filmmaker, curator, author, and trendsetter. Based in Brooklyn and Berlin, she is Co-Curator of Dance at the International Human Rights Art Festival. As the Founder and Artistic Director of Oxana Chi & Ensemble Xinren since 1991, also known as Oxana Chi Dance & Art, she has produced 18 performances including two commissioned works for the Humboldt-University, Berlin. Chi was trained in diverse classical and contemporary techniques including ballet, eurythmy, Raks Sharki, classical Javanese dance, and Cunningham technique. She developed her own transcultural fusion style, which inspired many dance-makers across the globe. In 2018, she was listed in the "A to Z of People Who Power The Dance World" (The Dance Enthusiast, New York).[5]

Chi has performed in France, Finland, India, the UK, Indonesia, Germany, Taiwan, Martinique, Turkey, and Singapore. Her work has been invited to venues including Hebbel am Ufer (HAU) Theater, Abrons Arts Center, Movement Research at Judson Church, Danspace Project, Dixon Place NYC, Werkstatt der Kulturen, Ballhaus Naunyn, Maison Heinrich-Heine (Cité internationale Paris), Théâtre de Belleville, Societätstheater Dresden, Volksbühne Berlin, Bronx Academy of Arts and Dance (BAAD!), LaMaMa, Performance Project @ University Settlement, and Aliwal Arts Center (Singapore). She appeared at festivals including Solo International Performing Arts (Surakarta), International Human Rights Art Festival, Taipei Fringe Festival, Jewish Music and Theater Week (Dresden), Black Herstory Night, Contemporary DansArt Bielefeld Biennale Passages, and Atelier de la Danse at the Cannes Dance Festival. She also performed at universities such as New York University (Tisch School of the Arts), University of Toronto, Tampere University Finland, Pratt Institute, City University of New York, Rutgers University Philadelphia, Humboldt-University Berlin, Bielefeld University, Mainz University, Yeditepe University Istanbul, and Goldsmiths University London, and at exhibitions such as Homestory Deutschland and EDEWA.

Awards, grants and residencies include Abrons Arts Center's AIRspace Grant for Performing Artists, Cité des Arts (Paris), Berlin City Council for the Arts, Fonds Darstellender Künste, Fonds Soziokultur, Gerda Weiler Feminist Foundation, and Fondation pour la Mémoire de la Shoah (Paris). Chi was also was honored at DOSHIMA (Jakarta) as Filmmaker of Inspiration and Ambassador of Peace for her art.

www.oxanachi.de

---

5   Chi, "Oxana Chi Dance Art."

OXANA CHI
17.09.2013 Berlin, Germany

Layla Zami: Oxana, the first time I saw you on stage was during a performance of your dance piece *Through Gardens [Durch Gärten]*. I was deeply impressed by your very aesthetic style, as well as your political content. Where and how do you draw inspiration for your art?

Oxana Chi: Through my travels. I have been traveling for nearly 31 years, beginning at the age of sixteen I traveled within Europe, and then at the age of twenty I realized that Europe is too limiting for me, and then traveled to India. India was quite an important experience for me, because I found a particular freedom for my choreography and dance, which is extremely important for my choreography. Namely, that I can treat time just as I wish. My movements need a wealth of time, and I want to deeply savor each movement – and this is what India taught me – something which may have gone lost in Europe, or which may never have existed in the first place. Then I traveled quite a lot to Indonesia, I went to Taiwan, I went to many islands and countries, in Asia, in the Pacific, in Australia, and also to America. In recent years, I also traveled to Nigeria and Martinique as well. All of these travels have shaped me, and above all, they provided me with a deep inspiration for my work. An inspiration which I cannot find in Europe. This makes my work distinctive.

L: By "my travels" you mean lengthier stays, right? Because in a short one-week trip you cannot find inspiration. So you stayed longer in these places?

O: Yes, for me "traveling" also means that I partially live there, or stayed for a minimum of one to three, or even twelve months. And really tried to immerse myself in the culture, simply to look at things, and also to participate. To study, to educate myself. Yes, that is quite important. So it is not a one-week package holiday, I simply do not do those types of travels.

L: You just told us about your travels, and the inspiration from your travels is clearly visible in *Through Gardens*. That is the first piece of yours I saw. That day, before your performance, you were interviewed on stage by the historian Susanne Jahn-Manske. Could you tell us a little more about that? I found it a very new, innovative, and communicative way to publicly present historical themes.

O: Yes, as to the inspiration for *Through Gardens*, I had just returned from China. Another long trip...first I was in Taiwan, then in Hong Kong, then in southern China, and there were many, many images in me, as Hong Kong is incredibly modern and high-tech, and following that I was in southern China, where there were still quite archaic structures in rural areas, where they really still tilled the fields with an ox and a plow [shows with a gesture]. The entire atmosphere was like a few hundred years ago, at least that is how I felt. This trip was extremely full of contrasts. Then I returned to Berlin, and it was like falling from paradise into hell. I always feel like this when I return from a trip. I went, despairingly, to the library, something which I almost never do...and looked at the dance section. There is actually just one small shelf in this enormous library with a few books on it, which are mostly somewhat out-of-date, there's basically nothing contemporary. I was quite frustrated, and thought, "Well, there's nothing here in the dance section, perhaps I'll take a look in the visual arts." I looked through a few books in the visual arts, found them all more or less boring and outdated as well, and then...on all of these dusty bookshelves, at the very, very top, there was a small white book. It completely stood out, because all the other books were grey and dusty, and this small white book simply glowed. I got a ladder – there are these small ladders in the library – and climbed up there, because I am only 1,60 meters, and the shelve was really over 2 meters high, and I took it down from the very topmost shelf. The cover read: *Tatjana Barbakoff, Dancer and Muse.*[6] The picture showed a very, very beautiful woman in a Chinese dress. And it totally spoke to me, it really hypnotized me, [laughs] because I had just looked at all these awful books, which actually had nothing interesting in them, and then suddenly there was this incredibly beautiful cover, and it was a catalogue of the [museum] August-Macke-Haus-Bonn.

I then leafed through the pages and saw that there were many photographs, and much of it felt kindred. I felt a certain affinity to this person, and looked at the kind of performances she had done, among others I read about her Bali and Chinese dances, dance styles I also enjoy, therefore I saw parallels to my work. I took the book home and read it through that evening, also something that I normally never do, I don't read, or very rarely. I read the entire book from the beginning to the end. Of course, I came across the terrible fate of Tatjana Barbakoff, well first [I came] across her successes, how she made incredibly beautiful dances, choreographed more than 60 dances, and how thus she achieved great success in Europe. It was also written that she was finally murdered in Auschwitz.

The next day, the next morning I said, "I would like to make a choreography in memory of Tatjana Barbakoff," so I resolved to do this. But actually, it wasn't only my decision or my desire, it was something greater than me. Not my self, but greater than myself. Yes, and that's how I came to choreograph *Through*

---

6   Drenker-Nagels, Goebbels, and Reinhardt, *Tatjana Barbakoff, Tänzerin und Muse.*

Gardens. The title is from a dance that Tatjana performed, a Chinese dance that she performed quite often.

L: And how did you have the idea of inviting the historian Susanne Jahn-Manske? What does it mean to you to be interviewed on stage by a historian before you dance?

O: The idea of working with interviews before I dance came about because I read a text about Yves Klein. Yves Klein had a period in which he only painted blue paintings, and he had an exhibition with blue paintings, and people asked what the point was, for all had the same format in the same size, and all the paintings looked the same. The exhibition was very badly received, I mean, it was met with absolute lack of understanding. Whereupon, Yves Klein repeated the exhibition with the same paintings, but asked a gallery owner who was very eloquent, to come and introduce the painting, in order to explain what kind of inspiration was behind the work. And he even went so far as to write different prices under the various paintings – [although] they were all the same. The art dealer then explained, for example, when one stands in front of this painting, one has this kind of a feeling, and that is why this painting costs so-and-so much. Another painting, which had exactly the same format, costs perhaps ten times the price...but this is because when one stands in this particular angle of the gallery and views the image, it is a completely different feeling. That is why it costs so-and-so much. He explained the art, the colors, and so on. I could say, or one could say that he introduced the works of art to the viewers. But it is also possible to say that he manipulated his audience.

I find it extremely important to prepare those who enter a space for that which they are about to see. Because then, the resonance will be very, very good. What happened with Yves Klein – all the paintings were then sold, the large majority of them, although previously no one wanted to see the paintings – that's precisely what I do with art, with my art, with dance. I find it very, very important that those who enter the space are prepared, particularly in Europe or Germany where dance is something that people almost do not know. In Berlin or Germany, people are not as interested in dance anyway, as they are in France or other countries. So it is important to prepare the audience, to tune them into what they are about to watch. For *Through Gardens* I found it particularly important, and especially began to do this, to give the audience an introduction.

It does not need to be about *Through Gardens*, but it can be a historical introduction/context. For example, Susanne Jahn-Manske told a story that did not really fully have to do with *Through Gardens*, she told a story about a father and son who hid in a garden in Wilmersdorf [in Berlin, Germany]. So she told of a historical event, that is also related with the Shoah. That was a very strong beginning – she also told it very beautifully, very, very deeply – to prepare the people for what they were about to see. Consequently, a story would be told which would also be told very beautifully, but which also has a certain depth, also has a certain sadness, and which also has a huge historical relevance for Germany, for Europe, and for the rest of the world. That is why I always do this before my dance performances, that I first give an introduction in order to prepare the audience. I have also noticed that the audience receives it extremely well, that everyone leaves the performance space extremely satisfied, and that no one says, "Oh, that was such an abstract choreography, I didn't understand it at all."

L: We just spoke about *Through Gardens*, and we'll remain with *Through Gardens*. In this piece you evoke in a poetic and complex way, the dancer Tatjana Barbakoff from the 1920s-1930s. I've seen various performances of the piece, and it is your dance art and specifically, *Through Gardens*, which inspired and shaped my doctoral project. I am particularly moved that through this piece, you promote an alternative narration of history which emphasizes resistance, and offer a personal practice of remembering, which brings the audience closer to an individual biography. Can you tell us more about *Through Gardens* with regards to history and memory?

O: Yes, Tatjana Barbakoff. This artist lived in Berlin in the 1920s and 1930s. She was Latvian-Chinese-Jewish, and moved to Dusseldorf, then to Berlin, and later emigrated to Paris. At first, I was interested in this topic because I took a similar path: I came from Dusseldorf, moved then to Berlin, then to Paris, and finally to Australia and back to Berlin. What's important to say is that I actually didn't choose to create *Through Gardens*. I didn't think, "I'll create *Through Gardens* now." Instead, as for the historical relevance, I didn't think at the time about creating a piece about the Shoah, but as I mentioned earlier, it was something greater than me. I was given the task. And then I thought, "Okay, if I'm given the task, then I'll do it." Then of course I immersed [myself], deeper and deeper, and deeper and deeper...and it was important to me to continually question, and to see how history actually functions in Germany. And who tells history. And how, where, and when history is told.

What I noticed then – but had also previously noticed – is that in dance historiography, only certain people appear, people with whom I cannot identify. Through this work on Through Gardens, I could for the first time identify with a figure, namely Tatjana Barbakoff. Tatjana Barbakoff helped me to call more and more into question: who actually, here in Germany, who actually, here in Europe, who actually in the world writes history, or is allowed to write history. Then it became clear to me that it is extremely important for contemporary artists like myself to write history themselves. And if I don't have the means to write a book, then I must stand on stage and dance this history out. I must add alternatives, or create alternatives to all this mainstream, which actually very cunningly narrates a single history, which is very, very limited to my taste. Instead [of this mainstream], I must widen the scope, without exclusion. This means that all the voices who have written history should be made audible, and Tatjana Barbakoff belongs to those. "Tatjana Barbakoff" is just a name. Behind Tatjana Barbakoff, millions of artists stand. Whether they were gassed, whether they are censored in other ways in present times, and cannot work, whether they are never mentioned by the media or in history books, that is not the point. Behind Tatjana Barbakoff there continues to be – all the way into today, and even beyond, into the future – other artists, who have distinctly helped shape our history, who have even created our history, but who are not named. This is why I find it very, very important that I attempt – in my own way, of course – but at least attempt to create alternatives, and to incite other artists to create alternatives to the narrative of history we encounter here. Because I believe that here, a great deal is left out that is actually extremely important.

L: Yes, thank you. That was very insightful. It is quite visible in your pieces that you genuinely demand an alternative historical narrative. In this case, you emphasized the resistance, and that very much moved me, because for example in school [in France and Germany], I was always confronted with medial representations of the Shoah that only show Jewish people as victims. Resistance was not a topic. There is a very important scene in your piece, I think you call it "The Struggle" (Der Kampf). Would you like to speak more about that?

O: Yes, I'd be glad to. When I was a child, I was also confronted often with anti-semitic discourses, and a violent language negating the resistance of Jewish people. I find it scandalously shameful that such a thing is even still said. I always paid attention to resistance, for instance with Tatjana Barbakoff. How many years she spent resisting! In Berlin, as she had to flee – and even before National Socialism came to power, she always had themes that focused on political issues. She always sought to view our society critically and to point out injustices in her performances. After her emigration, she still continued to choreograph and to work, even without a residence permit, without a work permit, and still she managed to make it into the newspapers, to make it into art books...and continued performing! That is a very, very strong resistance. Although she was a migrant, although she had to live underground, she still created incredibly beautiful choreographies, still had exquisite costumes...To achieve that, although you are actually being persecuted the whole time and constantly threatened by deportation, I mean, how can you reach that? For this reason, I believe that it is extremely important to show that she fought. I worked for very long on the scene "Der Kampf" (The Struggle) in my piece, I am still working on it, because it must become much, much more complex. The Jewish people, well not only the Jewish people, all people who resisted:

Sinti and Roma, Afro-Germans, and also all those who simply were not in agreement with the regime, many, many artists who simply did not create mainstream work, and rejected the 'Heimat-Abendland-Gedusel' [patriotic homeland blablabla], were persecuted, and tried to resist. That is simply how it was, and that must be shown. After the Struggle, there is the [scene of the] New Moon: the hope, because I believe that although Tatjana Barbakoff was put to death, and although so much art was destroyed here in Europe, she still left something here which gives us – me, or you, Layla, or all artists here – a certain strength to keep on going, and a fertile soil from which we can grow. And so I think that, even though she has passed away, she is still active and still resists, and that is also the case with many other artists.

L: Why do you prefer solo dances and solo choreographies? And are there points of contact, or parallels between your personal biography and the figures you perform on stage?

O: Well I danced in a musical once, and the only passages I liked were solos, two solos. All these group sequences, I found them absolutely awful. I always made mistakes, I always somehow danced the wrong steps, and the choreographer was incredibly frustrated, but I couldn't help it. I always made mistakes! Then I thought more about it, and realized that I probably found it uncomfortable to perform the same steps as nine other dancers the entire time. [I realized that] because of my personality – I am an individualist – I just somehow had no desire to dance like the other dancers. Then, of course it's also a financial issue: first of all, to employ other dancers as a choreographer costs quite a lot.

Also, I have done a few duos, and noticed that I had to look after the other dancer, yet I am simply very preoccupied with myself. I am quite a self-focused person. So when I dance, I try to pour myself more and more into the dance, and my body...to give everything that is possible to give. And if I must work with other dancers, I won't be able to give on stage what I would like to show. And I won't be able to develop myself the way I want to develop myself, because...I am a seeking person. I seek much in my own self. I can not manage that when I work with other dancers.

That is the first thing, and the other is that I have noticed, when attending dance performances, that I was most touched when a single person was dancing on stage...where I could fully concentrate on one dancer. I always incredibly enjoyed that. There are few group pieces that have moved me in the way that solo works did. I have also often noticed when watching group pieces that I think "I'll just watch this dancer, or that dancer," and then concentrate throughout the entire performance on one figure only. So I understood, more and more over the years, that I simply am not a group dancer, I am a solo dancer. That became clear to me in 1991. I danced my first solo then. And since then I have almost only danced solos, and am quite pleased with it, because then I can really give everything, and that is important to me.

L: Giving everything…I do see this when you are on stage, and this solo work is most likely reflected in your daily life and in your practice. You train nearly every day, right? In this way you can more freely shape your daily routine, or your training, than when you have to rely upon others, isn't that right?

O: Yes, first of all, I can arrange my time in a way that suits my body. Because it is also important to say this: I have not let myself be choreographed [by others], because here in Europe and in Germany, most people have a very, very different body than I do, and they need different time, they have a different nutrition – all of that does not fit at all with my energy and my body. My body is African, and my energy comes from many places. It's Eastern European, it's Asian… many energies come together, and build my energy. I have quite an individual energy. I also need to treat this energy in a certain way. I call this "housekeeping."

That is why it does not make sense for me to go to dance rehearsals of some dance group, to totally exhaust my energy there, and then to realize that it's too much for me, or that I am totally under-challenged, or whatever. I have always noticed that my energy does absolutely not fit with mainstream, does not fit with a white, Western, male-dominated society. It simply does not fit. Therefore, I work to my own rhythm, at my own pace. I always told myself that I have plenty of time to learn certain movements. I can not learn them in three years. Maybe I can learn them in twenty years. But then it's still early enough to bring the movement to the stage. For example, what I can do today on stage, I perhaps couldn't do twenty years ago, or not as well as [I can] today. And I continuously add new elements, and new movements from various cultures. It always becomes more dense, because my soul, my body and everything surrounding it, my energies become more dense.

Dance, to me, is a constant development of one's self. It is not one dance technique: classical ballet, modern dance and so on, all of that is not my thing. To me, dance is a very, very complex matter…akin to the soul. It is almost impossible to grasp. I wish to grasp it, of course, but it is impossible to grasp. And so it is important to constantly keep researching, like a scholar…and I can actually only present this work in a solo program. I can not expect this of anyone else. Besides, other people have other energies, and other focus in their dance.

Another aspect is that I have worked very biographically in recent pieces. About figures like Tatjana Barbakoff, Nefertiti and May Ayim. Those are figures to whom I have certain affinities. In very different ways, but all of them feel related to me. Not only through a biographical connection, but also through a soul-relationship. Therefore, it is good that I dance solo, because these pieces are extremely important to me, and that is how I wish to show them.

L: We met in Berlin at a public event, where a company named Mémoires Vives [Lively Memories] showed a piece about French colonial history. In your piece *Neferet iti* you also deal with colonial structures and discourses. How do you manage to contemporize the past in a way that is as multi-faceted as it is clear?

O: To contemporize the past...Well, past and present are deeply related to each other. I do not see a large rift between past and present. I actually intended to do something about a Pharaoh, the thought simply came to me. For me, it was about dancing a female personality, in order to bring women into the foreground, since women in Europe are always in the background. I told this to a friend, the actress Suheer Saleh. She is Egyptian-German, and she said to me: "Oxana, why don't you do something about Nefertiti? She is a very interesting Pharaoh, and that could be quite fascinating." A few days later [in Berlin], I stood in front of a larger than life advertisement picturing [the bust of] Nefertiti, with the legend "Nefertiti...the most beautiful migrant in town." That struck me. I thought, "migration" and "beautiful," in one sentence? In a public space, in Germany? That was a sentence that sounded nearly impossible to me. Because I have never heard such sentences. Certainly not in public spaces, or in the media. When the press reports about migration, it is always as a problem, never as an asset. The poster troubled me, because it became clear to me that migrants are gladly seen as a source of profit [to society], but when it's simply about being fair and living with one another, then migrants are always just seen as a problem. Because of the poster, I decided that I would make something about Nefertiti. When Suheer first suggested it to me, I thought, "Hmm, let's see," and "I'm not sure yet," but when I saw the poster, it became clear. And when I deal with Nefertiti, then of course the first thought is: art looting.[7] Of course, the topic is extensive, because art looting has to do with nearly all museums in Berlin. Not only in Berlin, also in Europe, or America...so art looting is actually a gigantic topic that cannot be captured in one small dance piece. That is why I framed my *Neferet iti* piece with a focus on details.

I assume that [the statue of] Nefertiti wakes up on the [Berlin] Museum Island, and travels the path back, or that she comes from Egypt and traces the path of her abduction. It was important to me to go at it purely through dance, to depart from dance styles. In this piece, I work with various dance styles that

---

7   The bust of Nefertiti is a looted work of art exhibited as major attraction at the Egyptian Museum in Berlin, drawing millions of visitors to the city each year. Egypt has been reclaiming the bust from German authorities for almost 100 years, without success. See Opoku, "Nefertiti in Absurdity."

could describe a journey. For this, I additionally studied Raks Sharki [Egyptian oriental dance] with Zadiel Sasmaz, a Turkish dancer, in order to feel my way in, to feel my way deeper and deeper into the movement. The journey actually describes various movement structures, from African to contemporary Hip-Hop, also classical ballet – for the classical ballet is actually an adaption of African movement. All of the leaps, the turns actually come from African countries, often from West Africa. I work through all of these adaptations in *Neferet iti*.

Because she is a Pharaoh, it was also very important to me to create a particular, spiritual, mood. I believe this worked quite well, because the way I combine the dances and choreographies with each other builds up a spiritual energy. And it ends with the Sufi dance, which comes from ancient Muslim cultures. Yes, it mattered to me, to work very choreographically, and yet still politically. It is still political, because before I even begin to dance, I first read a text which I previously wrote.[8] In this text, I express my opinion about the fact that Nefertiti "is" in Berlin, and my opinion about structures that do not view desecration of graves and art theft as criminal. I speak about this before I begin to dance. Therefore, I deal here, again, with a political topic, Nefertiti.

L: You just spoke of your dance styles, and how you actually mix different styles. I believe you actually call it "Fusion." Can you now tell us more about the process by which you work, and more concretely, how you create your incredibly beautiful performances, which you also always present with live music – which is also relatively rare [in the contemporary dance scene]?

O: Regarding my dance styles, I studied in various countries: with some of the greats like Christine Kono, who was at the Joffrey Ballet School in New York, or with Bu Endang Subono from STSI Solo [Sekolah Tinggi Seni Indonesia Surakarta], and with many different artists, Indonesian, Western... Through these experiences of training, it became clear to me what kind of dance I wanted to create. It also became clear to me that I did not want to create one style of dance. I also studied classical ballet for many years with Yvonne Wendrig from China/Holland.

At one point it became clear that I no longer wanted to do any of these styles, but instead that I had to develop my own style. Then I began to do "Fusion," an idea of various dance styles, as well as my own input. Some dances I did not even study, some styles are already in me: some Africanist dances, for example. Or "Oriental dance," by that I actually specifically mean Samudi and Raks Sharki. I can observe the forms a little, but actually they are already in me. I have developed these various styles into my own "Fusion-Trend" and I use this style in my choreographies. What I do, when I have a theme, I go

---

8   The text was published recently in Chi, "Neferet iti - Reloaded."

to the rehearsal room and I improvise. I let movement flow through me. I move, and I move, and I move, and at some point I think: "Yes, this movement is good, and this movement is good..." or "This beginning is nice," or "This middle is nice." It comes to me. I don't really think it up, instead all the styles just come to me...the movement, and the rhythm. And when I move then – I am always alone [in the rehearsal space] – it becomes more and more meditative.

From this meditative language of movement, I perceive how the music should be. First come the instruments, then I know, "there I need a violin," or "a hang would fit well there," or "there a bamboo flute, or a piano." They come one after another, and once I have the instruments, then I consider which musician would be fitting. Then I simply meet with musicians that I know – or don't know – and find out which musical language each one plays, and which ones would fit best with the piece. And then we begin to work in the rehearsal room together. I always work with images, I give them images. I tell them, for example, this is one image: the atmosphere must be very romantic, it must be like a park. Or I tell them, "This must really be brutal, right now we are in World War II. A bomb is about to drop on our house." I give them a mood, and sometimes I also give them composers that I find interesting. What is also important to say is [that] the musicians I work with are also simultaneously composers. They are artists, they create. Not only adapt, but also create: they invent the pieces for my performances. Some pieces are prior compositions, and if I really enjoy one piece, then I say: "Okay, I find this piece very interesting, but could you tailor it to me? It is like a beautiful dress I see, could you alter it so that it fits my shape?" Then they do that as well, and the second part of the process is that I work together with the musicians, and from there the dance emerges.

L: Oxana, you just told us about the process of your work, concretely about how you work together with musicians. I myself had the chance to be on stage with you, and experienced how you work together with others in the piece *I Step On Air*, which is dedicated to the Ghanaian-German poet, performer, and scholar May Ayim. How was the experience for you, having your performance art involved in scholarly-academic contexts? I would be interested in [hearing about] this.

O: Yes, I came to the theme of May Ayim through you, because you planned to make a film about May Ayim, and I had just met you then. From 2009 to 2012, I organized the Salon Qi every year in memory of Tatjana Barbakoff, and then in 2011 I had the idea of adding a May Ayim reading as well. Then you prepared texts that you had researched about May Ayim, and offered to give a presentation. I then had the idea of bringing in the actress Suheer Saleh. The two of you worked together and staged an incredibly beautiful lecture-performance, a scenic reading [szenische Lesung], which was half academic, half with presentation, but also theatrical. I programmed it at the Salon Qi. In the audience was Natasha Kelly, who teaches at the Humboldt University at the Gender Studies department, and we presented the reading again in 2012 at Dance Summer 12, a festival which I also organized together with you. In that same year, Natasha Kelly approached me, and commissioned me to choreograph a piece about May Ayim, Audre Lorde, Czinka Panna [known in English as Panna Cinka], and Delia Rosa Zamudio Palacios, female figures who were great and powerful personalities. I ended up choosing May Ayim and let the other figures flow in, but for me it was really about May Ayim.

That was very well received – and there was the contact to the university. We were then invited to perform it in various universities, at other exhibitions and festivals as well, but also in academic contexts. What was interesting was that it really fit in well there, because they had several presentations and lecturers, and our piece felt like release. It creates a good atmosphere, yet it is academic and complements the academic presentations. It was quite good to collaborate with the universities, and we decided to do it more often. It works well, has a receptive audience...and hopefully it will continue in this way.

L: Oxana, your dance pieces are transdisciplinary, as you mentioned earlier, and you yourself are a multi-talented artist who works with many art forms: choreography, dance, film, video installation, curation, and in addition, you have published texts on your art, which I can analyze for my work. But your heart seems to beat loudest in the dance arts. What is special for you about dance as a form of expression? Particularly with regards to time and space, life and consciousness?

O: It's true, I do like to film. I shot films for a while, and I also regularly write texts, not only about my dance, also about other things. I also love painting, I enjoy going to exhibitions, and have some friends who are painters, I find all of that wonderful. I love art in general. But for me, dance is the queen. Really the absolute greatest of all the arts. For me it is the purest form of art, because in the end, we humans can do without everything. We can do without books, without paintings, without images, we can also do without films...but we cannot live without our bodies. It simply isn't possible. Dance really is simply body, soul, heart. All of those are needed, otherwise one can't dance. It isn't possible otherwise. And so for me, it is the greatest of all the arts. That is why I dance.

Christiane Emmanuel in Choc(s) at Atrium Theater, Fort-de-France, Martinique 2011, photo courtesy of the artist.

Christiane Emmanuel is a dancer, choreographer, and dance pedagogue from Martinique (FWI). She created the Experimental Group of Contemporary Dance (GEDC) in 1989, now Compagnie Christiane Emmanuel. Her choreographic language is firmly inscribed in Martinican and Caribbean idiosyncrasy. The company is also enriched by the profile of various artists and choreographers. In 2010, the artist also became the Founding Director of the Maison Rouge/Maison des Arts, a socio-cultural dance center based in her home neighborhood in Fort-de-France, Martinique.

She holds a State Diploma from the Cuban Ministry of Education and Culture, and a State Diploma from the French Ministry of Culture. She studied dance for five years at the Escuela Nacional de Arte (ENA) in La Havana, Cuba, and for two years at the Académie Internationale de la Danse (AID) in Paris, France. She also trained in Dunham Technique, Contact Improvisation, and trained in traditional and contemporary Africanist styles with Elsa Wolliaston, Fred Lassere, Bruce Taylor and Marianela Boan, among others.

As a choreographer, Emmanuel received the "Utopia" Prize for Choreographic Creation (2011) from the Martinique Regional Council for whom she produced commissioned works. Her repertoire comprises 20 productions. The company has appeared throughout the Caribbean and beyond in Martinique (Tropiques Atrium, Fonds St Jacques Cultural Center, Aimé Césaire Theater), French Guyana (Auditorium de l'EnCRe, Musée des cultures Guyanaises); Guadeloupe (l'Artchipel), St Domingue (Edanco Festival); Venezuela (Caracas Dance Festival), as well as in Burkina Faso (FIDO Festival), and France (Tours National Choreographic Center, Avignon Off Festival).

Since 2016, Christiane Emmanuel has been the President of the Tropiques-Atrium Theater, the largest, state-sponsored performing arts venue in Martinique. She also entered politics and currently leads the Cultural Committee at the Martinican Regional Council.

christianeemmanuelcompagnie.blogspot.com

CHRISTIANE EMMANUEL
21.02.2014 Fort-de-France, Martinique

Layla Zami: At your talk at the Habitation Clément, you said that you "dig your Martinican self." Can you tell us more? From where do you draw inspiration?

Christiane Emmanuel: It was very clear to me, through my parents' education, that we are first and foremost Martinican [citizens]. Dad himself was immersed in reading Aimé Césaire, [Léopold Sédar] Senghor, and [was] a fervent supporter of the Martinican cause, so I had a good luggage, a full one, with the barcode label "Martinique". With this barcode, I went to study [dance] in Cuba. There, I felt confirmed in the feeling that I am Martinican, and mostly, Caribbean. Drawing on the training I got in Cuba – Afro-Modern Cuban dance, and traditional Cuban dances – and knowing the traditional dances of my own country, I quickly noticed that a local traditional dance is a strong base, a well, a stand on which you can rest, and bounce off in life. This does not mean that my choreographies are strongly influenced by my [Martinican] traditional dances, but there is a base...there is a knowledge of space, well is it inborn or not, is it conscious or not? But things are much easier if you dig [into] both spaces, the contemporary dance "space," and the traditional dance "space." My Martinican self is my forest, my location, the place where I live, the people I socialize with, the political space, the geopolitical space named Martinique, the cultural space, the dense forests of Martinique, the beaches, the inhabitants, the Martinicans themselves...

L: You just got back from Burkina Faso, and your company is now celebrating its 25th anniversary...How was your work received over there?

C: We had a flying start in the year. On January 14th, we left for Burkina Faso, upon invitation by a great dancer-choreographer, Irène Tassembedo, who organized the second edition of her festival [Festival International de Danse de Ouagadougou]. [...] Being an optimist, I always knew that one day I would eventually perform in Africa, maybe in a near future, to work with African choreographers who appreciate my work. And it happened! And actually the show I brought there, *Jazz Douss*, is an encounter between two contemporary dancers and a hip hop dancer, who dance to a [piece of] jazz music [*Olé* by John Coltrane], but use an element from a traditional dance from Martinique, not as a style, but as a form: the bèlè round. So the piece works around the circle, which is also the shape that jam sessions take, be it hip hop, or jazzmen in a street corner, it is always the same shape...The musicians stand somewhere, and immediately, the audience builds a circle around them, and in the middle the dancers express themselves. Therefore this recalls the traditional dance space arrangement. It was the fortieth death anniversary of [John] Coltrane, and I wanted to go down memory lane, so we brought this piece to Africa. The work was well received, because the audience understood my topic: how I used basics – without doing traditional dance on stage – the basics of a spine, the basics of the pelvis, how this pelvis moves in relation to everything that one learned, and added value to these basics, from this strong culture that flows into a way of being.

At the end of the day, I think that I choreograph our way of being, our way of being in Martinique, ways of moving...I think that unconsciously, it is inscribed in my choreographic dreams and creations...well, maybe it used to be unconsciously, but now I am conscious of it, because it is a recurrent theme! It all depends on the topic, if I am given a topic where one must dance the letter *i*, I think I would swing the *i*, because we can not be a straight *i*. We [in the Caribbean] have too much to express! Our walk is musical, our body is an orchestra, whether you look at the hips, the feet, the knees, the positions, the posture, the head nods, the gestures, the placing of the hands...we are a complete orchestra, it is all about putting it in symbiosis to make a choreography out of it.

L: Your mentioning of Coltrane resonates with my education, growing up with the sounds of Coltrane's *Africa Brass Sessions*. And you mentioned the circle, which indeed is recurrent in your work. You mentioned the relation between music and dance. Can you say more about your collaboration with other artistic partners?

C: In the case of Coltrane, the music already existed, since the artist no longer lives...I don't know if he may have enjoyed composing for the company? So in this case, the piece was directly linked to the music of *Olé*, which is really a very, very beautiful piece. And indeed this music is arranged similarly to a bèlè circle [dance and music style], because each instrument takes its turn of speech, like the tambouyé [drummer], like the bwatè [ti bwa player], the singer, the répondè [bèlè choir] and the dancer.[9] So I found an easy way through the musical space offered by Coltrane. But otherwise in my view, a true choreographic creation must be accompanied, meaning that the choreography must be the main art form, it must be the main statement that one carries.

I have a theme. I work with dancers according to the theme I need to develop, we do workshops, or excursions. For instance for the piece *An Kabel pou Lam*[10] dedicated to Wifredo Lam, and inspired by his painting *The Jungle*, we went

---

9   The bèlè is a dance and music style found in Martinique and other islands of the Caribbean, transmitted by Afro-descendent people over the generations.

10   The title means "One Kabel for Lam." The kabel is a traditonal dance step in Martinique.

out into the forests of Martinique...knowing that the catalyst for Lam to paint *The Jungle* was the famous walk he took with Aimé Césaire on the Balata road, so I took an excursion with the dancers on that road.

When I returned to other pieces such as *Paroles du bruit du dedans*, or *Mangrove*, or the *Petites choses de la vie*, or *Choc(s)*, it was first a choreographic creation, and then came the musical creation, the scenography, the costumes, and the light design. Often the scenography arose at the same time as the choreography, since one needs to work within the space arrangement determined by the scenography, or the scenography may become itself a partner, a dancer. So I often prefer to set up the choreography, and then... [the rest].

I have been collaborating with a great genius for years, his name is Jeff Baillard. We have been working in complicity for ten years, so we get to know each other better and better, and we always worked with a high esteem for each other's work, knowing that we both know our trade. What I appreciate about Jeff is his capacity to listen, and his suggestions. It is not someone who tries to persuade me to use a specific soundscore for a certain piece. No, Jeff puts his music, his whole self, his whole musical magical power in favor of the dance.

I can also mention Sylviane Gody who works with us, Line Backer Bonpin who works with us, Dominique Guédon, my light designer for over ten years. And honestly I can call on other people for specific tasks, but you don't change a winning team. [Laughter]

L: You just mentioned *Choc(s)*, in which the collaboration with the visual artist Valérie John is essential. Your movements are very aerial, but also grounded, there is a strong dynamic in this regard. The protagonist you embody seems to live in the rhythm between balance and unbalance...

C: This societal upheaval in 2009, this general strike that affected Martinique for two months...I was out there everyday, I participated in the movement, I watched TV, I listened to the people, I listened to the politicians...It came out from a great impetus and a great hope, but quickly, the house of cards collapsed, the sand castle dripped, the bricks fell apart...[Laughter] I won't say that I was disappointed, for it takes time...the life of a human being is very very short compared to History. History...if you draw a [graphical] curve, a century will be half a millimeter, so you can imagine that a human life is not even a dot on this curve [graph]. So I was shocked [by the politics], to see suddenly setbacks, people turning their shirts around [as the French saying goes], upside down, downside up, "nou mété tout moun d'ako" [Creole for the expression *we make everyone sing one song*] as the song goes.

So I was shocked. And I started thinking of strong moments in human history, I am not only talking about Martinique, but also the 1789 revolution, the abolition of slavery, civil rights movements, the women's rights movements, in Martinique the 1870 civil uprisings, the february 1974 uprisings, the 2009 uprisings. Some things have moved forward...I do not know at what cost, I don't know if there was an exchange of shirts, maybe it is common, I don't know, I was not there. But I keep in mind big names, all these people who fought, who pushed progress forward, who struggled, so there is a hope. I always keep the idea of hope, as I say in the artist statement for *Choc(s)*: I cling on, and I hang on to all these memories.

And so when you watch the performance, I start at a height of five meters above the ground, I run, and I recall myself running on the pavement of the main avenue of the Général de Gaulle boulevard...but here, in the performance, I run in the air, I do not know where I am going, I am lost, I run until I collapse out of exhaustion. And in the piece we are actually in a dynamic of "going around in circles," I run always in the same position, always facing front, never facing back, I reroute, I return myself, I turn around to run, still forward, in the opposite direction, but it is always a race going in circles. So I ask: am I bored, am I going around in circles, am I searching for something else? It all depends on the audience, and how they understand it. At one point, stop, we move on.

There is a very beautiful scenography designed by Valérie John, an artist who works with me, we are both great friends, longstanding accomplices. [...] She suggested this wall section that represents the crowd, all these shirts, these 250 shirts hanging on like bodies. And at one point, she set up, ahead of me, a wall section of shirts with collars, and long sleeves...and when I implemented this wall of shirts, I said "Oh no, I can't stand this, it's terrible!". It felt like an obstacle, like authorities that refuse to listen. Therefore when I worked on that piece, the authorities were present, onstage, but I defied them, and I allowed myself to laugh at them, saying "Where are we, where is this all going?" At one point there is also a "pool" made out of white shirts and linens. When I was choreographing at this specific moment, when I started to put on, and off, the colorful clothes I would find under this pile of white shirts, I recalled a quote by [Aimé]Césaire: "carnaval des autres" (the others' carnival).[11] Not even the whole sentence, only this expression. When I thought of this sentence, I laughed out loud, as I was dressing up, I was only thinking "carnaval des autres," "carnaval des autres." Those three words extremely motivated me and so I started to play with the dressing and undressing of the colorful clothes [on top of her white costume]. I experimented with this, until

---

11   "mon peuple [...] quand donc cesseras-tu d'être le jouet sombre au carnaval des autres" meaning "my people [...] when will you stop being the somber toy at the other ones' carnival." Maybe Césaire was thinking of his own complicity as a Martinican politician working within a French colonial system. Césaire, "Hors Des Jours Étrangers."

I decided that I would keep all these clothes on, heaping and stacking them on top of each other. Questions...

In *Choc(s)*, the number one question was consumption: prices. I find myself dressing up like a consumer, I never have enough, so I accumulate these clothes...out of fear of lacking tomorrow? Or am I simply a homeless person, who also searches, and is also in the fear of not having enough tomorrow? Or is it a behavioral disorder? There are strong, recurrent identity disorders in Martinique, people not knowing where they are at, or mimicking other cultures that are remote from their own. But I become aware of it, and I say "stop!" I explode into dance, and this pool of clothes becomes the idea of the bèlè circle, because the colors emerge out of it. So it is about the people, the people no longer in a uniform framework, like when we were running up the avenues [during the civil protests], but the people are now in a circle, and I dance for it, I say "But wait, we must return to matter, to the basics, we must search within our roots!"

At this point I call in three drummers, Micky Télèphe, Daniel Dantin, Marc Séraline, who play a rumba along to my dance. It starts with a *yambú*, and it ends with a *guaguancó*, which are part of the rumba cycle in Cuba. And here I do a phenomenal work, [connecting] my knowledge of traditional African dances, traditional Cuban dances and traditional Martinican dances. I start off with a simple *chacha lubafu*, to reach a *bel siyé*, for indeed the ancestor of the *bèl siyé* is the *chacha lubafu*. This is only one example, it was actually an array of research into my *Caribbeanity* if I may say [so], in my "Afro" resources. So when you speak of aerial, light dances that are also grounded, sure, that's right, but I would speak more of fragility. I walk a fine line. And at the end of the piece, you see that I draw a whole branch of shirts, which may be this fine line...on which cloth pieces appear. They may represent society, or simply the questionings that haunt me, the zombies I draw along with me, what I drag along. I leave it open to the audience – there may be different readings [of the piece] – and I am fine with that, every one may understand what they want, and often these different readings rejoin the choreography.

[Interview break]

C: So I was telling you that in *An Kabel pou Lam* and *Mangrove*, there is no specific [normative] gender. It is more of a "human being" dynamic. Well, not human, but rather living being, animal being, vegetal being. At what point are the dancers insects, at what point are they human, at what point are they vegetal? *Mangrove* is a subaquatic world, *An Kabel pou Lam* is a night world. When I look at [Wifredo Lam's painting] *La Jungle*, it is a thick forest, with various skin and light tones, but I see it as a nocturnal space. In both choreographies, there is a back and forth across gender. It is not about men/women. It is beyond. But surely in the rest of my repertoire, I do represent [cis-]women and [cis-]men, even when the [cis-]men wear skirts.

L: Let's conclude with the beautiful place where we are conducting this interview...

C: My most beautiful dream. Actually when I created this location, when I started planning this space, I called the project "the dreams in motion." I had been dreaming of this for more then twenty years: to turn the rooftop into a dance studio. Things moved on...[we are] on the rooftop of the Maison Rouge/Maison des Arts. It is the family house in which I was born, in which I was raised. We were ten children, all raised in this space filled with good spirits, loaded with foolishness, loaded with tricks made to each other. This is really a space that breathed...kindness, joy, cheerfulness, also pain (when you get punished), family spirit, parental love, and the love and respect my parents carried for each other. I say "carried" because Dad died. This year, he would have turned 100 years [old]. Mom is still with us, hopefully for long. [Her mother died in 2020, may she rest in peace]. They had a very warm and respectful relationship, we were imbued with it, and so it is a joyful house. And I am very glad to have turned it into [the Cultural Center] Maison Rouge/Maison des Arts, here in the neighborhood of the Terres Sainville.

It was a necessity. Musicians sometimes rehearse in one square meter, they work on their instruments. Architects, like us choreographers, are preoccupied with the use of space. They have a room where they work, and plan projects. And I was always in the position of depending on [space opportunities], having to ask for space in locations built for professionals. I don't even want to think of it now. All these small inconveniences led me to look for private funding. And I bought off the family house, without public funding, to turn it into a dance space. Today there are several projects here, including cooperations with the Solange Londas school, for the neighborhood children, and I am surrounded with professional dancers who work here. This is where we are at now. I have built, I believe, a highly cultural place.

Chantal Loïal in They Call You Venus at Moving Memory Festival, Berlin, Germany, 2016, photo by Layla Zami.

Chantal Loïal is a choreographer, dancer, and pedagogue. Born in Pointe-à-Pître, Guadeloupe (FWI), she arrived in France in 1977. She performed and toured with French, Congolese, and Belgian companies and artists such as National Congo Ballet, Ballet Theater Lemba, Georges Momboye, Tchico Tchikaya, Montalvo-Hervieu Company, Les Ballets C. de la B., and Raphaëlle Delaunay. Her training comprises traditional Guadeloupian and African styles. She also holds a State Diploma in contemporary dance from the French National Dance Center of Pantin.

In 1995, she founded her own dance company, Difé Kako. The group is known for a dynamic blend of modern jazz, West and Central African dance, ballet and Caribbean dances, accompanied by rich live-music, and for their irresistible enthusiasm as dancers and pedagogues. In 2015, she was awarded the Legion of Honor, for her 28 years of contribution to French culture through performances, events, classes and workshops.

The company receives funding from the French Ministry of Culture and the regional offices of Martinique and Guadeloupe, among others. They perform widely across France and the Caribbean. As a solo dancer, Loïal performed at various venues including the Kennedy Center and Maison Française (Washington), Festival d'Avignon, Bolzano Dance Festival, and Théâtre de la Villette (Paris).

www.difekako.fr

CHANTAL LOÏAL
01.03.2014 Paris, France

Layla Zami: Good day Chantal, thank you for taking the time for this interview, considering your busy schedule and the premiere of your new show, *Noirs de Boue et d'Obus*. Could you tell us more about it?

Chantal Loïal: It's a commemoration of World War I (1914-1918); The Great War. The idea is to continue the work I do: to be able to talk about the Caribbean, Africa, and about our roots. Therefore, we are still in this triangle that resides in me since the beginning of my [choreographic] work. The idea is to be able to let the soldiers from Africa, from the Caribbean, the [so-called] "tirailleurs," "La Force Noire," [The Black Force]] and France to coexist...to understand how the soldiers met in the trenches, how they fought war, what they endure during the war which was an atrocity. That's somewhat the idea.

L: With four dancers?

C: There are four performers, only [cis-]women as always – it is a known fact that my work revolves a lot around women. There will be three women soldiers who will perform, take us on a journey, and travel through all of the emotions that can be found in this war: fear, anguish, the trenches, the walk, monuments, letters from "les poilus," the wartime godmothers. There will also be excerpts of films which deal with difficult subjects that some of the soldiers have gone through during the war. The ones who refused to go fight were executed. We will have an excerpt of a film inspired by Kubric, and we will have "Le Camp de Thiaroye" by Ousmane Sembène, which covers the poor care given to soldiers, more precisely in terms of food. This movie, which is about the Second World War, corresponds to an excerpt where the "Moi-y'-a dit" language was established, in the First World War, for the Black soldiers, the "tirailleurs" to communicate amongst each other and also with France.

L: Ousmane Sembène is a Senegalese director...and I met you in Martinique where your show *On t'appelle Venus* was featured. A show, I must say, that moved me very much. I wrote an article about it already back then, it is also a work of memory...

C: It is true that my hobbyhorse is [cultural] memory. *On t'appelle Vénus* [They Call You Venus] revolves around Africa, but speaks of deportation, the triangular trade, and of a woman who was deported in the 1800s. She was deported simply because the Europeans deemed she had a different body type and ethnic practices. They wanted to make an effigy of her, so much, that when she arrived in England, she was displayed like a circus act, with animals, under the pretext that she had deformed buttocks, well as seen by the Europeans anyway. Furthermore, she was mistreated, arrived in England, than France, and found herself exposed, in cold weather, mistreated, sexually abused...and finally died of ailment. Painters wanted to draw her, and that's it. Suddenly, this becomes for France, since it's the naturalists' era, the opportunity to have racial slurs [...]. She became one of which we refer to when speaking of race.

L: You usually work in a group, whereas this time you presented a solo piece. What is the link between your personal trajectory and this solo? Did you dig in your autobiography to find inspiration?

C: While speaking of Venus, clearly! When a friend of mine, Jacques Martial, [the theater Director] at the Villette [Theater], mentioned it to me, it's because he knew on the one hand that I was working hard on memory, and on the other hand that I was committed to the [topic of] women. He told me: "I think you absolutely need to speak of this woman, there might be a comparison to be made with your body." Indeed, I realized there was a comparison to be made, since I have been working with contemporary choreographers for many years (even if I was using my body with humor), there were always the questions posed by the spectators: "Are these her real buttocks? Are these her real breasts?", the same questions would be raised when I went abroad. Therefore, it still needs to be addressed today, consequently, in 1802, Venus died, but I was able to come out of it, and to create humor...and the choreographers whom I worked with were interested in depicting that all bodies can dance, and that we need to accept the difference of otherness, but in Venus' era it wasn't what we accepted. This is why there was indeed a parallel to be made between what I was living on stage with the spectators' glance, and what Venus may have lived with the glance of these people who came to the circus, where the glance was pejorative, it was an atrocity. I doubt people of that era realized [this], or how conscious they were of it.

L: I felt you were tapping into that...as a spectator, we slightly are transported to a character of that era watching Venus, in the same breath, it is a contemporary show...

C: I did tap into that, I played on voyeurism, that's for sure. I certainly tried to make people feel uncomfortable. Physically, I was close to Venus, but I still tried to tell her story of suffering, what she may have lived, and to make people uncomfortable, put them in that state. There will always be those who enjoy and those who don't. Bringing up memory will always feel uncomfortable.

L: You just returned from South Africa where you presented this work. Was it received differently [there] than in France or in the Caribbean?

C: In the Caribbean, we feel close [to the topic], because throughout the show we speak of deportation, of slavery. In the Caribbean, I got very positive feedback, [as a] matter of fact, they said: "And it's a Caribbean [person] doing this show!"

We have this story about ship holds – Venus was brought back by boat. For the Caribbean people, it was clear, they got the message, and in the Caribbean, people are very demanding on this subject. In France, it's a bit harder, they felt way more uncomfortable, because they are responsible for what happened. Nelson Mandela had asked for [France to return] Venus' body and bones, so it can come back to South Africa, and that was cause for debate at the French Parliament! There is a situation of uneasiness. In South Africa, on the contrary, there isn't. They re-appropriated the body of Venus; it's their history. Seeing a foreign woman, well from the Caribbean, being able to communicate that, it was well-received, people were very touched. As a matter of fact, many have told me: "We feel that you are not from here, to be able to write such a show, and we have never seen Venus' story told this way." It was pretty moving.

L: How did you live it on a personal level, more so in terms of dance, since we spoke much about politics? I remember seeing video clips where you started in the Ballet du Congo, in group work..and now you return to Africa...in a solo.

C: Truthfully, I always used to work more with a group, whether in traditional African ballet or contemporary [European] companies. The idea of going towards a solo felt strange, because in my early years, watching contemporary dance [solos], I would say to myself: "But it's impossible not to share [with others], to be alone [on stage], it's hard to be isolated." Then, aging and gaining maturity, I told myself: "Why not?" It was a challenge to be alone on stage, but then, it fell on my lap as I was spoken to of this subject; it was the perfect timing for a solo. In the end, it's a beautiful experience, because one is left to rely on oneself, to defend a cause, and connect with an audience. Most of the audience members come out of the show crying, or feeling uneasy or screaming, and some are disapproving. The point is, my solo does not leave one indifferent!

In South Africa, I was proud and happy to retrace the steps Venus had taken. So far, I have only been to Cape Town, yet I would love to go where her ancestors were, between Cape Town and Port Elizabeth. It was extremely touching when I got on stage for the first time, in front of students of the university, I thought: "Finally, I am here." It was important for me to present this solo over there.

L: It is a beautiful story because in the show, in the South African music section, you actually bring her home in a way.

C: In any case I tried to be as close as possible to her story in order for people to understand clearly what had happened, where she left from, how she arrived, what she lived in Europe, and finally, how she left. I also paid tribute to her [posthumous] homecoming. Therefore, I think the idea of "going back" was important. I do hope to go back to Africa and tour cities other than Cape Town.

L: We first started speaking of the Caribbean, and you also current themes such as in *Zandoli pa tini pat* [Lezard has no legs].[12] You play with the connection between past and present, since we see Josephine Baker's bananas revisited by [the contemporary pesticide] chlordecone. There are some signs indicating the time period "1802"...

C: The initial idea was to speak of the environment, the garden, the nature. It just so happens that the show was created in the midst of Hurricane Dean in Martinique, in August 2007, if I'm not mistaken. So, in the middle of creation, I said to myself: "No, I can't pass on this." Hurricane Dean was able to bring forth a strong case of chlordecone history on the government level. For 13 or 15 years, we'd been fighting at the Senate and State levels for them to consider this issue, and it's Hurricane Dean that revealed the most about the history of chlordecone. I felt it was important to talk about it, because a year or two before, it had been Josephine Baker's 100th anniversary, which allowed me to make the connection. There were multiple photos and images of Ms. Baker everywhere in France, huge posters of shows about her. Josephine had a Black woman story as well, there was an ambivalence about this worshiped Black woman. There was again another voyeuristic side, which allowed me to continue riding this battle horse, the triangular link of the Caribbean, Europe and Africa, and to be able to dwell on another subject which is in a grave state, the environment. We suffer from health issues due to pesticides. Therefore, linking an internationally known character, who had been used in a "Banana" context, allowed me to speak of the past of Josephine de Beauharnais with Napoleon, in relation to Martinique and the Caribbean, reverting to Josephine Baker, who had been an international icon in the West. Painting Josephine Baker as a beautiful "banana figure," and then having a banana rotted by chlordecone, connected us to the past, to the duty of memory. That way, the youth stays connected, since our shows are very pedagogical, and the teachers hang on to the environmental themes throughout the school year.

L: You've mentioned a lot of triangular relations on the political, historical and social levels. What is the triangular in terms of dance, which is a mix of Afro-Caribbean-European?

C: My dance's identity is based firstly on Africa and the Caribbean. Indeed, I try to reconnect to movements from Central Africa, which are based essentially on hips and circular body movements, also movements from West Africa, which are more from the Mandingue dance style, with the head, the arms, the body's extremities, the jumps, and the Dooplé position, which represents a straight arrow statue. It's grassroots work we are developing, which can also be found in the Caribbean, either in Martinique with Bèlè, where we find the slightly

---

12   Zandoli is a lizard species found in the Caribbean.

different Dooplé position, and in Guadeloupe also. In Martinique, we find a dance that's much closer to West Africa, like in Benin, whereas in Guadeloupe we find something closer to Central Africa, characterized by more hip movements. Let's not forget that both Martinique and Guadeloupe have gained a lot from European styles such as biguines, mazurkas, polkas, quadrille, and court dance, what I call court dances. Often, what I say when teaching is: "[The] lower part of [the body], is Africa, [the] upper part, is France, the whole is Creole." It's an expression I developed while working. I use it in my teachings, because there is a specific attitude found in a Creole woman, which stems from these different African and European cultures, which in turn becomes Creole, it's reinvented, and I try anyway to convey this type of movement. Pointed shoes, arm dresses and haughty head dresses are elements found in Creole dance, where we are often "nagging" with hip sways. My work consists of that, preserving...and quite often mixing it with other knowledge, such as the one brought in by new performers who join the company. Actually, the company has a connecting thread, that we call "Afro-Creole."

Obviously, each performer brings their personal artistic baggage, their singular identity, which becomes a plural one within the company. This means that we accept each performer's singularity, while they adapt to the company's body of work. Therefore, these are people interested in the company's choreographic language, its connecting threads and artistic approach, and who want to do African and Caribbean dances. We integrate, for instance, hip-hop, contemporary, classical dances, and let's say, for a lack of better word, "oriental" dance. In general, performers arrive with their personal luggage, which is mixed with the company's luggage.

The [scope of the] company is very large. There is movement, we also use the voice quite a lot, the oral theatrical voice, the singing voice, and we know that in our [Afro-Caribbean] traditions, we do not segregate voice, music and dance. We know very well that in both Bèlè [from Martinique] and Léwòz [from Guadeloupe], we find voice, music and dance, it's not distinctive to one area, we all have it, and in Africa it's the same. Everything comes together, tightens up, and this is what I can say about the work I'm developing.

L: This is amazing! How long have you been doing this? You have created a lot of shows.

C: We have ten shows with Difé Kako, we are celebrating our 20 year anniversary in 2015. The idea is to develop and to make the world discover the Caribbean throughout carnivals, balls, dance conferences. The company is about 40 people, with approximately 15 musicians, ranging from percussions, bass, accordion, harmonica, violin...The percussions are West African (Djembe), Caribbean (Bèlè & Gwoka) and Central African (Ngoma). It's very, very, very diverse and [a] very large [ensemble]. What we find important is the use of a sense of humor. We try to write deep and serious shows while using humor, (and not every show is written as such), mostly they are created to speak of important subjects, with a light touch in this world of brutes. [Laugh]

L: It is indeed reflected in your shows. Thank you. Is there anything you would like to add?

C: Thanks to you. The only thing I hope for, is to get the next generation ready, that the youth are interested to keep going and that my company will be around for a long time!

Farah Saleh, Photo by Shareef Sarhan, courtesy of the artist.

Farah Saleh is a Palestinian dancer and choreographer active in Palestine, Europe and the US. She was born in Syria in a Palestinian refugee camp. She has studied linguistic and cultural mediation in Italy, and in parallel continued her studies in contemporary dance. She has been dancing and choreographing with Sareyyet Ramallah Dance Company since 2010, for which she created *Ordinary Madness* (2013) and *Hana and I* (2014). She also took part in and toured internationally with *Keffiyeh/made in China* (2012) and *Badke* (2013) co-produced by the Royal Flemish Theatre (KVS), A.M. Qattan Foundation and Les Ballets C de la B.

Since 2010, Saleh has also been teaching dance and coordinating and curating artistic projects with the Palestinian Circus School, Sareyyet Ramallah and the Ramallah Contemporary Dance Festival. In 2014, she won the third prize of the Young Artist of the Year Award (YAYA) for her installation *A Fidayee Son in Moscow*, and in 2016 she won the dance prize of Palest'In and Out Festival in Paris for the duet *La Même*. Recent performance works also include *Cells of Illegal Education*, and *Free Advice*, created with the support of the Artists-in-Residence program of the Federal Chancellery (BKA), KulturKontakt Austria and Tanzquartier Vienna.

In 2016, she was an Adjunct Lecturer at Brown University's Department of Theatre, Arts and Performance Studies, and a Visiting Scholar at the Pembroke Center.[13] She is currently a doctoral researcher in the Ph.D. by practice program at the University of Edinburgh and an Associate Artist at Dance Base.

www.farahsaleh.com

---

13   Saleh, "Farah Saleh."

FARAH SALEH
11.05.2014 Vienna, Austria

Layla Zami: I saw a short video trailer of *Ordinary Madness* on the Internet and I
was very touched by the performance. Can you tell us more about it please ?

Farah Saleh: Yes. We worked on *Ordinary Madness* in 2012/2013, it was a production of Sarrayet Ramallah, a company in Palestine with which I collaborate
with since...let's say, 2010. The idea of the performance was about the madness that the Palestinian people are living in, from the distorted social relationships that people are having, that are becoming very formal, without any
life anymore. So that's why we use a lot of gestures from greetings, and daily
life moments and relationships that are very distorted sometimes.

And of course we talk in a very subtle way also about political divisions, inter-
nal political division and also the Israeli Occupation in some moments, some
jokes here and there. I feel that the performance was thought (when we were
making it, the dancers and I), in a very light way, light and deep, but not in a
somber way.

L: So you choreographed the piece.

F: Yes, it's a piece of mine, it's 50 minutes long, but I like to work with the dancers.
It's me who gives the task, personally I think of states, or situations, I would
like to see. But it comes through improvisation and tasks with the dancers
so there is a lot of input from the dancers and then I put them together in a
dramaturgical way so that it would make sense also for the audience.

L: How was the feedback when you showed it in Ramallah?

F: I showed it in Palestine, in Occupied Golan, in Italy. So in Palestine it was in
the West Bank, in many cities and also in Jerusalem. The people liked it and
could relate to it because it had lot of gestures and situations that they could
relate to. They were interacting...there was also [a] little part where we had
interaction, one dancer would go down and kiss someone from the audience
and...people, yeah, didn't know what to do...and there were some more intimate moments...but...We thought that some things would shock the audience
but somehow, they were not very shocked but the performance brought something new to the stage. So we had interesting reactions from the people. And
also in Jenin, in Hebron or in other places where contemporary dance is not
common.

L: Yes, because yesterday at the conference you mentioned that you inspire yourself from Palestinian styles but that you make something more personal out
of it?

F: Yes, this was not about *Ordinary Madness*, it was about Badke, its a Belgian-Palestinian co-production, I dance in it, I am just a dancer so of course my input is there but Badke is a transformation of Dabkeh.

L: So in *Ordinary Madness*, you were not inspiring yourself from Dabkeh movements ?

F: Maybe not Dabkeh in general, but our daily life, Palestinian daily life, Palestinian gestures, greetings. For me, since I taught belly dance in Italy for a long time, it's really in my body somehow. So it is there somehow in my style of moving...a lot of movements not only in the belly but with the whole body related to belly dancing.

L: I think "belly dancing" is a wrong translation into English, in French also. Actually it means Dance from the East or something. I think it's just Europeans who called it belly dancing, no? Because it actually comes from the hips and the whole body.

F: Yes, it comes from everywhere in the body.

L: You were working with other dancers and you also work as a solo artist. What are the differences for you, how do you feel between working in a group and working as a solo artist?

F: I always had fears about working as a solo, because when I watched, or still watch solos, I feel "Wow!", you have the stage, you have to really be there, do things and be convincing otherwise it's really boring or not involving.
     My first solo was *Parole, Parole, Parole* and since the research was all about interaction with people and it was a miniature between 5 and 15 minutes, (mine was 9 or 10 minutes), it wasn't difficult at all, I enjoyed it very much. Because there was this interaction with the people I didn't feel that I was performing *for* people, but I was being *with* the people and feeling things with them, and making them feel things, and they were transmitting things to me. So it wasn't as difficult as I thought it would be. It gave me a lot of liberty, freedom. I liked it.
     And working with dancers is also very interesting of course. Sometimes it can be very difficult, because it's always about compromise, understanding the balance and knowing where everyone's role is, if it's division or collective work...but I like it, I like [them] both.

L: So you want to continue working with both?

F: Yes.

L: So you just mentioned *Parole, Parole, Parole*, for instance you're involving the audience, you send flowers to someone, what exactly do you want to reach when you interact [with] the audience, especially in different contexts? Because, as you mentioned in the program notes, this is about how difficult it may be to do something as easy in other contexts as sending flowers to someone, so when you present it here in Vienna, what is your artistic intent?

F: Yeah, for this miniature in general my intent is to make people feel this possibility of love, that very human simple thing that can happen when people
are close. And how easily I can do it with people that are very close to me, me
personally, and with the person I love...[across] this huge gap and distance,
not really physical distance but political distance, where I cannot reach this
person. And then from this intimacy, we go to the Skype chat, where for me
it's...where people really look for intimacy to talk together, to cook together, or
to have sex together but it's not real, there's no real contact. So yes, I intended
to try to make them feel this.

But, for me the Vienna audience was difficult. For instance, I performed at
least ten times in different countries. And the beginning here was difficult
because people were talking...they were not staggered in the space like we
asked them to. And so they lost the beginning, they missed it completely, this
contact. I think, it's what I felt, that many people missed it. And then usually
when I have contact with people, I can feel the contact. And I thought I was
trying and...not many really continued having it. And then there was a technical problem with the technical guy, he missed the cue...so I had to change the
end which didn't work as an end...but overall, I felt that the Austrian audience
was particular...but that's fine. It's a new experience!

L: It's interesting because yesterday when I was thinking about the piece, I
thought "Well, we're always talking about interacting with the audience,
making the audience react" but of course you have to react to the audience so
it's always...

F: Both sides!

L: Would you like to speak about *Sandwich Labné*?

F: It was the first piece where I was really a co-choreographer with other two
dancers from Sarayyet Ramallah. We worked over eight months on this 40
minutes piece, it took a long time because dancers at the time were not really
professionalized – not technically [in terms of training], but payment-wise [in
terms of employment status] so they had to work or study, etc. It was about
the Gaza war. And we were making fun of the humanitarian aid that was arriving after the war and helping the embargo! For us it is helping, and still now,
this humanitarian aid is just supportive to the colonial situation in Palestine.
It's just a game, it's money...it produces money for them and it makes us more
dependent so that we cannot really react and change the situation, it maintains the status quo. That was about it. And it was about the stories of two
little girls that were killed in the Gaza war. Through the story, even if it was
not narrative at all, they were coming in and out these girls...dancing, there
was no narration.

We were eight in the company, it was kind of collective as well, there was a
lot of input from everyone, and then we were putting it together and there

was the Artistic Director of the company who was the actual director, even if he wasn't really present. It was his idea. The idea of the girls, etc. It was a very interesting process for the group itself, because we had a lot of discussions, not only about dance, but also about the political, social, is it really necessary this humanitarian aid that we have...? It was very important to build the group, that's now still going. Not only as a group, each one is also becoming more independent, but it really brought individuals to understand that context which is really important for me. We toured in Palestine, Occupied Golan, again and Jordan, Lebanon. That was *Sandwich Labné*.

L: Listening to you, I understand the "dance as a form of resistance," which is what you talked about in your conference, is not only for the audience but for you also, right, and for the participating artists?

F: Yeah, especially! That's why for me it's not only about dance production but also about dance education. So for me it starts since you're little, but even if you start when you're older, it's good, that makes you think and feel, understand your emotions more and the surroundings, so that you can change whatever you like, so yes, in that sense it works on the dancers themselves.

L: Because we were talking about the Occupation, and you mentioned that you subscribed to the Cultural Boycott, so how does this materialize in your working process or in your daily art, your daily work?

F: The boycott movement has been growing lately in the past years. And for me it has been bringing results back. Because some Israeli people are thinking about it, they're very worried about it. They're becoming very worried about becoming an Apartheid state – which I think we already are – but now because of this movement, because of this campaign and because it is growing, the population in Israel is becoming worried and they're thinking – some of them – of changing the situation. Some are even boycotting settlement products – even though for me it's not the settlements which are the problem, or the only problem – but anyway. This is the boycott movement in general, that's economical. It's the Boycott Divestment Sanctions. But in it there is the Cultural and Academic Boycott Campaign and I subscribed to this one.

And as much as I believe that arts and culture can bring people together or build bridges, I also think that when you tell people "No! We're not equal, we can not make bridges when we're not equal." (and we make as if we are equal and as if things are normal), I believe this "no" can even change things more than these bridges that we pretend to build. So sometimes it's tricky because you think "Ah, maybe..., what if I meet this Israeli artist, or what if I see this Israeli performance" in Europe? Because as [a] Palestinian, I'm not allowed to go to Israel, and in theory they are not allowed to come to the Occupied Palestinian Territories, but they can. There is a small law that doesn't allow them but many Israeli friends of mine come, so it's just as if they don't really want to push themselves to go. I would be arrested [and detained] for six months in prison. For them, nothing would happen because nobody has been caught and put in prison [for going to Palestine] since many, many years. But anyway, sometimes I question myself a lot, also. If it's not blocking things from developing. But when I see the results on the ground, I believe, no it's working this campaign, and even Israeli artists are starting to change. Some are trying to do things on the ground. So sometimes the "no" also works, not only putting weak bridges or superficial ones.

L: You also organize a contemporary dance festival in Ramallah every year. How do you and participating artists react to the context of the Occupation during the festival ?

F: Since 2006 there is the Ramallah Contemporary Dance Festival which is an international dance festival, so it's Palestinian, Arab and international companies. 5000 international artists came to Palestine in these past nine years and they have been experiencing Occupation themselves as well. Problems on the bridge which is between Jordan and Palestine, it's the border, let's say, that's called the bridge. Problems in the airports, because they're coming to work with Palestinians so we send them invitation letters and sometimes they just take them for two, three hours [of interrogation], just because they are coming to dance...to Palestinian audiences. Nothing wrong, but it's a crime.

Until now no one was sent back, only some Arab artists didn't get permission, so they did not come. So performances were changing, adapted, unfortunately, but we were trying to find solutions. From the border, to the checkpoint that they have to pass, also their sets which they have to pass, sometimes it's a lot of problems, they open everything, they don't allow things, they do allow things... and the war, and the people, they see the situation, sometimes they visit refugee camps, that they have to cross, the main checkpoints which is Qalandia and sometimes on Fridays, there are some [...] clashes between young boys throwing stones and Israeli soldiers with really big guns and tear gas...so they see things with their own eyes. And they also meet Palestinians, for the first time [for] some of them, they don't see the Palestinian on the TV that they always see, the "terrorist" one or the one "covered all over with guns," they see normal people, humans. That's a big step already.

L: I think that's also what's specific about dance, to challenge. What you're saying, TV images, all these things or other media, they are giving us something and they don't want us to think at all. And what I like also about your dance is that it's abstract, as with all the choreographers that I am interviewing, they are telling very concrete things but in an abstract way, so that it's more complex. Once I go home, I still think about the performance or maybe I interpret things differently. So this is exactly what the project is about, to show that dance can be empowering or that it can change perception. You also mentioned, when someone asked a question in the conference, you said "Yes, I am talking about Palestine, but also people can see other stories," right, they can project, for instance you said that in Italy some people had different interpretations...

F: Yeah! Also they could relate to the stories of relationships that we were talking about, between men and women, between two men, two women, between a group of people, about superficial greetings and superficial circumstances we sometimes put ourselves in. Also the emotion that the performance transmits, you feel something, you live a process and you feel the emotions, it's not a final product, you act on emotion, so people feel the emotions themselves, and emotions are universal, [it's] not [about] Palestinian emotions and Italian emotions!

L: The last question would be, in which ways does your autobiography, well of course you already talked about your daily context but maybe your autobiography in the sense of the places you lived in, in which ways does it reflect your dance on stage?

F: Well, I was born in Syria, then grew up in Jordan. I lived the first five years of my life in Syria and then seven more in Jordan, and then seven more in Palestine, and then seven more in Italy, and then back to Palestine, but in the period between 2009 and 2014, which are five years, I had a base in Palestine but I had many months also in Europe, in France and in Belgium, and sometimes also in Italy. So for me this kind of continuous movement makes me feel a citizen of the world.

I am very much connected to Palestine, because it's a cause, so I want Palestine to be free, for its people, and I'm part of its people also, but I believe once Palestine is free, I come back only to my idea of [a] citizen of the world, so I can then go live in Japan, or in India,...because I feel this world is owned by everyone, not by certain persons, populations or nations. And this is very much reflected in my performances. I feel that I am universal or a citizen of the world. As I said before, on the gestures that I use, they come really from daily gestures that you can see on the streets here in Vienna or in Palestine. Same for the situations. It's also because I lived all these situations everywhere and I feel that they exist everywhere and people everywhere are really the same with the different causes that they live for and dedicate their lives for.

L: Thank you, is there anything more you would like to say?

F: Good luck for your research!

Zufit Simon in all about nothing at Moving Memory Festival, Berlin, 2016, Photo by Layla Zami.

Zufit Simon is a German-Israeli performer and choreographer born in Israel, living in Berlin. She studied at the Amal Alef Performing Arts School in Israel, and graduated in Contemporary Dance at the University for Music and Performing Arts in Frankfurt on the Main, Germany.

In 2005, she won the third prize of the euro-scene Leipzig for the best German dance solo with *fleischlos*, and the third prize of the International Choreographers' Competition in Hanover for *Meine Mischpuche*. Her awards also include the Best German Dance solo (Euro-Scene Leipzig), and the Audience Prize (Vorort-Festival Münster).

As a performer, she worked with Anja Hempel, Marco Santi, Sommer Ulrikson, and Christoph Winkler, who choreographed the solo *We are time* for her. Simon has appeared at international festivals in Italy, Austria, Tanzania, Poland, France, Czech Republic, Russia and Germany.

In Germany, her work was shown among other places at the festival Tanz im August and selected twice for Tanzplattform Deutschland. She was invited to the German Dance Platform in 2012 with *Wild Thing* and in 2014 with *I LIKE TO MOVE IT*. She performed at the Theaterhaus Jena with director Moritz Schönecker and the production *Die Zofen* in 2015, and with her own works in 2018. Her solo work has received funding from the Hauptstadtkulturfonds Berlin and the Berlin Senate. The piece *all about nothing* was in residency at the Munich Tanztendenz, as a part of her trilogy *un-emotional* about the relation between body language, expression and gestures.

www.artblau.de/Simon.html

Zufit Simon
30.06.2014 Berlin, Germany

Layla Zami: Memory plays an important role in your work, for instance in the piece *Meine Mischpuche*, you processed your family history in relation to the German past and present. Can you say more about it?

Zufit Simon: The piece Meine Mischpuche is about relations. Foremost, family relations and memories are a way to produce the piece. Memories are like a bag of emotions that we carry everywhere, no matter where we go, whether we are sleeping or awake...[Memory] is what we always take with us, [it] influences our character, how we act, react. That is something one can never let go of, never get rid of. *Meine Mischpuche* deals with the chain reaction of emotions within family, about how fragile family relations are. It was a fascinating process, with two other dancers, and it was also a very intensive process, living and working together for about ten weeks. During the process we worked with approximately 1000 [clay] eggs, that somehow contributed, that broke in pieces and are also very fragile. That was also a very exciting process.

L: How long was the work process?

Z: The process was about ten weeks, a long phase of "ups and down."

L: When did you decide that it would be a group work? Did you know it from the start?

Z: I knew from the start that this piece, *Meine Mischpuche*, would be a group piece with two more dancers. I come from a family of three children, I am in the middle, the "sandwich-child," so it was clear to me that I needed two more dancers to even be able to create different constellations and relations to and with each other. The process ahead of the rehearsals was long, a long preparation process and research. For a long time I had wanted to produce a performance about family relations and about my family story.

L: How do you work in practice? When you have an idea, before collaborating with others, do you improvise in the space?

Z: I started by doing research, I got a stipend for this production and I flew to Israel with a photographer. We interviewed and photographed various people in my family. We also confronted diverse people. It was enthralling to talk about things that were never spoken of before. Very slowly, like an onion peeling, we uncovered layer after layer. My father and his sister talked about memories from their childhood, things they had never discussed before. It was exciting, but also very fragile.

L: The dance generated change, because you found out through your research what you did not know of before. Did it trigger a new perception, a deeper perception maybe in daily life of how you deal with emotions?

Z: Actually not, it is just a bag that you carry everywhere with you. But my grandmother and grandfather came to the performance, my family came specially from Israel, it was also very interesting and exciting for them. For several months later, they kept discussing it, actually talking about what they had exchanged with each other in the interview. [Laughter]

L: Last month I had the chance to see your solo *all about nothing*, it was the premiere. This is also about memory, as you wrote in the program notes. But different kinds of emotions, it seems to me...

Z: The solo *all about nothing* handles emotions, mostly emotions. Memories are actually just a way to create diverse situations, diverse images that inhabit us...our minds...from our childhood or daily life, or emotions that we witnessed in other people. The solo deals with various emotions and moods that slowly rise up and slowly shift. The emotions result [from] the various moods that were developed slowly, that may be interrupted. It is about how emotions may be manipulative, in me, or in the audience.

L: I felt that strongly, because at the beginning, there was a party atmosphere, but then it changed, toppled over, and I did not know exactly when.

Z: The music plays an important role here, the music is consciously also very manipulative. The relation, the gravity between dance and music changes constantly. The music is not only in the background, sometimes the music generates various images that appear and disappear, and so is the dance: it generates images that slowly appear and disappear, the atmosphere switches from one instant to the other.

L: How did you collaborate, did you develop the choreography with music from the start?

Z: The musician accompanied the process quite early, we had a lot of discussions, exchange of ideas, we experimented a lot, in order to use the music consciously as a manipulative tool in some moments in the piece, but not only. We just researched into various moods of music. It was a very intensive productive collaboration with the musician Robert Merdzo, we kept working until a few minutes before the dress rehearsal.

L: And now on stage, is there some improvisation?

Z: Some aspects are composed, predetermined, and some are improvised, and it depends on the mood and the moment. Because the piece deals with emotions, one can not pinpoint "after three seconds, you start this and that," or that kind of cue. The perception of temporality can be stretched. There is also a part where we constantly react to each other, like a ping-pong effect between us. I take in some aspect of the music, the musician takes on some of my mood. It keeps going back and forth.

L: We talked about your pieces *Meine Mischpuche* and *all about nothing*. How does your solo work differ from group collaborations, in general?

Z: In solo work, where I am myself on stage, communication flows totally differently. I can directly implement, try out something and reflect with myself in the moment. [When] working as two people, then it is also direct communication, "one-on-one," but also the first level of exchange; three people is already a small group. Then there are various elements, various levels in the way one transmits something. Which moods are in the group? Which constellations are there between three people? There are various interpretations and variations. There is not only the work itself, but also the communication and how it flows, which also makes the process productive, rich, and exciting.

L: Is three a difficult number? You also choreographed duos...

Z: Three is already a small group. It is no longer one-on-one. From three onwards, the communication flows like this [hands draw a zig-zag]. Someone understands this way, the other one that way. There are all kind of possibilities.

L: Maybe we can also discuss your solo *ich(a)*? In this piece you deal with gender stereotypes and you question societal norms of being-woman or being-man, I found that interesting, can you say more about it?

Z: I was in a very long process, for several years I wanted to work with the theme. It was mostly about self-perception: how is one's own body and how is it perceived by society, what is seen as feminine, what is seen as masculine, what is seen as erotic, which body parts are erotic, what makes a body erotic. It also relates to media, fashion, different cultures. *ich(a)* is one of the works that matters the most to me, because it is a theme I have been dealing with for a long time and that had to "boil" for very long, until it could reach the stage, or even the rehearsal room.

It deals with the body, and disassembles it to the basic: flesh. The audience's reception varied strongly between [cis]-men and [cis]-women. I performed it several times and received different feedback each time. The light design allowed me to really watch the audience's faces.

It was a collaborative work with video artist Carlos Bustamante. On stage there were four big flat screens. The piece really deals with body, flesh and blood. It deals with human beings, and their various cognitions, and at the same time I show something personal and see how the audience reacts. I was very surprised by how the reactions differed between [cis]-men and [cis]-women. Many women identified with the piece, with what happens on stage, with the question mark, with the question of what and how one feels as a human being, as a woman, and their body. And the men...for many men it was difficult to watch the piece, to confront me, the body and the flesh.

L: So it probably means that the piece was a success, if your intent was to desta-
      bilize and show how gender may be a societal construct.

Z: Yes, well the piece does not contain a statement in itself. It is a question mark.
      And I had not guessed that the reception would be so different in terms of
      gender.

L: Where did you perform it?

Z: I performed it here [at Uferstudios, Tanzfabrik Berlin] and in Braunschweig
      and Hannover. Later I performed it again in Berlin. Because my pieces contin-
      uously develop further, the process does not stop at the premiere, it is contin-
      ually developed and reflected further from one show to the other. Therefore
      the last performances in Berlin were very strong. And also within me many
      things developed further.

L: There is no spoken language in it, right?

Z: No. It was a conscious choice to not use language, because otherwise it relates
      directly to a specific culture or country. In the solo *all about nothing*, I clearly
      use text and voice, and create various layers...between body language, voice,
      text content, and facial expression. It all piles up and the elements overlap.
      They do not create one common image, they do not complement each other,
      but rather overlap with diverse requirements as a background.

Wan-Chao Chang in Keep Her Safe, Please! at Silk Road Festival, San Francisco, photo by Shalom Ormsby, courtesy of the artist.

Wan-Chao Chang is a choreographer and dancer who was born and raised in Taiwan, where she is now based. She founded Wan-Chao Dance in 2008, a blend of many virtuoso dance disciplines, giving them a unique character. The company performed at West Wave Dance Festival, San Francisco Ethnic Dance Festival, Cultural Encounters at the de Young Museum, Festival of the Silk Road, Consulate General of the Republic of Indonesia in San Francisco, and Eve's Elixir. In 2010, she received a nomination for Outstanding Choreography by the Isadora Duncan Dance Award (Izzies) for the work *Follow the Footprints*.

Chang studied music for ten years in college, and studied Chinese Dance at the Guang Dong Dance Academy (廣東舞院大專班). She moved to San Francisco in 1995, where she graduated with a BA Magna Cum Laude in Dance Ethnology (1999) and an MA in Creative Arts (2001) from San Francisco State University (SFSU).

Chang performed with EMBAJE dance company (currently San Francisco State's University Dance Theater), Gadung Kasturi Balinese Music and Dance, Lestari Indonesia, and Gamelan Sekar Jaya. She was also a principal dancer of the Chinese Folk Dance Association, and a founding member and lead dancer at the Harsanari Indonesian Dance Company. As the Dance Director of the Westwind International Folk Ensemble (2000-2002), she performed throughout the San Francisco Bay Area. In 2005, she joined Ballet Afsaneh as a Principal Dancer, and toured internationally in venues such as the British Museum in London, Museum of Fine Arts, Houston, and in the Persian Iranian New Year Parade in New York.

www.wanchaodance.com

WAN-CHAO CHANG
05.09.2015 Taipei, Taiwan

Layla Zami: Hello Wan-Chao, would you like to introduce yourself?

Wan-Chao Chang: Sure. My name is Wan-Chao, last name Chang, Wan-Chao Chang. I call myself an "ethnic contemporary dancer." I founded Wan Chao Dance about, let me count...about six or seven years ago, in 2001 in America. And I was very fortunate to dance and work with many different talented dancers and put [together] some choreographies. Why did I call it "ethno-contemporary?" It's really interesting that I have been learning many, many different styles of dance, because I really am interested in different cultures and their traditional dance. But they have so many different dance vocabularies and body styles, so after dancing other peoples' dances [for] about ten years, I started to think, "What's my *own* dance?" The dance I want to make, deep inside, is rooted in traditional dance movement, but giving a different meaning, a more contemporary meaning. So I was looking for the terminology – how do I call my own dance style? Because when people asked me "What kind of dance are you doing?" I didn't know how to answer. Actually my husband, Bernard, helped me to find this term, "ethno-contemporary." So I kind of call it "ethno-contemporary dance." And since then, it's been very abundant, and I feel very blessed and, should I say, I've been neutralized with different cultures and many dance communities. Yeah! [Laughter]

L: You mentioned some styles you were learning or cultures you are interested in. Can you name some?

W: Oh yeah, there's a lot, actually! Let me see...Like a lot of kids, I took some dance classes, simple movement, or so-called ballet, and a little bit of Chinese classical dance. In college here, I started to very seriously learn ballroom dance, international styles, and I had very, very good teachers. I really appreciated it because I learned a lot. The couple dance, the connections with the partner. But you have to risk – you have to dance with another person. What happens if you don't have another good partner to dance with? And so I felt there is something else I want to try. Until there was a day I was invited to perform ballroom dance in a performance. That was an international folklore dance performance. I saw that – wow, there is abundance, there is a Filipino dance, a Balkan dance. So from that time I started to – I was very hungry – took all kinds of dance classes, and learned Bulgarian, Romanian, Hungarian, East-European, Malaysian and Filipino [dances]. Just a little bit. Everything just a little bit. And then, in order to be a good dancer, I started to go back to the ballet...

L: Did you also learn Iranian dances?

W: Yeah, that's right. That I actually did when I went to America. When I went to America I entered this dance ethnology program. I started to take Indian dance, because there were many dance styles I was very interested in, but it wasn't available in Taiwan at the time. So when I went to America, in addition to taking Flamenco, Indian Dance, Modern, after class I went to take dances like Russian, Ukrainian, and Indonesian dance. After school, after graduation, I also performed with a Central Asian dance company. I did a bit of Tajik, Iranian, and Afghan and Uzbekistan, that kind of dance. But of course I still continued doing Indonesian dance, because it's very beautiful, and there are very, very articulate dance movements from Indonesian dance. So I think that's my main source: one is Indonesian dance, and another one is Central Asian dance. And probably a little bit of Chinese classical training!

L: Yes, yes it is! I don't know many people with such a great mix [besides Oxana Chi, who introduced me to Wan-Chao Chang]

W: There are actually many. But most dancers choose – when they try different styles of dance, they pick the one they really like, and that they feel really touched their heart, and they really devote [themselves] to it. But I was too hungry! [Laughs] When my Kathak teacher told me, "Oh, you need to take ten years to master it," I thought "I don't have ten years!". I want to take these ten years to do different things as well. So [I have a] lot of influence from different dance styles.

L: And actually I can see this in *Keep Her Safe*, because they're using several vocabularies.

W: Right. *Keep Her Safe* is a piece inspired by an incident happening in Indonesia. My parents were born and raised in Indonesia, and later on they moved to Taiwan. So there is some experience – the culture, the history that they are familiar with. When I was a kid I wasn't really connected, until I was an adult, until I was away from home, then I finally got the opportunity – the desire to trace the roots. Of course, I found out – my goodness, I have so many roots I don't know what to pick! But that story really inspired me, that accident that happened.

There were two waves of anti-Chinese movements. I wanted to make a piece, not particularly to describe the history of the accident, but a piece inspired by the conflict. Not only by conflicts, but also by peace that we actually can make. Because after 9/11, when I was in America, I really saw a lot of splits. I was struggling – of course we are different, but we are the same, too. We share the same earth, but why do we see differences more than we see the similarity? And since then, I started to find the vocabulary that can connect individual cultures. Why did I choose the Indonesian for that piece? That's because at that time, I danced a lot of Indonesian dance, and my dancers were interested in it. And I was very fortunate to have an Indonesian Gamelan musician and Indonesian dancers to work with. That's a great resource! That's why I used Indonesian movement. But I also worked with many different dancers who had never learned Indonesian dance. They came from different backgrounds. That's why for that piece, not only Indonesian dance and Chinese – the main inspiration – but also some other material developed, inspired by those various dance vocabularies. Or the prop, or the music, or whatever they can think about.

L: So you didn't start alone yourself in the rehearsal room? You started from the beginning with people? Or you first started alone?

W: That's a very interesting question. Because usually I choreograph very slowly. I try not to waste my dancers' time, so I try to choreograph some movement before [rehearsal]. But I also realize that – coming from the modern dance class – dancers play a very important role in the creativity process, and it's a powerful resource. It would be such a waste if you don't have space for them to develop. Because what they come out with might be a much better surprise than what you have in mind. So actually there are two ways: I try in the beginning of the process to make the piece, to do a lot of improvisation, or creative exercise, to try to encourage them to come out with something: some gesture, some movement. Or to utilize different props, or space, or interaction with other dancers. That's one way. And another thing is, I try to come up with some movement and teach them, to see how they can take it. Because for dancers who never learned those traditional movements, the result is very different. After I teach them, I have to quickly adjust and find out – how can I make them feel comfortable with this movement? And also not only fit them into the movement I choreograph, but develop the movement to become theirs. That's actually a very challenging process, but I really enjoy that because the result is different from what I had in mind originally. But it has more spice, more...how do I say it? More feeling than what I originally created, so it's good.

I also think for the improvisation process, for the dancers it's actually very interesting, because in traditional dancing – we usually just learn steps, we just copy in the beginning. Especially for Asian dance, or the dance that I am familiar with, usually you learn [a] specific dance style, you have specific dance steps, and you don't have much space to improvise.[14] So it's very interesting to see how ethnic dancers struggle with the exercise. But you can tell that when they start to explore the possibility, you're happy for them. Because you see

14   This is also true to for ballet and other forms of dance established in the West.

they already go beyond the boundary, go out of the box. You see them actually start to develop their own things. I feel very happy that after we work together, some dancers actually start to develop their own form of choreography, or start to do their own work. I think that's really very fruitful. I think that's the creative process – usually not only about my creative movement, but also to do some exercises with dancers to see what's coming out, and then put it together.

L: The solo *I Thought Here Is My Home*, you mentioned this before we started recording [this interview], is a part that could almost be independent from the whole piece, right?

W: Right.

L: It's your solo, I could say?

W: Yes. I've just combined a solo and a group piece.

L: Oh, the group is also still a part of it?

W: Yes.

L: So I really like this image at the beginning...

W: For the solo work?

L: Yes. The circle. Okay, I don't need to say my interpretation now [laughter], but I could really relate to that, this idea of home, and that you could transport it or take it away. So maybe you want to say something about this. And also about being a solo dancer.

W: Right. I start to answer the first question about identity, home and roots. As I mentioned before, my parents were born and raised in Indonesia, so they moved to Taiwan, but since I was a kid, we have never been identified as Taiwanese. So there was always some division. We have a home – my parents have a hometown in Indonesia, and my hometown is supposedly Taiwan, and I do believe so. But for some reason, people, some people don't really recognize it. It's a very complex issue. I don't want to say it's right or wrong, because there are many aspects from a historical point of view. But from my personal experience at that time, when I was a kid, I was still searching "Where is my home?". Because it's not China, it's not really Indonesia, and is it Taiwan? Yes, it should be, right? And then I moved to America and became a foreigner, they called it "alien!"

L: Yes, they also called me an "alien." [legal term in the US for people who are not US nationals]

W: Right! And I devoted many years over there, a lot of my professional network is over there. But still, I was called a "foreigner" and I couldn't stay. Also when we go abroad, people ask us "Show your cultural dance. Show your culture," and then I start to struggle. My culture? Should I show Chinese dance? Well, I'm ethnic Chinese. But I'm not really coming from China, right? Should I show the Taiwanese Aboriginal? Well, I'm coming from Taiwan, but I'm not Aboriginal! Where's my culture? So it was a struggle at that time for me, because I was still searching for roots, and there is a stage where I recognized that, well – how do you define culture, actually? It's the environment I grew up with. Taiwan is the place I was born and raised, [where I] spent 30 years before I moved to America. In America I spent 15 years, and in the meantime, I spent a lot of time with different ethnic groups. I danced with them, I dined with them, I played with them, so they are part of my culture. I feel that it's very difficult: I have to split myself. You have "It's your culture" or "It's not." So on stage, *Where Is My Home?* is the beginning of the process, because I feel that I've always been an "alien."

At that time I was searching, where is my home? In that piece I feel a little bit lonely, and use a lot of material from Indonesia and China. That was actually the beginning of the source for *Keep her Safe, Please!* I usually start from a very small piece, and put it together and develop it further. *Where Is My Home?* actually is a solo development. Later on, another part became a group piece. The group piece actually works with a live percussionist, and it's very powerful. What I want to say is that, after a journey of searching for the roots, or trying to find the answer, or trying to find what's right or wrong, Black or white, I just want to embrace the colors, embrace the diversity, and just recognize that I have the strength, no matter where I come from. Those are elements which enrich me. In the group piece, different dancers start developing from a solo, until the break. A long tail starts to build up until you can say it's a celebration...different groups just merging together and...bump!

L: We were talking about music just now, so *Keep Her Safe, Please!* was your first experience working with live music?

W: Not the first time, but it's the first time I created a piece starting from scratch. I mean, the music is basically from scratch. Because I used to work with live music, but basically already composed. So I set the choreography on the composed music, but *Keep Her Safe, Please!* was the first time I worked with a composer to try to build music for that piece.

L: And you put together Chinese drum with Indonesian Gamelan?

W: Oh yes, right. Those are the two main ethnic groups for the theme. Then I realized, they are all percussion instruments! It's quite interesting, we did not worry about rhythm, that was a good experience. There are so many ways and so many different styles, and the musicians all work differently.

L: Very different rhythms also, right? The Gamelan music...

W: Very different.

L: Was it Gamelan from Java, or Bali?

W: The instrument is Balinese Gamelan, but the composer [Midiyanto] is Javanese. Midiyanto tried to compose music particularly for the Balinese Gamelan, but with also a flavor of Sundanese, Javanese, or Balinese. I like the composition, it's very beautiful. [...]

L: Talking about your solo, *Impressions*, would you like to tell us more?

W: Sure. *Impressions* is a new experiment for me, because it's my new solo work, with another musician who also composed the music. It's also a piece that I created after I moved back to Taiwan. The work environment in Taiwan is very different from America, the Bay Area I used to work in. So when I first came back, I had a hard time to restart, because I didn't know many people here at that time...unlike in the Bay Area, where I had a whole team, a whole cast, a crew I can work with, where I didn't need to worry about stage management, or sound engineer, or lighting designer. But when I moved back to Taiwan I wanted to do something. Even though I came back home I still felt lost, because I felt that my mind and my mindset were still in America...Which is a very strange feeling for me, because I am supposed to feel that I am comfortable here [in Taipei]. But I was actually not, and I realized that, after 15-16 years, there is a lot of memory in the past that I couldn't let go of. And I still think about that.

Impressions is a piece where I try to recall those memories from the past, the different segments. It intends to put them together, to call back the memory...like an album. That time, by coincidence, I had the opportunity to work with the musician Klaus Bru, to create this "memory" environment or atmosphere. I feel that in terms of movement, maybe it's a little bit traditional, but with the music, it is a new concept, segment by segment...it's a kind of experimental work for me. I am glad I did that, because after I brought back those memories, now I can say, "Good, I'm glad I did those." And I can move on to try different things.

L: It's awesome. Really great.

W: I finally bring it back to memory? [Laughter] [...]

Solo work is not easy. Especially for the Fringe Festival, you don't have much time to set up. You have to consider your constraints with the set up time and strike time. So you can't really do things as desired. And how can you retain audience attention for 40 minutes? It's very challenging to me. After that I was just exhausted! But actually, 40 minutes is quite a long piece for solo work. Oxana's piece [Neferet iti, performed at the Fringe Festival 2015 in Taipei] is also 40 minutes, right?

L: Yes. She has other pieces which are even longer, like 60 minutes. Indeed, you have to get used to the venue, and exactly like you say, you have to get used to the context, especially with the lighting. [...]

I could really relate to what you were saying about being a migrant, and always feeling "alien," and all of these things, because I have a similar – maybe completely different history – but my family is also mixed from many places, and also I travel. It's interesting what you say about Taiwan, because my family partly comes from Germany, originally – part of my family, [which] was Jewish. But now I moved back to Berlin, and my grandparents were German, but I don't feel [fully] German. But when I am in France, I also don't feel [fully] French. So I could really relate to it, and it's also why I like your dance because I could find my own stories inside it, or [I could] relate to your stories.

W: Yes. I think it's a struggle, because of course you can always say "Everywhere is my home," but deep inside, you always have that question. Also, how people really accept you for who you are – that also matters. At some point, I thought San Francisco-Bay Area was my home – but that's a basic fact that I couldn't stay. I am still a foreigner! And here, after I came back, I still feel that I am a stranger too. A lot of things are still new, or I can never be used to [them] anymore. So I think this constant journey to find inner peace, it's...it's still a topic, it's still a theme that can be developed a lot. Especially in Taiwan, there are so many immigrants here. How do they define, how do they see themselves in a different country. Do they feel that they abandoned their culture? Or how do they embrace their own culture? It's very interesting how a lot of immigrants, when they travel abroad, keep their tradition. They don't want to touch it. It has to be that way.

L: But even the story of Taiwan, right, people come from many different places in China. So I guess it's also kind of a mix of people.

W: It's a mix – actually it's a mix. "Are you Taiwanese?" That question is always a little sensitive. Why, why do you ask this question? It's just like asking people "Are you American?" I mean, we are human! [Laughter] We live here now, we do our work here, we contribute ourselves here, we are local. So why do we have to divide ourselves into differences? But unfortunately there are still differences, there are still conflicts. I think people are scared of the unknown, that's why they exaggerate the differences, and they are afraid of that. I think I want to see the similarities.

L: I like that you say that. And I think that dance can bring people together a lot, you know?

W: I hope so.

L: For sure. I believe so.

W: If music can do that, why not dance? It's just a different medium. Some people use artwork, and painting, and dance can be too. We all have [a] different vocabulary, so how can we use this vocabulary to build a sentence that both of us can understand. And both of us feel the same – maybe we don't see this exact same pattern, but the meaning is the same.

L: We understand the same.

W: Right. For dancers, the good thing is: they don't have a language barrier. So I think that's one of the powerful languages we can use. For the diversity, I think it can be a blessing. And also for myself, for example, even though I learned many, many dance styles, there are still certain styles I am more comfortable with. That's my body memory, that's the source when I choreograph movement. But I also like to take different classes, or seek different inspirations, or music, and try to help me to think out of the box, and to develop, to come out from this memory. [...]

I try [to deconstruct the dance]. The method I try is: after having this movement, I try to use a different music. Or just no music at all. I force myself to come out – to keep my memory for a certain stage and move on to find different things. It's...how do I say it? Not an easy journey, but when you find something different that belongs to yourself, I think it's a treasure. So, when I think back, I am really grateful for having this opportunity to put [together] those works with those dancers who are open-minded and willing to work with me, and also with those musicians, willing to take risks.

L: But they are also lucky that they worked with you, right?

W: Yeah, I hope so! [Laughter].

L: I like what you said about the treasure. I like that. Memory and treasure.

André M. Zachery in Untamed Space at Danspace Project (St Mark's Church), 2017, photo by Oxana Chi, courtesy of Oxana Chi.

André M. Zachery (b.1981, United States) is a Chicago bred and now Brooklyn-based interdisciplinary artist, scholar and technologist with a BFA from Ailey/Fordham University and MFA in Performance & Interactive Media Arts from CUNY/Brooklyn College.

He is the artistic director of Renegade Performance Group (RPG), a Brooklyn-based dance company exploring Black artistic aesthetics and expressions through dance theatre, visual performance, and film/media. RPG has received several residencies and awards. These have included a CUNY Dance Initiative, Performance Project Residency at University Settlement, ChoreoQuest Residency at Restoration Arts Brooklyn, 3LD Art & Technology Center, HarvestWorks, and a Movement Research AIR. Awarded grants have been from the Brooklyn Arts Council, Harlem Stage Fund for New Work and a Slate Property SPACE Award. Commissions have come from the Brooklyn Museum, Five Myles/BRIC Biennial and Danspace Project. Zachery was a 2019 Jerome Hill Foundation Fellow in Choreography.

Zachery has been a creative lead on collaborative teams ranging from music videos, theatre works, films and operas with artists such as Daniel Bernard Roumain, The Clever Agency, Kendra Foster, and Spike Lee.

The artist has taught at Brooklyn College and been a guest faculty member at the dance programs of Florida State University, Virginia Commonwealth University, The Ohio State University and University of California Los Angeles. He has presented research and been a panelist at conferences at Duke University, Brooklyn College, and Massachusetts Institute of Technology.[15]

www.renegadepg.com

---

15   Zachery, "Renegade Performance Group."

ANDRÉ M. ZACHERY
01.12.2015 New York City, US

Layla Zami: Hi André, thank you so much for making time, can you please introduce yourself?

André M. Zachery: I am André M. Zachery and I am the artistic director of Renegade Performance Group. RPG is a Brooklyn-based dance company that has three artistic components: dance theatre, site-specific performance, and film and media. Most recently, the major project that we have been mounting, and [which] just premiered our season, is the *Afrofuturism Series*. It is a platform where Black culture and aesthetics and practices are being remixed and reimagined through dance and technology and its relationship to 21st century culture and the global diaspora presence of Blackness.

L: I was impressed and moved by your performance *Digital Middle Passage (DMP)*, can you tell me more about this piece, how was the process of working on it and what was your intent?

A: The solo *DMP* was a self-exploratory work that was a true linking of past, present and future ideologies, frameworks, and concepts surrounding my own cultural heritage and my own experiences from traveling, researching, and interactions with experiences of Blackness around the globe. The work now asks what those experiences mean to me personally moving forward. In the sense of relating it to the Middle Passage, I wanted to capture the transitory experience of the soon to be enslaved Africans in-between [the] process of literally being autonomous and free to an existence completely defined by subjugation and itemization if you will.

So I am now asking: well, how do we remix that experience to reconsider that moment of transformation for this idea of Afrofuturism? In the sense of relating it to Sun Ra's *Space is the Place* (the movie where he leaves Earth and he finds another planet to exist in liberation), this solo is about a speculative experience for Blackness in the present moment. What is it that, where is it that we can metaphorically go from this state of constant, you know, resistance and revolution within our bodies and in our psyche, to a space where we can define a landscape, or planet, galaxy, atmosphere of an existence independent from whatever circumstances that we had prior, meaning on Earth, or in the United States or wherever you're from in this realm of the diaspora.

And so that's what *DMP* is really looking at: what does this cocoon-like transition feel like spiritually, physically? What happens to the body, mind and spirit? What is released? Do the ancestors come with you? Do the ancestors guide you? I'm trying [to reclaim] the horrors from the Middle Passage into a moment of self-actualization. In another sense I was thinking the transformation was about submergence into the seas to get permission from the ancestors that were lost on the voyage. That I had to literally almost drown myself to find their spirits under the water, to then get permission to move forward.

L: Thank you. I felt that drowning at certain points, I felt it could be as much about the Middle Passage as it could be about the present of a Black man in America. So how do you concretely work when you're in the process of rehearsal, and you have this idea. Does the music come at a later point, or do you choreograph first?

A: In the case of *DMP*, the solo, the music was composed by Ivonne K. Paredes. She is a composer and an MFA graduate of Brooklyn College's Conservatory of Music – Composition Program. We met at Brooklyn College and shared similar ideologies on sound and performance. I was really interested in Ivonne's work after I heard it in an electro-acoustic ensemble recital. I thought it was really wonderful, so I approached her about collaborating on this project. I knew she had done some compositions for cello, and I was specifically interested in having a cellist arranged electronically. In this piece, she actually used a lot of her Peruvian roots and cultural traditions to lend to this praxis of intersectionality within Afrofuturism. That it is not solely about people of African descent, but this idea of "How are you taking your own heritage and legacy, and taking with you, and moving forward?". Through our discussions I saw that's a big part of her work as well, so we were able to relate that to the sound. She created the score into three sections, which I really like.

The past few years I have begun working directly with composers – Ivonne and with RPG Resident Composer Jeremy Toussaint-Baptiste. It is really an intrinsic partnership that builds the work simultaneously akin to the collaborative relationship between John Cage and Merce Cunningham. I'm really interested in creating soundscapes in which the movement is encapsulated. Time and space for me are truly malleable, and it's not something where I'm always concerned [about] building exact counts or placement of movement. But it's like ok, this idea is coming here, and is framed by the sound saying something, here, and I'm interested in moving here, or the piece finalizing with this, so that is the picture [of] how, you know, the path within the relationship to the sound, it's flowing together, it's juxtaposing...I'm informing it, it is informing me and that's how this piece [DMP] was built and most work now I do with composers. I enjoy it and have some really great relationships creatively and personally. I can't really stress enough how incorporating live sound, with the Black body, is under-used presently in performance. It is something you [Layla] and Oxana do that really inspires me. That's something Jeremy and

I talk about, you know, I think that I would like to see more choreographers doing, bring[ing] that relationship back.

L: Yeah, it makes sense. That is one of the aspects I appreciate about your work and Oxana Chi's work. It is true that not many choreographers work with live-music. It also has a cost. It makes such a difference when you have this live interaction.

A: I actually want to talk about that a little bit more. That's actually something I was talking about with [RPG Resident Composer] Jeremy Toussaint-Baptiste. We realized not many choreographers of color work intimately with a live sound artist in NYC. At least we don't see it happening that much. It's something within our creative relationship we've been doing since we've met.
In one sense it happens on a mass level within social dance and social gatherings, in that, you know the DJ gets on, and the groove is there and magic is happening because it's a shared, intrinsic thing that we [Black people] do. Especially within this realm of dance and performance, the investigations that we're doing with digital music and digital sound in conversation with Black movement, concepts and performance structures we feel offers another perspective to expand on Black artistry. For us this is merely an extension of the traditional relationship from the mother continent with a drum/string/horn orchestra for classical forms of African (specifically West African) dances such as Sabar, Doundounba, Manjani. But now with this idea of Afrofuturism: yeah, ok, in how many ways can we recreate and remix the generation and initiation of this sound?
Black music and Black dance is a synonymous marriage. It continues to produce forms (jazz, hip-hop, reggae, zouk, kompa, soca, house, rock-n-roll, rhythm and blues) that feed an entire hemisphere. There is no separating the two. It's interesting then that the partnership between live sound makers/composers and dance makers of color does not happen regularly! I mean living artists! I'm not talking about dead. That's another thing. I can say I was inspired to see this happening with choreographer Adia Whitaker and rock artist Tamir Kali at AFROPUNK at Harlem Stage.
Within Afrofuturism and the work of RPG, I am really, really interested in contemporary artists across disciplines working together. That is something I would like to challenge more choreographers, older and younger than me, to really consider. We can ask ourselves, Who is a sound artist doing interesting work now, that's pushing something fresh?" and begin to really work there because that is a relationship that will really broaden our art and really bring generations [together]. Looking at AFROPUNK, it exists at an amazing level for Black sound and Black music, whereas Black dance and performance it's not quite at the mass level of appeal independently. So I think there is something that we can ride with [hands connect in a snake-like move], and build

amongst ourselves. Especially Black women composers and sound artists, let's find and support them. Those doing interesting work such as yourself [Layla], we must acknowledge Black women's presence within new sound, new music, remixing from our own cultural heritage. That is very important and part of the work of *Afrofuturism Series* and that should be a part of more choreographers of color moving forward.

L: So while you were talking about this, I was thinking on another totally different level, of *Dapline!*, where you make another big challenge which was to present a piece with Black male dancing with no sound. You know you had this great review [in the NY Times], people were really thrilled by your work, so maybe you want to talk about that. It's a totally different process, you're choreographing a group. You're still dealing with, I feel, memory, time and space, reimagining past imageries of Blackness to give new possibilities of imagining for the future but in a totally different way. Also telling the difference between working as a solo artist and choreographing with visual artist LaMont Hamilton.

A: The piece *Dapline!* was built from a relationship with artist-practitioner LaMont Hamilton and his visual series Five on the Black Hand Side.[16] What LaMont really was doing with his photographic project was anthropological work into Black cultural practice. 21st century anthropological work on breaking down African-American or more broadly African diaspora social practices of daily life. I think one of the things for the non-Black person viewing this work is to understand that there is deeper meaning in how we as a people [Black people] move and communicate.

Dr. Brenda Dixon-Gottshild elaborated on this at a Judson Church performance in September 2015. [...] Her artistic explorations show how the Black body moves in a white space or one that is framed by whiteness, versus a space that is really formed by Black experience. Black movement is very different. So the idea of "the Dap" [André simulates a dap with his two hands], for us, for me, living in Brooklyn New York, living on Eastern Parkway and Nostrand, is a gesture of love. Even if it's between two older men doing it, even if it's between two young men doing it, even if it's between two gang bangers doing it. All three of them have just showed love to each other. Usually, from a white frame of context, that is an absolute action of resistance. And that's how we begin to really tell the truth about race society and specifically this country – the United States of America. *Dapline!* is rooted ultimately in the personal experience of being a Black male in this country. Whether you're a Black male that identifies in a myriad of ways: hetero, trans*, homosexual, gay. Your gender pronoun is not necessarily the issue or the focus, but it's on

---

16   See Hamilton.

that shared experience of "Yeah, my body in space moves in a certain way. And I know how it impacts the people with whom I'm sharing space." I feel, and we all feel in our own unique ways, the experiences of this in the good, the bad, the sad, the happy, the triumphant. *Dapline!* is about setting a space for all of these emotions to exist and be translated through this one gesture – dap! Because that fist bump, no matter who does it, is powerful. But especially when two Black fists dap. It's a unifying and empowering experience that is loud! In that sense, we knew there needed to be no "added" sound or other acoustic element besides the rising of the breath, the bodies making contact with the floor and each other. In a way it made them [the *Dapline!* performers] hyper-aware of each other while in action. It's something that we didn't really need to explain. They just realized it themselves within the movement.

Dapline! is a piece that is very hard for me to watch. We created it quickly, because I mean, what did I need to investigate besides our own lives? If I don't know myself after all these years on Earth then there is a problem! It was literally my/our everyday actions with each other as Black men shared openly. Me, LaMont and the rest of the crew, we just decided to open up a conversation and let the world see it. It's something that our mothers have seen, that our sisters that support us and love us, have seen, and have held us and laughed with us, cried with us. Something our fathers, uncles and cousins gave us by birthright. But outside of that, it was something that...for people to see it so un-stylized was eye-opening. And I'm speaking for the non-Black here. For every Black person in the room, they knew what the piece was, and we worked our best to again, not stylize it. It was really stripped away, just be...your experience is real but just be...that became so clear and evident within that [first] group of men that we had, that we were so grateful they embodied. I think that is the real truth in the piece. That it is an honest assessment of our everyday existence. It doesn't need a soundtrack.

Working collaboratively with LaMont, he was able to bring a visual art perspective to help create these frames, these tableaux, and vice-versa: I was able to look at the tableaux that he was using as [a] reference point and say "this is work, how to get into action, how it flips out." From my own readings...I was really into the book *Pedagogy of the Oppressed* [by Paolo Freire] at that time, and LaMont was heavily taking on the work of Fred Moten. All of these considerations went into the work, all of that was shared with the performers, all of that was given to them whether they read it or not. We simply said, this is what we're thinking about and this is what we're all going to consider. And that simple [dap] gesture, you know, again, I think that's the depth of us as Black men in this diaspora. That head nod or hug...is love. From the oppressive standpoint, it's a tactical action of resistance that can be used to kill us. And that's the truth. But that's the power of our existence in this country, and that's why I'm saying that it's the truth about this concept of race. That's why the piece is hard, and it is heavy, but it's necessary.

L: You just touched upon a lot of things. I was going to ask you if your Black diasporic heritage is a daily source of inspiration or struggle or both, you totally answered that. I feel that's the power of your work and maybe that has to do with Afrofuturism too. How do we make work that's inspiring to our communities and that speaks in certain codes…Let's say a Black man would see your work and feel that it's about love and it's empowering and still it's relevant, in my eyes, to any audience, whether they are white Americans or not familiar with the US-context at all. Because you know there is body movement, there is emotionality, it's political and people might interpret it in different ways but still it will touch them. It's really interesting what you just said because I feel this was achieved with *Dapline!*, hearing the feedback from certain white people in the audience who might have read certain codes in certain kinds of ways before watching the piece [and expressed how the work gave them new perspectives]. Let's go back to Afrofuturism. You are also a media designer. In *Digital Middle Passage*, you use projections which you made yourself. Do you want to talk about the interaction between bare, raw movement and the technological realm?

A: As I was mentioning, the *Afrofuturism Series* was about looking at many forms and iterations of Black cultural practices or African diasporan cultural practices and artistically addressing them in a various contexts, re-imagining them or re-purposing them in new spaces such as a digital realm. One of the things I've said is: how do we access our spirituality through this digital realm? Are we able to still contact our ancestors in this virtual space? How does this happen? In that sense, yes, the framework for all the digital pieces, the digital media within the performed work was really built with this in mind.

I put these considerations into practice when building the technology aspect for the season. I was especially looking at the different viewpoints of how I was able to interact with my own body in the space. By using data from the livefeed to achieve interactivity, through capturing the movement to slightly alter the projected image. It's asking: my body is here in the space, but does one see the same or another body in this virtual realm? Bill T. Jones asked similar questions when he was experimenting with digital media, in the work *Ghostcatching*. More specifically, how does one translate the experience of the Black body in the virtual realm to the corporeal world? Is the feedback the same?

In the program *Untitled Distances*, my point of departure was tracing the use and application of iconography and symbolism from the African continent to the American Hemisphere. I started with images of the Bakongo cosmogram which serves as a symbol of the eternal life cycle. Shaped as a cross, kalfou, carrefour or crossroad if you will. Its extension in the Diaspora is especially relevant in the *loa vèvè* in Haitian voodoo. In the United States, because so much Africanism was stripped away all we had left to create our eternal life circles were our Black bodies. This is how the ring-shout practices [which are referenced in the piece] have survived and become remixed over time in the jazz improvisation jams, doo-wop circles, hip-hop cyphers and especially, dance gatherings. So we have all this imagery and symbolism and now I'm asking can we create that same energy in the virtual space – this idea of a digital ring-shout. Again it's not necessarily having answers. It's asking: what if we just place that there? What happens? I think this idea (especially within "elite" artistic circles that are mainly cis-white) is that "oh you know, Black people don't really experiment with their cultural..." and myself and many others are responding: Are you sure about that? Even hip-hop itself was an experimentation. Some DJs taking some records to find and isolate the "breakbeat." Even scratching the recording to get the sonic result of the vinyl being skimmed by the rock rhythmically?! That's a laboratory setting if I ever heard of one, you know? In a way they did a one-up on John Cage, who was not a fan of records as music mediums, and instead used the properties of the record as the sound generator itself and not solely the music within it's grooves! [Laughter]

To say that that [the doing and creating of hip-hop by Black people] is not really high art, but then see the constant co-opting of Blackness and it being resold in the "high" art market, or the "high" performance realm, is explicitly stating that Black people can be removed even when our artistic innovations, developments, and cultural realities birth these movements. I'm explicitly looking at Black cultural practices through movement, performance, and this digital filter of technology – and I don't know what's gonna come out on the other side! It's going to be received differently from each viewer [on] the other side. Digital media is a space that several choreographers of color use and have used in various ways. For myself it's always an integral part of the artistic process, it's never ever just an aesthetic layer. It is an absolute realm and body in itself that I seek to program to translate and extend the artistic message. Luckily, I had some space at 3LD [Art & Technology Center in NYC] where I was able to really look at "How are these dancers' bodies and energy interacting with the projections and affecting the space?"

In the other full-length piece, the *Inscription Project*, there are several interactive moments that translate Black presence and existence. At one point the dancers are creating the digital graffiti with the use of connected devices and the projections are absolutely speaking to what's happening in the space from a literal standpoint and historical standpoint. The work references practices of segregation in the United States like "red lining," and I projected these red lines with which the performers respond to in real-time. I think this is where the application of digital media moves forward from being an aesthetic element to being able to create another context in abstraction. In my personal experience, this again is such a cis-white male realm – especially because of the money that is needed to access this equipment and the time to spend with the education. For me now, digital technology in performance will look completely different if you put the equipment in the hands of a queer Thai woman and say "create a piece, you have a year!" It's going to look completely different than what a company like Elevator Repair Service would do with digital work. And I think that this room must be created within our art and performance world to really exist with equity.

And it's going to blow their minds up. It really will. People say "everything has been done before." Yeah, everything has been done before, but not everyone's story has been told. I think that's the thing that's so important that I am realizing now. Who is the person that's doing it? Who is the person that's telling it? The story will sound totally different and have [a] totally different meaning from each person and experience from who is allowed to get on the mic or get on the dance floor or get behind the computer and do the work. I'm just playing my part with my own experimentation. I love doing it. I think it's the next step for choreographers: using their own equipment, using their own lenses, cameras, and sound boards. But there must be encouragement to say we can do it. Don't think it's behind your reach. No, you can do it too. I'm doing it, I need someone else to do it too and be like, "Oh ok you do it like that, Im gonna try this..." We need that. We must become our own enablers, say let's just "nerd out." [Laughter]

L: Thank you very much André, I think a lot has been said and our time is up. Maybe just one more question that came to my mind while you were talking: you choose really different people to perform together, you have a way of putting together dancers that have very different bodies, aesthetic styles, training as much in *Dapline!* as in the *Afrofuturism Series*. I also really like that about your work, do you want to say one more thing about that?

A: Working with performers from different backgrounds, different ways of identifying, different bodies, different techniques, it feeds me. That literally keeps me engaged with how they're going to approach my own movement. In the sense of me being a choreographer, I do have a very specific style that I definitely have developed through a lot of alone time and experimentation. I am then able to relate to somebody and say "Ok, I need you to do this movement." I am not so much a choreographer that needs them to do exactly what I do. I don't need a personal reflection. But I think it's interesting to see all these different responses to what I'm doing and then see them collectively come together and negotiate how they all navigate the space together. What is most important for me – and I am not speaking for all choreographers – is that I have to be very clear on my own intentions prior to coming into the space with the performers. So my research, my trajectory with the piece, with the work, about what it is, where it is going and how we get there as a group – that always for me has to be refined. Whatever the movement is that comes out is going to be "André." That's where the various leanings and understandings of these different bodies, identities, techniques, come into play.

A specific task in *Hidden Tracks* was this idea of cultural residue. I asked the performer to consider this. "Okay, if someone was to metaphorically trace your path to where you are now from a certain place in your life, what would be the things that you have dropped along your way that have led you to where you are now?" The performer's first response was merely "What?", but then to see each person's interpretation of that is pretty amazing! Another time I created a phrase that I remember, "Struck fear into their hearts" and the performers said, "Wow this phrase is so hard." But then they work tirelessly to get on the material in effect saying, "This is how we're going to negotiate, this is what we're going to do," and I get performers that don't mind doing the dirty work. I get performers that are not interested in being pretty. My work is not interested in saying, "Oh I look so good doing this." I don't care what you "look" like, I'm interested in how you're doing what you [are] tasked with in the space. That's most interesting for me. I am beyond honored and lucky to work with each one of them, past, present and future.

TU(R)NING OUT
TRANSFORMING THE BODY INTO A SPACETIME OF RESIST(D)ANCE

It's hard to stop rebels that time travel...[1]

...says a voice at the beginning of Janelle Monáe's music video *Q.U.E.E.N.* The announcement is meant to welcome incoming visitors to the "Living Museum." As the people step into a white box-like gallery space, they find the bodies of political artists on display, "legendary rebels" that have been "frozen into animation."[2] The visitors take a look at the bodies of lead singer Janelle Monáe and her band Wondaland, who seem suspended in time. The narrating voice goes on, and explains that the "Time Council" has been "hunting the various freedom movements that [the band] Wondaland disguised as songs, emotion pictures and works of art."[3] Two of the visitors liberate the displayed bodies; by playing a vinyl of their own music, they animate the band back into life. A mise-en-abyme happens here, as the first beats coming from the vinyl are actually the beginning of the music video's soundtrack. Janelle Monáe slowly regains her corporeal agency, starts singing the song and dancing, as does her band, which begins to move and play music.

This scene epitomizes the power of perforMemory in postmemorial times. It suggests the possibility of a complex relation between art and resistance, between physical and political movements, between archival and performative practices of cultural memory. If music can destabilize power relations by conveying emotional and political meaning, so can dance performances intervene into hegemonic narratives, and bring a memorial status quo into movement. The ability to propel oneself across time – moving back and forth between past, present, and future – invigorates the capacity to rebel against hegemonic power. The seven dancing protagonists of my research not only invite their audiences to "time travel," they incite them to re-imagine the very consistency of time.

---

1   Monáe, *Q.U.E.E.N.*
2   Monáe.
3   Monáe.

Much time has flown by since I began this research, and the artists keep moving forward, on stage, and in the spacetime of their careers. We all flow through life. As this book is about to go to print, I am working on completing my documentary *Memory2Go* as a future audiovisual companion to the book. Farah Saleh is herself now pursuing a doctorate under the auspices of the "PhD by practice" program at the University of Edinburgh, College of Art, and she is a mother. Christiane Emmanuel entered politics and is a President of the Regional Cultural Committee of Martinique, while remaining an active dancer-choreographer.

Oxana Chi and I are back in Brooklyn, where I teach at Pratt Institute. We are both Co-Curators of Dance at the International Human Rights Art Festival. Since I completed the initial version of this manuscript, Oxana developed two new pieces. In her *Psyche* trilogy, she deals with her own embodied memory, in a quest to grasp, process and access knowledge of the soul's essence. The artist was also in the first historical cohort (2017-2018) of the AIRspace Grant Program for Performing Artists at the Abrons Arts Center. There, we developed a new performance, called *feelingJazz*, a duo between a body and a saxophone that has inspired dancers across the whole New York dance scene, and beyond. In 2018, Oxana Chi was listed in *The Dance Enthusiast*'s A to Z of People Who Power the Dance World.

André Zachery developed a new work in the *Afrofuturism Series*, called *Untamed Space*. In the Fall of 2017, I facilitated a pre-performance talk for the premiere at Danspace Project, in the St. Mark's Church in the East Village. In this 75 minute ode to the survival of Black bodies, Zachery and his dancers Candace (now Zachery-Thompson), Nehemoyia Young and Kentoria Earle maroon across space (Haiti, Southern USA, Chicago) and time (from the 18th to the 21st century). In the meantime, Zachery was also a Guest Professor and Artist-in-Residence at Virginia Commonwealth University, 100 miles northwest of one of the largest historical maroon communities, on the site of the Great Dismal Swamp in the United States.

The performances addressed here deal with such various topi as the European Holocaust, the Maafa or Transatlantic Slave trade, and the displacement of Palestinians, Chinese, and other citizens of the world. In this book, I strived to show how the dance productions generate a performance that not only represents, but also enacts memory from a contemporaneous perspective. I introduced the new idea of perforMemory, which is open for further development. PerforMemory is a corporeal intervention into Western hegemonic discourses and practices of history and geography. In my readings of the works of seven choreographers, I demonstrated how they respond to what bell hooks calls "the need to create spaces where one is able to redeem and reclaim the past, legacies of pain, suffering, and triumph in ways that transform present reality."[4] Consequently, I emphasized the empowering aspect of their dances. I validated the hypothesis that dance can contribute to

---

4   hooks, "Choosing the Margin as a Space of Radical Openness," 154.

"a politicization of memory" and to a "remembering that serves to illuminate and transform the present."[5]

As a reader, I invited you to travel with the dancing rebels of perforMemory through memory as a site of movement, through diasporic dance moves, and through intensity as a spacetime of memory. I argued that the place the dancers call home is the body they inhabit, and its electricity is the vitality they put in setting their body-homes into e-motion. I also showed how performers dance the past in the present tense, moving audiences forward through diasporic dancescapes. I defined perforMemory as a mobile memory2go, and highlighted spinning, jumping, and crossing as three corporeal sites of connection between physical and conceptual resistance. Thus, I aimed to show how the dancers not only become whom they imagine, to paraphrase Marquié,[6] but also re-imagine how to become... a narrative, a story, a motion, a memory, all that contributes to a human's humanity.

The book also demonstrates that the dances of perforMemory may transform memory matter, body energy, space and time. I explored the ways in which the performances shift conventions of linear time, physical space, home, and identity to perform counter-hegemonic memories, and thus intervene in dominant modes of collective memory transmission. Therefore, the seven solos in my repertoire of perforMemory epitomize the feat of a political corporeal rebellion that moves fluidly across spacetime, and eventually generates new forms of storytelling that may help us to understand, and transcend, historical trauma. While bell hooks speaks of the possibility to choose the "margin as a space of radical openness,"[7] I find that the dancer-choreographers no longer accept being confined to the margins, rather they move center stage, shifting the very definition of margin and center. They re-create diaspora on stage, and within themselves. Dancing, they permanently transform their own reality through kinesthetics, and transform the audience's relation to reality by propelling past memories and future possibilities into the present spacetime of performance.

A common element linking the seven solos, as well as other works by these choreographers, is that they move within a triangle connecting life, resistance, and memory (as an archival and as a performative practice). For instance, in the choreobiography *Through Gardens*, Tatjana Barbakoff earns an afterlife on stage through the contemporary body of Oxana Chi. While Barbakoff's figure can mostly be found in paintings and museums, Oxana Chi embodies her story in her former medium of expression, dance. Barbakoff was murdered in Auschwitz, a place that strangely enough, people visit like a "museum" today. Chi transforms the concert dance stage

5   hooks, 155.
6   Marquié, *Non, la danse n'est pas un truc de filles!*, 101.
7   hooks, "Choosing the Margin as a Space of Radical Openness."

into a space of memory, where contemporary audiences may engage with an anti-
semitic past in relation to present issues of discriminations. In *They Call You Venus*,
Chantal Loïal embodies the story of Sawtche, whose actual, bodily remains were on
display in a French museum until 1974. The performance returns corporeal agency
and dignity to a historical figure, and liberates her narrative from a double containment, the violence inflicted on a body that was exhibited alive as well as posthu-
mously. In *Digital Middle Passage*, André M. Zachery personifies historical and contemporary Black diasporic journeys, representing the capture, but also enacting the
survival of his ancestors throughout slavery, and his own contemporary survival in
a Black body in the USA. In *all about nothing*, Zufit Simon addresses traumatic violence, and uses at times large, energetic, and at times microscopic motions to
process the emotions stored in her body. In *Parole, Parole, Parole*, Farah Saleh centers love, and movement as resistance against an oppressive, restrictive geopolitical
context. When physical borders impede individual mobility, and thus the possibility of a relationship, her dance creates intimacy with the audience, and her play
with balance negotiates (in)stability. In *Choc(s)*, Christiane Emmanuel races, in the
air and on the ground, searching for stability on an island marked by historical and
contemporary racial inequity. In *Impressions*, Wan-Chao Chang dances the memories of her life, melding past, present and future moments into the spacetime of
movement. All these works suggest that perforMemory cannot be frozen in a "Living Museum," rather they reify the possibility of a "Living Archive."[8] Through the
live art of dance, perforMemory keeps the remembering, and its audience, alive.

Dances of perforMemory attempt to counter the physical and political immobility that dominant systems enforce on minoritized subjects. In them, perforMemory represents an emotional, rather than a factual connection to memory. Furthermore, they embrace the dancing body as a site and source of constant, and
conscious transformation. This is a quality specific to dance, as noted by dancer-
choreographer and scholar Hélène Marquié, for whom dance is a "perpetual metamorphosis," in which the body "plays with gravity, spatiality, temporality, direc-
tionality, senses, and the self's relationships to the world."[9] Marquié helps us to
understand how in molding of these variables, the body acquires the capacity to
transform itself, in awareness of itself. I addressed these parameters in relation
to the dancing body as a vector of memory, and explored how the postmemorial
aesthetics and kinesthetics of the dancer-choreographers transform memory, and
how this may in turn shift consciousness for the performer as well as for someone
sitting in the audience. I argued that perforMemory blurs artificial boundaries of
spacetime, and blurs the differences between the visual and other realms of cognitive perception.

---

8   Diallo and MID Redaktion, *The Living Archive*. See chapter one "Memory dancescapes."
9   Marquié, *Non, la danse n'est pas un truc de filles!*, 98. [My translation]

In order to offer a differentiated reading of the performances, I placed my personal interpretations in conversation with such diverse sources as performance studies, memory studies, literature, and dance theory. I drew from such diverse perspectives as decolonial feminist research, a TEDx talk on quantum physics, theological reflections on time, and the testimonies of Holocaust survivors. Further, I engaged in personal conversations with each artist, and offered you to read the full transcripts of these strong encounters. Beyond the end of this book, PerforMemory offers so much more to explore. In future research, I am interested in developing further the physicality and materiality of perforMemory, and the connection between gender and non-linear time. It would also be interesting to assess audience embodied reception and the range of emotions involved in the reactions to perforMemory. I would also be interested in further exploring convergences and divergences in individual and collective performances of memory.

In the very first pages, I wrote about the commemorative stones called *Stolperstein* placed by Gunter Demnig on streets across Europe. A *Stolperstein* incites passersby to pause and read names and information about individuals killed during the Nazi regime. I described how Oxana and I commissioned one to be placed for Tatjana Barbakoff in front of the Renaissance Theater in Berlin. Barbakoff's stone inscribes into physical space the memory of the time when she used to perform there. It literally influences the urban choreography of passersby, provoking them to watch their steps, walk around the stones or stop and look at the ground. The stones, like the performers, shape public spacetimes of memory. They link time and space, geography and history, to perforMemorialize biographies that often go missing in the historiography of the city, and of the country.

Many questions remain to be excavated, like memory, stone by stone, step by step. A few days after I completed the first iteration of my manuscript, a Berlin news website reported that a construction worker digging out grounds in a sports stadium accidentally found a gigantic swastika engraved under the lawn.[10] The swastika, known as "Hakenkreuz" in Germany, is an ancient symbol often used in Hinduism and other religions, but now systematically associated with the European Holocaust in Western contexts since it was appropriated and misused by the Nazi regime.[11] This massive swastika, made out of concrete, is thought to be the remnant of a Nazi monument that belonged to the stadium, itself built in 1929. While the monument was removed after the war, its foundation remained. What does this finding say about the grounds that we walk or dance on? How deeply is historical trauma rooted beneath our society, and how does it affect negotia-

---

10   See "Baggerfahrer Legt Riesiges Hakenkreuz Frei." *Der Spiegel*, November 21, 2017.
11   For an overview of the international history of the swastika symbol, see Campion, Mukti Jain. "How the world loved the swastika - until Hitler stole it."

tions of diaspora in contemporary spacetimes? How can perforMemory create new timescapes?

A few months after my doctoral defense, I traveled to the South of France with Oxana Chi, on the footsteps of Tatjana Barbakoff. We presented a lecture-performance at the Atelier de la Danse n°8 called *Traversées*, a dance symposium on the topic of trajectories of mobility, choreography, and gender, organized by the University of Nice Sophia-Antipolis in partnership with the 2017 Cannes Dance Festival. Oxana Chi performed an excerpt from *Through Gardens*, starting with the scene of The Journey. Oxana had asked me to open the performance with a brief musical prelude played on the chalumeau instrument, and to contextualize her dance by highlighting biographic and choreographic parallels between Chi and Barbakoff. On this trip, we were accompanied by Silvia Wojczewski, a Doctoral Fellow at the University of Lausanne, who was conducting research on Afro-German mobility. Both Oxana Chi and I are main protagonists in the upcoming publication of her dissertation. I had just earned my doctorate, and was now becoming myself a subject of doctoral research!

After Cannes, Oxana and I spent a short time in Nice, the city where Barbakoff was arrested by the Gestapo in January 1944. We could feel her soul accompanying our every step, along the magical ocean blue, into the Georgian puppet theater, and through the Chagall Museum and its palm trees. We reflected upon the role of dance as a practice of historiographical survival. We spoke again about Through Gardens, and how Oxana Chi gives Tatjana Barbakoff an embodied, afterlife in perforMemory, without re-enacting her choreography or biography, but rather enacting the possibility of her presence. I thought about the last four years of research, and the moving words of Oxana when I interviewed her at the very beginning of my research in 2013:

> [...] I believe that although Tatjana Barbakoff was put to death, and although so much art was destroyed here in Europe, she still left something here which gives us – me, or you, Layla, or all artists here – a certain strength to keep on going, and a fertile soil from which we can grow. And so I think that, even though she has passed away, she is still active and still resists, and that is also the case with many other artists.[12]

These thoughts will always give me hope that if we can dismantle the historic foundations of our society of inequity, we will find a fertile ground onto which to build, and to dance a better world. What her words suggests to me is the importance of survival as a trope of resistance: resistance of bodies to immobility/death, resistance of souls to trauma, resistance of knowledge to erasure.

---

12   Chi, Interview.

In the context of the Americas, we can also think of Audre Lorde's reflections on survival, which remind "those of us who live at the shoreline" that being alive should be celebrated as a triumph when you "were never meant to survive."[13] Deconstructing the very notion of historical victory, Alejandro Murguía's offers another compelling reflection on survival. The author explores his Mexican-Native-Californian genealogy in relation to history:

> History – as the saying goes – is written by the victors, never by the vanquished. I am neither of the victors nor the vanquished. If anything, I am of the survivors – the curious survivors who have brooded on the past and wondered about the future.[14]

Alejandro Murguía posits survival as an alternative to binary conceptions of historical trauma, spacetime, and diaspora. Chi, Lorde, and Murguía hint at memory as a source of power, as a site of inspiration for contemporary struggles. This spirals back to the question of narratives and perspectives at the opening of this book. Centering survival makes it possible to re-think historical trauma constellation beyond the binary distinction between perpetrators and victims, victors and vanquished, hunters and lions. On this journey, each chapter was a window onto the dancescapes of perforMemory.

If memory can be a "site of resistance,"[15] perforMemory may be the spine of resist(d)ance. The artists of perforMemory, in my interpretation of their works and words, merge dance and resistance, generating what I propose to call resist(d)ance: a live art of survival ensuring continued diasporic presence across centuries and miles. Luckily, not only trauma and concrete survive the passage of time, humans also do, and sometimes they blossom. To perforMemory then, is to be in the intensity of the dancing moment, and to perform the conscious possibility to transform one's body into a spacetime of resist(d)ance.

How to conclude a work on the topic of ongoing movement? Memory, like life, quantum matter, and dance, keeps on moving. Embarking on diasporic journeys, I traveled with choreographers who dig, sink into, jump towards, and reach out to memory. Moving with and within distinct aesthetics, cultural backgrounds and intentions, they share a common goal: to clear the grounds of memory in order to define subjectivities firmly anchored in the present, and already moving towards the future. As I write the final words of this spiral-book, many images and memories come to my mind. Dancers gracing the stage with movements infused by power, versatility, subtlety and creativity. Bodies jumping, falling, spinning, arms and legs wandering in all directions, diving into or rolling on the ground. Arms

---

13   Lorde, "A Litany for Survival."
14   Murguía, *The Medicine of Memory*, xiv.
15   hooks and Mesa-Bains, *Homegrown*, 110.

and legs tracing instant drawings on an airy canvas. Cores inflating and shrinking. Hands floating, joining, shaking, caressing. Faces playing all the arpeggios of the known human emotional scales – and beyond. Humans gathering and parting. Not only do humans stand on the shoulders of those who preceded them, they sometimes dance on the grounds shaped by the steps of their predecessors. Hopefully, the dances of perforMemory will help humanity to stop shipwrecking against the loads of its painful past, and to start levitating through the galaxies of its infinite cultural legacy.

Bibliography

Ahmed, Sara. *Queer Phenomenology: Orientations, Objects, Others*. Durham: Duke University Press, 2006.

———. *The Cultural Politics of Emotion*. New York: Routledge, 2004.

Ahmed, Sara, Claudia Castañeda, Anne-Marie Fortier, and Mimi Sheller, eds. *Uprootings/Regroundings: Questions of Home and Migration*. Oxford: Berg, 2003.

AK Forschungshandeln, ed. *InterdepenDenken: Wie Positionierung und Intersektionalität forschend gestalten*. wissen_bewegen. Berlin: w_orten&meer, 2015.

Ali, Kazim. *Orange Alert. Essays on Poetry, Art, and the Architecture of Silence*. Poets on Poetry. Ann Harbor, Michigan: University of Michigan Press, 2010.

Allain, Paul, and Jean Harvie, eds. *The Routledge Companion to Theatre and Performance*. New York: Routledge, 2014.

Allen, Zita. "What Is Black Dance?" In *The Black Tradition in American Modern Dance*, edited by Gerald E. Myers, 22–23. Durham: American Dance Festival, 1988.

Altınay, Ayşe Gül, María José Contreras, Marianne Hirsch, Jean Howard, Banu Karaca, and Alisa Solomon, eds. *Women Mobilizing Memory*. New York: Columbia University Press, 2019.

Amra, Widad. *Le Souffle du Pays. Nabd El Jayzirah*. Paris: L'Harmattan, 2010.

Angelou, Maya. *And Still I Rise: A Book of Poems*. New York: Random House, 1978.

Anzaldúa, Gloria E. *Borderlands - La Frontera*. 3rd ed. San Francisco: Aunt Lute Books, 2007.

———. *Light in the Dark/Luz En Lo Oscuro: Rewriting Identity, Spirituality, Reality*. Edited by AnaLouise Keating. Durham: Duke University Press, 2015.

Anzaldúa, Gloria E., and AnaLouise Keating, eds. *This Bridge We Call Home: Radical Visions for Transformation*. New York: Routledge, 2002.

Anzaldúa, Gloria E., and Cherríe Moraga, eds. *This Bridge Called My Back: Writings by Radical Women of Color*. New York: Kitchen Table, Women of Color Press, 1981.

Appadurai, Arjun. "Archive and Aspiration." *Archive Public* (blog). https://archivepublic.wordpress.com/texts/arjun-appadurai/

———. *Modernity at Large. Cultural Dimensions of Globalization*. Minneapolis: University of Minnesota Press, 1996.

Asantewaa, Eva Yaa. "Hamilton and Zachery at University Settlement's Performance Project." *Infinite Body* (blog), July 31, 2015. http://infinitebody.blogspot.com/2015/07/hamilton-and-zachery-at-university.html

Assmann, Aleida. *Der lange Schatten der Vergangenheit: Erinnerungskultur und Geschichtspolitik*. München: Beck, 2006.

———. *Erinnerungsräume: Formen und Wandlungen des kulturellen Gedächtnisses*. Kulturwissenschaften. Munich: C. H. Beck, 2006.

"Attitude." *American Ballet Theatre* (blog). http://www.abt.org/education/dictionary/terms/attitude.html

Ayim, May. *Blues in Schwarz-Weiss*. Berlin: Orlanda Frauenverlag, 1995.

Baldwin, James. *Just above My Head*. (1. 1978). London: Penguin Books, 1994.

Ballé Moudoumbou, Marianne. "Erste Annäherung zu Maafa." In *Interdepen-Denken: Wie Positionierung und Intersektionalität forschend gestalten*, edited by AK Forschungshandeln, 112–33. wissen_bewegen. Berlin: w_orten&meer, 2015.

Batiste, Stephanie. "Aquanova: Collapsing Time in the Lives of Sharon Bridgforth's *Delta Dandi*." In *Solo/Black/Woman. Scripts, Interviews, Essays.*, edited by E. Patrick Johnson and Ramón H. Rivera-Servera, 238–54. Evanston: Northwestern University Press, 2014.

Bauer-Zhao, Lisa. "*Moderne Kunst*": Betrachtung eines Topos im Kontext der Globalisierung des Kunstdiskurses. Bielefeld: transcript, 2020.

Benston, Kimberly W. *Performing Blackness: Enactments of African-American Modernism*. New York: Routledge, 2000.

Bernabé, Jean, Patrick Chamoiseau, and Raphaël Confiant. *Eloge de La Créolité*. Paris: Gallimard, 1989.

Boyarin, Daniel, and Jonathan Boyarin. *Powers of Diaspora: Two Essays on the Relevance of Jewish Culture*. Minneapolis: University of Minnesota Press, 2002.

Boyarin, Daniel, Daniel Itzkovitz, and Ann Pellegrini, eds. *Queer Theory and The Jewish Question*. Lesbian, Gay, and Bisexual Studies. New York: Columbia University Press, 2003.

Bragin, Naomi. "Shot and Captured: Turf Dance, YAK Films, Nad the Oakland, California, R.I.P. Project." *The Drama Review* 58, no. 2 (Summer 2014): 99–114.

Brah, Avtar. "Diaspora, Border and Transnational Identities." In *Feminist Postcolonial Theory. A Reader*, edited by Reina Lewis and Mills, 613–34. Edinburgh: Edinburgh University Press, 2003.

Brandstetter, Gabriele, and Gabriele Klein, eds. *Dance [and] Theory*. Critical Dance Studies. Bielefeld: transcript, 2012.

Brandstetter, Gabriele. "Dis/Balances. Dance and Theory." In *Dance [and] Theory*, edited by Gabriele Brandstetter and Gabriele Klein, 197–210. Critical Dance Studies. Bielefeld: transcript, 2012.

Bruns, Claudia. "Antisemitism and Colonial Racism: Transnational and Interdiscursive Intersectionality." In *Racisms Made in Germany*, edited by Wulf D. Hund,

Christian Koller, and Moshe Zimmermann, 99–121. Racism Analysis, Yearbook 2. Berlin: Lit, 2011.

Bruns, Claudia, Asal Dardan, and Dietrich, Anette, eds. *"Welchen der Steine du hebst" - Filmische Erinnerung an den Holocaust*. Berlin: Bertz+Fischer, 2012.

Butler, Judith. *Bodies That Matter: on the discursive limits of "sex."* New York: Routledge, 1993.

———. *Gender Trouble: Feminism and the Subversion of Identity.* New York: Routledge, 1990.

———. *Parting Ways: Jewishness and the Critique of Zionism.* New York: Columbia University Press, 2013.

Cadeau, Valérie. "Chantal Loïal - La diversité par la mise en danse du corps." *Point d'Afrique*, Mai-Juin 2011.

Cahyaningtyas, Alexia. "The Gambyong Dance: A Small Intro." *Cahyaningtyas* (blog), January 22, 2011. https://acahyaningtyas.wordpress.com/2011/01/22/the-gambyong-dance-a-small-intro/

Camacho, Dakota. "Matao: Queerly Navigating Indigenizing Creative Practice." Edited by Rosy Simas and Ahimsa Timoteo Bodhrán. *Movement Research Performance Journal*, no. 52–53 on "Sovereign Movements: Native Dance and Performance" (Fall 2019): 58-61.

Campion, Mukti Jain. "How the world loved the swastika - until Hitler stole it." *BBC Magazine*, 23 October 2014, Kiev. https://www.bbc.com/news/magazine-29644591 (Accessed August 1, 2020)

Campt, Tina M. "Black Feminist Futures and the Practice of Fugitivity." Barnard Center for Research on Women, July 10, 2014. http://bcrw.barnard.edu/videos/tina-campt-black-feminist-futures-and-the-practice-of-fugitivity/

———. *Image Matters: Archive, Photography, and the African Diaspora in Europe.* Duke University Press, 2012.

———. *Listening to Images.* Duke University Press, 2017.

———. *Other Germans: Black Germans and the Politics of Race, Gender, and Memory in the Third Reich.* Social History, Popular Culture, and Politics in Germany. Ann Harbor, Michigan: University of Michigan Press, 2005.

———. "The Crowded Space of Diaspora: Intercultural Address and the Tensions of Diasporic Relation." *Radical History Review* 83 (2002): 94–111.

Cándida Smith, Richard, ed. *Art and the Performance of Memory: Sounds and Gestures of Recollection.* Studies in Memory and Narrative 13. Oxfordshire: Routledge, 2002.

Caponi-Tabery, Gena. *Jumping for Joy: Jazz, Basketball, and Black Culture in 1930s America.* University of Massachusetts Press, 2008.

Capra, Fritjof. *The Tao of Physics: An Exploration of the Parallels between Modern Physics and Eastern Mysticism.* 5th ed. Boston: Shambala, 2010.

Carter, Julian. "Embracing Transition, or Dancing in the Folds of Time." In *Transgender Studies Reader 2*, edited by Susan Stryker and Aren Z. Aizura, 2nd ed., 130–43. New York: Routledge, 2013.

Castro Varela, María do Mar, and Nikita Dhawan. "Europa Provinzialisieren? Ja, Bitte! Aber Wie?" *Femina Politica* 2, no. 2009 (2009): 9–18.

Césaire, Aimé. "Hors Des Jours Étrangers." In *Ferrements*. Paris: Points, 2008.

Chakrabarty, Dipesh. *Provincializing Europe: Postcolonial Thought and Historical Difference*. Princeton: Princeton University Press, 2008.

Chang, Wan-Chao. *I Thought Here Is My Home*. San Francisco: CounterPULSE, 2009. https://www.youtube.com/watch?v=3OmLm8-OxbQ

———. "Impressions." Wan-Chao Dance. Accessed March 26, 2017. http://www.wanchaodance.com/Performance.htm

———. "Wan-Chao Dance." Wan-Chao Dance. Accessed March 26, 2017. http://wanchaodance.com

———. Interview by Layla Zami. Taipei, September 5, 2015.

Chatterjea, Ananya. *Butting Out: Reading Resistive Choreographies Through Works by Jawole Willa Jo Zollar and Chandralekha*. Middletown: Wesleyan University Press, 2004.

Chatterjee, Sandra, and Cynthia Ling Lee. "'Our Love Was Not Enough': Queering Gender, Cultural Belonging, and Desire in Contemporary Abhinaya." In *Meanings and Makings of Queer Dance*, edited by Clare Croft, 45–65. New York: Oxford University Press, 2017.

Chatterjee, Sandra, Cynthia Ling Lee, Shyamala Moorty, and Anjali Tata. "Post Natyam Collective." Post Natyam Collective - Process, Praxis, Performance. http://www.postnatyam.net/

Chi, Oxana. "E-Mail an Laszlo Moldvai, 01.01.2010." In *Tanzende Erinnerungen - Mémoire dansée. Femmage an die Tänzerin Tatjana Barbakoff. Katalog zur Ausstellung des Salon Qi 2011 in Berlin und in Paris*, edited by Oxana Chi, 12–13. Berlin: li:chi e.V., 2011.

———. "Neferet iti - Reloaded." *UnGehörig. Humboldt-University*, November 2016.

———. "Oxana Chi Dance Art." Oxana Chi. Accessed March 26, 2017. http://oxanachi.de

———, ed. *Tanzende Erinnerungen - Mémoire dansée. Femmage an die Tänzerin Tatjana Barbakoff. Katalog zur Ausstellung in der Galerie Gondwana im Rahmen von Salon Qi*. Berlin: li:chi e.V., 2011.

———. "Von Hier Nach Dort - I Step On Air." In *Sisters and Souls. Inspirationen von May Ayim*, edited by Natasha A. Kelly, 201–15. Berlin: Orlanda, 2015.

———. Interview by Layla Zami. Berlin, September 17, 2013.

Chi, Oxana, and Layla Zami, dir. *Durch Gärten Tanzen - Dancing Through Gardens*. Berlin: li:chi movie, 2014, DVD.

Chivallon, Christine. *L'esclavage, du souvenir à la mémoire - Contribution à une anthropologie de la Caraïbe*. Esclavages. Karthala, 2012.

Chung-hing. *Chants de Thé*. Paris: Delatour, 2012.

Clifford, James, Lawrence Grossberg, Cary Nelson, and Paula Treichler. "Travelling Cultures." In *Cultural Studies*, 96–112. New York: Routledge, 1992.

Cohen, Robin, and Carolin Fischer, eds. *Routledge Handbook of Diaspora Studies*. London: Routledge, 2019.

Cole, Teju. *Open City*. New York: Penguin Random House, 2012.

Collins, Patricia Hill. *Black Feminist Thought: Knowledge, Consciousness, and the Politics of Empowerment*. 2nd ed. New York: Routledge, 2000.

———. "Learning from the Outsider Within: The Sociological Significance of Black Feminist Thought." In *The Feminist Standpoint Theory Reader - Intellectual and Political Controversies*, edited by Sandra Harding, 103–25. New York: Routledge, 2004.

Commander, Michelle D. *Afro-Atlantic Flight: Speculative Returns and the Black fantastic*. Durham: Duke University Press, 2017.

Conyers, Liana D. "Shedding Skin in Art-Making: Choreographing Identity of the Black Female Self Through Explorations of Cultural Autobiographies." Master of Fine Arts Thesis, University of Oregon, 2012. https://scholarsbank.uoregon.edu/xmlui/bitstream/handle/1794/12380/Conyers_oregon_0171N_10368.pdf?sequence=1

Cooper Albright, Ann. "Embodying History: Epic Narrative and Cultural Identity in African American Dance." In *Moving History / Dancing Cultures. A Dance History Reader*, edited by Ann Dils and Ann Cooper Albright, 439–54. Durham: Wesleyan University Press, 2001.

Cooper, Julie E. "A Diasporic Critique of Diasporism: The Question of Jewish Political Agency." *Political Theory* 43, no. 1 (2015): 80–110.

Coorlawala, Uttara. "Ananya and Chandralekha - A Response to 'Chandralekha: Negotiating the Female Body and Movement in Cultural/Political Signification.'" In *Moving History / Dancing Cultures. A Dance History Reader*, edited by Ann Dils and Ann Cooper Albright, 398–403. Durham: Wesleyan University Press, 2001.

Cox, Aimee Meredith. *Shapeshifters: Black Girls and the Choreography of Citizenship*. Durham: Duke University Press, 2015.

Cvetkovich, Ann. *An Archive of Feelings: Trauma, Sexuality, and Lesbian Public Cultures*. Durham: Duke University Press, 2003.

Cyrille, Dominique. "Musique, Danse et Résistance En Guadeloupe et En Martinique," in *Les Armes Miraculeuses. Paroles, Chants, Poésie, Littérature, Rites et Mémoires*, Africultures, vol. 98, Paris: L'Harmattan, 2013, 116–24.

Cyrulnik, Boris. *Je Me Souviens*. Textes Essentiels. Le Bouscat: L'Esprit du Temps, 2009.

DeFrantz, Thomas. *Dancing Revelations: Alvin Ailey's Embodiment of African American Culture*. Durham: Duke University Press, 2006.

DeFrantz, Thomas F., and Anita Gonzalez, eds. *Black Performance Theory*. Durham: Duke University Press, 2014.

DeFrantz, Thomas, and Tara A. Willis. "Black Moves: New Research in Black Dance Studies." Edited by Thomas DeFrantz and Tara A. Willis. *The Black Scholar* 46, no. 1 (2016).

Desmond, Jane C. "Engendering Dance: Feminist Inquiry and Dance Research." In *Researching Dance - Evolving Modes of Inquiry*, edited by Sondra Horton Fraleigh and Penelope Hanstein. Pittsburgh: University of Pittsburgh Press, 1999.

———, ed. *Meaning in Motion: New Cultural Studies of Dance*. Durham: Duke University Press, 1997.

Diallo, Aïcha, and MID Redaktion, eds. *The Living Archive: Kulturelle Produktionen Und Räume*. Berlin: Heinrich-Boell-Stiftung, 2013. http://heimatkunde.boell.de/tags/living-archive-kulturelle-produktionen-und-raeume

Diawara, Manthia. "Conversation with Edouard Glissant Aboard the Queen Mary II (August 2009)." In *Afromodern: Journey Through The Black Atlantic*, 59–63. Liverpool: Tate Publishing, 2010.

Diggs Colbert, Soyica. "Black Movements: Flying Africans in Spaceships." In *Black Performance Theory*, edited by Thomas F. DeFrantz and Anita Gonzalez, 129–48. Durham: Duke University Press, 2014.

Dixon Gottschild, Brenda. "Dance Is a Message in a Cultural Envelope. Urban Bush Women, Jant-Bi, and Diasporan Dialogues." Brenda Dixon-Gottschild. Writer on Dance and Culture, 2009. http://brendadixongottschild.files.wordpress.com/2010/07/dance-is-a-message-in-a-cultural-envelope.pdf

———. *Digging the Africanist Presence in American Performance: Dance and Other Contexts*. Contributions in Afro-American and African Studies 179. Westport: Greenwood Press, 1996.

———. "'Racing' in 'Place': Dance Studies and the Academy." Duke University, 2015. http://humanitiesfutures.org/papers/racing-in-place-dance-studies-and-the-academy/

———. *The Black Dancing Body: A Geography From Coon to Cool*. 1st ed. New York: Palgrave-Macmillan, 2003.

Dolan, Jill. *Utopia in Performance: Finding Hope at the Theater*. Ann Harbor, Michigan: University of Michigan Press, 2005.

Drenker-Nagels, Klara, Günter Goebbels, and Hildegard Reinhardt. *Tatjana Barbakoff (1899–1944) – Tänzerin und Muse*. Edited by Verein August-Macke-Haus. 43. Bonn: August-Macke-Haus, 2002.

Ellis, Nadia. *Territories of the Soul: Queered Belonging in the Black Diaspora*. Durham: Duke University Press, 2015.

El-Tayeb, Fatima. *European Others: Queering Ethnicity in Postnational Europe*. Difference Incorporated. Minneapolis: University of Minnesota Press, 2011.

———. *Undeutsch. Die Konstruktion Des Anderen in Der Postmigrantischen Gesellshaft*. Bielefeld: transcript, 2016.

Emmanuel, Christiane. "Choc(s) - Artist Statement," 2011.

———. "Rencontre." Conference presented at the Exhibition LAM CESAIRE PICASSO, Habitation Clément, Martinique, December 15, 2013.

———. Interview by Layla Zami. Fort-de-France, February 21, 2014.

Etoke, Nathalie. *Melancholia Africana: L'Indispensable Dépassement de la Condition Noire*. Coll. Mémoires Du Sud. Paris: Editions du Cygne, 2010.

Fabre, Geneviève E. "The Slave Ship Dance." In *Black Imagination and the Middle Passage*, edited by Maria Diedrich and Henry Louis Gates, Jr., 33–46. W.E.B. Du Bois Institute. Oxford: Oxford University Press, 1999.

Firmino Castillo, María Regina, Daniel Fernando Guarcax González, and Tohil Fridel Brito Bernal. "Beyond the Border: Embodied Mesoamerican Transmotions." Edited by Rosy Simas and Ahimsa Timoteo Bodhrán. *Movement Research Performance Journal*, no. 52–53 on "Sovereign Movements: Native Dance and Performance" (Fall 2019): 34-41.

Fischer-Lichte, Erika. *Ästhetik Des Performativen*. Frankfurt a.M.: Suhrkamp, 2004.

Foster, Susan L. "Choreographies of Writing." Performed Lecture presented at the Susan Foster! Susan Foster! Bodies of Work: 3 Lectures: Performed, Pew Center for Arts & Heritage, Philadelphia, March 22, 2011. http://danceworkbook. pcah.us/susan-foster/choreographies-of-writing.html

———, ed. *Corporealities: Dancing Knowledge, Culture and Power*. New York: Routledge, 1996.

———. *Reading Choreography: Bodies and Subjects in Contemporary American Dance*. Berkeley: University of California Press, 1986.

———. "Worlding Dance: An Introduction." In *Worlding Dance*, edited by Susan L. Foster, 1–13. Studies in International Performance. NYC: Palgrave-Macmillan, 2011.

Fox, Robert Elliot. "Diasporacentrism and Black Aura Texts." In *The African Diaspora: African Origins and New World Identities*, edited by Isidore Okpewho, Carole Boyce Davies, and Ali A. Mazrui, 367–78. Bloomington: Indiana University Press, 1999.

Fuentes, Marisa J. *Dispossessed Lives: Enslaved Women, Violence, and the Archive*. Philadelphia: University of Pennsylvania Press, 2016.

Gabriel, Teshome. "Ruin and The Other: Towards a Language Of Memory." *Teshome Gabriel - Articles & Other Works* (blog). Accessed February 9, 2016. http:// teshomegabriel.net/ruin-and-the-other

Gebske, Jennifer. "Performativität zwischen Zitation und Ereignis. Vergleich der Performativitätsbegriffe von Judith Butler und Erika Fischer-Lichte." Magisterarbeit, Friedrich-Alexander-Universität, 2009. https://opus4.kobv.de/opus4-fau/files/1593/MagisterGebske.pdf

George-Graves, Nadine. "Diasporic Spidering: Constructing Contemporary Black Identities." In *Black Performance Theory*, edited by Thomas F. DeFrantz and Anita Gonzalez, 33–44. Durham: Duke University Press, 2014.

———, ed. *The Oxford Handbook of Dance and Theater*. Oxford: Oxford University Press, 2015.

———. *Urban Bush Women: Twenty Years of African American Dance Theater, Community Engagement, and Working It Out*. Studies in Dance History. Madison: University of Wisconsin Press, 2010.

Glissant, Édouard, and Sylvie Sémavoine Glissant. "La Pensée Du Tremblement." *Contemporary French & Francophone Studies* 20, no. 4–5 (2016): 526–29.

Glissant, Édouard. *Le Discours Antillais*. Paris: Seuil, 1981.

Goebbels, Günter. *Tatjana Barbakoff: eine vergessene Tänzerin in Bildern und Dokumentation*. Düsseldorf: Freundeskreis Kulturbahnhof Eller e.V., 2009.

Gopinath, Gayatri. *Impossible Desires: Queer Diasporas and South Asian Public Cultures*. Perverse Modernities. Duke University Press, 2005.

Green, Jill, and Susan W. Stinson. "Postpositivist Research in Dance." In *Researching Dance: Evolving Modes of Inquiry*, edited by Sondra Horton Fraleigh and Penelope Hanstein, 91–123. Pittsburgh: University of Pittsburgh Press, 1999.

Ha, Kien Nghi, ed. *Asiatische Deutsche. Vietnamesische Diaspora and Beyond*. Berlin: Assoziation A, 2012.

———. "Die Fragile Erinnerung Des Entinnerten." Bundeszentrale für politische Bildung, October 23, 2012. http://www.bpb.de/apuz/146985/die-fragile-erinnerung-des-entinnerten?

———. "Macht (T)raum(a) Berlin: Deutschland Als Kolonialgesellschaft." In *Mythen, Masken Und Subjekte. Kritische Weißseinsforschung in Deutschland*, edited by Maureen Maisha Eggers, Grada Kilomba, Peggy Piesche, and Susanne Arndt, 105–17. Münster: Unrast-Verlag, 2009.

———. "People of Colour." In *Rassismus Auf Gut Deutsch. Ein Kritisches Nachschlagewerk Zu Rassistischen Sprachhandlungen*, edited by Adibeli Nduka-Agwu and Lann Hornscheidt, Transdisziplinäre Genderstudien 1:80–84. Wissen & Praxis 155. Frankfurt a.M.: Brandes & Apsel, 2010.

———. "Rostock-Lichtenhagen: Die Rückkehr Des Verdrängten." Heinrich-Boell-Stiftung, January 9, 2012. https://heimatkunde.boell.de/2012/09/01/rostock-lichtenhagen-die-rueckkehr-des-verdraengten

Hall, Stuart. "Cultural Identity and Diaspora." In *Colonial Discourse and Postcolonial Theory*, edited by Patrick Williams and Laura Chrisman. New York: Columbia University Press, 1994.

Hamilton, LaMont. LaMont Hamilton. Accessed July 4, 2017. https://www.lamonthamilton.com/

Han, Byung-Chul. *Duft der Zeit. Ein philosophischer Essay zur Kunst des Verweilens*. 12th ed. x texte. Bielefeld: Transcript, 2015.

Hardt, Yvonne. "Engagement with the Past in Contemporary Dance." In *New German Dance Studies*, edited by Susan Manning and Lucia Ruprecht, 217–31. Chicago: University of Illinois, 2012.

Harry J. Jr Elam. *The Past as Present in the Drama of August Wilson*. Ann Arbor: University of Michigan Press, 2006.

Hartman, Saidiya. *Loose Your Mother: A Journey Along the Atlantic Slave Route*. New York: Farrar, Straus and Giroux, 2007.

———. "Venus in Two Acts." *Small Axe* 12–2, no. 26 (June 2008): 1–14.

Hayes, Jarrod. "Queering Roots, Queering Diaspora." In *Rites of Return: Diaspora Poetics and the Politics of Memory*, edited by Marianne Hirsch and Nancy K. Miller, 72–87. New York: Columbia University Press, 2011.

Hernández, Dava D. "Dancing Mestizaje: The Choreodramas of The Guadalupe Dance Company." Master of Arts, Texas Woman's University, 2015. http://poar. twu.edu/xmlui/bitstream/handle/11274/7027/Hernandezc2.pdf?sequence=1 &isAllowed=y

Hirsch, Marianne. *The Generation of Postmemory: Writing and Visual Culture After the Holocaust*. Gender and Culture. New York: Columbia University Press, 2012.

Hirsch, Marianne, and Nancy K. Miller. *Rites of Return: Diaspora Poetics and the Politics of Memory*. Gender and Culture. New York: Columbia University Press, 2011.

Holley-Bockelmann, Kelly. "TEDx Talk: The Spacetime Symphony of Gravitational Waves." TEDx Talk, Nashville, May 23, 2016. https://www.youtube.com/ watch?v=DTKGAE4voNM

hooks, bell. "Choosing the Margin as a Space of Radical Openness." In *The Feminist Standpoint Theory Reader - Intellectual and Political Controversies*, 153–59. New York: Routledge, 2004.

———. *YEARNING: Race, Gender, and Cultural Politics*. Boston: South End Press, 1990.

hooks, bell, and Amalia Mesa-Bains. *Homegrown*. Engaged Cultural Criticism. Cambridge, MA: South End Press, 2006.

Hornscheidt, Lann. "Aber wie soll ich das denn machen? Interdependenkend forschen: Methodologische und Methodische Handlungsvorschläge." In *InterdepenDenken: Wie Positionierung und Intersektionalität forschend gestalten*, edited by AK Forschungshandeln, 194–212. wissen_bewegen. Berlin: w_orten&meer, 2015.

———. *feministische w_orte: ein lern-, denk- und handlungsbuch zu sprache und diskriminierung, gender studies und feministischer linguistik*. Vol. transdisziplinäre genderstudien. 5 vols. wissen & praxis 168. Frankfurt a.M.: Brandes & Apsel, 2012.

———. "Postkoloniale Gender-Forschung: Ansätze Feministischer Postkolonialer Studien." In *Schlüsselwerke Der Postcolonial Studies*, edited by Alexandra Karentzos and Julia Reuter, 215–28. Wiesbaden: Springer VS, 2012.

Hornscheidt, Lann, and Susanne Baer. "Transdisciplinary Gender Studies: Conceptual and Institutional Challenges." In *Theories and Methodologies in Postgraduate Feminist Research: Researching Differently*, edited by Rosemarie Buikema, Gabriele Griffin, and Nina Lykke, 165–79. London / New York: Routledge, 2011.

Ingrisch, Doris. *Wissenschaft, Kunst Und Gender. Denkräume in Bewegung*. Image 44. Bielefeld: transcript, 2012.

Jewish Voice for Peace. "Facing the Nakba." https://jewishvoiceforpeace.org/facing-the-nakba/

John, Valérie. "De lieu en lieu(x)." In *L'Art à l'épreuve du lieu*, edited by Dominique Berthet, 127–38. Histoire et Idées des Arts. Paris: L'Harmattan, 2004.

Johnson, E. Patrick, and Ramón H. Rivera-Servera, eds. *Blacktino Queer Performance*. Durham: Duke University Press, 2016.

———, eds. *Solo/Black/Woman. Scripts, Interviews, Essays*. Evanston: Northwestern University Press, 2014.

Jones, Omi Osun L. *Theatrical Jazz: Performance, Àse, and the Power of the Present Moment*. Columbus: Ohio State University Press, 2015.

Kabir, Ananya J. Kabir, A. J. (2020). "Creolization as balancing act in the transoceanic quadrille: Choreogenesis, incorporation, memory, market." *Atlantic Studies : Global Currents*, 17(1), 2020, 135-157.

———. "Oceans, cities, islands: Sites and routes of Afro-diasporic rhythm cultures." Atlantic Studies: Literary, Cultural and Historical Perspectives, 11, no. 1 (2014), 106-124.

———. "Plantation, archive, stage: Trans(post)colonial intimations in Katherine Dunham's L'Ag'ya and Little Black Sambo." *Cambridge Journal of Postcolonial Literary Inquiry*, 2(2), 2015, 213-231.

Kanaaneh, Rhoda Ann. *Birthing the Nation: Strategies of Palestinian Women in Israel*. Berkeley: University of California Press, 2002.

Kapitan, Alex. "Ask a Radical Copyeditor: Black with a Capital 'B.'" *Radical Copyeditor* (blog), September 21, 2016. https://radicalcopyeditor.com/2016/09/21/black-with-a-capital-b/

Karentzos, Alexandra. "Postkoloniale Kunstgeschichte: Revisionen von Musealisierungen, Kanonisierungen, Repräsentationen." In *Schlüsselwerke Der Postcolonial Studies*, edited by Alexandra Karentzos and Julia Reuter, 249–66. Wiesbaden: Springer VS, 2012.

Katrak, Ketu. *Contemporary Indian Dance: New Creative Choreography in Indian and the Diaspora*. Studies in International Performance. New York: Palgrave-Macmillan, 2011.

Kelly, Natasha A. *Afrokultur: Der Raum zwischen gestern und morgen*. Berlin: Unrast-Verlag, 2016.

Kilomba, Grada. *Plantation Memories: Episodes of Everyday Racism*. Münster: Unrast-Verlag, 2008.

Kimmerer, Robin Wall. *Braiding Sweetgrass: Indigenous Wisdom, Scientific Knowledge and the Teachings of Plants*. Minneapolis: Milkweed, 2013.

King, Rosamond. "Untamed Space: What Can Black Creativity Look Like?" Danspace Project, September 27, 2017. (Edited by André Zachery) https://danspaceproject.org/2017/09/27/untamed-space-what-can-black-creativity-look-like/ (Accessed August 1, 2020)

Klein, Gabriele, and Sandra Noeth, eds. *Emerging Bodies: The Performance of World-making in Dance and Choreography*. Critical Dance Studies. Bielefeld: transcript, 2011.

Klein, Gabriele. "Dancing Politics: Worldmaking in Dance and Choreography." In *Emerging Bodies: The Performance of Worldmaking in Dance and Choreography*, edited by Gabriele Klein and Sandra Noeth, 17–27. Critical Dance Studies. Bielefeld: transcript, 2011.

Klüger, Ruth. *weiter leben. Eine Jugend*. Göttingen: Wallstein, 1994.

Kukuwa, Ellen. "Kukuwa." Kukuwa, www.kukuwafitness.com

Küppers-Adebisi, Adetoun. "Nationalisierung interdepenDenken." In *Interdepen-Denken: Wie Positionierung und Intersektionalität forschend gestalten*, edited by AK Forschungshandeln, 134–47. wissen_bewegen. Berlin: w_orten&meer, 2015.

Kusser, Astrid. *Körper in Schieflage: Tanzen im Strudel des Black Atlantic um 1900*. Bielefeld: transcript, 2013.

Kwan, SanSan. *Kinesthetic City: Dance & Movement in Chinese Urban Spaces*. Oxford University Press, 2013.

Laframboise, Sandra, and Michael Anhorn. "The Way Of The Two Spirited People: Native American Concepts of Gender and Sexual Orientation." *Dancing to Eagle Spirit Society* (blog). Accessed July 4, 2017. http://www.dancingtoeaglespiritsociety.org/twospirit.php

Landsberg, Alison. *Prosthetic Memory: The Transformation of American Remembrance in the Age of Mass Culture*. New York: Columbia University Press, 2004.

Lauré al-Samarai, Nicola. "Inspirited Topography. Über/Lebensräume, Heim-Suchungen und die Verortung der Erfahrung in Schwarzen deutschen Kultur- und Wissenstraditionen." In *Mythen, Masken und Subjekte. Kritische Weißseinsforschung in Deutschland*, edited by Maureen Maisha Eggers, Grada Kilomba, Peggy Piesche, and Susanne Arndt, 2nd ed., 118–34. Münster: Unrast-Verlag, 2009.

Lepecki, André. *Exhausting Dance: Performance and the Politics of Movement*. New York/London: Routledge, 2006.

———. *Singularities: Dance in the Age of Performance*. New York: Routledge, 2016.

Lespiaux, Sophie. "Durch Gaerten, une performance musicale et chorégraphique d'Oxana Chi." *Une Chambre à Soi* (blog), November 24, 2014. http://sophielespiaux.blogspot.de/2014/11/durch-garten-une-performance-musicale.html

Levy, Daniel, and Natan Sznaider. *Erinnerung im globalen Zeitalter: Der Holocaust.* Frankfurt a.M.: Suhrkamp, 2001.

Lightman, Alan. *Einstein's Dreams.* London: Vintage, 2004.

Lin, Yatin. "Kinesthetic City: Dance and Movement in Chinese Urban Spaces by SanSan Kwan (Review)." *Dance Research Journal* 46, no. 1 (April 2014): 129–33.

Lockward, Alanna. "Diaspora." In *Rassismus Auf Gut Deutsch. Ein Kritisches Nach-schlagewerk Zu Rassistischen Sprachhandlungen*, edited by Adibeli Nduka-Agwu and Lann Hornscheidt, Transdisziplinäre Genderstudien 1:56–71. Wissen & Praxis 155. Frankfurt a.M.: Brandes & Apsel, 2010.

Loïal, Chantal. "On T'appelle Vénus - Dossier de Diffusion." Compagnie Difé Kako, 2015. http://www.difekako.fr/wp-content/uploads/DOSSIER-VENUS-WEB-0717.pdf

———. Interview by Layla Zami, Paris, March 1, 2014.

Lorde, Audre. "A Litany for Survival." In *The Black Unicorn: Poems*, 1978.

———. "Foreword to the English Language Edition." In *Showing Our Colors: Afro-German Women Speak Out*, edited by May Opitz-Ayim, Katharina Oguntoye, and Dagmar Schultz. Amherst: University of Massachusetts Press, 1992.

———. *Zami: A New Spelling of My Name.* New York: Persephone Press, 1982.

Lori L. Tharps. "The Case for Black With a Capital B." *New York Times*, November 19, 2014.

Lykke, Nina. "This Discipline Which Is Not One: Feminist Studies as a Postdis-cipline." In *Theories and Methodologies in Postgraduate Feminist Research: Researching Differently*, edited by Rosemarie Buikema, Gabriele Griffin, and Nina Lykke, 137–50. London / New York: Routledge, 2011.

Mandel, Naomi. *Against the Unspeakable: Complicity, the Holocaust, and Slavery in America.* Cultural Frames, Framing Culture. Charlottesville: University of Virginia Press, 2006.

Marquié, Hélène. "Le genre, un outil épistémologique pour l'historiographie de la danse." In *Actes du colloque international*, edited by Roxana Martin and Martina Nordera, 211–22. Université de Nice-Sophia Antipolis: Honoré Champion, 2009.

———. *Non, la danse n'est pas un truc de filles! Essai sur le genre en danse.* CULTURE DANSE. Toulouse: Editions de l'Attribut, 2016.

Martin, Randy. *Critical Moves: Dance Studies in Theory and Politics.* Durham: Duke University Press, 1998.

McCarren, Felicia. *French Moves: The Cultural Politics of Le Hip Hop.* New York: Oxford University Press, 2013.

Mignolo, Walter D. *Local Histories/Global Designs: Coloniality, Subaltern Knowledges, and Border Thinking.* 2nd ed. Princeton: Princeton University Press, 2012.

Miller, Nancy K. *Getting Personal: Feminist Occasions and Other Autobiographical Acts.* New York: Routledge, 1991.

Mohanty, Chandra Talpade. "Crafting Feminist Genealogies: On the Geography and Politics of Home, Nation, and Community." In *Talking Visions: Multicultural Feminism in a Transnational Age*, edited by Ella Shohat, 485–500. New York: New Museum of Contemporary Art MIT Press, 1998.

Monáe, Janelle. *Q.U.E.E.N.* Atlantic Records, 2013. https://www.youtube.com/watch?v=tEddixS-UoU

Morrison, Toni. *Beloved: A Novel.* New York: Vintage Books, 2004.

———. "The Site of Memory." In *Inventing the Truth. The Art and Craft of the Memoir*, edited by William K. Zinsser, 183–200. New York: Houghton Mifflin, 1998.

"Moving Memory - International Symposium-Festival." *Performing Memory: Interventions* (blog), 2016. http://movingmemoryberlin.tumblr.com/event2016

Muñoz, José Esteban. *DISIDENTIFICATIONS. Queers of Color and the Performance of Politics.* Cultural Studies of the America, vol. 2. Minneapolis: University of Minnesota Press, 1999.

Murguía, Alexandro. *The Medicine of Memory: A Mexica Clan in California.* Austin: University of Texas Press, 2002.

Native Resistance Network. "Mother Earth – Manna-Hata – A Native Perspective." POC Zine Project, May 2012. https://issuu.com/poczineproject/docs/nrn_zine_motherearth_may_2012

Nduka-Agwu, Adibeli, and Lann Hornscheidt, eds. *Rassismus auf gut Deutsch. Ein kritisches Nachschlagewerk zu rassistischen Sprachhandlungen.* Vol. Transdisziplinäre Genderstudien 1. wissen & praxis 155. Frankfurt a.M.: Brandes & Apsel, 2010.

Nelson, Alondra. "AfroFuturism: Past-Future Visions." *Colorlines: Race, Culture, Action*, Center for Third World Organizing, 1, no. 3 (Spring 2000): 34–37.

———. "The Factness of Diaspora. The Social Sources of Genetic Genealogy." In *Rites of Return - Diaspora Poetics and the Politics of Memory*, edited by Marianne Hirsch and Nancy K. Miller, 23–39. Gender and Culture Series. New York: Columbia University Press, 2011.

Okach, Opiyo. "Cleansing." Gaara Projects. Accessed November 1, 2016. http://www.gaaraprojects.com/cleansinggaara.htm

Omise'eke, Natasha Tinsley. "Black Atlantic, Queer Atlantic: Queer Imaginings of the Middle Passage." *GLQ: A Journal of Lesbian and Gay Studies* 14, no. 2–3 (2008): 191–215.

Opoku, Kwame. "Nefertiti in Absurdity: How Often Must Egyptians Ask Germans for the Return of the Egyptian Queen?," June 28, 2011. https://www.modernghana.com/news/314307/1/nefertiti-in-absurdity-how-often-must-egyptians-as.html

Oral Historian Association. "Principles and Best Practices." Oral History Association, 2009. http://www.oralhistory.org/about/principles-and-practices/

Oyěwùmí, Oyèrónkẹ. *The Invention of Women: Making an African Sense of Western Gender Discourses.* Minneapolis: University of Minnesota Press, 1997.

Paris, Carl. "Reading 'Spirit' and the Dancing Body in the Choreography of Ronald K. Brown and Reggie Wilson." In *Black Performance Theory*, edited by Thomas F. DeFrantz and Anita Gonzalez, 99–114. Durham: Duke University Press, 2014.

"Performing Memory." Blog. http://movingmemoryberlin.tumblr.com/

Petrowskaja, Katja. *Vielleicht Esther*. Berlin: Suhrkamp, 2015.

Phelan, Peggy. *Unmarked: The Politics of Performance*. New York: Routledge, 1993.

Pinto, Samantha. *Difficult Diasporas: The Transnational Feminist Aesthetic of the Black Atlantic*. New York: New York University Press, 2013.

Plate, Liedeke, and Anneke Smelik, eds. *Performing Memory in Art and Popular Culture*. Routledge Research in Cultural and Media Studies 48. New York: Routledge, 2013.

Quayson, Ato, and Girish Daswani. "Introduction – Diaspora and Transnationalism: Scapes, Scales, and Scopes." In *A Companion to Diaspora and Transnationalism*, edited by Ato Quayson and Girish Daswani, 1–26. Oxford: Blackwell Publishing, 2013.

Quijano, Aníbal. "Coloniality and Modernity/ Rationality." *Cultural Studies* 21, no. 2 (2007): 168–78.

Ramón H. Rivera-Servera. *Performing Queer Latinidad: Dance, Sexuality, Politics*. Triangulations. Lesbian/Gay/Queer. Theatre/Drama/Performance. Ann Harbor, Michigan: University of Michigan Press, 2012.

Rossen, Rebecca. *Dancing Jewish: Jewish Identity in American Modern and Postmodern Dance*. Oxford University Press, 2014.

Rothberg, Michael. *Multidirectional Memory: Remembering the Holocaust in the Age of Globalization*. Cultural Memory in the Present. Stanford: Stanford University Press, 2009.

———. "W. E. B. Du Bois in Warsaw: Holocaust Memory and the Color Line, 1949-1952." *The Yale Journal of Criticism* 14, no. 1 (2001): 169–89.

Rovelli, Carlos. *Reality Is Not What It Seems: The Journey to Quantum Gravity*. New York: Riverhead, 2017.

Saleh, Farah. "Farah Saleh." Vimeo. Accessed March 26, 2017. https://vimeo.com/user13826099

———. "Note D'intention. Parole, Parole, Parole," December 2012. http://miniatures.officinae.fr/parole-parole-parole-farah-saleh/

———. "On Art Production as a Form of Daily Protest." Tanzquartier Vienna, September 5, 2014.

———. Interview by Layla Zami. Vienna, June 30, 2014.

Saleh, Farah, and Nicole Bindler. Free Advice and an Interview with Farah Saleh. Thinking Dance, April 27, 2016. http://thinkingdance.net/articles/2016/04/27/Free-Advice-and-an-Interview-with-Farah-Saleh

Schneider, Rebecca. *Performing Remains: Art and War in Times of Theatrical Reenactment*. NY: Routledge, 2011.

Schwab, Gabriele. *Haunting Legacies: Violent Histories and Transgenerational Trauma.* New York: Columbia University Press, 2010.

Scolieri, Paul A. *Dancing the New World: Aztecs, Spaniards, and the Choreography of Conquest.* Latin American & Caribbean Performance Series. Austin: University of Texas, 2013.

Sharpe, Christina. *In the Wake: On Blackness and Being.* Durham: Duke University Press, 2016.

Shea Murphy, Jacqueline. *The People Have Never Stopped Dancing: Native American Modern Dance Histories.* Minneapolis: University of Minnesota Press, 2007.

Shehadeh, Raja. "Palestinian Choreographer Finds Expression in Modern Dance." *Al-Monitor - The Pulse of the Middle East,* April 15, 2013. http://www.al-monitor. com/pulse/originals/2013/04/ordinary-madness-ramallah-   contemporary-dance-festival.html

Shohat, Ella. *Taboo Memories, Diasporic Voices.* Next Wave. New Directions in Women's Studies. Durham: Duke University Press, 2006.

Simon, Zufit. "All about Nothing." Art Blau - Zufit Simon. Accessed March 26, 2017. http://www.artblau.de/Simon.html#all%20about

———. Interview by Layla Zami. Berlin, May 11, 2014.

Simpson, Leanne Betasamosake. *As We Have Always Done: Indigenous Freedom Through Radical Resistance.* Minneapolis: University of Minnesota Press, 2017.

Sirri, Lana. "Führt geografische und religiöse Positionierung zu Ausschluss? Feministische akademische Wissensproduktion hinterfragen." In *Interdependenz-Denken: Wie Positionierung und Intersektionalität forschend gestalten,* edited by AK Forschungshandeln, 158–71. wissen_bewegen. Berlin: w_orten&meer, 2015.

Der Spiegel. "Baggerfahrer Legt Riesiges Hakenkreuz Frei." *Der Spiegel,* November 21, 2017. https://www.spiegel.de/panorama/gesellschaft/hamburg-baggerfahrer-legt-riesiges-hakenkreuz-frei-a-1179496.html# Accessed December 4, 2017.

Spitz, Emilia, and Linda Uruchurtu. "Bag of Steps: Turns." *The Ballet Bag* (blog), October 31, 2009. http://www.theballetbag.com/2009/10/31/bag-of-steps-turns/

Straus-Ernst, Lou. "Bei Tatjana Barbakoff." *Die Weltwoche.* May 25, 1934.

Taylor, Diana. *The Archive and The Repertoire: Performing Cultural Memory in the Americas.* Durham: Duke University Press, 2003.

Thompson, Candace. "Of Circles and Bright Colors." *Instagram,* November 23, 2016.

Thurner, Christina, and Julia Wehren, eds. *Original und Revival: Geschichts-Schreibung im Tanz.* Materialien des Instituts für Theaterwissenschaft Bern (ITW) 10. Bern: Chronos, 2010.

Tighe, Claire. "Middle Passage in Twenty Minutes: The AFROFUTURISM Series." *Culturebot - Maximum Performance,* November 10, 2015. http://www.culturebot.org/2015/11/24930/middle-passage-in-twenty-minutes-renegade-performance-groups-the-afrofuturism-series/

Tillet, Salamishah. *Sites of Slavery: Citizenship and Racial Democracy in the Post–Civil Rights Imagination*. Durham: Duke University Press, 2012.

Trouillot, Michel-Rolph. *Silencing The Past: Power and the Production of History*. Boston: Beacon Press, 1995.

Walcott, Derek. "The Sea Is History." In *Selected Poems*, 137–39. New York: Farrar, Straus and Giroux, 2007.

Walkowicz, Karolina. *Die Kampfkunst-Tänzerin. Der Gender Diskurs Im Interkulturellen Vergleich Des Tanzes*. Marburg: Tectum Verlag, 2010.

Wehren, Julia. *Körper als Archiv in Bewegung: Choreografie als historiografische Praxis*. TanzScripte 37. Bielefeld: transcript, 2016.

Welsh Asante, Kariamu. "Commonalities in African Dance: An Aesthetic Foundation." In *Moving History / Dancing Cultures. A Dance History Reader*, edited by Ann Dils and Ann Cooper Albright, 144–51. Durham: Wesleyan University Press, 2001.

Wojczewski, Silvia. 2019. "À la recherche d'un enracinement. De l'importance des voyages au sein des itinéraires de féministes activistes afro-allemandes." *ethnographiques.org*. no. 37 (2019). https://www.ethnographiques.org/2019/Wojczewski (Accessed August 1, 2020)

Wright, Michelle M. "Others-from-Within from Without: Afro-German Subject Formation and the Challenge of a Counter-Discourse." *Callaloo* 26, no. 2 (Spring 2003): 296–305.

———. *Physics of Blackness: Beyond the Middle Passage Epistemology*. Minneapolis: University of Minnesota Press, 2015.

Yung-Hing, Renée-Paule, ed. *Art Contemporain de La Caraïbe: Mythes, Croyances, Religions et Imaginaires*. Paris: HC, 2012.

Zachery, André M. "Artist's Journal: Futurity and the Containment of Blackness in Twenty-First-Century Performance." *Theater - Yale School of Drama* 46, no. 3 (2017): 62–82.

———. "Physical Propulsion." Brooklyn Studios for Dance, 2016. Accessed April 24, 2016. http://bksd.org/event/flying-low-andre-zachery/2016-04-26/

———. "Renegade Performance Group." Renegade Performance Group. Accessed March 26, 2017. http://www.renegadepg.com/untitled-distances.html

———. "Untitled Distances." Renegade Performance Group. Accessed March 26, 2017. http://www.renegadepg.com/untitled-distances.html

———. Interview by Layla Zami. New York, December 1, 2015.

Zambrano, David. "Flying-Low - Dance Technique." *David Zambrano* (blog). http://www.davidzambrano.org/?page_id=279

Zami, Layla. "Dancing the Past in the Present Tense. Queer Afropean Presence in Oxana Chi's Dancescapes." *Lambda Nordica*, Postcolonial Queer Europe, no. 2–3 (2017): 126–50.

———. "Danser le passé au présent. Oxana Chi et Chantal Loïal, chorégraphes de la mémoire." *Recherches En Danse* 7 (2019). https://doi.org/10.4000/danse.2736

———. "Ein all_zu_täglicher Tag*." In *InterdepenDenken: Wie Positionierung und Intersektionalität forschend gestalten*, edited by AK Forschungshandeln, 72–83. Berlin: w_orten&meer, 2015.

———."Of Circles and Cycles: Remembering, Ritual, and Rhythm in Black Queer Female Dances." *Movement Research Performance Journal* on "Spatial Practice", no. 54 (Summer 2020): 46–47.

———. "Oxana Chis Tänzerische Wissensschaffung: Biographische Erinnerung an Tatjana Barbakoff Aus Feministischer Perspektive." In *Sichtbar Unsichtbar. Geschlechterwissen in (Auto-)Biographischen Texten*, edited by Maria Heidegger, Nina Kogler, Ursula A. Schneider, and Annette Steinsiek, 259–74. Gender Studies. Bielefeld: transcript, 2015.

———. "Oxana Chi von Zopf bis Fluss: Transkulturelle Tanzkunst und alternative Geschichtsschreibung." In *The Living Archive: kulturelle Produktionen und Räume*, edited by MID Redaktion and Aicha Diallo, 52–61. Berlin: Heinrich-Boell-Stiftung, 2013. http://heimatkunde.boell.de/2012/12/18/oxana-chi-von-zopf-bis-fluss-transkulturelle-tanzkunst-und-alternative

———. "Mit Oxana Chi Durch Gärten." *Nah & Fern. Das Kulturmagazin Für Migration Und Partizipation*, 2010.

———. "Rendre sur scène son corps à Sawtche." *Madinin'Art*. February 2011.

———. "Research Diary - Unpublished Manuscript," 2013-2017.

———. "Tanzkunst als lebendige Erinnerung: Oxana Chis performative Erinnerung an Tatjana Barbakoff." In *Neues Judentum – altes Erinnern? Zeiträume des Gedenkens*, edited by Dimitrij Belkin, Lara Hensch, and Eva Lezzi, 267–88. Berlin: Hentrich&Hentrich / ELES, 2017.

Zenenga, Praise. "Power and the Body: Revisiting Dance and Theatre Aesthetics of Resistance in the Academy." *Dance Research Journal* 43, no. 1 (2011): 65–69.

———. "The Total Theater Aesthetic Paradigm in African Theater." In *The Oxford Handbook of Dance and Theater*, edited by Nadine George-Graves, 236–51. Oxford: Oxford University Press, 2015.

Cultural Studies

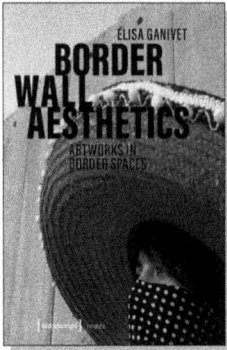

Elisa Ganivet
Border Wall Aesthetics
Artworks in Border Spaces

2019, 250 p., hardcover, ill.
79,99 € (DE), 978-3-8376-4777-8
E-Book: 79,99 € (DE), ISBN 978-3-8394-4777-2

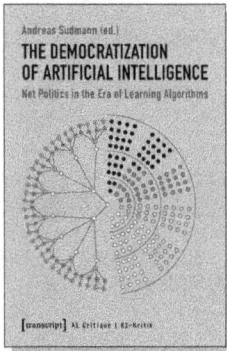

Andreas Sudmann (ed.)
The Democratization of Artificial Intelligence
Net Politics in the Era of Learning Algorithms

2019, 334 p., pb., col. ill.
49,99 € (DE), 978-3-8376-4719-8
E-Book: free available, ISBN 978-3-8394-4719-2

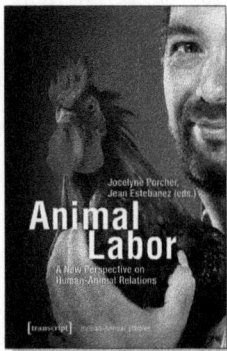

Jocelyne Porcher, Jean Estebanez (eds.)
Animal Labor
A New Perspective on Human-Animal Relations

2019, 182 p., hardcover
99,99 € (DE), 978-3-8376-4364-0
E-Book: 99,99 € (DE), ISBN 978-3-8394-4364-4

**All print, e-book and open access versions of the titles in our list
are available in our online shop www.transcript-verlag.de/en!**

Cultural Studies

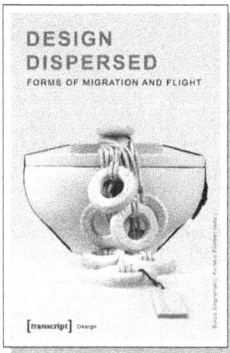

Burcu Dogramaci, Kerstin Pinther (eds.)
Design Dispersed
Forms of Migration and Flight

2019, 274 p., pb., col. ill.
34,99 € (DE), 978-3-8376-4705-1
E-Book: 34,99 € (DE), ISBN 978-3-8394-4705-5

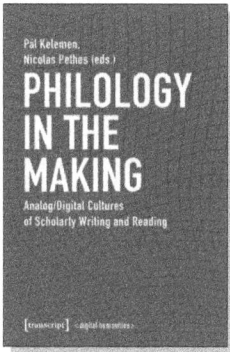

Pál Kelemen, Nicolas Pethes (eds.)
Philology in the Making
Analog/Digital Cultures of Scholarly Writing and Reading

2019, 316 p., pb., ill.
34,99 € (DE), 978-3-8376-4770-9
E-Book: 34,99 € (DE), ISBN 978-3-8394-4770-3

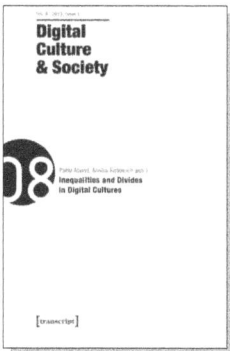

Pablo Abend, Annika Richterich,
Mathias Fuchs, Ramón Reichert, Karin Wenz (eds.)
Digital Culture & Society (DCS)
Vol. 5, Issue 1/2019 –
Inequalities and Divides in Digital Cultures

2019, 212 p., pb., ill.
29,99 € (DE), 978-3-8376-4478-4
E-Book: 29,99 € (DE), ISBN 978-3-8394-4478-8

**All print, e-book and open access versions of the titles in our list
are available in our online shop www.transcript-verlag.de/en!**

GPSR Authorized Representative: Easy Access System Europe, Mustamäe tee
50, 10621 Tallinn, Estonia, gpsr.requests@easproject.com

www.ingramcontent.com/pod-product-compliance
Lightning Source LLC
Chambersburg PA
CBHW070058030426
42335CB00016B/1937